PUNJAB
FROM
BRITISH ANNEXATION
TO
LAHORE RESOLUTION
(1839-1939)

Gurprit Singh

First Published 2022

ISBN 978-93-83723-95-9

Published by
LG Publishers Distributors
49, Lane No. 14, Pratap Nagar
Mayur Vihar Phase I, Delhi 110 091
Tel : 011 2279 5641 email: lgpdist@gmail.com

Typeset at
Arpit Printographers, Delhi

Printed at
Sapra Brothers, Noida

Contents

Preface

Although I have been attracted to the reading material on Punjab since childhood, it was much later that my passion to know about Punjab seriously was rekindled. My interest about the Colonial Punjab also stemmed from the fact that my great grandfather was a Commandant in the cavalry of Maharaja Ranjit Singh and over the years the family members including my late father S. Hardial Singh often talked about the anecdotes dating to those glorious days of the Sikhs and their kingdom in the Punjab.

It was Maharaja Ranjit Singh who took the border of Punjab and India so close to Afghanistan, so similar to what Emperor Ashoka had done more than two thousand years ago. I was fortunate enough to have got hold of the classic book on Partition by Kirpal Singh. I did not know how invaluable the book was. It belonged to S. Gurdial Singh, a family relative (1911-1991) and one of the founders of the Punjab and Sind Bank. I took this book from his library as asked to by Mrs Singh.

Freedom at Midnight was another such book which depicted a broader picture on Partition but covered some heart-wrenching stories on Punjab. Ishtiaq Ahmed's *Punjab Bloodied, Partitioned and Cleansed* is another unique work in this genre. I read the book and came into contact with the author. At his request, I translated his work into Hindi and it got published by Aakar Books, Delhi.

Rajmohan Gandhi's book on Punjab is another excellent work. Every decade in the history of the Punjab has been eventful and there is no dearth of reading material either in book form or in e-book format for any period. The British have chronicled the history of the Punjab very well even though they have been biased at times.

I have tried to keep the book size well within limits bearing in mind that a book need not be too detailed or too concise, for that matter.

I can be reached at *gurpritwb@gmail.com*.

Gurprit Singh

Acknowledgements

First of all, I would like to acknowledge the great support received from my wife Kawaljit Kaur and son Satwinder Singh during all stages of this work. Their patience and continual support have enabled me to study, analyse and compose this work. My late father S. Hardial Singh infused in me a keen interest in the history of Punjab, particularly Anglo-Sikh relations. I developed a keen interest in the history of Punjab and Afghanistan.

For doing this type of work, which demands delving into the past, one needs material from various sources which includes the Internet, printed books and e-books.

I got help from the Archive.org, National Digital Library of India—IIT Kharagpur, Archaeological Survey of India asi.nic.in collections digitized at Indira Gandhi National Centre for the Arts (IGNCA) for downloading a number of e-books.

I am highly indebted to Shri Rahul Saxena of LG Publishers Distribution for publishing this book. Without his efforts and words of encouragement, this work would not have been possible.

Introduction

Punjab was generally called 'the Lahore Province' or 'the Lahore Kingdom', after the name of the capital city during the Sikh reign of Maharaja Ranjit Singh. The Lahore Kingdom stretched from Sutlej in the east to the Khyber Pass in the west.

The British had arrived in India in the second half of the eighteenth century but it was only in 1849 that they could annex Punjab, a full 92 years after the fall of Plassey to them.

After the Mutiny of 1857, Delhi and Hissar of present Haryana was added to the Punjab Province. From the Punjab, the areas to the west beyond the Indus were separated in 1901 and a separate province NWFP (presently KPK) was formed. It was away from the administrative control of the Lieutenant Governor of the Punjab and placed under the charge of a chief commissioner, directly responsible to the Indian Government.

The great development of Punjab took place under the British, particularly the building of canals and extension of irrigation facilities. The canal network was one of the biggest in the world. The British established educational institutions and other infrastructure. They developed Lahore like never before. Railways and telegraphs reached Punjab, not to mention electrification of the towns. An efficient bureaucracy, justice, administration and revenue collection schemes were developed by them. Many social evils like *sati* and *thuggee* were put to an end by the British. A lot of Punjabi youth, especially from North Punjab benefited as they were recruited for the Army.

Under the Viceroy Lord Curzon and in 1912, the capital Delhi was separated from the Punjab. Under the British rule, it came to be called 'the Province of the Punjab' and after independence, the Indian portion of the Punjab got the name 'East Punjab'.

When the call for Swadeshi was made, Punjabi youth abroad got involved in the Ghadar movement and the Jallianwala Bagh Massacre further distanced the Punjabis from the British. But the Communal Award was used by the British to divide the communities and already the minority quota during elections had been enforced. The INC was busy fighting the British during the Second World War with its Quit India movement and its leaders were jailed. The Muslim League found this an opportune moment to forge ties with the British to create its own pure land called *Pakistan*. Already the Lahore Resolution of March 1940 had paved the path for such an Islamic country.

1

Chaos in the Lahore Kingdom After Ranjit Singh

Death of Ranjit Singh

Ranjit Singh had lived life to the full, having ruled for nearly four decades and his health did not permit any more campaigns. He was attended by English doctors, Murray in 1826 and McGregor after his paralytic seizure in 1834. But the prescriptions were ineffective and he did not refrain from drinking strong liquor, either. He also tried electricity and galvanism, as a cure.

The marriage festivities of Prince Nao Nihal Singh, in March 1837, did the Maharaja no good. He thought that it was a part of hospitality that he should set an example of drinking. It made him weak.

In the cold weather of 1838, a second stroke of paralysis, caused by excesses, anxiety and excitement really brought Ranjit Singh's time close to end. Till the rest of his life, he was only half alive, yet he still tried to conduct business, and was sometimes carried in his palanquin to a parade of his troops. But everyone knew that the end would come soon.

During his last illness, Fakir Azizuddin, his medical adviser was beside him administering the medicine and keeping him informed of news from all quarters. Sadly, Ranjit Singh refused to see the English doctor whom the Governor-General sent him. But medicine could not cure him and the native pharmacopoeia, did him no good either. He summoned to his bedside Prince Kharak Singh, his son, and proclaimed him his heir, with Dhian Singh as minister; a big triumph for the wily Dogra. It was a grave judgmental error on the part of a great man like Ranjit Singh to keep in employment these Dogra and other Brahmin ministers from Meerut like Khushhal Singh. They had become a part of the central decision-making process.

Before his death, the Maharaja gave away Rs 2.5 million in alms to the poor and to the priests of Nankana and the Dera Baba Nanak where the first Guru was born and died, respectively. Thereafter, the great Maharaja was moved, as per age-old custom, from his bed to a carpet on the ground, where he breathed his last on the June 27, 1839.

Self-Immolation by the Maharaja's Queens

On June 28, 1839, Maharaja Ranjit Singh was cremated in Lahore and four of his queens and seven maid girls burnt themselves on his funeral pyre. They were not forced to commit *sati*, but perhaps had no other option. The Sikh Gurus had denounced the notion of the inferiority of women and had protested against their historic subjugation.

What followed after his death was ritualism befitting a Maharaja but not a devout Sikh. Guru Nanak had urged for the equality of women. Guru Amar Dass had also condemned the practice of women burning themselves on their husband's funeral pyre.

Perhaps the court of the late Ranjit Singh felt like honouring old martial traditions of India and the sati custom was followed in spite of its condemnation by the Gurus.

Raja Dhian Singh, the Prime Minister, declared that he would also burn to death with the Maharaja and ordered his effects to be given to charity. However, the court nobles persuaded him to change his decision. They pleaded that the Maharaja had chosen Raja Dhian Singh, amongst all men because of his wisdom and it was in the greater interest of Punjab that he should attend to the affairs, run the state and guide the crown Prince Kharak Singh. Raja Dhian Singh, however, refused to listen. Prince Kharak Singh then, walked up to him and convinced him to change his mind. Was the whole thing a drama? Nobody can say for sure.

Character and Policy of Ranjit Singh

Ranjit Singh was no less remarkable than either Mehemet Ali or Napoleon. At the age of seventeen, the affairs of his *sirdaree* fell into his hands. He defeated those who opposed him, converted enemies to friends. Ranjit Singh succeeded, with minimal bloodshed, in elevating himself from a simple sirdar, to be the sovereign of a large kingdom, including Hindus and a Muslim majority, as well as rival Sikhs; the only state in India not substantially under British dominion.

The habit of hearing papers read in Persian, Punjabi, and Hindi, and his keen attention to the minutest of business, gave Ranjit an opportunity to transact business rapidly even though he was completely unlettered. With natural intelligence, and a sharp memory he remembered the minutest details of circumstances.

He had a lively imagination and there was a frankness and naiveté about his conversation, and his observations and remarks were full of short, terse, incoherent phrases, or in the shape of interrogatories.

He took infinite delight in hunting from his earliest years which was the most innocent of his recreations, and often he was accompanied, as a soldier-king, by a full camp and every luxury was taken care of.

At his court, Kashmiri nautch-girls of the rarest beauty enacted their voluptuous dances. He had a band of Amazons, consisting of about 150 of the most beautiful girls of Kashmir, Persia, and the Punjab, who frequently appeared on horseback, for the amusement of the Maharaja.

He had a passion for horses and watching military parades and display was another hobby and he spent nearly half of every day in reviews, examining equipment, or in some way studying to promote the different branches of his army.

He was active in restraining the Akalis and other zealots and for a certain number of hours every day he had the Granth Sahib read before him by gurus. He was liberal in alms to fakirs and men of reputed sanctity, not excluding Brahmins. He was not opposed to Christianity and he requested that an English missionary see him privately in 1830 to explain to him the doctrines of Christianity.

With respect to the policy and internal government of Ranjit Singh, there was no Western type of management. His career throughout was that of a seizer of all within his reach; but what he possessed he did not subject it to any specific administration. The same was entrusted to the farmers, with full power to deal with the lives and properties of the producing classes of the population.

Ranjit's extortions were directed from the old Sikh families, and his own state officers; merchants and traders were protected, and the duties and taxes were moderate. Forty percent or two-fifths of the produce was the proportion nominally taken by the state. No constitution, or fixed form of government was put in place by Ranjit Singh in Punjab. All powers were vested in the hands of the sirdars, jagirdars, and renters. The revenue-farmer was judge, magistrate, and often custom-master, within his jurisdiction.

Some districts were tolerably administered and others oppressed. A rich source of revenue was the *adalat*, or the nominal court of justice since a fine was the punishment usually awarded. The vagabond thief, urged to plunder lost his nose or ears; but the wealthy robber escaped with fines.

The state treasury was getting substantial sums of money, thanks to guarding of customs and checking of every pass and ferry. Ranjit, overthrew the old political institutions of the Sikhs, but substituted them with none. Treating the chiefs of all his subjected states merely as jagirdars, he forced them to furnish quotas of troops for his most distant and dangerous expeditions, thus saving the *khas* troops of the state.

To the British, the standing army, ever ready for active service, forming the whole machinery of administration made the Lahore Durbar seem like pure despotism. The entire power and authority was centred in the single individual placed at the head of affairs. Ranjit Singh had neither the opportunity to include in civil administration, the European aspects and practical knowledge, from which he derived so much advantage solely in his military affairs. In a superior civil capacity, the only foreigner he employed was Dr. Harlan, an American, a man of ability and enterprise, who was placed in Gujrat, but he soon lost the Maharaja's favour.

The Successors of Ranjit Singh (1839-1845)

While Maharaja Ranjit Singh was dying, the army was assembled, and Dhian Singh was assiduous in his mournful attentions as if he was taking orders from the departing sovereign. As the dying

Maharaja was being carried in a solemn journey, from time to time, the apparently obedient and yet wily Dhian Singh made it public that a dying Ranjit Singh had declared that the Prince Kharak Singh would succeed him and that he (Dhian Singh) would be the *wazir,* i.e. minister of the kingdom.

On the night of June 27, Rani Mehtab Devi, the Katoch princess of Kangra, made the Dogra and Kharak Singh exchange mutual pledges of confidence and good-will. They were asked to swear on the body of the late Maharaja as well as the Holy Scriptures, promising to abide by their bond. The period of mourning came to an end with the ceremony of *Kriya* on the thirteenth day.

The Army watched the proceedings in silence and consented. The British Government sincerely offered its congratulations, to the new and seemingly unworthy master of the Punjab.

The slow-witted (or as Cunningham calls him 'imbecile') Kharak Singh was acknowledged as the master of the Punjab. He was not a young immature person but a 38-year-old man. He was the oldest child of the late Maharaja, born to Raj Kaur or Datar Kaur in 1801. He and his father had an age difference of just 21 years.

It may be recalled that during the last days of the Maharaja's reign, the Dogras held very important positions in the court as well as army. They nurtured great ambitions which came out in the open once the Maharaja was dead. The Durbar or the Sikh Empire was now divided into many houses just like the Mughals when they declined in the mid-eighteenth century. Therefore, to have a clearer understanding, it is proposed to depict who was against whom and which group was against which other group as the situation unfolded.

Scenario in July 1839

The Maharaja was cremated on June 28, 1839.

Table 1.1

<table>
<tr><td>Prince Kharak Singh who would be king</td><td rowspan="2">Versus</td><td rowspan="2">Prince Sher Singh</td></tr>
<tr><td>Wazir Dhian Singh Dogra</td></tr>
</table>

Sher Singh is Disgruntled

The thirteen days of mourning were no cakewalk for the king to be, Kharak Singh. Sher Singh, his stepbrother also had an eye on the throne. Sher Singh was born to Mehtab Kaur, the daughter of famous and ambitious Sada Kaur. He was born in 1807 and along with his twin, Tara Singh and was 6 years junior to his step-brother Kharak Singh. He had increased the force on his estate in Mukerian to 1500 men while the Maharaja was dying. He hastened to Kangra when he knew about the Maharaja's death and also, he sent a confidential message to the British Agent at Ludhiana asking the British authorities for aid and promising to reward them by a cession of territory on the left bank of the Sutlej.

It may seem preposterous that a son of Ranjit Singh would stoop so low to acquire power, unlike the Europeans who would normally never compromise with their patriotism. The Europeans would bribe other native kings to capture power for their country and would hunt in a pack and here we see the prince at the highest level of society engaged in unbelievable machinations for power.

Sher Singh was clearly junior to Kharak Singh who was the eldest son and Ranjit Singh had explicitly nominated him for the succession. Moreover, Sher Singh's paternity was questionable as per the people of the Durbar. But Sher Singh was mentally better equipped than Kharak Singh. Towards the end of his life, Ranjit Singh had developed a liking for Sher Singh. However, his twin, Tara Singh remained in the background. Sher Singh was popular with the army, and had interacted with the British who liked him too.

In March 1837 Prince Sher Singh met Sir Henry Fane, Commander-in-Chief of the British forces, and in early 1838 received Lord Auckland, when the Governor-General visited Lahore and Amritsar. Prince Sher Singh, assisted by Sardar Lehna Singh Majithia looked after him. Miss Emily Eden, Lord Auckland's sister, spoke of Sher Singh as 'our dear friend' and the latter had succeeded in creating the sympathy of the British.

When Dhian Singh came to know about Sher Singh's endeavours in Kangra he took pre-emptive steps as any battle for succession would have been exploited by the British. As early as December 1838, Lord Auckland had expressed his wish to Ranjit

Singh to station a British Resident at Lahore. The Maharaja turned down the proposal. The British, in any case, were garrisoned in Ferozepur and had set military posts in Sindh.

Dhian Singh the Powerful Wazir

Following the death of Ranjit Singh, one person who emerged as the most powerful contender was Dhian Singh Dogra. Dhian Singh assured the senior officers of the Durbar that their estates, privileges and jagirs would remain intact and he wanted to announce the date of the formal ceremony of accession (Raj Tilak) by Kharak Singh. A date in September was arrived at. After getting the news from the commandant of the Kangra fort, orders were sent to the governor and commandants of other garrisons to be vigilant.

Personal letters were sent to Princes Sher Singh and Nau Nihal Singh by Dhian Singh Dogra. He advised Sher Singh to come to Lahore to take part in the ceremony, promising him all the security needed. Kharak Singh signed the document confirming Dhian Singh's words. Nau Nihal Singh was fully apprised of the situation. Sher Singh had approached the British for their support but was refused and Captain Wade clarified that Kharak Singh would be recognized as the new Maharaja.

Kharak Singh is Made the King (1839)

The investiture of Kharak Singh took place on September 1, 1839. He sported the Kohinoor diamond and his forehead was anointed with a saffron mark by the Hindu and Sikh priests. The Durbaris then made their obeisance. The absence of Prince Nau Nihal Singh, Kharak Singh's only son became a topic of gossip. The Prince was on his way to Delhi from Peshawar and although Kharak Singh knew about it, the ceremony was rushed through as if the Maharaja and his young companion, Chet Singh Bajwa, expected the Prince to create same disturbance.

Kharak Singh's friendship with Chet Singh Bajwa may have earned the displeasure of Prince Nau Nihal Singh and Dhian Singh Dogra but it would be far-fetched to insinuate that the Prince intended to usurp his father's rights.

Surely the Prince wanted to see the establishment of an efficient government, which could retain the respect for the

Khalsa and he was aware of his father's imbecility and knew that Chet Singh was not the right friend for his father. Nau Nihal Singh also knew about the popularity of Sher Singh with the army and the British Government and the Dogras' influence in the court with the backing of the Sikh family priests of the Maharaja. In the prevailing situation the Prince was possibly left with no other alternative than putting all he had into preserving the Lahore Kingdom.

Kharak Singh was the eldest of Maharaja Ranjit Singh's eight sons, but sadly, he was the most wimpish. The homeopathic doctor Dr. Honigberger disliked him even more than Ranjit Singh and declared his ascending the throne on September 1, 1839 as a dark day.

Murder # 1 (Victim: Chet Singh Bajwa) and the Beginning of Kharak Singh's fall

Maharaja Kharak Singh's friend Chet Singh had good looks and a smooth manner and that was all he could boast of. He was related to Kharak Singh on his wife's side and he gained the Maharaja's confidence.

Table 1.2 Scenarios in Early October 1839

Kharak Singh the King	*Versus*	*Prince Sher Singh*
Kharak Singh the King Chet Singh Bajwa (Kharak Singh's friend) Misr Beli Ram (head of treasury) Ram Kishan (Raja's household controller) Priests Ram Singh and Gurmukh Singh	Versus	Wazir Dhian Singh Dogra Nau Nihal Singh (son of Kharak Singh) Chand Kaur (wife of Kharak Singh)

Kharak Singh unnecessarily extolled Chet Singh's virtues and almost treated him as a minister. It created unpleasantness and insecurity in the minds of Dhian Singh and other dignitaries of the court affronted by Chet Singh's arrogance and extra-constitutional powers.

Dhian Singh and Chet Singh each decided to teach a lesson to the other by plotting each other's downfall. Dhian Singh was smarter and acted faster. A rumour was going around Lahore that Chet Singh was a vassal of the British to enable them to annex

Punjab. That was enough for Dhian Singh to rope in Rani Chand Kaur, Kharak Singh's senior Maharani, to transfer power from Kharak Singh to her own son, Nau Nihal Singh. It was a very shrewd but destructive move by Dhian Singh and it was just the beginning of the long chains of events of suspicion, murder and revenge. It was the same Dhian Singh, who had vowed before a dying Ranjit Singh to safeguard the Khalsa Empire and be ever faithful to Kharak Singh.

The mother and son were thus secretly taken into confidence and Dhian Singh Dogra planned his next move of the chess-board. He very secretly interacted with important ministers to line up things the way he wanted. He wanted Nau Nihal Singh to be a puppet in his hands and he would be the king maker. A deputation consisting of Raja Dhian Singh, the Sindhanwalia Sardars, Jamadar Khushal Singh and Sardar Lehna Singh Majithia, made the prince believe that their loyalty and devotion towards him and his family was assured, they would not take orders from Chet Singh. They requested, on October 7, 1839 to accept their resignations or size up the intolerable Chet Singh. The prince promised to set things right.

Dhian Singh had to act fast now. Misr Beli Ram, head of the treasury, his brother Ram Kishan, controller of the Maharaja's household, and the Sikh priests Ram Singh and Gurmukh Singh, were sympathetic towards Chet Singh. Dhian Singh's party in the early hours of the morning of October 8, forced an entry into the Maharaja's sleeping apartments. Kharak Singh tried to shield his friend physically but to no avail. But Dhian Singh, the avowed saviour of the Sikh Raj could not be stopped. Violating every iota of protocol, the pusillanimous Dhian Singh separated Chet Singh from Kharak Singh and got him hacked to pieces. Beli Ram and his brothers were thrown into a dungeon. Kharak Singh was ejected from active administration and Prince Nau Nihal was installed in his place to carry on the affairs of government in his father's name. Chet Singh's brother, Gurdit Singh, was murdered too and a number of his relatives were rounded up.

Thus, Chet Singh's murder and Kharak Singh's removal by force was the first of a series of violent acts resulting in the liquidation of the Sikh kingdom. Dhian Singh, the Prime Minister was the initiator of the bloody streak. It is hard to say that if Kharak Singh had followed his father's advice and reposed faith in Dhian Singh, all activities of the court would have proceeded in a normal fashion.

Nau Nihal Singh

At 19, Nau Nihal Singh assumed supreme power of the Lahore Kingdom but allowed Kharak Singh the title of Maharaja. Nau Nihal had no great personal ambition and wanted the good of the state while Kharak Singh was too addicted to alcohol and opium and his mental faculties were at their lowest ebb. Perhaps the young prince thought that to retain the Sikh character of the state, leaving all critical decisions to a Dogra Hindu would do it no good. As executive head of the state, Nau Nihal Singh followed the advice of Dhian Singh and Aziz-ud-din diligently in foreign affairs, particularly the British. For domestic affairs he made decisions himself; proving to be a tough administrator.

In the areas of the North-West and beyond, widespread unrest existed and the Pathans of the areas beyond Attock refused revenue and hoped to throw off the Sikhs. The Zamindars of the uplands of Muzaffarabad were creating trouble. Painda Khan of Darband defied the authority of the Sikh governor of Hazara and collected a force of tribesmen and ravaged the countryside between Pagh Dhamtaur and Muzaffarabad. He occupied the fortress of Kishengarh from its Sikh commandant. After February 1840, the Lahore government restored Painda Khan's jagir.

Around Hassan Abdal the banditti of Gandgarh looted nearby areas and made the highway between Rawalpindi and Attock unsafe, bringing the caravan trade between Northern India and countries of Central Asia to a standstill. The Chief of Gandgarh now defied the government. Chattar Singh of Attari was ordered to proceed to Gandgarh to bring Khan Zaman to book.

The state treasury was in dire straits. During the five weeks before the death of Ranjit Singh, a sum of Rs 3.1 million was drawn in cash and cheques from the central treasury for purposes of charity. Gold and silver, richly caparisoned horses and elephants, milch cows and utensils, were given to religious institutions. The monsoons had failed during two successive years (1837-39) and the peasantry was quite hard pressed to pay their dues. Nau Nihal Singh called Diwan Sawan Mal from Multan and General Mian Singh from Kashmir and ordered them to clear their arrears.

The Iskardu Expedition of 1840

In conquering Ladakh in 1834, the Dogra General, Zorawar Singh, returned triumphant from Ladakh and came to Ranjit Singh to seek permission to extend the frontier further into Tibet. Ranjit Singh was wise and did not want to provoke the Chinese and the British and put a full stop to another expedition.

The ever clever and ambitious Wazir Dhian Singh Dogra had other ideas. He persuaded Nau Nihal to let the expedition be undertaken. Dhian Singh's brother Gulab Singh was the employer of Zorawar Singh and the Dogra brothers had extensive estates in Jammu and Kashmir. They thought they stood to gain by expansion of the Jammu and Kashmir kingdom.

Zorawar Singh took advantage of the division among the Iskardu (in the Gilgit-Baltistan area of Pakistan) ruling house, and made Iskardu a tributary to Lahore in May 1840. But for the next 12 months, operations had to be deferred owing to complications with the British.

Expedition to Mandi and Kulu, 1840

Zorawar Singh was given permission for the expedition against Iskardu and simultaneously General Ventura and Sardar Ajit Singh Sindhanwalia were ordered to march with their troops to the hill states of Mandi and Kulu to ensure from their rulers the payment of their stipulated dues to Lahore. The Sikh army encountered stiff resistance and reinforcements had to be sent from Lahore. However, Nau Nihal's attentions being divided, the expedition against Mandi and Kulu, like the one against Tibet, was suspended.

Relations with the British

Political relations between the Sikhs and the British had deteriorated. Nau Nihal Singh, despite his youth, handled the issue tactfully to save his kingdom. There was a tripartite treaty between the Sikhs, British and the Afghans and under the terms, Shah Shuja was to be restored as the King of Afghanistan without annexing any areas of the Sikh kingdom. In August 1839, the British reached Kabul and proclaimed Shujah, the King of Afghanistan.

Macnaghten (1793-1841) was an ambitious, arrogant and

megalomaniac British political officer in Kabul, who wanted rapid expansion of the British-cum-Durrani kingdom. He went west to acquire Herat and advised his government to snatch Peshawar district from the Sikhs. This was totally against the Sikh-British friendship and a gross violation of the Tripartite Treaty. The Sikhs were assured of their domains between the Indus and the entrance to the Khyber Pass.

British policy under Auckland had stooped to the lowest level of meanness. Macnaghten and his colleagues provoked the Yusafzais and other Muslim clans under the Lahore kingdom rousing the religious sentiments against the Sikhs and bribing them with gold and Khillats. Captain Wade also danced to Macnaghten's tune to get the government declaration of Yusafzai clans of Swat and Buner independent of the Sikh government. He asked Durbar officials in Peshawar to stop collecting revenues from the area pending an enquiry into their claims. He convinced the Muslim zamindars and jagirdars of the Yusafzai to be a part of the Kabul government.

Macnaghten made a false charge against the Lahore Durbar of monetary aid to the fugitive, Dost Muhammad Khan. Prince Nau Nihal was mentioned specifically as a culprit. To discuss the matter Fakir Aziz-ud-din was deputed by the Lahore Durbar to meet George Russell Clerk at Ludhiana. The British Agent dissuaded his own government from entertaining Macnaghten's proposals, once he was satisfied with the Sikh claims. But Lord Auckland's government took the opposite course and deadlock persisted.

Under these circumstances of suspicion, the two governments met to discuss the passage of British troops returning from Kabul, delineation of boundaries between Sikh and Afghan areas near Peshawar, maintenance of the Derajats, the regulation of tolls on the Indus and Sutlej. The most urgent of these was the return of British troops from Ghazni via Punjab.

The British troops were denied permission by Ranjit Singh to pass through his territory on their way to Kabul. Later, the British Agent paid a courtesy call to Prince Sher Singh and when the subject was re-opened a few days later, the Durbar under Nau Nihal Singh agreed to the British proposal only for the one emergency case; that its route should be via Dera Ismail Khan not

Lahore. The British Agent accepted these conditions and again after three months the question of passage for British troops was raised; this time to help Shah Shujah. Captain Wade had resumed his position of Agent of Ludhiana. And there was no love lost between him and Nau Nihal Singh.

The British army in Kabul was in trouble and Lord Ellenborough decided to restore Russell Clerk to his post in Ludhiana (March 1840). For supplies and a military convoy to proceed to Kabul by the Khyber route, the latter was successful in getting permission.

Another matter related to a contingent of 5000 Muslim soldiers which the Durbar had undertaken. Captain Wade and Macnaghten recommended to their government that Article 15 of the Tripartite Treaty whereby Shah Shujah was bound to pay Rs 0.2 million towards the maintenance of this force should be abrogated. The Durbar objected to this and Russell Clerk recommended that the unwelcome abrogation should not take place. This was agreed to by the Governor-General.

The British government next took up the revision of a commercial treaty. The British wanted to use the rivers for commercial and political purposes. Steamers could easily be modified into warships and the Indus could be used for transporting troops and artillery. In the end the solution was arrived at amicably and like his grandfather, Nau Nihal Singh proved himself as informed and tactful. He expressed his desire to talk to the British without compromising any of the interests and prestige of the Sikh kingdom.

Administration of the Durbar

One of Nau Nihal Singh's problems on the domestic front was his wayward and addicted father, Maharaja Kharak Singh. The year 1839 was almost coming to a close and he used to preside over the Durbar. He was quite upset and bitter about the throwing of Misr Beli Ram and his brothers into the dungeons, and often threatened to take British help. In December 1839, when he was apprised of Sir John Keen's intended visit to Lahore, he looked forward to it as an opportunity for speaking his mind to the Commander of the British forces. On December 31, 1839, he stole away from the palace, causing embarrassment to the court.

Nau Nihal Singh knew that a total break in relations between himself and his father might benefit the British, he ordered that the Misr family should be released. Beli Ram submitted an apology for his past conduct and agreed to abide by the orders of Dhian Singh. The wily Dhian Singh was not happy at all with the release of Beli Ram and his brothers.

Sher Singh, the step-brother of Kharak Singh was a constant source of irritation to Nau Nihal Singh. Since Nau Nihal Singh was having a difficult time with the British, Sher Singh was always hopeful of sitting on the throne at a suitable opportune moment. Sher Singh applied for a month's leave of absence from the court for visiting Hardwar and other holy places but he was informed that Maharaja Kharak Singh was planning a similar pilgrimage and if the brothers went together, it would be convenient.

Dhian Singh had become powerful independently and rather be a loyal subject, he continually bargained for some benefit and it accentuated the friction between the Dogras and the Sikhs. The Prince had to look after Durbar's interests as well as keep the ministers in good humour. He got along well with Dhian Singh Dogra; for the moment, at least.

Table 1.3 Scenario in 1840

Kharak Singh the King Misr Beli Ram (head of treasury) Bhai Gobind Ram, Brahmin priest Priests Ram Singh and Gurmukh Singh Ajit Sindhanwalia, Attar Sindhanwalia Jamadar Khushhal Singh	Versus	Wazir Dhian Singh Dogra

The release of Misr Beli Ram caused a serious difference for the first time. Dhian Singh wanted to go home and was granted a fortnight's leave on January 20, 1840. Dhian Singh was despised by the priests Bhai Ram Singh and Bhai Gobind Ram, the Sindhanwalias, Ajit Singh and Attar Singh, and Jamadar Khushal Singh. These men attempted to widen the breach between Dhian Singh and the Prince who told them about his own regard for Dhian Singh's abilities.

Death/Murder # 2 (Victim: Kharak Singh)

Kharak Singh was a weak and avaricious man; he was regarded as a fool by even the nobles. The crown prince was frequently drunk; wine and women mattered more to him rather than the matters of state. He was addicted to copious amounts of opium and had little time for royal advisers. The prospect of serving such a man did not go down well with the *durbaris*.

Though his coronation came later on September 1, 1839, Kharak Singh had assumed the title of Maharaja immediately after his father's funeral in June 1839. He threw lavish parties, got drunk for days on end, ignored his Wazir (the highly ambitious Dhian Singh) and alienated the most powerful nobles in his realm. The religious Khalsa despised his behaviour. The new Maharaja's generals and advisers were fed up with him. Even if his lecherous ways of his love of drugs, drink and dancing girls is forgiven, his inability to focus on matters of state was unpardonable. A plan was hatched, just four months into his reign i.e. in early 1840 to get rid of Kharak Singh.

Who else but Dhian Singh was involved in it as the circumstantial evidence points to but this was achieved in a very clandestine manner? The Maharaja's daily food and wine was mixed with *rus camphor* (a compound of mercury) and *Sapheeda kaskaree* (white lead). At first, the poison simply mimicked drunkenness. Kharak Singh's speech became a little more slurred than usual, and he had coordination problems for longer periods of time.

Then the Maharaja started to lose his eyesight and a mysterious and merciless itch took over his body. Kharak Singh's joints burned with pain within weeks and skin lesions appeared all over his body. Six months after the poisoning began, his organs started to shut down in July/August 1840. Kharak Singh lay in bed in agony, unable to get up and awaited death.

The poisoning caused a slow death which occurred after eleven months of struggle by Kharak Singh to survive and Nau Nihal Singh had already been recalled to the capital. Dhian Singh was always suspected to be the mastermind behind the plot of poisoning the Maharaja although it was never proven. Nau Nihal, in all possibility, did not have any hand in his father's murder, even though his attitude towards his own father was of utter indifference. As he awaited his death and struggled in pain, he begged to see his son every day. However, the crown prince rarely visited his father, as noted tersely by Dr. Honigberger. When death finally came to Kharak Singh on November 5, 1840; the pain was gone forever.

The official announcement talked about a sudden mysterious illness, but no mention of the months of suffering was made. Nobody really missed Kharak Singh or seemed to be bothered about the way he died.

Once again, Dr. Honigberger found himself with a ringside seat at a Punjabi state funeral. Describing the event in his memoirs, Honigberger said: *'Three of his wives were burnt with him; and I was present at that horrid, yet remarkable spectacle ...'* Eleven slave girls also burned to death that day, but Honigberger, perhaps was overawed by the horrors of *sati* and failed even to mention them.

Nau Nihal performed the last rites for Kharak Singh the same way as Kharak Singh had lit his own father's pyre. In contrast to his father, he looked a king perfectly. He was popular with the court as well as the masses and he had taken the reins during his father's 'sickness'. Though not yet nineteen, he possessed a maturity beyond his years, and to those who had longed for leadership, Nau Nihal seemed worthy to wear the Koh-i-Noor.

There was a bad omen during the occasion. While Kharak Singh's funeral pyre was still burning, Nau Nihal Singh felt very ill. He complained of stomach-ache and as he vomited, he was taken to the shade near the shrine of Maharaja Ranjit Singh. Ram Singh and Gobind Ram, the Bhais gave him medicine for sunstroke. Or was there an attempt to poison him too? It was November and it could not have been very warm in Punjab.

Later, when the mourners proceeded towards the river to perform the traditional bath, the Prince felt strong enough to join them; holding the hand of his friend Mian Udham Singh, son of Raja Gulab Singh.

Death/Murder # 3 (Victim: Nau Nihal Singh)

Maharaja Nau Nihal Singh was on his return from bathing, and just before entering Roshnai Gate, he took the hand of his constant companion Mian Udham Singh, the eldest son of Raja

Gulab Singh, brother of Dhian Singh. The two young men entered the archway together. As they emerged from it stones, and tiles fell from above, and the Maharaja and Udham Singh were struck to the ground. While Udham Singh died on the spot, Nau Nihal Singh lay on the ground. Nau Nihal had received head injuries and he tried to rise, and cried out for water. Dhian Singh also received injuries on the arm.

Sadly, Nau Nihal's skull was fractured and had an arm broken. Bhai Gobind Ram, the family priest felt his pulse and pronounced him as dying (*waqt-i-akhri-ast*). It was on the afternoon of November 5, 1840 that Nau Nihal Singh met with the fatal accident and was carried into the palace in a senseless condition with brain haemorrhage. He would never speak again. His initial injury was described as slight by an eye witness to the accident. The crafty minister circulated the news that the young sovereign had only received a slight injury, and would soon recover.

Apparently reserving all his devotion and care for the young King, Dhian Singh rushed up, pushing aside the dead body of his own nephew. The Prince was removed to the baradari of the Hazuri garden and the premises cleared of people; Dhian Singh, personally, using 'hand and stick' to persuade anyone who lingered. The two Bhais, the Fakir brothers, Aziz and Nur-ud-din, the Sindhanwalia Sardars and Jamadar Khushal Singh remained there and the rest were evacuated. The gates of the garden were closed. Admission was denied to all.

Several of the prominent Sardars begged to see the Maharaja including the relations of the royal family. Also, in vain was Nau Nihal Singh's mother's request. In a paroxysm of rage and anxiety, she came and beat the fort gates with her own hands. Admittance even to the fort was not given and into the Maharaja's apartment, there were greater restrictions. None of the female inmates, not even his wives, were allowed to see him.

Nau Nihal Singh expired probably the same day, just three days short of thirteen months since Chet Singh's assassination had made him de facto ruler of Punjab. Raja Dhian Singh and Dewan Dina Nath were among others who suffered injuries.

An emergency meeting of the Sardars decided to invest Raja Dhian Singh with the highest executive authority and only those orders that bore the *sahi* and seal of Raja Dhian Singh were to be treated as official.

The fact of his death was kept secret and towards the evening the body of the Prince was conveyed to the fort. Late at night communication was sent to Sher Singh at Kahnwan, 80 miles from Lahore, to make a quick journey to the capital. Upon his arrival on November 7, 1840, the news of Prince Nau Nihal Singh's death was officially released. His head was now severely crushed and the courtiers were shocked to see the body. The obsequies were performed the next morning on November 8.

Did Dhian Singh Plan Nau Nihal's Murder?

Dhian Singh was the main player during the sad events in Lahore and so his enemies and rivals suspected him. Some felt that the sudden fall of masonry was pre-planned by him and Gulab Singh using men who were in the bad books of the prince. But no concrete evidence emerged. Dhian Singh was a shady character and it was known to all the courtiers. The execution of a plot of murder could not easily pass without detection.

It is not known with certainty that the Rajas of Jammu including Gulab Singh designed to remove Nau Nihal Singh; but it is difficult to acquit them of the crime, and can be said for sure that they were capable of committing it. There was no love lost between the Hill Rajas and the Khalsa since the days of Guru Gobind Singh. It is also quite certain that the prince was contemplating their degradation, and, perhaps, their destruction.

A Russian traveller, Soltykoff, who visited the site a year after the accident wrote: 'I tremble every time I pass a gateway of Amritsar on an elephant and ....many such gates, half ruined and threatening to fall at any time.' Nau Nihal Singh's death at that particular moment is believed by most of the authors to be accidental but the impact of the tragedy was tremendous.

Alexander Gardner (1785-1877) was an American soldier, mercenary and a traveller. He was in Lahore when the event unfolded there. His details are sure to raise suspicions. He writes:

> Nao Nihal Singh was taken inside the palace by 5 palanquin-bearers....2 of them were later liquidated, 2 escaped...., the fifth could not be traced....One palki-bearer confirmed that while the prince was put into the palki.... he saw that above the right ear there was a wound accompanied by not much blood.... but when the room was opened, blood in great quantities, both fluid and coagulated,

was found around the head of the cloth....when the doors were opened the Sindhanwalias found the young Maharaja dead, Dhian Singh lying prostrate on the ground, and Fakir Nuruddin, the royal physician, feeling helpless....

Who Would be King Now?

It was now the second week of November 1840. Nau Nihal Singh had been cremated; he was just 19 years old at the time of his death. Six princes were now claimants to the throne: Sher Singh and his twin brother Tara Singh born in 1807; Peshaura Singh (b. 1818) and his brother Kashmira Singh (b. 1819); Multana Singh (b. 1819) and Duleep Singh (b. 1838).

Sher Singh was the eldest, having failed in his attempt to overtake Kharak Singh, but he was the senior-most surviving son of Ranjit Singh and the notables agreed, on November 5 to place him on the throne. Sher Singh was formally proclaimed Maharaja on November 9, 1840. Rani Chand Kaur, widow of Kharak Singh and mother of just dead Nau Nihal Singh, backed by the Sindhanwalia chiefs, put forward a claim that she was expecting a child from her daughter-in-law Sahib Kaur who should be considered for the throne. She asked to be accepted as a regent during the pregnancy. The claim was admitted but the question was whether she would remain a regent till the child came of age.

The most important courtiers came to be divided into two sharply opposed groups.

Table 1.4 Scenarios in Late 1840

Rani Chand Kaur (widow of Kharak Singh) Sahib Kaur (widow of Nau Nihal Singh) Attar Singh Sindhanwalia Ajeet Singh Sindhawalia Lehna Singh Majithia Bhai Ram Singh; Gobind Ram (priest) Jamadar Khushal Singh and his nephew Tej Singh (Brahmins from Meerut) Sardar Fateh Singh Mann, Sardar Gulab Singh Povindia Sheikh Ghulam Mohi-ud-din	Versus	Sher Singh Wazir Dhian Singh Dogra Raja Gulab Singh Dogra Bhai Gurmukh Singh Granthi Sardar Sham Singh Attariwala Sardar Dhanna Singh Malwai Fakir Aziz-ud-din and his two brothers Senior European officers including Ventura and Court

Dhian Singh Dogra expressed concern that if a woman remained in charge it could prove quite unsafe for the Sikh kingdom as the British marched across it to Kabul, routinely, sending troops, stores and ammunition. The Rani's supporters expressed fears for the life of the unborn child if the ambitious Sher Singh was around. A solution needed to be found.

On November 27, 1840, it was decided by the council of ministers that Sher Singh would retire to his estate with his minor son, Partap Singh, representing him on the council till the birth of Nau Nihal's child. Consequently, Chand Kaur became a regent with Dhian Singh, Khushal Singh, Attar Singh Sindhanwalia and Lehna Singh, four ministers, acting as her advisers.

Thus, Chand Kaur's party seemed to have won. Sher Singh watched helplessly as the order was issued. But the real problem arose where day-to-day functioning was involved as there was no lack of factional spirit, with both Chand Kaur and Sher Singh having grand opinions about themselves. They did not consider the opinion of their ministers. The devious Dhian Singh was blessed with sharp intelligence and had a firm grasp of administrative complexities and this caused jealousy among his colleagues.

Dhian Singh, finding himself in a quandary did not come to the court for five weeks i.e. almost till the end of 1840. When he realised that even Chand Kaur was collaborating with other ministers, against him, he chose to go to Sher Singh's camp.

Dhian Singh went on leave to Jammu and sent a secret message to Prince Sher Singh to be prepared to take charge, and also advised the officers of the army, close to him, to join the Prince when the call came. Dhian Singh's influence with the regiments of the army having European officers was great. During Dhian Singh's absence the administrative machinery came to a standstill and Chand Kaur found to her chagrin that Dhian Singh was indispensable. She asked him to return to Lahore. What else could she do?

A clever Dhian Singh did not reply but instead sent word to Sher Singh to proceed to Lahore. The Prince with 300 men reached the vicinity of Lahore on the morning of January 13, 1841 to encamp on the site of an old brick kiln known as *Budhu da Ava* staying with his junior, Jawala Singh who tried to convince the troops to defect to their side and the desertions to his camp happened soon. Ventura was one of them. Soldiers were followed by civilians.

Rani Chand Kaur was not a dumb woman; she brought Gulab Singh Dogra to her cause who with Teja Singh and Attar Singh Sindhanwalia, attempted to get the support of soldiers quartered about the fort.

Gulab Singh gave away 0.3 million and Sher Singh half a million during the twenty-four hours before hostilities commenced on January 16, 1841. The Khalsa soldiers had almost become mercenaries, prepared to fight for the highest bidder. On the evening of January 15, Sher Singh had a force of about 26,000 infantry, 8000 cavalry and a park of artillery comprising 45 guns, also Generals Ventura, Court and Mahtab Singh Majithia, in his camp. Two hours after sunset, he marched from his camp till he reached the wicket gate of the city adjoining the Badshahi mosque.

Dhaunkal Singh's battalion, which was on guard, betraying the Rani, opened the gate. At the three other gates named the Delhi, the Yakki and the Taxali gates, the same process was repeated. Thus, before sunrise on January 16, Sher Singh was master of most of the city. He called upon the defending troops to surrender. Rani Chand Kaur prepared for battle. Gulab Singh, Teja Singh and Attar Singh Sindhanwalia were on her side.

Next Sher Singh ordered his artillery to open fire. The Hazuri Bagh gate was blown and two to three hundred Nihangs made a charge but nearly a hundred Nihangs died in a double cannon fire from the fort. The second Nihang charge met the same fate. Meanwhile the Dogra infantry poured deadly fire and in 10 minutes all the attackers evaporated; either killed or taken prisoners. Some including Sher Singh fled back. Another attack on the Eastern gate was repulsed. The fewer Dogras proved heavy for a vast number of Sikh soldiers.

The status quo prevailed and for Rani Jindan, the queen, no British help was forthcoming either. For two days there was a stalemate. She directed Bhai Ram Singh to see Clerk's munshi, Harsarn Das, who wrote to Clerk that the Rani would accept a British Resident in Lahore and be guided by him in forming a ministry. She offered the province of Kashmir, or one-fourth of the annual revenues of the entire Punjab to the British in return for their help. She added that state troops in Lahore numbered no more than 20,000 and so on. What a proposed treachery!

Because of Gulab Singh's continued support of the Rani, Sher Singh was now nervous and desperate. He sent an urgent summon to Dhian Singh in Jammu. On January 18, the Prince and the Minister mounted on the same elephant, rode to the city, much to the relief of the troops and the people.

The few days of fighting made the lives of people miserable. The soldiers were uncontrolled, had been without wages for months and in absence of any sensible control, they pillaged and looted the shops, shopkeepers, traders and merchants. As the people lived without much to eat or drink, the soldiers looted the Gulab Khana stocked with delicacies, wines, dried fruits, nuts and preserves of all kinds. It was free for all and the Khalsa sepoys feasted for two days. For the first time since 1799, the situation resembled the one during the attacks by the barbarous Afghan hordes of Abdali's time.

Dhian Singh asked Chand Kaur to renounce all claim to the throne; against a jagir valued at Rs. 0.9 million per annum, and Raja Gulab Singh and his Dogra troops were to be granted a safe conduit out of the fort; Sher Singh was to be Maharaja and Dhian Singh Chief Minister. It was a difficult offer for ambitious Chand Kaur but she accepted it; Gulab Singh vacated the fort and it was occupied by Sher Singh on January 20, 1841. Gulab Singh and the treasurer, Misr Beli Ram, paid homage to Sher Singh who was presented the Koh-i-Noor after Chand Kaur and Gulab returned to his home in Jammu. In this way ended the seventy days of Chand Kaur's regency. The British were to discover the chasms in the body politic of the Khalsa to exploit it at the opportune moment and turn it to their own advantage.

Sher Singh and Chand Kaur had each treacherously offered slices of Ranjit Singh's kingdom to the British. We will not find the British guilty of the similar disloyalty to the crown, i.e. sacrifing EIC or British interests for personal gains. But India has been a country of Mir Zafars else how can one explain the foreign rule over it for a thousand years?

Moreover, the negotiations for personal gains leaked to the British Agent a great deal of sensitive information regarding the

Sikh state. After the accession of Sher Singh, Lord Ellenborough began making plans for the conquest of the Punjab.

In the last 70 days, soldiers were pampered by the contesting parties for their support and the soldiers developed an opinion of their indispensable support for king making much to the detriment of the dignity of the state and the ruler. Sher Singh was quite responsible for the situation.

Sher Singh is Crowned King

Sher Singh was invested as Maharaja formally on January 20, 1841. Baba Bikram Singh Bedi of Una applied the saffron mark on the Prince's forehead and blessed him and his son Kanwar Partap Singh. The chiefs present included Attar Singh Sindhanwalia and others who had sworn to compel Prince Sher Singh to retire to his jagir. They wanted Rani Chand Kaur as a regent at least for eight months. At this moment things promised well. The supporters of Chand Kaur departed from the court. Attar Singh, was soon to follow his nephew Ajit Singh Sindhanwalia who had already left. The British seemed to have accepted the present situation.

The army now started demanding the emoluments promised by Sher Singh, his Chief Minister, Dhian Singh, and his friend, Jwala Singh. There was barely any money in the treasury and over and above, Chand Kaur and Gulab Singh had removed cartloads of cash, gold and jewellery from the *Toshakhana* (treasury). For days, the soldiers deserted their posts, claiming that the pay-clerks were fraudulent (this particular grievance was well founded); and that their commanders were unnecessarily harsh. They not only plundered homes and shops but also hunted, maltreated or killed the fraudulent clerks and those rigid officers. General Court, Jamadar Khushal Singh and Lehna Singh Majithia were considered too harsh. For eight to ten weeks, the city was hellish. Even the Ministers and secretaries of the government were treated with disdain and Sher Singh, was warned that unless he paid up, Rani Chand Kaur would be restored.

Revolt by soldiers spread. In Srinagar, the governor, Man Singh, had been hacked to pieces on April 19, 1841. In Mandi the murder of Commandant Foulkes took place in March 1841. In Hazara the murder of Major Ford took place on April 8 and in Amritsar, the garrison commander Sobha Singh was killed.

General Avitable abandoned Peshawar and sought shelter at Jalalabad, and Diwan Sawan Mal, governor of Multan, somehow escaped.

This state of lawlessness continued for at least six months and was a paradoxical situation. With the soldiery both Sher Singh and Dhian Singh had been popular. Dhian Singh had charge of the whole of the Westernised military force and got tremendous support for Sher Singh from the same Army. Even the financial demands of the army were partially met. The pay-rolls of March 1841-February 1842, show that the scale of pay was raised and each man was rewarded with a gratuity equal to one month's salary.

It seems probable that the grievance of the army had roots in the battle against Chand Kaur when Dhian Singh Dogra's brother Gulab Singh literally destroyed the Sikh attackers. This combined with the measures he was forced to take to check the turbulence of the soldiers made him even more unpopular. He was responsible for transferring vitriolic Sikhs more often and also the new recruits were mostly non-Sikhs, including the Dogras and this aroused suspicion of him.

The soldiers were distressed to see the decimation of Sikh Panthic principles through dissension between members of the ruling family who were ready to partition the state for their selfish gains. The soldiers thought of reviving old traditions, the formation of Panchayats, and calling of the *Sarbat Khalsa*, as a representative of the Sikh people.

Although Sher Singh was seated on the throne, the prospects of Nau Nihal Singh's widow giving birth to a male child, must have worried him. Also, Attar Singh and his nephew, Ajit Singh Sindhanwalia, had been in British India to bolster the claims of Chand Kaur whom they supported.

Death/Murder # 4 (Victim: Chand Kaur)

A feeling of great insecurity gripped Sher Singh and he could only think of liquidiating his rivals to come out of it. His first victim was the widow of Nau Nihal Singh, pregnant Kanwarani Sahib Kaur. He first circulated rumours that the news of her pregnancy was false and a maid girl was bribed to administer drugs to Sahib Kaur. It brought about a miscarriage.

Chand Kaur was Sher Singh's next target whom in fact he offered his hand for marriage. Such were the complex games the rulers played to hang on to power. Chand Kaur was not satisfied with the offered Jagir and she resided in her mansion within the city ostensibly waiting for Sher Singh to take her as a bride.

She was in touch with the Sardars, the army and the British. The British needed help at Kabul, Kandahar, Ghazni and Jalalabad. Maharaja Sher Singh readily agreed to help provided the British assured him of support against Rani Chand Kaur, who was still actively plotting against him and whose agents were in British India. There was no way Clerk could not give this assurance.

Ajit Singh Sindhanwalia was told to go to Calcutta to wait upon the Governor-General. Attar Singh was instructed to come to Ferozepur, much closer to Lahore. When Sher Singh returned to the capital after attending Holi celebrations in Amritsar, the Khalsa soldiers surrounded the palace, also insulted him; threatening to replace him by Rani Chand Kaur.

The Maharaja kept quiet, but wanted to take a revengeful decision. Briefing Dhian Singh about the clandestine operation to be carried out, he went on a hunt around Wazirabad. Dhian Singh roped in Mahan Singh, Thanedar of Lahore, and Ichar Singh, Jamadar of the guard at Chand Kaur's haveli. Four of the Rani's women attendants were bribed with gifts to kill their mistress. They first infused poison in a beverage she used to take but this day she did not. Next while she was asleep, her skull was battered with a stone. After three days of agony, she died, on June 12, 1841.

She was cremated in the precincts of Mai Nakain's garden. Dhian Singh had now Sher Singh perpetually obliged to him. Dhian Singh always had a grudge against the Sindhanwalias.

On some of the state documents, his signature occurs, in Roman letters: Sher Singh. He ordered the minting of coins unlike his predecessors and it is possible that Sher Singh's departure from this tradition, was a sign of his insecurity about the *gaddi*.

Death/Murder # 5 (Victim: Jawala Singh)

Jawala Singh was the administrator of Sher Singh's jagirs and over time became a close confidant of the latter. Jawala Singh was with Sher Singh when the latter marched on Lahore in January

1841, and they were together also during Dhian Singh's absence from the scene between January 13-17. Later he took over the estates of the Sindhanwalias.

The position of Chief Minister was his aspiration. But he was no match for the wily Dhian Singh Dogra who created a suspicion in Sher Singh's mind regarding his proximity with the arch enemies, the Sindhanwalias. The crooked Dhian Singh also warned Jawala Singh that he had lost the Maharaja's good-will. The hot-headed Sardar soon revolted. He won over the Chahär Yari horse of irregular cavalry, comprising about 5000 men, and set up a camp near the Shalimar Gardens in May 1841. When called by the Maharaja, he refused to present himself. Then Dhian Singh cautioned Sher Singh that, if Jawala Singh was not handled with an iron hand, treason would be a fallout.

Despite the Maharaja's order, the soldiers refused to surrender their leader. Sher Singh achieved his object with a cash donation of Rs 30,000. Jawala Singh was led into Lahore in chains. He was tortured and thrown into a dungeon. After forty days he died.

The Brave Zorawar Singh

Colonel Zorawar Singh made the state of Iskardu as a tributary to the Lahore Durbar in 1840. He resumed hostilities against the Tibetans in April 1841. In May 1841 he proceeded against Gartok (in Lhasa) and he occupied the town with the help of Ladakhi troops in June. He was intercepted by a force sent from Lhasa, but he forced the Tibetans to withdraw on August 29 and succeeded in occupying Tuklakote, a town near Lake Mansarovar, the source of the Indus and Sutlej. The dominion of Lahore was thus brought close to the frontiers of Nepal by him.

Before undertaking the long march to Lhasa, Zorawar Singh decided to spend the winter in Tuklakote, to rest his troops and muster his resources. The great victories of Zorawar Singh alarmed the British who were wary of losing the wool traffic from Lhasa. Russell Clerk came to Lahore in October 1841 to remonstrate with the Durbar. He pointed out that a satisfactory agreement between them and the Chinese would be jeopardised by the Durbar's adventures. The Maharaja was requested to recall his troops from Lhasa by the middle of December 1841.

The Chinese government had not been unaware that

Zorawar Singh had reached Lake Mansarovar. A well-planned counter attack was launched against him and the Dogras were overwhelmed. Zorawar was struck and pierced by a lance. The Lhasa in the next five months recovered Tuklakote, Gartok, Rohtak and Iskardu and threatened Ladakh. There, Mian Munga Ram, with 400 Dogras fought the Lhasa troops till the end of May 1842. Led by Wazir Ratnu and Diwan Hari Chand, reinforcements arrived from Jammu. Diwan Hari Singh and Wazir Ratnu went in pursuit of the retreating Chinese but the British again intervened, drawing the Lahore Durbar's attention to the agreement concluded by Clerk in October 1841 which restricted the Khalsa up to Ladakh.

Diwan Hari Singh persuaded the ruler of Lhasa to send the raw wool and tea produced in his territory to Ladakh and to recognise the sovereignty of Lahore over Ladakh.

The assassination of Shuja-ul-Mulk on April 5, 1842, raised another issue between the two powers and the question of the validity of the treaty was considered and the British proposed a fresh treaty to the Khalsa government. The Durbar's draft included clauses whereby (1) Sikh possession of Swat, Buner, and Panjtar would be formally recognised, (2) As it infringed on the sovereignty of the Sikhs, the passing of the British troops through the Punjab must be stopped.

The first proposal was acceptable to the British but not the second one. The Governor General was not prepared to give up the concession of passage for his troops, which his government had extorted from the Durbar on one pretext or the other. Further, he insisted that the Durbar permit Dost Mohammad to pass through the Punjab on his way to Kabul and the Durbar contracted a treaty of amity and friendship with Dost Mohammed independent of the British. Dost Muhammad was set at liberty by the British and returned to Kabul as ruler. On his way he stayed in Lahore (January 25-February 15, 1843) as the guest of Maharaja Sher Singh and the opportunity was taken, of drawing up a friendly agreement.

The Anglo Fiasco in Afghanistan

The Afghans hated the way the British tried to put Shah Shuja on the throne of Kabul against their wishes. An extremely irate

Afghan mob surrounded the houses of Sir Alexander Burnes and Broadfoot on the morning of November 3, 1841, and slaughtered every inmate. An unnerved General Elphinstone decided to surrender. Hunger, frost and Afghan bullets accounted for most of the British men. Out of thousands of men almost the sole survivor, Dr. Brydon somehow arrived in Jalalabad to tell the tale of disaster.

The British planned the occupation of the Punjab at the very time when the Sikhs were fighting Britain's battles at Ali Masjid, Jalalabad and Kabul. Not only this, Ellenborough was planning a personal meeting with Maharaja Sher Singh and his ministers to chalk out a policy regarding Afghanistan.

Clerk arranged that a mission from the Lahore Durbar, should meet him at Ludhiana on December 15, 1842. In this regard, Sham Singh Attariwala, Fakir Aziz-ud-din and Lehna Singh Majithia went to Phillaur to meet Ellenborough. Conducted by Clerk, the Governor-General in his camp at Ludhiana was to receive Lehna Singh. The Sardar remained at Phillaur expecting to be found in his own camp while Clerk waited half-way between Ludhiana and Phillaur. The Vakil of the Lahore Durbar in league with the crafty Dhian Singh misled Lehna Singh to discredit him both with the Maharaja and the British.

Table 1.5 Scenario in Late 1842

Sher Singh Bhai Gurmukh Singh, General Ventura, Bhai Gobind Ram Diwan Kirpa Ram	Versus	Dhian Singh Dogra
Sher Singh	Versus	Attar Singh Sindhanwalia Ajeet Singh Sindhawalia (nephew of Ajeet) Lehna Singh Kehr Singh
Attar Singh Sindhanwalia Ajeet Singh Sindhawalia (nephew of Ajeet) Lehna Singh	Versus	Dhian Singh Dogra

The Maharaja had to send Raja Hira Singh, Raja Suchet Singh and Jamadar Khushal Singh to join Fakir Aziz-ud-din and proceed to Ferozepur where the Governor-General had gone. Later, Lord Ellenborough was happy enough to receive Sher Singh's son the young Partap Singh and pay a return visit to the Lahore camp.

Power Struggle in the Lahore Durbar

Sher Singh was not gifted in the handling of affairs; after all he had little education. His weakness was exploited by others. In Ranjit Singh's immediate family the Sindhanwalia family were next of kin. Attar Singh, Lehna Singh [not Majithia] and their two nephews, Ajit and Shamsher Singh, represented the family at court. Attar Singh was a renowned soldier and as a champion of Khalsa, came after only Hari Singh Nalwa in the Sikh annals.

Sher Singh was considered an upstart and usurper by the Sindhanwali and when the former came to power, Attar Singh sought refuge with Baba Bikram Singh Bedi at Una and was later joined by Ajit. But Lehna Singh and Kehr Singh were brought to Lahore in chains, and dispossessed of their estates, weapons, stables, etc., valued at Rs. 4 million.

Sher Singh was getting tired of Dhian Singh's control of affairs. After Chand Kaur's death, the Sindhanwalias wanted to make peace with Sher Singh to regain their status at the court and challenge the supremacy of the Dogras. Attar Singh and Ajit Singh were advised by their friends and by Clerk, the British Agent, to return to the Punjab, and try to form an 'all-party' government. So, Ajit Singh made a request to the Maharaja to be allowed to return. This move was for ousting Dhian Singh from power and to accomplish this goal, Ajit Singh Sindhanwalia arrived in Lahore in the first week of November 1842, while his uncle Attar Singh awaited the development from Thanesar. Ajit Singh was welcomed and reassured by the Maharaja, given a cash grant and their family property was restored to the Sindhanwalia. Lehna Singh and Kehr Singh were received in Lahore with the honour due to their rank once they were released from the Mukerian jail. Ajit Singh and Sher Singh had known each other since boyhood and soon they resumed their drink-and-dancing soirées. Sher Singh now neglected his urgent work and ignored ministers and secretaries. He was drawn to the shikar and chase too often during the day. Some of the elder Ministers such as Lehna Singh

Majithia, Lehna Singh Sindhanwalia, Fakir Aziz-ud-din, and Dhian Singh counselled him but Sher Singh began to think of means to rid himself of Dhian Singh. He invited Diwan Kirpa Ram, disliked by Dhian Singh to return to Lahore. Bhai Gurmukh Singh, General Ventura, Bhai Gobind Ram and several others of the anti-Dogra faction, became close to him. There was grave mutual distrust between the Maharaja and his Chief Minister and they had to swear good-will to each other every third day of the week. The crisis came in the month of July 1843 when Dhian Singh and Aziz-ud-din decided to leave Lahore in separate parties.

The Sindhanwalia Sardars watched the situation. It was a complex scenario. The Maharaja suspected his Chief Minister Dhian Singh Dogra; the Sindhanwalias despised the Dogras as they had to be in exile for three years because of them. They disliked Sher Singh as well since they had earlier supported Chand Kaur, the widow of Kharak Singh. The Sindhanwalias hoped to exploit the misunderstanding between the Maharaja and the Chief Minister to get rid of both.

Dhian Singh perceived during the summer of 1843 that his influence over the Maharaja had reduced a great deal and he had good reason to be wary of the machinations of Gurmukh Singh. The minister then again began to talk of the boy, Duleep Singh, and tried to make the Sindhianwala chiefs believe that they had been deceptively brought to Lahore for their ruin.

Ambition in the Sindhanwalia Sardars to seize sovereignty was not a new phenomeaon. Ajit Singh drew the Maharaja's attention to the fact that Attar Singh and his escort, were at the moment (March 23, 1843) at Una. He suggested that the Maharaja should come personally to take him home. Sher Singh agreed but remained indifferent about it. Lehna Singh and Ajit Singh sought a private audience with him to press the matter on August 16 some months later. Sher Singh was cordial, but non-committal quoting Dhian Singh that their wishes defied the regal decorum.

This annoyed both the Sardars greatly and was precisely what the Maharaja had wanted. It was decided to invite Dhian Singh to the palace and get him murdered. The Maharaja was assured by Ajit Singh that Dhian Singh's brother Suchet Singh was in accord with him and willing to undertake the responsibilities of government. The Maharaja agreed. Somehow Dhian Singh got to know of the plot and slipped away. The day of reckoning came a month later for him as well as the Maharaja.

Although Ajit Singh was a good companion of the Maharaja; he was nevertheless himself ambitious for power. He and his uncle believed in taking Sher Singh's life to save their own.

Death/Murder # 6, 7 and 8 (Victims: Maharaja Sher Singh, Kunwar Partap Singh and Dhian Singh Dogra)

On September 15, 1843 which was the first day of the Bikrami month and a *sangranth*, the Maharaja rode out of the city early in the morning and there was no *Durbar* for him to attend. In Tej Singh's garden tents were put up for his son, Kanvar Partap Singh and Sher Singh alighted there. He moved on the Shah Balaval to fulfil the morning's engagement where sitting in the pleasure house, he enjoyed watching wrestling-bouts, with Buddh Singh his armour-bearer and Diwan Dina Nath. After he had dismissed the wrestlers with due charity, the Sandhanwalia Sardars, who had followed him with 150 horse and 300 foot, requested him to inspect their troops. Ajit Singh went to the garden house at Shah Bilawal where the Maharaja was encamped. Ostensibly for muster and inspection, he took his newly raised levies with him,

Sher Singh agreed and came out of the room without an iota of suspicion. After the parade, Ajit Singh wanted to show the Maharaja a carbine which he had procured from an Englishman in Calcutta. It was a trap. The Maharaja was a lover of weapons and as he stretched out his hands to inspect the said rifle, Ajit Singh pressed the trigger, emptying bullets into his chest. The Maharaja said, 'Oh, Sardar, what deception!' as he dropped to the ground dead. Ajit Singh rushed forward and with a single blow of the sword, beheaded him.

The attendants of the Maharaja Budh Singh, Nikka Singh and Ashraf, who challenged the assassins were killed right there; Sardar Hukm Singh Malwai was severely wounded.

While Ajit Singh was thus engaged, his uncle, Lahna Singh, went in search of Prince Partap Singh, who was distributing alms in the garden of Jawala Singh. He seized the 12-year-old boy and with one blow severed his head from his body. For conducting the ceremony, the two priests Hira and Jawahar who were summoned, were also killed.

With contingents of 500 horse and foot, the Sindhanwalias proceeded to the city and on the way, they met Dhian Singh who was going to the Shah Bilawal garden to pay his respects to the Maharaja. To settle the future of the government the Sindhanwalias pressed him to accompany them. Dhian Singh had no choice but to comply. The party had hardly reached the gun foundry inside the fort when a pistol shot from behind killed Dhian Singh and another ended the life of his devoted attendant, Fateh Khan Gheba. It was September 17, 1843 and Dhian Singh was 47 years old then.

There are many other versions of the story but the fact remains that since these kinsmen of the Maharaja returned to Lahore, a contest for power was inevitable. Although there is no proof, but it can be safely said that the British were watching the developments in Punjab very keenly and the Company's corrupt influence had been employed in fanning and fomenting these plots.

Sher Singh's reign ended in violence, as it had begun; in violence. He ruled for two years and eight months, a period marked by events which accelerated the dissolution of the kingdom. The Prince had shown his capabilities as a soldier and held command in the most difficult areas like Peshawar and the uplands of Hazara. This enabled him support at court. But he belied their hopes. He became a reckless sensualist and alcoholic. His own character, and that of many of those closest to him was marred by insecurity and self-seeking.

Hira Singh the New Prime Minister of the Punjab

Hira Singh was a great favourite of Ranjit Singh and was allowed privileges similar to what were given to the Princes, Kharak Singh and Sher Singh. Suchet Singh, his uncle was a soldier of fame. The Dogras, Hira Singh and Suchet Singh got the fullest support of the Khalsa army.

Hira Singh sought support from the troops under the command of Generals, Court and Avitable and General Ventura commanding the *Fauj-i-Khas*. He then addressed Sikh soldiers winning their support and he then told them about the Sindhanwalias and their close relations with the British. He pointed out that the hand of the British was clearly discernible in all the recent intrigues and killings. Hira Singh tried to bribe the army by promising an increase in pay if they helped in decimating the traitorous Sindhanwalias.

Table 1.6 Scenario in September 1843

Hira Singh General Ventura, Khalsa Army	Versus	Attar Singh Sindhanwalia Ajeet Singh Sindhawalia (nephew of Ajeet) Lehna Singh Misr Beli Ram Bhai Gurmukh Singh Mehr Ghasita

Death/Murder # 9, 10 (Victims: Ajit Singh Sindhanwalia and Lehna Singh, his uncle)

Around the citadel of Lahore on September 16, 1843, nearly 40,000 men with some 200 guns had taken up positions. It was the day of destruction as the troops went berserk and looted shops. Under Lehna Singh the garrison offered strong resistance. A few breaches in the walls enabled the Durbar Khalsa soldiers to charge in and about 1,000 defenders were killed. A wounded Lehna Singh was discovered hiding under a vault and was promptly killed. Ajit Singh was shot dead while attempting to jump over the wall of the fort.

Dhian Singh's body was discovered in a foundry pit and was conveyed with due honour to his mansion. Hira Singh carried the severed head of Ajit Singh to his stepmother who along with 17 mistresses of Dhian Chand committed sati on the pyre of Dhian Singh.

Sher Singh's obsequies were performed on the same day and all the ceremonies befitting a king were followed.

The men suspected to have participated in the murder of his father, Dhian Singh were now on the radar of Hira Singh for liquidation. They were Misr Beli Ram, the Chief Treasurer and his brother Ram Kishen, Mehr Ghasita, manager of the Sindhanwalia estates, Bhai Gurmukh Singh Granthi, the religious adviser of the late Sher Singh, and quite a few of their friends and relatives.

These men were secretly put to death, jailed or dismissed from service. Lal Singh had helped carry out the purge. He was to achieve notoriety later.

Hira Singh had Prince Duleep Singh (b: 1838) proclaimed Maharaja and himself assumed the position of Prime Minister. Duleep Singh, at this time five years old, was the youngest surviving son of Ranjit Singh. Two other princes, Peshaura Singh and Kashmira Singh, were about the same age as Hira Singh. With either as sovereign, Hira could not have authority as he would have with the child Duleep Singh on the throne. How the Khalsa agreed to this system is surprising.

Rani Jind Kaur was to continue to look after her son, and her brother, Jawahar Singh was to supervise his education. Secretaries were instructed to submit their papers through Pandit Jalla, whose influence on Hira Singh was too great and his advice in matters regarding civil and revenue matters were to be regarded as final.

Hira Singh retained the charge of the army and to keep soldiers happy, he enhanced their salary and paid the soldiers who had taken part in the siege of September 16-17, 1843, a gratuity equal to one month's salary.

Duleep Singh's maternal uncle was raised to a position he did not deserve; he loitered in the streets of Lahore 'drunken and debauched.' Jawahar Singh thought about removing Hira Singh from power and started parleys with Suchet Singh Dogra. The approval of Jind Kaur was obtained and she was familiar with Suchet Singh, manager of her household for 6 years. Suchet Singh prepared himself to make a bid for the Prime Ministership. He did not get the support of his elder brother, Gulab Singh who was in Lahore.

Table 1.7 Scenario in Late 1843

Hira Singh Pandit Jalla Khalsa Army	Versus	Suchet Singh (uncle of Hira Singh) Jawahar Singh Rani Jindan
Hira Singh	Versus	Kashmira Singh Pashaura Singh Attar Singh Sindhanwalia

As Hira Singh was informed by some loyal soldiers regarding Jawahar Singh's misdemeanour as he kept repeating that he would take Duleep Singh to British territory as he was not safe under Hira Singh. Jawahar Singh was taken in chains and his position in the young Maharaja's household was given to Lal Singh, a clerk of the *toshakhana*.

Gulab Singh restrained Suchet in Jammu but he hated Pandit Jalla and he could not be silenced. Gulab Singh got an assurance from Colonel Lawrence that he would be allowed to retain his possessions if Punjab was divided, provided he remained loyal to the British. Gulab Singh took away Dhian Singh's treasure by offering handsome tips to the Khalsa army. Now he was involved in Hira Singh's schemes for ejecting Kashmira Singh and Peshaura Singh from their jagirs in Sialkot which was close to the borders of Jammu. Hira Singh mischievously charged the Princes for having conspired with the Sindhanwalias against Dhian Singh.

The Princes had to seek sanctuary in the monastery of Mahtab Singh at Kotli Loharan, whose good offices and the fear of the Khalsa compelled Hira Singh to keep away from them. They could return after signing a pledge of loyalty to the government and undertaking to show clemency to Kapur Singh. However, Prince Kashmira Singh ignored his promise and a few weeks later had the informer Kapur Singh flogged to death.

The Princes got help from two regiments of irregular infantry and a number of men from irregular battalions going to Peshawar. Suchet Singh, from Jammu was moved to offer help; and Mussalman Najib battalions sent for besieging Sialkot, declined to open fire upon the sons of their late Maharaja unless the Khalsa joined in. Then the old Dogra battalions of Dhian Singh forced the defenders to lay down arms.

Kashmira and Peshaura Singh were harassed and harangued for three months and this roused the Khalsa against the Dogras. Between March 21-23, 1844, the army panchayats held meetings and decided to pressurise Hira Singh to concede certain demands or else he must be removed from power. The order of the Khalsa was:

- that he must release Jawahar Singh,
- remove the guard placed at the residence of Misr Beli Ram and set free his relatives and dependents,

- raise the siege of Kuryanwala and Sialkot, and
- give an undertaking that the Princes, Kashmira Singh and Peshaura Singh, would not be ill-treated in future.

They also demanded the surrender of Misr Jalla, Sheikh Imam-ud-din and Raja Lal Singh. Hira Singh did not allow the delegation's blunt way of expressing their opinion to really perturb him and he readily promised compliance. Suchet Singh had returned to Lahore as asked to by some troops and Hira Singh knew about it. Hira Singh tried to win back the confidence of soldiers by entertaining and feasting with them.

Suchet Singh had come with 40 of his followers and he took up position to fight it out with his devoted comrades. The Khalsa liked none of the Dogras. Hira Singh summoned Pandit Jalla for consultation who advised him to liquidate his rival for ever. A force of about 20,000 men with fifty light guns was despatched. Suchet Singh and his 40 companions came out to face this army but the small band was overcome and annihilated (March 27, 1844).

The death of Suchet Singh further embittered the relationship between Hira Singh and Gulab Singh whose jagirs yielded Rs. 0.7 million annually. The biggest revenue from farming in the state came from him. He had estates on contract, including salt mines worth about Rs. 1.1 million.

Early in the spring of 1844, Hira Singh faced another challenge. The monastery of Bhai Bir Singh in the village of Sarhali on the right bank of the Sutlej was very popular among the Sikh peasantry and the people of Malwa. Many disaffected came to the monastery and the general opinion being, that the Prime Minister should be a Khalsa Sikh.

Even the British became interested in Bhai Bir Singh as an alternative to Hira Singh who in his turn kept aware of the developments at Bir Singh's derah. He could not garner support of the army against 'this God-inspired man.' He dropped the negotiation attempt in 1844, when reports of the Sikh brotherhood between Bir Singh and Attar Singh Sindhanwalia were confirmed. Among the people residing in the monastery were Jawahar Singh Nalwa, son of Hari Singh and the Princes, Peshaura Singh and Kashmira Singh.

Death/Murder # 11, 12 and 13 (Victims: Attar Singh Sindhanwalia, Bhai Bir Singh and Prince Kashmira Singh)

The news that Attar Singh, as advised by the British had accepted an invitation from Bhai Bir Singh and crossed the Sutlej, spread in the city like wild-fire on May 3. Hira Singh explained to Army panchayats the British policy and reminded them that 'The Sindhanwalia Sardars' were thrust upon Maharaja Sher Singh, and this provoked the Khalsa Army against Attar Singh. On May 5, 1844, a strong force under Gulab Singh Calcutteea marched to Naurangabad (Sarhali) and a deputation of senior officers with him then went to Bhai Bir Singh to request him to retire from the conflict.

During the course of negotiations, an angry Attar Singh shot Gulab Singh Calcutteea dead. The Durbar troops instantly launched an attack; princes Kashmira Singh and Peshaura Singh having deserted earlier to save their lives. Attar Singh and Bhai Bir Singh were killed. A large number of peasants fled and many were drowned in their attempt to escape. The triumphant army was accorded a royal welcome by Hira Singh by ordering a salute of guns from the citadel. It was in fact an act which was avoidable and it was going to prove dangerous for Hira Singh. The Khalsa were hurt.

The reception of the troops in their barracks was quite different as they were taunted with the epithet, *gurumar*, murderers of a guru; and for all this Hira Singh and Pandit Jalla were held responsible. Hira Singh tried to appease the troops by liberal gifts of gold medals and ornaments. He also promised to build a *samadh* over the ashes of Bhai Bir Singh and grant a jagir for the maintenance of the Sarhali gurdwara. It came too late.

For quite some time, it was suspected that Ventura and Avitable were informing the British about the Lahore Durbar. The Khalsa troops at Sarhali were outraged seeing the British interference for fomenting trouble that they were willing to attack Ferozepur. Hira Singh, seeing the anti-foreign wave, discharged all the remaining Europeans. Ventura and Avitable had departed soon after the death of Sher Singh.

Suchet Singh had a sizeable amount of treasure in gold, silver and bullion, conveyed to Ferozepur. In February 1842 Suchet Singh had asked Colonel Lawrence to be allowed to retain possession of his property in future. The Ferozepur 'treasure' was stored in three huge copper vessels. Lord Ellenborough decided that the treasure should go to Suchet's heirs and not to the Durbar.

Meanwhile Sir Henry Hardinge replaced Lord Ellenborough as Governor-General in May 1844. Hira Singh, hoping for better results, had Duleep Singh write a personal letter to Lord Hardinge requesting for the property which Suchet Singh's widow claimed entirely as hers and her adopted son's. The matter was not resolved and was lost due to the non-relenting British who hid their real intention of not parting with the treasure behind their so-called legal proceedings.

Another issue between the two governments was regarding the village Mauran whose ownership the British would not return to the Durbar.

The movement of British troops, the building of additional barracks in cantonments at Ferozepur, Meerut, Ambala, Kasauli, Simla and Sabathu; purchase and storage of large quantities of wheat and other provisions caused uneasiness to the Lahore Durbar. The British explained this assembly as a plan for moving to Sindh. Hira Singh, during the first three months of 1844 moved Khalsa regiments from Lahore to Mangat, to Kanha Kacha, and on to Kasur.

This did not go down well with the British but Hira Singh replied that when the British troops in Ferozepur left for Sindh, he would consider recalling his own troops from Kasur.

There was trouble in the frontier districts of the Punjab and Hira Singh was in touch with Malik Fateh Khan Tiwana, who defied the Durbar. His father had submitted to Ranjit Singh in 1819. When trouble started in Hazara, Tiwana was quick to be on the scene. Tiwana got moral and material support from Raja Gulab Singh whose relations with his own nephew Hira Singh, were again strained. Tiwana continued to defy the Durbar. He remained at large till Hira Singh's death.

In the meanwhile, Kashmira Singh, the sixth son of Ranjit Singh and whose mother was Daya Kaur, was killed with Attar Singh Sandhawalia and hundreds of Bir Singh's followers in the heavy cannonade on May 7, 1844. Baba Bir Singh as he was sitting in service to Guru Granth Sahib and at that time a piece of mortar fired by Dogra army fell on him. In August 1844, trouble for the Khalsa *durbar* spread towards Muzaffarabad, Baramullah and in the Jhelum valley. The Muslim-dominated area from Peshawar to the Jhelum was in an anti-Sikh state and this hatred spread to Multan, Dera Ghazi Khan and Dera Ismail Khan. Accompanied with the sudden death of Diwan Sawan Mal. Sikh sovereignty was under a great challenge.

The trouble in Hazara was started by Sardar Habib-ullah Khan of Pakhli who attacked the Sikh garrison at Khori but reinforcements from Srinagar got Habib-ullah Khan killed. His son with other Muslim chiefs of the valley, launched a crusade against the Sikhs. The allies took Khori and then Muzaffarabad. Soon the chiefs of Uri and Dobheta joined in the rebellion and occupied Baramulla and closed in on Srinagar. Muslim troops under the Governor of Kashmir joined the rebels. Gulab Singh, the Raja of Jammu circulated the rumour that the Sikh government was fast disintegrating. However, in November 1844, the whole of the Jhelum valley and the bordering region of Muzaffarabad was reconquered by Hira Singh.

The financial resources of the state dwindled rapidly. The numbers of troops and their salaries had risen significantly.

Table 1.8 Number of Troops and Salary

Year	*Troops (all branches)*	*Total Salary (Rs)*
1839-40	35,242	42,11,292/-
1843-44	51,452	87,30,108/-

The Lahore Kingdom was spending on its army in 1843-44, a sum of Rs. 133,36,528 nearly twice the amount Ranjit Singh used to pay. Often, large quantities of cash, gold and silver were taken out of the state vaults for distribution as largesse by Chand Kaur, Sher Singh and Hira Singh.

Jagirdars, Rosinadars and *Dharmarthwalas* often usurped state lands adjacent to their *jagirs,* thus depriving the state from the due revenue. Hardly any step was taken to boost the income of the state. Arrears from governors and big farmers such as Raja

Gulab Singh, Diwan Sawan Mal and Sheikh Ghulam Mohi-ud-din were more than a crore of rupees. To restore financial stability, it became urgent that taxes should be increased, expenditure on the army curtailed, and the feudal nobility induced to pay their dues.

Death/Murder # 14, 15, 16, 17 (Victims: Hira Singh, Pandit Jalla, Mian Sihan Singh, Mian Labh Singh)

An investigation of the title deeds of *jagirdars* was ordered by Hira Singh and the former were told to produce the original *patanama* and Pandit Jalla was made the investigating officer whom the Sikh Chiefs refused cooperation and many left Lahore in disgust.

To celebrate the day of *Sangranth* in December of 1844, Rani Jindan collected a number of wanted pieces of gold and silver to be given away in charity. Using allegedly abusive language, Pandit Jalla questioned her action. The Rani, through her brothers, appealed to the Khalsa soldiers for protection with promises of cash and salary hike. This added fuel to the fire. A few days before this, Hira Singh had ordered the discharge of five hundred troopers.

Some of the Khalsa regiments deserted cantonments and once again demanded the surrender of Pandit Jalla. This was refused. Hira Singh and a party loaded with cash and jewellery on elephants left their residence in the early hours of December 21, 1844, quietly. They were noticed by a company of Sikh soldiers near the Taxali gate. Immediately, 6,000 troopers led by Sham Singh Attariwala went in pursuit. They overtook Hira Singh and his so-called accomplices at a distance of twenty-one kilometres. Those who were killed included Hira Singh, Jalla, Mian Sohan Singh son of Gulab Singh, and Mian Labh Singh; all Dogras. Their severed heads were hung with chains on the branches of trees outside the Lohari gate and displayed for the public for many days.

Therefore, we see the death or murder of 16 prominent persons including kings, princes and Prime Ministers taking place in about 5 years after the death of Maharaja Ranjit Singh.

Punjab Inches Towards British Annexation

The army and the Sardars of the Lahore Durbar, headed by Rani Jind Kaur and her brother decimated the Dogras of the Durbar.

There was no working machinery in place and the interests of the army, the chiefs and the Rani were multi-directional. It was an anarchic situation now and towards the end of 1844, the Sardars and the Rani appeared to be united against the Khalsa army even tempting it to go to war against the British. The Sikh Empire was destined to doom from the day Hira Singh Dogra was killed. There was intrigue all over and no unity among all the Sikh heads who were the masters once again like 50 years ago.

Jawahar Singh, brother of Rani Jind Kaur went to Hira Singh Dogra's house and captured treasure worth Rs. 3 million. Two days passed in revelry and then a grand Durbar was held at which the Sardars exulted for getting rid of unwanted Dogras who had established their unwanted rule. Jawahar Singh asked for Prime Ministership. The army as well as the chiefs were unwilling to offer such a post to the son of a kennel-keeper. Attar Singh Kalianwala was rejected as he was a *naherna*, or a barber, by caste. Thus, we see that the Jats dominated the Lahore Durbar and even Sikhs of the so-called 'inferior castes' were denied posts in the court.

[A story of Qumedan Rattan Singh (1785-1865 CE), belonging to the regular cavalry of the Sikh Army is another good example of casteism. Being a Non-Jat (tonk-Kshatriya), he was not allowed by the Jats to build a house in village Othian, Ajnala, Amritsar in the year 1810 or so. It was only when some Royal troops came at the behest of Maharaja that the Jats relented. He was later addressed as the 'Sardar' in the village. The Jagir of 200 acres given by Ranjit Singh got divided into many parts and sub-parts. He was this author's great-grandfather and still some land remains under the ownership of the author].

Rani Jind Kaur, in any case, was in no hurry to fill the post of Chief Commander of the army which her brother had aspired to, having herself a different disposition at heart.

Peshaura Singh thought it was a good time to try his luck for becoming chief adviser to the Durbar as he was a descendant of Ranjit Singh and the Dogras had been removed from the court. Keeping the British agent informed, Peshaura Singh left Ludhiana but upon his arrival at Lahore on January 1, 1845, he was advised by Rani Jindan to accept a jagir worth Rs. 40,000 and live a quiet life, away from Lahore. She won over the army to give the Prince the same advice.

Meanwhile the government was not working and for administration a group was set up with Jind Kaur as president, her brother Jawahar Singh and Bhai Ram Singh as members. She was assisted by Bakhsi Bhagat Ram, Diwan Dina Nath and Fakir Nur-ud-din as senior secretaries. The Army controlled all military affairs. Turbulence and disorder spread in the capital and soldiers maltreated the citizens. Sikh chiefs were ensconced in their fiefdoms and carried on their jobs without any responsibility.

The hilly districts of Hazara, Chhach and Attock and the Sindh Sagar Doab were in chaos or in a state of ferment. Collectors of revenue were expelled. Sheikh Mohi-ud-din, Governor of Kashmir, himself threatened to form an alliance with the British.

Gulab Singh had appropriated the properties of his brother Suchet Singh and his nephew Hira Singh, earning the jealousy of the Khalsa. His unpaid dues were a crore of rupees and to recover it the Khalsa planned an expedition to the hills. It suited Rani Jindan who wanted a lion's share of the army away from Durbar in any venture or misadventure so that she could control the court unchallenged. The excesses now being committed by the Khalsa soldiers would even put Abdali to shame.

As the army marched to Jammu, the Rani sent senior Sikh chiefs to Gulab Singh to negotiate with the Raja. The party included Sardar Fateh Singh Man, Diwan Rattan Chand Dugga, Sardar Sher Singh Attariwala and Baba Mian Singh Bedi. The Raja entertained them and cleverly enough, he entertained the army which reached there after a few days. He warned the army of the danger of letting the revenues be wasted by the Durbar. Both the parties thought that the Rani was mismanaging the situation and her brother was playing dangerously with the state revenues. Both the parties failed to pursue the matter when they were sent to Jammu.

Negotiations were concluded on February 28, 1845. As earnest of the full discharge of his obligations to the state Gulab Singh agreed to pay Rs. 0.4 million. When the money was handed over, an altercation which took place between Sardar Fateh Singh and Wazir Bachna. When the party emerged from the belt of thorny bushes which surrounded Jammu, it was fired upon and Fateh Singh and Bachna were killed; Diwan Ganpat Ram who was on the same elephant, was mortally wounded. The money was brought back to Jammu.

Gulab Singh decided to accompany the soldiers to Lahore personally to settle his accounts. He arrived at Shahdara on April 4, 1845. Jawahar Singh did not like it but he was ushered into Lahore on the morning of April 7 by the Rani. The next day, he was invited to the palace and introduced to the Maharaja and the Rani by the reluctant Raja Lal Singh and Jawahar Singh. He was offered the position of Wazir but Gulab Singh knew about the dangers involved and he politely refused the offer and managed to persuade the government to accept Rs. 2.7 million as arrears and got the lease of his revenue-farms extended for two years and managed to reach Jammu in July 1845.

In the meantime, the cholera epidemic spread in Lahore, killing hundreds of people a day. Taking advantage of the situation, Rani Jind Kaur decided to install Jawahar Singh as the *Wazir*. It was formalized on May 14, 1845. Jawahar Singh did not amend his lowly ways and one of his cronies was Bishen Singh, the adopted son of Jamadar Kushhal Singh. Bishen Singh had already earned the wrath of soldiers of two units of infantry. The soldiers wanted to take action but were persuaded by Gulab Singh and Bhai Ram Singh to exercise restraint.

Death/Murder # 18 (Victim: Peshaura Singh Another Son of Ranjit Singh)

Gulab Singh had encouraged Peshaura Singh to make a claim for the throne and it stayed in Jind Kaur's mind. So, to pre-empt any such move, she asked General Mehtab Singh to march towards Sialkot. The Prince and his soldiers tried to stop the Lahore Army but failed. The Prince and his family, however, somehow escaped. They crossed the Sutlej to seek British help. Also, Mehtab Singh was instructed by the Khalsa Army not to molest Peshaura Singh as he was a son of Ranjit Singh and they could play him against Duleep Singh, if need be. Peshaura Singh wandered about in the area between the Indus and Jhelum for four weeks in the predominantly Muslim areas while his family stayed back in the British area. Peshaura Singh then occupied the Attock fort and with help from locals, declared himself as the sovereign on July 17, 1845.

Jawahar Singh was a married man and he wanted to eliminate Peshaura Singh. For this he selected Chhattar Singh Attariwala whose daughter was betrothed to Duleep Singh. He agreed very reluctantly. Fateh Khan Tiwana was also roped in to besiege the fort of Attock.

The Prince agreed to accompany Chhattar Singh to Lahore, being assured of his safety and all his claims. But on August 31, 1845, as he was preparing for the journey, he was captured and thrown into a dungeon and then later strangled.

In this way, another son of Ranjit Singh died tragically. He was born in 1821 and died in 1845, aged just 24.

Chhattar Singh sought temporary asylum in Raja Gulab Singh's territories while Fateh Khan returned to Dera Ismail Khan. Jawahar Singh made the crime an occasion for rejoicing and the city was illuminated at night.

Death/Murder # 19 (Victim: Jawahar Singh, Brother of Rani Jind Kaur)

The killing of Peshaura Singh hastened Jawahar Singh's downfall. His attempt to escape with the young Maharaja into British territory had already enraged the Khalsa and his conduct was unacceptable, which particularly in the matter of Peshaura Singh was highly deplored. Raja Gulab Singh also added fuel to the fire.

The army panchayats resolved on September 19 that Jawahar Singh must die as a traitor and Rani Jindan (Jind Kaur) was told to hand over her brother, or else, she and the young Maharaja would be harmed. She sent Fakir Nur-ud-din, Diwan Dina Nath and Attar Singh Kalianwala to negotiate but the latter two were detained by the Khalsa.

Jind Kaur was informed that Jawahar Singh must present himself to the new government on the 21st or else all living inside the fort would be liquidated. Four battalions of infantry, in fact, marched from Mian Mir towards the city. On the afternoon of the 21st Rani, her son and Jawahar Singh left for Mian Mir and arrived there soon after sunset.

The Maharaja, his mother, and attendants were taken safely to their tents and Jawahar Singh was put to death, by sword and musket in the howdah of his elephant and the next morning his body was handed over to the Rani for cremation. Diwan Dina Nath and Attar Singh Kalianwala were allowed to return with her to Lahore.

The army committees represented in the Sarbat-Khalsa, which manifested their power, revived the old ways of the pre-Ranjit Singh days; with the words Panth Khalsa the seal of authority was inscribed and above this was the invocation *Akal Sahai* (God is our help). The names of Maharaja and Rani were dropped from official communications.

The soldiers even toyed with the idea of putting Sher Singh's son Sahdev Singh on the throne after the death of Peshaura Singh. In the early 1845, Jind Kaur and Gulab Singh tried to involve the British in Lahore Durbar's matters. The British communications show that the Rani was ready for a subsidiary position in an alliance. Hardinge indicated if some influential Khalsa persons were permitted to retain their jagirs they were ready to compromise with their sovereignty with some nominal powers given to Duleep Singh.

In January, while the Khalsa troops were marching to Jammu to collect the dues from Gulab Singh which he owed the Durbar, Gulab Singh sent Bhai Ram Singh to ask for help from the British. He asked for retaining his present possessions and Jammu and the neighbouring territories with an income of Rs. 1.2 million a year, be guaranteed to him and his heirs for ever.

The Rani and her chosen coterie of chiefs aroused the passions of the soldiers by warning them of imminent British invasion. A council of army officers and Sardars was called in the Shalimar Gardens early in November, where the court was encamped on its way back from Amritsar. Diwan Dina Nath confirmed some of these reports and reminded the Khalsa that the British had not returned Suchet Singh's treasure, nor had they restored Mauran village. He drew attention to the depleted state of the treasury—no money was coming from Kashmir or Peshawar.

The appointment of Lal Singh as a wazir as the Rani's proposal was communicated by Dina Nath. Tej Singh was to be made a commander of the armies who would be given full powers in the event of hostilities. Neither Lal Singh nor Tej Singh had any distinction to recommend them. Tej Singh was the nephew of Jamadar Kushhal Singh, the Gaur Brahmin from Meerut who converted to Sikhism.

Raja Lal Singh (d. 1866) was the son of a Brahmin shopkeeper named Misr Jassa Mall whose roots were from Jhelum district in

West Punjab. He entered the service of the Sikh Durbar in 1832 as a writer in the treasury.

Hira Singh enjoyed immense power for some time. Lal Singh influenced those in power and grabbed some power himself. He displayed ingratitude towards Raja Hira Singh who had throughout been in his favour. Not only was Lal Singh made the controller of the Toshakhana, Hira Singh had appointed him as young Duleep Singh's tutor removing Jawahar Singh. Moreover Hira Singh made him 'Raja Lal Singh' and granted jagirs to him at Rohtas. Lal Singh joined hands with Rani Jindan and her brother, Jawahar Singh to bring about Hira Singh's downfall when the relations soured between Jind Kaur and Hira Singh.

He was appointed a member of the Council of Regency in December 1844, under her. After the assassination of Jawahar Singh he was made Wazir on November 8, 1845. As a commander and a *wazir*, Lal Singh showed disloyalty to the Sikh Durbar in the Anglo-Sikh war of 1845-46.

The Sikh army was to be divided into seven divisions, each with an approximate strength of 8,000 men. The distribution was to be 1) to remain in Lahore; 2) Peshawar; 3) towards Sindh; 4), 5), 6), 7), the remaining four, after crossing the Sutlej, were to proceed towards Ropar, Harike, Ludhiana and Ferozepur respectively. On the morning of the 19th, Lal Singh and Tej Singh were formally confirmed to their posts.

Sir Henry Hardinge did not want to start a war as his preparations were not complete. Also, he was not in favour of safeguarding the interests of a few sardars to maintain a puppet on the throne. Nor did he think that the Sikhs had given him cause for war. To his Agent, Major Broadfoot he replied on October 23, that in his view nothing had occurred *'to justify the seizure of our friends' territory, who, in our adversity assisted us to retrieve our affairs.'* Further, he said *'abstinence from all interference or aid, by whomever solicited, defensive measures for the protection of our territory and destruction of those who violate it, must be our policy.'*

He authorised Major Broadfoot to inform the Lahore Durbar that if Maharaja Duleep Singh *'was deposed by violence the Governor-General would not recognise his successor.'* This removed Rani Jind Kaur's fears and her view of the British as potential allies got strengthened. Major Broadfoot continued to foment trouble.

2

The Anglo-Sikh Wars

Anglo-Sikh Relations Deteriorate

Both the British and the Sikhs believed that war was now inevitable. Lord Ellenborough even dated it to November 1845. The British expansion was restricting the Sikh kingdom by capturing states around it either directly or as subordinate states. The East India Company had established a military cantonment at Ferozepur, and had begun increasing its military strength, only a few miles from the Sutlej river. In 1843, they conquered and annexed Sindh and the British did not gain any respect in the Punjab, and such acts increased doubts about British motives.

The actions and attitudes of the British, under Governor General Lord Ellenborough and his successor, Sir Henry Hardinge was controversial. Their perception of a Sikh threat was an excuse for expansionism and on the contrary, the British military preparations were offensive in nature like preparation of bridging trains and siege gun batteries.

The new political agent in the frontier districts, Major George Broadfoot influenced the British attitudes. The British earnestly wanted to expand their rule and control Punjab, the only remaining state not under their rule so far.

Table 2.1 British Army Power

Year	*Location*	*Men*	*Resources*
1838	Ludhiana	3000	12 Guns
1838 (End)	Ferozepur	1000	12 Guns
1842	(plus) Ambala, Kasauli, Simla	17,612	66 Guns

1843	Ludhiana, Ferozepur, Ambala and Meerut	40,612	94 guns, 1100 picked horses and mules, 500 elephants, 700 camels and bullocks in large number
1845	Ferozepur (additionally)		60 Large boats

Major Broadfoot behaved as though a war was imminent and took upon himself to train and drill the troops. Sir Charles Napier held his troops in Sindh in readiness to cross into the Punjab. Broadfoot was most unpopular when he passed through the Punjab escorting the families of Shah Shuja and Zaman Shah in April 1841. Moreover, Broadfoot intervened in a domestic quarrel among the Sodhis of Anandpur and placed military in the town and its adjoining villages. It was quite a provocation.

Major Broadfoot'a actions irritated the people of the Punjab no end. When the sentiments of the Khalsa were already inflamed by reports of British troop movements towards their frontier, Broadfoot occupied two villages of the Durbar on the pretext that they were giving safe havens to the criminals from British territory.

First Anglo-Sikh War

On about November 20 British troops at Ambala and Meerut were instructed to get ready and between December 2-10, 1845 these were moved towards Ferozepur. Brigadier Wheeler, with about 5,000 infantry, two regiments of cavalry and twelve field guns, marched from Ludhiana to Ferozepur.

The Governor-General Hardinge arrived at Ambala on December 2. The next day he severed diplomatic relations with the Durbar by dismissing its Vakil (representative) from his camp on the plea that the Durbar had not cared to explain the reason for movement of its troops. The Vakil had in fact, asked for explanations of Broadfoot's actions and for British military activities on the Punjab borders. On December 6, Sir Henry Hardinge himself, marched towards Ludhiana and a week later the Commander-in-Chief Gough proceeded to join him.

On December 13, 1845, the Governor-General proclaimed

war on the Durbar. He annexed its cis-Sutlej territories, on the excuse that the Khalsa army had crossed the Sutlej. The British marched to Ferozepur via Ambala, Rajpura, Sirhind, Ludhiana, Rajkot, Bassian, Adhni, Chirakh and Mudki, which they reached on December 18, and where the first battle of the war was fought.

Sikh troops began to move on November 24. Four brigades of the *fauj-i-ain*, under Tej Singh, arrived at Qadian between December 9-11 and then went southwards through Jhangi and Nathianwala, to cross the Sutlej near Harike on the 12th. It took 23 boats and three days to get the war material to the other side of the river. Between Attari and the small stream of Sukhne camp was pitched at Ludhiana in the Durbar's cis-Sutlej territory on December 16.

The irregular cavalry under Lal Singh moved towards Harike. An unwilling Lal Singh was made to cross the Sutlej and they reached Mullanwalla on the 16th from which they could easily communicate with the regular army. Having annexed the cis-Sutlej areas, the British declared war and Lal Singh was provoked by his soldiers to attack Ferozepur. The British had 10,500 men (7,000 as per Gough). They had 5,000 fighting men at Ludhiana with 12 guns. Another 10,000 British men were located at Ambala, Kasuali and Subathu. At Meerut were 9,000 British men with 26 guns. It may be noted that all the soldiers of the British Army were not truly British; there were a vast number of 'native' soldiers.

The Sikh army consisted of 18,000 infantry, 16,000 ghorcharas and 85 guns. But Lal Singh had already informed the British about his friendly intentions and no harm would come to the garrison at Ferozepur. Leaving one brigade of the regular army and a few ghorcharras with 6,000-7,000 men and 20 field guns to monitor Ferozepur, he moved towards Mudki on the 17th.

Having commandeered grain from the village, the British army began preparing their first proper meal for some days. An advance guard of the Sikh army, commanded by Lal Singh, spotted the British cooking fires and advanced. A flat sandy plain was the terrain there with villages at random. The Durbar troops lost their way. After a whole night's wandering, they arrived, not at Mudki but Pherushahr and got a message that the Governor-General had arrived at Mudki. Even though tired, the Sikh

Army marched towards Mudki and was ready for battle except Lal Singh who marched with only half the troops keeping the other half with the excuse that Sardar Tej Singh might require the remainder in Lulliani. Lal Singh reached Mudki at about noon, and an hour or two later was faced by Sir Hugh Gough's force of about 1,000 men of all arms with 40 guns.

Table 2.2 Battle at Mudki

	Sikh Army	*British Army*
Generals	S.Lal Singh S.Tej Singh	Sir Hugh Gough Sir Henry Hardinge
Strength (men)	11,000 – 12,000,	10,000
Guns	22	42
Killed		215
Wounded		657

The British were ordered to form the line of battle, the time being now about four o'clock in the afternoon. The cavalry, together with the horse artillery, advanced under Sir Hugh Gough and formed a line in front of the Sikh position, the guns occupying the centre. The infantry formed up in second line and moved forward; Wheeler's brigade on the extreme right, and Brigadier Bolton, with Native Infantry on their left.

The field battery of the British joined the Horse Artillery. The cavalry on the right and then also on the left, were ordered to make flank movements to turn the Sikhs' flanks as these threatened to turn the British left and right. Brigadiers Gough and White with cavalry swept out to the right, and fell upon the Sikhs' left flank. The Sikh horses withdrew, and the British and native cavalry followed them behind the Sikh infantry, and Brigadier Mactier, going from the left, fell upon the Sikh right in similar style, and averted the danger of the British line being outflanked. Had there been no jungle, the British cavalry would have harmed the Sikhs much more.

Meantime the British infantry advanced upon the Sikh line from the right, Sir Harry Smith's division leading, and fired heavily on the Sikhs with the artillery support. The Sikh infantry and guns stood with determination and fought resolutely but were steadily driven back by the British infantry. Darkness put an end to the pursuit, but the conflict was maintained in an irregular manner for another hour, clouds of dust making the visibility poor.

After opening the attack, Lal Singh vanished from the field. The fighting lasted for about a hundred minutes and the Sikhs fought very bravely and a cavalry regiment charged upon the British with such force that the confused British began firing upon their own men. General Havelock with two European regiments made a timely intervention.

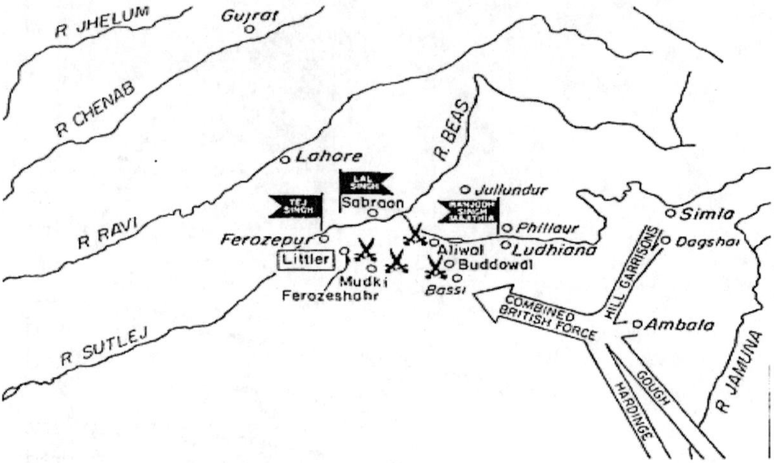

Fig 2.1 Map Showing First Anglo-Sikh War

Night allowed the leaderless Sikh army from further disaster. They had lost a number of men and 17 guns were captured on the field. It might have been success for the British but it came with a severe loss, particularly among the distinguished offcers of the army. Sir Robert Bale, Quartermaster-General of the British troop, Sir John McCaskil and Brigadier Bolton, of H.M.'s 31st were killed in the battle while being in Sir Harry Smith's Division; Brigadiers Mactier and Wheeler were severely wounded, also were Lieutenant-Colonel Byrne, commanding H.M.'s 31st Foot and Major Pat Grant, Deputy-Adjutant-General of the army were severely injured. Another senior officer who was killed was

Major George Broadfoot. He was earlier the British representative to the Punjab and at the time of his death was on Hardinge's staff pool. The brunt of the fighting was faced by Sir Harry Smith's Division. The native British infantry fought fairly well and, in the darkness, some British troops were fired upon by their own colleagues by mistake.

When the darkness fell the fighting stopped. The Sikhs had lost 17 guns but there is no record of the Sikhs' dead and wounded. However, the British losses in men and officers, were heavy.

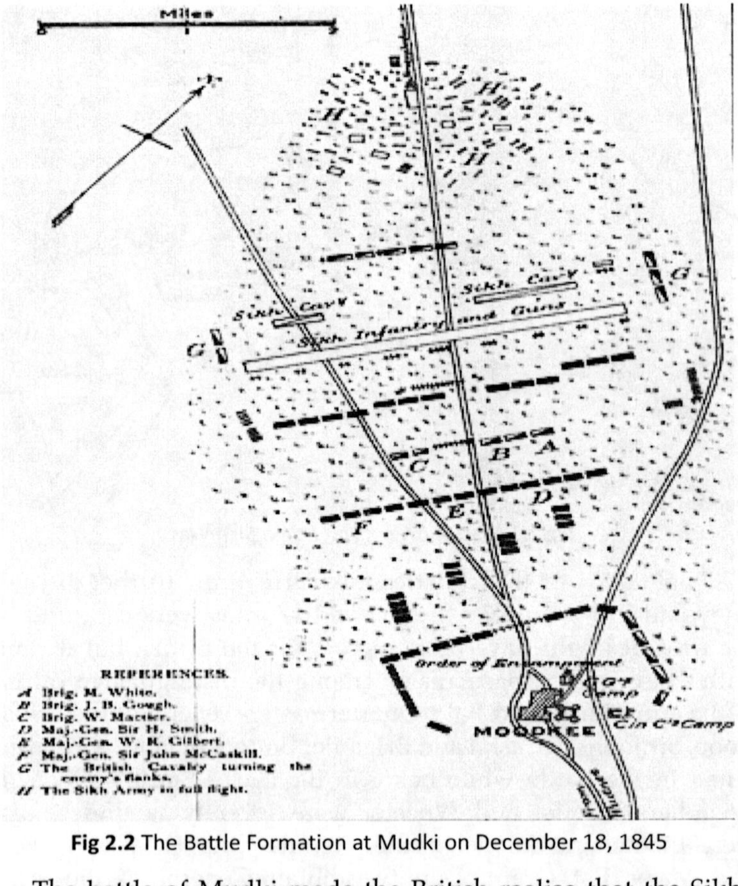

Fig 2.2 The Battle Formation at Mudki on December 18, 1845

The battle of Mudki made the British realise that the Sikhs were no spent force. This was the first great fight of the British with the Sikhs. Their gallantry and discipline in the fight evoked the admiration of the British. They could not inflict the crushing defeat upon them without reinforcements. The Khalsa were therefore able to retire unmolested to Pherushahr. Though the adversaries remained very close to each other both at Ferozepur and Mudki there was no movement of troops on the 19th or 20th.

While the Sikhs were poorly led and did not have a strong strategy to attack the British repetitively before they could combine their distributed forces at Ferozepur, Ambala, Ludhiana and so on, the British used the two-day interval very effectively. Possibly, the Sikhs fought traditional war with the only strategy of facing the British head-on, the latter adopted all clever manoeuvres including diplomacy and the famous 'divide and rule' policy. The British Generals Hardinge and Gough were vastly experienced but they were shaken, no doubt.

[The author's great-grandfather Qumedan Rattan Singh was a part of the cavalry that took part in the battle. He took a bullet in his leg and was taken care by a Muslim family in a nearby village where he hid and recuperated].

Battle of Pherushahr (Part of First Anglo-Sikh War)
(Pherushahr is also known as Ferozeshah)

Sir Henry Hardinge ordered Sir John Littler to help European troops from the hills to speed up their arrival to Mudki where they reached on the evening of December 19. Sir John Littler's forces left Ferozepur on the morning of December 21 with 5,000 infantry, 2 regiments of cavalry and twenty-one guns. Although an army of 20,000 trained Sikhs hovered at a distance of only six miles, they were not allowed to molest the British soldiers.

Battle at Pherushahr

	Sikh Army	*British Army*
Generals	S.Lal Singh S.Tej Singh	Sir Hugh Gough Sir Henry Hardinge
Strength (men)	25,000	16,700-18,000
Guns	130	69 and 2 Howitzers
Killed/Wounded	4,000 (killed + wounded)	694/1721

The critical time was lost and the British got enough time to re-organise into a formidable force. He joined the main British force at 1:30 in the afternoon and thus there were now 17,000 men, with 69 guns.

Day I: December 21, 1845

At Pherushahr, the Sikh army had 12 battalions of infantry, 4 regiments of cavalry and 50 guns of the *Fauj-i-Ain* and some 15,000 of irregular horse; thus, the total strength was about 25,000-30,000 men. The Sikhs grouped in a formation about a mile long and half a mile deep. The soldiers prepared up the earthworks, with help from expert technicians. In any case, their Generals were already purchased by the British.

The artillery and cavalry of the British were the same as they had at Mudki. At 10:30 am, the Sikh forces were approachable and the British soldiers settled for a breakfast as their General went in for reconnaissance. Till then Littler with his forces had not yet arrived.

Tej Singh led Sikh forces waited to the north of Ferozepur and Lal Singh led another combination at Pherushahr. *[Both these generals were born Hindus and were baptised as Sikhs in Ranjit Singh's time]*. The Sikh formation was horseshoe-shaped. The central part of the Sikh entrenchment facing southwards lay parallel to the British line of marching. The British had a major problem: whether to wait for John Littler's arrival from Ferozepur or attack with sufficient daylight remaining. The Governor General wanted to wait and Hugh Gough, the commander and superior to Governor General at the war field wanted to attack straightaway. By 1 pm, Littler had arrived nearby, bypassing Tej Singh's entrenchment. The British were relieved to know that.

The day was short but Hugh Gough gave orders for storming the Sikh entrenchments at 3.30 pm. Sixty-six-year-old Hugh Gough was positioned at the right, 60-year-old Henry Hardinge at the centre and 62-year-old John Littler at the left wing of the assailing force. By the time attacks could be carried out it was already 4 pm.

The British army was positioned such that it faced the southward and westward faces of the Sikh entrenchments with Wallace at the centre and Gilbert on the right. The powerful battery consisting of heavy guns was placed between Wallace and Gilbert's positions and the horse artillery was on the flanks.

It would be wrong to say that Tej and Lal Singh led the Sikh Army as Generals. They were just the 'Generals' for the saying. They did not lead their forces like the British Generals at all. They were seeking personal favours by causing minimum damage to the British, taking the hapless troops as the lambs to the slaughter. The Sikh troops however rose to the occasion and fought as disorganised small units without a command or direction. The Sikh Army was destined to lose.

The Sikh gunners opened fire when they could see the British. But for reasons best known to them, the British continued to advance. Littler's troops who marched against Sikh right or west positions became an easy target, coming under tremendous fire. Seven officers and 97 men were killed and another 11 officers and 184 men were wounded. The Regiment was alone and the Sikh cavalry constantly challenged their left. Brigadier Reid was compelled to tell his troops to retire. Another 51 men including officers were killed and 180 injured. These comprised the Brigade staff and native infantry. The Sikh sepoys started to celebrate as the pall of gloom descended on the over-confident and yet very optimistic British troops.

Now advance from the right was planned. H.M.'29th in advance under Brigadier Taylor marched, supported by H.M.'s 80th and after them the 41st Native infantry under Hugh Gough himself. Henry Hardinge was at the centre. The British force came under heavy artillery fire.

Thus, one of the British regiments (the 62nd Foot) lost almost half its men and was driven back. Part of General Gilbert's division could break into the Sikh encampment, but his own right flank was threatened by large numbers of Sikh irregular cavalry. The Sikh horsemen fought against a British cavalry regiment, the 3rd Light Dragoons.

Then siege guns were brought into play by the British for checking the Sikhs.

[Siege guns are heavy guns designed to bombard fixed targets like fortifications and are capable of firing heavy cannonballs or shells requiring enormous transport and logistical support to operate—Author]

This enabled some of the British foot soldiers to leap over the mud entrenchments of the Sikhs and physically fight with the Sikh gunners on a one-to-one basis. Seeing the problem of the gunners, the Sikh musketeers came forward and fired so rapidly that within ten minutes two hundred of the English soldiers were killed or crippled, and Littler got belittled, retiring for the moment. Harry Smith was also repulsed, but he was successful in inflicting severe damage to the elite *Fauj-i-khas* of the Sikhs.

Walter Gilbert and General Wallance taking a tremendous risk captured a few Sikh batteries, losing 270 men in the process and they continued their assault till night fell. Half of the British soldiers under Littler and Harry Smith were outside the Sikh entrenchments, but the other half was within which was unable to advance; thus, the British now found themselves in a precarious position. Some of their officers were scared and advocated retreating to Ferozepur. But the views of these British cowards were overruled by their own two war veterans in command. The Governor-General was acutely aware of the precarious position of the British. He had no reserve of troops, while the Sikhs had Tej Singh close at hand. And in case it should be necessary to retreat to Ambala or Delhi, the march through 160 miles of Sikh territory lying between the Sutlej and the Jamuna, would be extremely hazardous.

The Sikhs might have won had they been possessed of a worthy leader at this crucial point. Lal Singh had spent the day of battle hidden in a ditch; and at night stole away to Amritsar. Gough and Hardinge re-formed their troops before dawn and summoned Smith and Littler from their camps.

Day II: December 22 1845

Gough and Hardinge decided to take advantage of the dimness before sunrise and make an immediate attempt to dislodge the Sikhs. The Khalsa who had exhibited such courage a few hours earlier was leaderless with many dead and wounded, besides 73 pieces of cannon, stores, camp equipment and ammunition.

The following morning of December 22, 1845 saw both the British and Sikhs mixed up in disorder. Gough and Hardinge engaged with the troops in encouraging banter. In fact, Hardinge was getting ready for the defeat the next day. He sent word to the camp at Mudki that the state papers in his baggage were to be burned in this event, and gave his sword which once belonged to Napoleon Bonaparte to his aide-de-camp.

However, when the dawn broke, the British found that they held most of the camp, and had captured seventy-one guns; as per British accounts. After reforming their line, Gough and Hardinge advanced north-west and by noon they had repelled Lal Singh's army from the field but in the process suffered heavy losses from the remaining Sikh artillery.

Gough's troops almost ran out of ammunition and were already exhausted. The British were aware that Tej Singh's army was approaching from the west. As they formed up again, and came under fire from Tej Singh's guns, a retreat was considered so that the wounded could be saved from the massacre.

Ironically, some of his horse artillery ran out of ammunition and this saved Gough's army. It was ordered to withdraw to Ferozepur to replenish, and much of the British cavalry was ordered to escort them.

Tej Singh pretended to guard Ferozepur and arrived between 9 and 10 in the morning at the battlefield when Lal Singh's army was already in fight. He might have defeated the British force which was exhausted and famished but he made a shadow attack and withdrew when the British had exhausted their last round of ammunition. What a treacherous leader!

The battle of Pherushahr was gained by the British after it had been lost. *'Another such action,'* General Havelock observed, *'will shake the Empire.'* British losses amounted to more than 2200, killed or wounded; their ammunition ran short and they were left with some siege guns only. Thus, the Sikhs were able to re-cross the river into their own country. The Khalsa casualties as estimated by Sir Henry Hardinge was 4,000.

One reason for the withdrawal of the Sikhs was that they were not holed up in their own bastions. They had advanced and crossed the Sutlej and it must have weighed heavily in their heads that they were perhaps fighting in the enemy territory and fighting the British in the latter's territory was a different proposition. Moreover, they had nobody to lead them; they were taken across the Sutlej to fight and get decimated so that the crooked generals like Tej Singh and Lal Singh could continue as the powerful Chiefs with none to challenge them at court; neither Duleep Singh nor Rani Jindan nor the Khalsa army.

Battle of Aliwal

The war scenario now shifted to the upper Sutlej between Ferozepore and Ludhiana. Opposite Ludhiana on the right bank of the river, the Sikhs had a military post at Phillaur with about 1,000 men. The British garrison moved to Bassian to guard the provisions depot. As the Khalsa asked for more men to bolster its strength of the Phillaur garrison; a force of 10,000 men with sixty pieces of artillery was therefore despatched under Sardar Ranjodh Singh Majithia. Although it crossed the Sutlej on January 17, 1846, Majithia failed to take advantage of country which was wide open as the British were holed up in Mudki.

But the British got enough time to move towards Ludhiana and protect the convoy of guns, ammunition and treasure that were on the way from Delhi.

Although Harry Smith had planned an attack on Runjodh Singh's army at Buddowal but he made some changes when he came to know about the Sikh strength, and moreover he was instructed by Gough to take his troops via Jagraon. There a British regiment joined him to reach Ludhiana ahead of the Sikh main body. The Sikh irregular cavalry (the Gorchurras) continually attacked his rearguards as he left Buddowal on January 21. Most of Smith's baggage animals (mules, bullocks and elephants), were captured by the Sikhs who cut down any straggling troops. Ranjodh Singh did not escalate the attack; instead he was content with the capture of baggage and transport cattle. Joined by a brigade of four battalions Ranjodh Singh Majithia resumed his march and his force comprised now 15,000 men. With his troops exhausted, Smith somehow succeeded in reaching Ludhiana. As reinforcements, a brigade of troops from Delhi, including two Gorkha battalions arrived.

Ranjodh Singh and Harry Smith had a small battle near Buddowal which ended in victory for the Sikhs.

Table 2.3 Battle of Aliwal

	Sikh Army	*British Army*
Generals	S. Ranjodh Singh Majithia	Sir Harry Smith
Strength (men)	15,000	12,000
Guns	69-70	30-32
Killed	2,000	673-850

Sir Harry Smith, being reinforced by a division commanded by Brigadier Wheeler prepared (January 28) to give battle. Awaiting reinforcements, the Sikhs withdrew to Aliwal on the Sutlej, and on January 28, Smith cautiously advanced against them.

A fierce encounter took place at Aliwal, where the Sikh soldiers gave ample proof of their bravery. The Sikhs had occupied a position along a ridge between the villages of Aliwal, on the Sutlej, and Bhundri and was almost 4 miles long. The Sutlej ran dangerously close to their rear.

Smith determined that Aliwal was the Sikh weak point which became obvious after the initial artillery salvos. He sent two out of his four infantry brigades to capture the village and a deadly struggle seemed ahead as the Sikh ranks were steady firing incessantly; but the holders of the post were battalions of hill-men not as militant as the Sikhs and were rather indifferent to the interests of the Khalsa. After a while, they fled as they were leaderless once again and, raised because their demeanour was sober, and their hearts indifferent to the Khalsa, leaving the brave Sikh artillerymen at the mercy of the conquerors. The British cavalry of the right made at the same time a sweeping and successful charge, and one-half of the Sikh army was broken apart and dispersed. Then the Sikhs on their own apparently outflanked their opponents in spite of the relentless fire by the English infantry and artillery; the more regular battalions were in line, and the Sikh soldiers would not easily give in.

A regiment of European lancers, supported by one cavalry was launched against the Lahore infantry since a strong and quick effort was necessary. The Sikh soldiers knelt to receive the orderly but impulsive charge of the English warriors, moved alike by feelings of revenge; but at the critical moment, the unaccustomed discipline of many of the Sikh soldiers failed them. They rose, reserving their fire till the English were very close and delivering it till the mass had been three times ridden through and then only the Sikhs dispersed.

The bodies of victorious horsemen outnumbered those of the beaten infantry of the Sikhs. However, the Sikhs retreated across the Sutlej leaving behind more than fifty pieces of cannon.

Circumstances Leading to the Battle of Sobraon in 1846

Gulab Singh first reproached the vanquished Sikhs for rashly engaging in hostilities with their colossal neighbour, and then entered into negotiations with English leaders. The Governor-General had realized the impossibility of capturing the Punjab in one stroke. It meant defeating an army as numerous as his own and laying siege to Multan, Jammu, and Peshawar in a few months; a task of enormous difficulty and tremendous risks.

The English soldiers had to face very warm weather and tropical diseases and sometimes the epidemics. It was also felt that the natives were hostile to the English and any warfare of longer duration might further spread the hatred against them which might transform to continued skirmishes and battles all over, particularly the north-western part.

The first English objective was to force the Sikhs across the Sutlej to their own side of the river. This depended on the unconditional submission of the chiefs and the delegates of the army. For the final success of the English, it was thought to be necessary since even petty native chiefs would assert their independence.

But the total defeat of so large and so well-equipped body of Sikh troops, known for their bravery could not be accomplished by one defeat. The English intimated to Gulab Singh their readiness to acknowledge a Sikh sovereignty in Lahore if the army were disbanded; but this was beyond the capacity of Gulab Singh. A treaty under the walls of Lahore was essential to the British reputation; and there was to be a tacit understanding that the Sikh army should be attacked by the English, and once beaten, the Sikh Army was to be abandoned by its own government! Further, for the English, the road to the capital must be laid open including the unopposed passage over the Sutlej. From the

Sikhs' point of view the battle of Sobraon was fought under such shameless treason.

The Sikhs brought the greater part of their force on the left bank of the Sutlej along-with 67 pieces of artillery in battery, and nearly 20,000 men and not all of them were regular troops. The entrenchment lacked unity of command and of design; and at Sobraon also the Sikh soldiers did everything and their leaders nothing. Each junior commander defended his position on the front according to his means and skill. The right flank was mainly guarded by a line of two hundred *'zamburuks'* or 'falconets'.

The Sikhs were somewhat demotivated by the defeat at Aliwal but the self-confidence soon returned as they captured an unguarded post of observation established by the English. But a realisation dawned upon them that there was no escape from domestic chaos or from imminent foreign subjection. They were led by the grey-headed 56-year-old chief Sham Singh of Atari.

The British confidence was great too, fresh from the success achieved at Aliwal, and early in February a formidable siege train with a large cache of ammunition arrived from Delhi. It was decided that the Sikh Army would be attacked on February 10, and various plans were laid down for ascertaining English victory. The officers of artillery wanted their guns to be used as per the established rules of the engineer. But the consensus was that the entire heavy ordnance should be planted in masses opposite particular points of the enemy's entrenchment, and that when after shaking the Sikhs by a volley of shelling, the weakest part would be assaulted by the strongest of the three investing divisions comprising 15,000 men.

The precise mode of attack was not divulged and the evening darkness of February 9 was thus occupied with busy preparations.

Battle of Sobraon

The decisive battle of the campaign was fought at Sobraon on February 10. The Ferozepur front had remained quiet after Pherushahr; the British having learned something of their adversaries: 'toughness'. Reinforcements of men and officers of known repute were called for from all over British India and the resourceful magistrate of Delhi, John Lawrence, was asked to supply ammunition from the local magazine without delay.

When all resources had been put to place the British resumed their offensive. The Sikhs were ready during this period but were inactive due to the developments in the Durbar where various negotiations were going on.

To persuade the Khalsa to begin fighting the signal had to come from Gulab Singh. Persuasion was not necessary: the Khalsa were only too impatient to grapple with the enemy. By the close of the first week of February, the Sikh army had constructed formidable entrenchments on the British bank of the river near Sobraon. Their batteries were placed as high as the stature of a man and protected by deep trenches. For about two and a half miles these defensive works extended and a bridge of boats connected them with the right bank of the river.

Table 2.4 Battle of Sobraon

	Sikh Army	*British Army*
Generals	S. Tej Singh S. Lal Singh S. Sham Singh Attariwala S. Ranjodh Singh Majithia	Sir Hugh Gough Sir Henry Hardinge
Strength (men)	26,000	20,000
Guns	69-70	35 Siege Guns, 30 Light Guns
Killed	5,000	2,300
Wounded	Unknown	2,063

Some 20,000-25,000 men, and 70 guns were placed behind these entrenchments. But ironically, the Durbar courtiers were determined to see the Khalsa beaten. Lal Singh was re-imposed on the army. Two days before the battle, the traitor sent Shams-ud-din to Major Lawrence with details of Sikh formations. The right flank was the weakest point of the Sikh defence where the loose sand did not allow building high parapets or place heavy guns; it was to be protected by ghorcharras and light camel guns. These could fire balls one or two pounds in weight; unfortunately for the Sikhs, the flank was being commanded by the traitor Lal Singh himself.

Cunningham wrote on the basis of the intelligence reports:

> *....the whole of the heavy ordinance should be planted ....opposite particular points of the enemy entrenchments, and ...... when the Sikhs had been shaken by continuous storm of shot and shell, the right or weakest point of their position should be assaulted ...by together mustered nearly 15,000 men.*

The British divisions advanced in silence, amid the darkness of night and the Sikhs seemed everywhere taken by surprise, and they came up quickly. The English batteries opened at sunrise, and for upwards of three hours fired routinely on the Sikhs the general mass of the enemy. The round after round exploded but all was in vain and the Sikhs stood unmoved, replying fire with fire. The battle field was full of battle cries, roars and reverberations from explosions.

When the sun rose, the British realised that they had achieved little so far and it would be the endeavour of infantry to achieve success by any means with assistance from directed artillery power.

The left division of the British army advanced in even order and they were aware of the Sikh weakness on their right flank due to the sandy field. The British moved in a line formation instead of in column and the shots fired by the Sikhs put them in disarray and the greater part of the division was driven back by the firepower of muskets and swivels and enfilading artillery of the Lahore Durbar.

On the extreme left, the regiments effected an entrance and the British comrades on the right were boosted by the partial success and formed themselves into wedges and masses, and rushed forward. While cheering on his ardent followers Sir Robert Dick was mortally wounded close to the trenches. The British Third Infantry Division was under him. He was 58 years old.

The British soldiers leaped into the ditch, and climbed onto the ramparts or the hurriedly prepared structures of the Sikhs and captured cannon, a sure signal of victory at that place. Even though the British effort was great; the Sikhs fought with calmness and determination; their guns from the interior now directed against the tired British soldiers. This was the second charge by the British, the earlier one having failed. Now their central division was brought forward, and the supporting regiments moved in line. Thus, even higher Sikh ramparts than the earlier barriers had to be overcome.

The British were assailed mercilessly by the firing Sikhs, sending them in utter confusion; but reaching at a close distance, they marched with bravery and discipline. The second assault was aided on the left, by the already present victorious first division British soldiers in the trenches. In this way, the regiments of the centre after a fierce battle captured many of the Sikh batteries which lay in their front.

The British soldiers were seeing oscillating fortunes and the battalions on the right, who were the victors of Aliwal, were up against the opposite flank of the Sikhs and destruction awaited the British there as well. The first line fell in heaps, and the second moved rapidly to the assault. The two lines moved forward in masses and the right flank of the Sikhs was attacked by the British cavalry to create gaps to penetrate further as the infantry of the British was exhausted by this time.

The Sikh army was leaderless and openings were thus created in the Sikh entrenchments. Single Sikh batteries still held out; the interior was filled with courageous men, who fought fiercely for every inch of ground. The traitor, Tej Singh instead of strengthening the weak right flank of the Sikhs, fled after the first assault, and, sank a boat in the middle of the bridge of communication.

Sham Singh Attariwala (b: 1790) was born in the town of Attari, Amritsar in the house of well-known Sikh farmers. Educated in Gurmukhi and Persian, he rendered his services to the Maharaja of Punjab, Ranjit Singh who made him a 'Jathedar' of 5,000 horsemen. He participated in the campaigns of Multan, Kashmir, Frontier Province, etc. In 1817 Sham Singh Attariwala joined the Sikh military and took part in the Battle of Attock, Battle of Multan, Battle of Peshawar during the Afghan–Sikh wars, and also in the 1819 Kashmir expedition. He served on the council of regency for Maharaja Duleep Singh and his daughter was married to Prince Nau Nihal Singh.

At Sobraon, he was not the type of person that Lal Singh and Tej Singh were made of. Like an old Sikh warrior Sham Singh remembered his vow, being a true Khalsa soldier. He dressed in simple white attire, as one devoted to death, and calling on all around him to fight for the Guru; he rallied his broken ranks time and again.

In the first phase of the battle he was present everywhere urging the Sikhs to fight bravely. When he saw that all was lost, he charged forward waving his sword against the 50th regiment, calling his men to follow him. His call was obeyed by about 50 of the Sikhs but they were driven back into the river. Sham Singh Attariwala pierced by seven balls, fell dead from his horse a martyr, over the bodies of other slain soldiers. Other Sikhs stood waving defiance with their swords, or telling the gunners where the English clusters needed to be targeted. The parapets bloodied and the trenches were filled with the dead and the dying.

The Sikhs' defensible positions were gradually captured, and they were pressed towards the scarcely fordable Sutlej river. In any case, they were not running away, even though they were leaderless. They were being assailed from both sides by British cavalry and infantry but no Sikh would surrender and none of them asked for quarter. They faced the British everywhere with their chests thrust forward. Many rushed forward to meet their inevitable death.

The indomitable courage of the vanquished drew the astonishment of the British and did not strike at the helpless and the dying who lay on the ground. But the British, despite their admiration for the Sikhs, fired batteries and battalions chased the remaining Sikh soldiers so that they forded the river Sutlej and went to the other side, which was still under the Lahore Durbar. It completed the British victory.

On the night of the victory some regiments were pushed across the Sutlej opposite Ferozepur; no Sikh soldier was visible; and on February 12 the fort of Kasur was occupied without opposition. On the following day the army encamped there and even though the Sikhs numbered 20,000 in the direction of Amritsar but the Khalsa Army had lost its power. The first Anglo-Sikh war was over.

Lahore After the War

The soldiery readily assented that Gulab Singh should have full powers to deal with the English who had agreed already to recognising a Sikh government in Lahore. On February 15, 1846, Raja and several other chiefs were received by the Governor-General at Kasur, and they were told:

- that Duleep Singh would continue to be regarded as a friendly sovereign,
- the conquerors (the British) would retain the country between the Beas and Sutlej, and
- that for the expenses of the war £1.5 million to be paid as some indemnity

Reluctantly the terms were agreed to and the young Maharaja tendered his submission in person, and the British army arrived at the Sikh capital on February 20. Two days later, a portion of the citadel was garrisoned by English regiments, symbolising the British presence in Punjab.

The Governor-General wanted to chastise the Sikhs for their aggressions and chose the Beas, as commanding positions instead of the old boundary of the Sutlej. He initially thought that Raja Gulab Singh be made independent ruler in the hills of Jammu. But the Raja was silently thinking positively for the viceroyalty of Punjab with a weaker Army. The chiefs appointed Gulab Singh as a Wazir.

Peace Treaty

Frederick Currie drafted and negotiated the peace treaty. It was signed on March 9, 1846. The same parties, on March 11, 1846, signed a supplement, comprising eight Articles of Agreement. A British force was to remain in Lahore till the end of the year, under the terms of the treaty so that 'during the reorganisation of the Sikh Army, protection could be provided on the person of the Maharaja and the inhabitants of the City of Lahore'. It is said that the Lahore Durbar was afraid of its own army and the supplementary agreement was requested by them. From the city the Lahore army was to depart and for the British troops convenient quarters were to be provided and the Lahore Government was supposed to make the payment for the extra expenses.

The bona fide rights of *jagirdars* in the Lahore territories would continue as per the Agreement and these people would continue to assist the Lahore Government in recovering the revenue arrears just like they would do for the last government from the *Kardars* and managers in the territories. This was as per the provisions of Articles 3 and 4 of the Treaty.

The Treaty of Amritsar

As reparations for the cost of the war the British demanded payment of Rs. 15 million (one and a half crore). The whole of this sum could not be paid by the Lahore Government immediately and had to cede some areas including Hazara and Kashmir equivalent to Rs. 10 million. Apart from this, the Maharaja was required to pay Rs. 6 million immediately.

The Lahore treasury was almost empty, and in the meantime the Governor-General tried to appease Gulab Singh in a befitting manner sufficiently agreeable to the Raja himself. As two-thirds of the indemnity in money required from Lahore could not be given, Kashmir and the hill states from the Beas to the Indus were cut off from the Punjab proper, and like auction, transferred to Gulab Singh as a separate sovereign for a million pounds sterling.

On March 16, 1846, the Treaty of Sale was concluded and signed by Gulab Singh, Hardinge, Currie and Lawrence. Consequently, Gulab Singh became the founder and the first Maharaja of the princely state of Kashmir and Jammu.

This transaction was highly debatable and unworthy of the British greatness. Gulab Singh was to pay Rs. 6.8 million (£680,000), as a fine to the Lahore Durbar, before the war broke out but now, he was owner of the Lahore provinces as an independent prince. His rise to sovereign power roused the ambition of people like Tej Singh, who offered Rs. 2.5 million for a crown and a province! He was rebuffed. Gulab Singh was invested with the title of Maharaja at Amritsar on March 15, 1846. On this occasion the new 'Maharaja' Gulab Singh stood up, and, with joined hands, expressed his gratitude to the British viceroy, adding that he was indeed his *'Zurkharid'* or gold-bought slave.

The terms of payment were made easier for Gulab Singh, as he was a legal heir to the money which his brother Suchet Singh had buried in Ferozepur.

As per the British agreement, a key clause was that a Resident British officer, with assistants, was to remain at Lahore, as appointed by the Governor-General. These persons were fully authorised to direct and control all matters of the state. A Council of Regency composed of leading Chiefs and Sirdars replaced the Regent, Maharani Jind Kaur, mother of the Maharaja. She was awarded an annual pension of Rs. 1,50,000. Those chiefs were to act under the control and guidance of the British Resident. Thus the British acquired the effective control of the government.

Lal Singh was pleased that his influence with the mother of the Maharaja would soon enable him to remove Gulab Singh and all his treasons were directed towards his own success at the cost of the state. Gulab Singh put the Governor-General in a quandary by asking what he was to get for all he had done to bring about a speedy peace, and to size up his own army.

Lahore Durbar is Now Under the State of Lahore

Lal Singh became minister once more but along with other traitor chiefs he knew that handling the downsized Army would also be a problem for him and the departure of Gulab Singh did not make him fully comfortable. Thus, the decision of the British to station a force in the capital till December 1846 was agreeable to the chiefs who would get enough time to reorganise the army.

The end of the year came; but the chiefs were still helpless and were quite willing to see the English in power till Maharaja Duleep Singh came of age. While the Governor-General and Commander-in-Chief remained at Lahore at the head of twenty thousand men, portions of the Sikh army came to the capital to be paid up not disbanded. The brave Sikh soldiers showed neither the despondency nor the effects of any loss in the war.

The Sikh soldiers talked of their defeat as the chance of war and they inwardly dwelt upon their future destiny with unabated confidence. Later the Punjabi hard-working men served the British army with zeal and the synergy made Punjab quite prosperous by the end of the nineteenth century.

The British soldiers were lent for a time to preserve the semblance of a government, but in reality, the British wanted to keep possession of the advantages already gained, until the end of the year by which time the Governor-General would annex the whole of Punjab to the British possessions, if necessary.

By the Treaty of Lahore, the fort and town of Kangra and

some hilly area between the Sutlej and Beas were ceded to the British. In command of some 300 men in fort, Sunder Singh Ailadar would open the gates to no one except the Maharaja of Lahore.

The province of Kashmir and the estates of Jammu and Kohistan were transferred to Gulab Singh by the Treaty of Amritsar. The implementation of these clauses was left to the Lahore Durbar which encouraged the local zamindars and jagirdars of Kohistan to create disturbances. Ostensibly, to please the British the Durbar ordered the governor at Jasrota to spare no pains to bring the zamindars to book. A cryptic message was sent to Misar Rup Lal, the governor who retired leaving arms, ammunition and provisions within the fort which were seized by the rebels thereby spreading the revolt. Gulab Singh with great endeavour and resources occupied Poonch, Bhadarwah, Sumruth, Ramnagar and Jasrota.

Ghulam Mohi-ud-din, who had been governor of Kashmir, was succeeded in 1844, by his son Shaikh Imam-ud-din. During their tenures as collectors of revenue in Jalandhar, both father and son had amassed private fortunes but they were among the worst defaulters of revenues to the state which amounted to Rs. 4.5 million. With the decline of the government in Lahore the chiefs of the valley surrounding the hills of Uri, Muzaffarabad, Rajauri and Kurna were in for reviving Muslim domination of the region. The governor thought he might succeed like Gulab Singh in acquiring a huge land mass. Lal Singh was encouraging the Shaikh to resist the occupation of the province. He issued a *parwana* from the Durbar exhorting the soldiers to help Shaikh not to deliver the province to its new ruler.

On August 30, Shaikh, the governor of Kashmir defeated the troops of Raja Gulab Singh in battle. Wazir Lakhpat Rai, the commander to the Dogra army, was killed, and Wazir Ratan Singh was forced to seek asylum in the fort of Hari Parbat.

This did not please Lord Hardinge at all as the winter was approaching and military operations in the valley would become difficult. Under orders from Calcutta, the Lahore Durbar was roused to action. The landed property of the Shaikh in Jalandhar and Hoshiarpur, was confiscated and a large force from Lahore was ordered to move towards Kashmir. Sir John Littler also marched towards Jammu to be ready to proceed to Kashmir if necessary. Sir Henry Lawrence supported by a British force from Jalandhar under Brigadier Wheeler arrived in Kashmir on October 21, 1846. Imam-ud-din tendered his submission to Captain Herbert Edwardes on October 31, 1846.

Captain Edwardes a young officer learnt that the Shaikh had been authorised in his action by Lal Singh and he went deep into the matter. A court of enquiry with Sir Frederick Currie as president, Lt. Colonel Lawrence, Sir John Littler, John Lawrence, and Lt. Colonel Goldie as members began its proceedings. Dignitaries of the Durbar included Attar Singh Kalianwala, Sher Singh Attariwala, Tej Singh, Diwan Dina Nath and Khalifa Nur-ud-din. Lal Singh and Imam-ud-din were summoned before the court. Three letters signed by Lal Singh, two to Imam-ud-din and one to the Durbar soldiers were produced. The evidence was found conclusive. Lal Singh was held to be unworthy of the chief ministership both by the Durbar and the British government. Accordingly, he was stripped of his office and ordered to leave Punjab. After a week's detention in Lahore, he was conducted to Ferozepur, thence to Agra and Dehra Dun.

The Rani Jindan-Lal Singh government never commanded respect in any quarter. After Lal Singh's dismissal, the powers of government were invested in a council of four, Tej Singh, Sher Singh Attariwala, Diwan Dina Nath and Khalifa Nur-ud-din. A circular, was sent to all government officers that no *parwana* was to be considered valid unless it bore the seal of all four councillors. This government, however was not intended to last long and the Governor-General formulating an alternative form of administration.

The Treaty of Bhyroval

That the British troops would not remain in Lahore after the end of 1846 was specified in the supplementary articles of agreement,. When the British were to leave, the Durbar requested that the troops should be retained till the Maharaja attained the age of 16. Agreeing to this, the British added new articles of agreement in the Treaty of Bhyroval. The 13 members of the Durbar, Currie and Lawrence signed this on December 26, 1846 and it was later ratified by Hardinge and the young Maharaja.

The agreement, consisting of eleven articles was finally ratified by Sir Henry Hardinge and Maharaja Duleep Singh when the latter was induced to visit the Governor-Gencral at Bhyrowal on December 24, 1846. By it the Regency Council was doubled in size by the addition of Sardar Attar Singh Kalianwala, Shamsher Singh Sindhanwalia, Ranjodh Singh Majithia and Bhai Nidhan Singh. The eight councillors were mentioned by name and it was stipulated that no change be made without the consent of the British Resident acting under the orders of the Governor General. Article 6 stated that the British Resident assisted by an efficient staff 'shall have the full authority to direct and control the duties of every department' ; the allowance of the Maharani was fixed at Rs. 1,50,000 and the arrangement was to continue till September 4, 1854, when Maharaja Duleep Singh should attain the age of sixteen.

The preamble of the treaty emphasised that the British government had taken over the administration, and agreed to keep their troops in the country at the request of the chiefs of the state at their own free will. The British resident backed by an army then, 'virtually became the successor of Ranjit Singh on the throne of Lahore.'

The Maharani, having been outwitted by British statesmanship was now being considered a burden and an embarrassment. Sir Frederick Currie in his personal correspondence with the Governor-General recommended that she be removed from Lahore; but the latter objected.

A few months later, Sir Henry Lawrence found, in what came to be known as the *Prema Plot*, an excuse indeed. It was alleged that Prema secretly plotted to murder the British Resident and Tej Singh but no incriminating documents of any significance were produced by the prosecutors, and since the Maharani's munshi had met Prema once or twice, she was implicated too. The Governor-General, however, stayed the expulsion of the Queen-Mother.

Six months later, an incident put Rani Jindan in trouble. The Resident, Henry Lawrence, wanted the Maharaja to honour some Sikh Chiefs who had rendered services to the British during the war, on August 7, 1846. At the exact moment fixed by the court astrologer, the Maharaja refused to apply the saffron mark on the forehead of Tej Singh, alleged by the Resident that the Maharaja had acted under the influence of his mother. The Council recommended that the Rani's personal movements be restricted within the four walls of the palace and she be stopped from giving audience so freely and frequently to people of her choice.

The Resident was not satisfied with this step and he wanted the Rani away from day-to-day working and got permission from the government to send Rani Jind Kaur to live in the fort of Sheikhupura, and reduce her allowance from Rs. 1,30,000 to Rs. 48,000 per annum. Lawrence did not share this action with the Regency Council till the hour of the departure.

Three people including Kahan Singh and Ganga Ram were hanged by the resident on charges of sedition. Ganga Ram was employed by the Rani, and she was alleged to have given bribes to him. The Rani's private papers were subsequently searched but she could not be proven guilty and the Resident preferred to drop the matter but yet he wanted to carry out constitutional proceedings to remove her. He obtained the approval of the Regency Council to banish the Rani from the Punjab and a further cut in her allowance.

The Resident was reorganising the administration. The Lahore treasury was almost empty; it had to meet the British demand for Rs. 2.2 million per annum for the maintenance of a thousand troops in the capital. The new government had to tap fresh sources of income. The standing army of the state, by the Treaty of March 1846, was to be limited to 25 battalions of infantry and 12,000 cavalries. Every day a number of soldiers were paid arrears in salary and discharged. The scale of pay of retained troops was reverted to Ranjit Singh's times.

Henry Lawrence hoped to reconcile the soldiers by offering some compensatory benefits. Leave rules were relaxed; regular monthly payment was ensured and an allowance known as *bhatta* was introduced.

The Durbar had neither an organised judiciary nor a codified system of law. Lawrence established appellate courts to deal with cases the panchayat had not been able to settle. This was an intermediate authority between the District Collector and the Maharaja. Regarding revenue matters, Lawrence was anxious to render the Collector, 'as innocuous as possible.' He appointed a number of British officers and to the outlying districts were appointed: Herbert Edwardes to Bannu, James Abbot to Hazara, Herbert to Attock and George Lawrence to Peshawar. They were to collect information regarding the resources of the district and they were vested with wide discretionary powers. Each officer thought that the Punjab had passed into the hands of the British, and that he represented his government. The weekly reports submitted to the Resident reflected the 'superiority complex' of the officer. Towards Diwan Daulat Rai, the governor of Bannu province, Edwardes' behaviour was arrogant and rude and the former was replaced by him with Commandant Cortland. Similarly, George Lawrence replaced Autar Singh, governor of Peshawar, with Gulab Singh Povindia, who he found more amiable. These incidents sowed the seeds of dissension.

The banishment of Jind Kaur was one of the major decisions taken by Henry Lawrence in his capacity of Resident. He went to Simla in August being in a poor state of health, to return in November on a brief visit before sailing for England in furlough, on the same boat as the Governor-General Hardinge.

Henry's younger brother John (b: 1811), became acting Resident till Sir Frederick Currie could take charge. John Lawrence had sympathy for the common man and he felt that a prosperous peasantry could be the backbone of the country. Land and customs reform were on the top of his priority list. He felt that fifty per cent of gross produce, which the state took as its share, was exorbitant and the further unauthorised taxes, which collectors levied made the burden on peasants very harsh and these could be minimised if regular records were available. The appointed officers were to guide the collection figures of the past few years in the Durbar account books, and all the Kardars were asked to give receipts for the amounts obtained from Zemindars and enter this in a register which was maintained in a village as a permanent record of all such transactions. These new changes benefited the peasants.

But many peasants found the rigid enforcement of the rule tough as all payments were to be made in cash and often, they tended to leave some of their land uncultivated. Bigger landlords rued that the encroached land under them could not be exploited by them, being restricted by the record of rights.

Almost every article of trade was subject to state duty under the prevailing system. John Lawrence exempted daily necessities such as corn, ghee and fuel. Transit and town duties were abolished to eliminate extortion by officers of the Customs Department. Only import and export duties were retained. John Lawrence, in his report to the government on this matter said that the loss to the treasury would amount to Rs. 2,23,000 per annum.

John Lawrence regulated the working hours in public offices and the officials were required to observe them. Civil and Criminal Procedure Codes were developed and a beginning was made towards the establishment of a public postal system. John Lawrence tried to curb certain social menaces like female infanticide, sati and burying of lepers.

British officers were seen busily going to and fro with parties of land surveyors, carrying measuring chains, telescopes and other paraphernalia which changed the complexion of things and the seeds were sown for rapid social and economic changes. Then John Lawrence proceeded on furlough leaving his successor, Currie to reap the benefits.

Heading Towards the Second Anglo-Sikh War

The Outbreak at Multan (March–May 1848)

Multan was added in 1818 to the Sikh kingdom by Maharaja Ranjit Singh, for it had been held by Divan Sawan Mal since 1821. On Sawan Mal's death in 1844, his eldest son, Mul Raj, was confirmed in the Governorship of Multan. The condition was that he would pay a *nazrana* (succession fee) of Rs. 3 million to the Lahore Durbar. Mul Raj did not pay any part of this amount as there was no regular Government at Lahore. It was agreed in 1846 after mediation by the British Resident that the Diwan should pay Rs. 2 million in all on account of the *nazrana* and for his arrears. Also all lands north of the Ravi comprising one-third of the province was to be given up by him and that the revenue of the area under him to be increased by more than one-third for three years beginning with the kharif of 1847.

Lord Hardinge was succeeded by the Earl of Dalhousie (b: 1812), who arrived at Calcutta on January 12, 1848. At 35, he was the youngest Governor-General ever. The British army's strength at strategic positions was 50,000 men and 60 guns on both sides of the Sutlej. A standing British army of 9,000 men held the Sikh capital, and about the same number were at Ferozepur; these men could be moved anywhere in the Punjab at a day's notice. The Sikh army, which 4 years ago had 85,000 men and 350 guns, was reduced to 24,000 men and 50 guns and that too in distributed places.

Under such comfortable circumstances, Lord Dalhousie assumed office. A British sycophant boasted 'Not a shot is fired from the Indus to Cape Comorin against our will.' But events belied this wishful thinking, and the prophecy of Lord Hardinge about at least 7 years of peace from 1848 onwards proved to be wrong from the very beginning.

The tranquillity was rudely shaken by a comparatively insignificant outbreak at Multan, on the south-west frontier of the Punjab, but which eventually led to the absorption of the Punjab in the British dominions.

But soon new difficulties arose which were basically created by the British in the Diwan's way which made him resign his office. The Treaty of Bhyrowal gave the British Resident complete control of the administration of the Punjab. Under his influence the archaic octroi duties of Punjab were abolished and some articles of trade were declared to be duty free. The new system was also to be introduced in Multan, and as this was surely going to affect his income more harshly. Mul Raj requested some concessions but John Lawrence, the officiating Resident would have none of it. Mul Raj could not lower his personal honour for making appeals for remission and he came to Lahore in December 1847, and tendered his resignation on the 18th of that month. But John Lawrence pressed him to continue with the administration of Multan till at least March 10, 1848; no one else could recover the revenues from Multan in the middle of the harvesting season. Lawrence had different plans for Punjab and he thought he would be busy in those ventures. Mul Raj agreed but requested that his resignation be kept a profound secret, till the winter revenue had been paid.

John Lawrence agreed to it and also submitted to the Government of India, proposals to depute two British officers—Messrs. Cocks and Agnew to Multan to learn about the administration before Diwan Mul Raj resigned.

As the appointment of John Lawrence as Resident at Lahore was only a stop gap arrangement, the Secretary to the Government ordered that Sir F. Currie (the permanent incumbent) should be awaited and he would issue orders as need be. Currie was handed over the charge by Henry Lawrence on March 6, 1848 and he began making arrangements for the government of Multan. He met the Durbar and its members accepted the British proposal to nominate a Sardar as the Nazim of Multan to oversee the administration on behalf of the Durbar for a fixed salary of Rs. 30,000 per annum. He was to act in conjunction and by the advice of a British Political Agent.

The post of Nazim was conferred on Kahan Singh Mann and that of Political Agent at Multan was to be filled by Mr. P.A. Vans Agnew, and Lieutenant Anderson was appointed to assist him at Multan. The real power, naturally, rested with the British.

The two British officers and Sardar Kahan arrived at Multan on April 18, and it was arranged that Mul Raj should make over the fort to the new Governor the next morning which was done via a ceremony on the 19th. The two British officers then addressed the old garrison who tried to dispel their fear of losing employment, assuring them of their old positions.

As the cavalcade including the British officers crossed the bridge over the ditch, a sepoy of Mul Raj who was sitting in the first gate made a thrust at Mr. Agnew who was on horseback with a small spear which knocked him off his horse, and he was severely wounded. Mul Raj rode off as he was afraid of his own life. Lieutenant Anderson and Agnew were rescued. But not for long.

Mul Raj was in a predicament. He was the Diwan and his soldiers supported him but when he accompanied the Sahibs to Multan, the atmosphere was charged and the normal patriotic zeal became vitriolic and ultimately it turned into violence. The soldiers belonging to different communities vowed to stand by him, and a war-bracelet was fastened on Mul Raj's wrist. This happened on April 19, 1848. The following day, the troops from Lahore also joined the Multan garrison. No sooner had this become known than an over-zealous rabble rushed towards the Idgah where the British officers were stationed and killed them. Sardar Kahan Singh Man was made a prisoner. When Mul Raj heard of the murder of Agnew and Anderson, he was angry but he could not do much.

These events took place against the wishes of Mul Raj and were the handiwork of the Multan troops against anticipated English domination in Multan. They had their own apprehensions and the sight of foreigners wresting Multan from the Diwan made them very angry. The troops could not accept the replacement of the Diwan who was in power for about 28 years. Moreover, there were apprehensions that mass sacking of soldiers in Lahore, would occur if the British were to rule Multan. They thus rebelled against the foreigners, and proceeded with the ceremony of investing the unwilling Diwan with the leadership of the rebellion. However, Mul Raj had nothing to do with the murders.

Though the British Resident expressed his unwillingness 'to expend British blood' in a service which the British Government was treaty-bound to perform and for which they pocketed Rs. 2.2 million a year out of the Punjab revenues, he considered it absolutely necessary that the British Government should avenge the murder of its officers.

For this purpose, the Resident Currie recommended to the Commander-in-Chief that a British force should move upon Multan to suppress the rebellion without delay. But the Government of India under the British wanted the rebellion to spread enough to prepare a handy excuse for annexing the Punjab.

Lord Gough advised Currie to enter on operations against Multan till the rains were well over, and the cold season commenced but Currie wrote back about risks if operations were postponed to the period mentioned. Lord Gough believed that Multan was too strong and a very large expedition would be required to produce any decisive results. He also observed that the rebellion was against the Durbar and it was its business to quell it and that the employment of the Bengal troops (comprising Hindusthani or Eastern UP and Bihar-based troops) would make the situation more volatile if a general Sikh rising occurred.

The views of Lord Gough were endorsed by Sir Currie as well as the Governor-General Dalhousie. Sir Charles Napier subsequently declared that he thought they were right.

Such was the decision of the British Government and three

weeks had passed since the muder of the British officers, during which Mul Raj consolidated his position and did not do much to control the spreading revolt.

Dalhousie seized this opportunity of allowing the local outbreak at Multan to annex the Punjab as per his policy. As early as May 10, 1848, he wrote to Sir George Couper, his best friend about his desire to annex Punjab soon.

In various letters, Lord Dalhousie made no secret of the *'heavy reparation'* which he wanted the State of Lahore to make, once the English had conquered Punjab. *'If not in my days'* he wrote on August 4, 1848—*'If not in my days.... in my successor's the curtain will fall on the Sikh dynasty.... The right to annex Punjab is beyond cavil....'*

On September 18, he made a more definite admission: *'I can see no escape from the necessity of annexing this infernal country'*. In a letter to Henry Lawrence, dated October 15, 1848, he bluntly said *'The task before me is the utter destruction and prostration of the Sikh power....and the subjection of its people. This must be done promptly, fully, and finally.'*

Advance of Edwardes in June and July 1848

Edwardes's Multan adventure in June and July 1848 with limited serious military equipment is amazing. Edwardes on April 22 in his camp at Dera Fateh Khan (in Dera Gazi Khan) received Agnew's appeal for help, before he was murdered. He reached Layyah and came to know of the fate of Agnew and Anderson. He also heard that Mul Raj intended marching against him.

He got a document, a summons from the Sikh soldiers in the Multan fort to the regiment of Sikhs, Fateh Paltan, under him and he was clever enough to decide that a meeting between his own Sikh regiment and Mul Raj's soldiers must be prevented. Accordingly, he came back to Dera Fateh Khan and awaited General Cortlandt, in charge of Dera Ismail Khan, and to whom Edwardes had addressed soon after the Multan outbreak. On May 4 he was joined by Cortlandt, with a Muslim regiment and six guns, whereupon Mul Raj who was following retreated.

The next day Edwardes wrote to the Resident requesting him to ask Bahawal Khan to send a strong force to assist him, as the operations had been deferred. A general plan was made by Frederick Currie to use the time interval between May and October; five columns were to operate for the pacification of the Multan province. Three of them consisted of Sikh soldiers under Sikh Sardars, of whom Sher Singh was the most prominent. One was from the army of the Nawab of Bahawalpur, and the fifth of the troops collected by Edwardes.

The Sikh Columns had hardly marched two-thirds of the way to Multan, when it was halted by the Resident's orders and the Bahawalpur troops did not dare to march alone, and so the whole scheme fell through. A belligerent Mul Raj crossed the Chenab with 6,000 men and 15 guns, and advanced towards the Indus and he planned to overrun Cortlandt's forces, separated from that of Edwardes, before the forces could combine.

Edwardes marched fast to join him. The combined forces would have numbered about half of Mul Raj, and so he fervently requested Sir Currie that the Bahawalpur troops should be immediately asked to join them. On May 19, at the right bank of the Indus, opposite Dera Deen Punnah, he advanced southwards in the meantime, joining Cortlandt. Two days after Edwardes's forces had combined with Cortlandt's forces, he received news from the south. Ghulam Haidar Khan had succeeded in bringing about the surrender of the fortress of Dera Ghazi Khan, which he hoped would make Mul Raj withdraw to Multan.

Keeping Edwardes in the dark, Currie wrote to Bahawal Khan to cross the Sutlej in the Bari Doab and to march on Multan. The Bahawalpur troops known as *Daoodputras* were on their way to Multan. On June 18, a Multan force under Ram Rang gave them battle at *Kineyri* on the Chenab river, nearly twenty miles from Multan. The Multan army was defeated by the Bahawalpur troops, which were joined the same day by about 5,000 men and ten of Edwardes' guns, and 25 zamburas. The battle lasted for nine hours. Now, emboldened by victory, Edwardes began to advance upon Multan; further strengthened by Shaikh Imam-uddin's force, 4,000 strong, on June 28, on which day also arrived Lieutenant Lake, virtually the commander of the Daoodputras.

On July 1, 1848 the battle between Mul Raj and Edwardes was fought at Suddosam and it resulted in the defeat of Mul Raj, who was now forced within the walls of Multan.

The First Attempt to Siege Multan (July to September 1848) and Sher Singh's Desertion

Soon after the battle of Kineyri, Edwardes thought of besieging Multan itself, and decimating the rebellion in its nascent state. He applied to Currie for some heavy guns and mortars and for permission to launch the action. It was June 22, 1848. Major Napier was requisitioned to plan operations. Currie consulted Major Napier who reassured him 'with every prospect of success' with a single brigade, ten guns, and twenty mortars and howitzers from the British Army. This opinion was forwarded by Currie to Gough on June 28 for concurrence.

Gough kept Governor General in the loop adding that the smallest force he could recommend would be a) two brigades of infantry (with a European regiment attached to each), b) one native cavalry brigade, c) two troops of horse artillery and d) a siege-train with foot artillery.

While Currie was waiting for his decision, the news reached him (on July 10) of Edwardes' victory at Suddosam. Currie now decided to use the special powers allowed to him for acting in emergency, and ordered a British force, partly from Lahore and partly from Ferozepur, to move upon Multan with a siege-train duly equipped under General Whish. He at the same time asked Sher Singh to continue his advance and cooperate with Whish.

On July 22 the Resident issued a proclamation to the people of Multan, informing them of the advance of a British force; and the two British columns from Ferozepur and Lahore reached Multan on August 18-19, 1848. On September 4 Whish issued a proclamation asking people and the garrison of Multan to surrender unconditionally, but the people defied it.

On September 6, Whish prepared a plan of attack on the fort and city of Multan. Trench works began on September 7 and on September 9 an unsuccessful asault was made on the fortress. On September 12, the British advanced by half a mile.

Two days later, an unexpected event took place as Sher Singh defected to Mul Raj, taking with him all the troops under his command. A Council of War held by the General concluded that the siege was not feasible and, on September 15, the siege was raised, and the British troops took up an entrenched position.

The defection of Sher Singh resulted from many factors. The high-handed and very unpopular acts of the British in the Punjab during the time gap between the first outbreak at Multan and the siege of the citadel. It provoked and alarmed many Sikh Sardars and soldiers, who saw in these British acts an intention to end to Sikh independence.

The exile of the Maharani from the Punjab and her virtual imprisonment at Benares was the first cause of resentment of the Sirdars. She was opposed to the British ascendancy in the Punjab but in her forced retirement at Sheikhupura she could do no harm to them.

Soon after he went over to Mul Raj, this national grievance was given a prominent place in the manifesto which Sher Singh issued. The feeling of indignation was further intensified by other acts of the British officers. The province of Hazara had been transferred to Gulab Singh, but it was subsequently exchanged and handed over to the Lahore Durbar. This was placed under Sardar Chattar Singh Attariwala (the father of Raja Sher Singh), who was to be 'aided and advised' by one of the Resident's Assistants, Captain Abbott. But soon Abbott crossed swords with Chattar Singh, and began to ill-treat him. This combined with the news of the Maharani's exile, led Chattar Singh to suspect that the British had decided upon his doom as also that of the house of Ranjit Singh.

His daughter was betrothed to Maharaja Duleep Singh, and he wrote to his son, Raja Sher Singh, to ask the Resident, through Herbert Edwardes, to fix a date for the marriage ceremony. The reply of the resident was so evasive that it increased suspicion. Shortly after the outbreak at Multan, Abbott thought that the Sardar was at the head of a conspiracy for the expulsion of the English from the Punjab.

He moved to a residence fifty-six kilometres away from that of Chattar Singh and thus all personal communication with him was aborted. Soon a crisis developed. A very few troops of the brigade of the Durbar troops stationed at Pukli, near the Sardar's residence, started marching to Multan in order to join the insurrection, totally unsupported by their offcers but Abbott tried to brand them as rebels going for participation in the Multan insurrection. These troops belonged to Chattar Singh.

Early in August 1848, Abbott roused the armed Muslim peasantry to rise and destroy the Sikh forces and closed the passes which blocked any movement of the Durbar troops. On August 6, the mountaineers in large numbers surrounded the town of Haripur where Sardar Chattar Singh was staying. In self-defence, the Sardar ordered Colonel Canora, an American, who had been for some years in the Sikh service, to place his guns in position but he refused to move his battery without Abbott's permission. Canora loaded his guns and ordered his havildar to fire at the infantry. The havildar refused but he was killed by Canora. In the melee, Canora himself was killed. This was a case of unwanted homicide and finding it to be a good chance; Abbot sent the Resident an utterly false account of the incident, charging the Sardar with a cold-blooded murder.

But although the Resident vas absolutely sure of the Sardar's innocence his Nazamat was withdrawn and his Jagir was confiscated. Chattar Singh was now a bitter man and there was no doubt in his mind that he was to be victim number one in the general subversion of Duleep Singh's kingdom. In desperation, he raised the standard of revolt and dedicated himself to one last struggle for Sikh independence.

Early in September, Sher Singh received letters from his father couched in terms of despair at citing the ill-treatment which the British representatives were meting out to him. In spite of these letters which had a great influence on him, he remained steadfast in his resolve till the failure of the besiegers' attack on September 9; then for three days he wavered, but on the 13th, despite the successes of the previous day he finally resolved to make an effort, at any cost. This was to be for: a) rescuing his injured father, b) for the survival of the Sikh sovereignty itself.

Along with his troops he went over to Diwan Mul Raj on September 14, 1848 and consequently General Whish was forced to raise the siege.

Sher Singh received anything but a cordial reception from Diwan Mul Raj, who regarded his movements with distrust and suspicion and therefore the raising of the siege seemed to be the only effect of Sher Singh's defection. The Diwan asked him to encamp in the Hazuri Bagh under the guns of the fort and refused him admission into Multan. Mul Raj's suspicions were increased by a fictitious letter addressed to Sher Singh, which Edwardes ensured that it came into Mul Raj's hands. Sher Singh was soon fed-up as he was viewed with suspicion. He marched out from Multan on October 9 to join his father. Sher Singh issued a manifesto calling upon all good Sikhs to expel the tyrannous and crafty British under whom both their possessions and religions were threatened. The response was overwhelming and the old soldiers of the Khalsa flocked to join Sher Singh.

The Sikh Rising; Outbreak at Hazara

In the meantime, Chattar Singh had opened communications with Amir Dost Muhammad and the Sikh troops in Peshawar; and by the end of October the British officers in Peshawar including George Lawrence had to evacuate Peshawar. Early in November, Peshawar was taken by Chattar Singh. This forced Sultan Muhammad to hand them over to him. Shortly afterwards, Attock fell into Chattar Singh's hands, and the Bannu troops too, as soon as they heard the news of Sher Singh's defection, rose in rebellion and killed Malik Fateh Khan Tiwana, and marched off to join Sher Singh.

The British authorities were silent. Though George Lawrence and Nicholson had demanded in September and October for a British brigade to the north-west, absolutely nothing was done by the British authorities. The British plan was that the army should not move till it had adequate strength to encounter the Sikh nation in arms.

The defection of Sher Singh was a turning point but it was waiting to happen as the Sikh nation had not yet folded up and for more than 50 years, the Sikhs had been the major force in Punjab. The insurrection became a revolt against British control; awaiting the final trial of strength. Gough had his own military policy. He believed that a rebellion against the Durbar had to be quelled by the Durbar. After Hardinge, the Army had been downsized and sufficient battalions were not there at the disposal of the British to be deployed at frontier areas, as and when required, on a piecemeal basis.

Also, the British had suffered heavily at the hands of the Sikhs in the first war despite getting too many guns of the defeated army. The British garrisons were located quite apart and mobilising meant using animals and litters which moved really slowly, if we compare them with motorised movements of the present day.

Therefore Gough wanted to keep a big centralised army to face the Sikh nation in the big war like scenario, when need be and their mobilisation to frontiers could weaken the big main army.

Also, in the specific case of Multan, it was advised that it would be dangerous for European troops to move in the hot weather, while sepoy regiments, i.e. native army, without European support, could not be relied on to fight their best. Also sending a detachment in July for attack on Multan would not have served much of a purpose. Also, in September Mul Raj had adequately strengthned himself with a greater number of troops which he had gathered.

On the other hand, the despatch of an overwhelming force, might have helped in capturing Multan; but it could have roused the whole Sikh nation to arms.

So, instead of sending any force, big or small, the decision was taken to collect a big army to defeat the entire Sikh nation and such a synergised Army would take months to collect. The required force, according to Gough's calculations would include some 24,000 of all arms, with 78 field-guns and 50 siege-guns. Carriages were in short supply and troops would have to be brought up even from Calcutta; the sepoy army was already heavily downsized by Lord Hardinge; further reduction was due to troops absent on furlough.

Gough's opinion did not count when Sir Currie sent troops in Multan months back. Now the second expedition being planned, Whish's forces were to be detained till the fall of Multan in January.

Since Sher Singh's defection, the siege of Multan was of secondary importance; the focus was now shifted to the northern districts of Hazara, Peshawar, etc. The real drama was to be seen in the upcoming contest in the more northern districts. The main object of bringing down Multan was to get the engaged troops free for further deployment in the north. Plans were made to despatch a column from Bombay as Mul Raj was strong enough to withstand the onslaught of the British troops actually deployed.

It has already been observed that during the month of August, while Sher Singh was still supporting Edwardes before his father, Chattar Singh rebelled in the north. In the north Peshawar used to be the main citadel of a large body of Sikh troops, under the loyal and aged governor, Gulab Singh 'Povindia' and the British representative was Major George Lawrence. Kohat lay to the south-west of Peshawar where Sultan Mohammed was the governor and who had always expressed the strongest personal attachment to George Lawrence. But he was well-known for his spells of treachery. There was no British officer at Kohat.

Across the Indus, in the Hazara district, Chattar Singh was the Nazim or governor. Not only was he in touch with his son Sher Singh but he opened communications with Gulab Singh of Kashmir, and also with the Amir at Kabul, and with Sultan Mohammed.

Dost Mohammed who had been at loggerheads with the Sikhs in the previous decades was contacted to acquire Muslim support. Chattar Singh offered the control of Peshawar to Dost in return for his support.

In Peshawar, George Lawrence had enough loyal Sikhs for a long time. At the end of October that loyalty waned. The British officers were compelled to evacuate under a humiliating scenario for them. They needed Afghan escort to Kohat; and as prisoners they were handed over to Chattar Singh. *[George Lawrence, the elder brother of Henry and John Lawrence was also arrested by Chattar Singh and was released thrice on parole. He was a free man at the end of the Anglo-Sikh War in February 1849 – Author]*

In September and October, Lawrenee and Nicholson pressed Sir Currie for a Brigade to be sent to the north-west but Hugh Gough was opposed to any idea of reducing the centralised pool of soldiers which he was preparing for the 'big day'.

In the early days of November, Multa n under Mul Raj was still lying uncontrolled; in the western Punjab proper, the old Khalsa soldiers were coming in support to Sher Singh; while Peshawar and the northern part of the Sindh Sagar Doab had declared the revolt; the only check on them being Lieutenant Herbert, who had come in place for Nicholson at Attock, with a Muslim garrison, and Major Abbott with the Hazara tribesmen.

Attock stubbornly held at great odds by Herbert but

ultimately with Dost Muhammad's support, Herbert himself was captured by the Sikhs while trying to escape and sent to join the other prisoners in Chattar Singh's captivity at Peshawar. The fall of Attock took place by January 3, 1849.

In the east, Ram Singh, son of the Wazir of Nurpur, one of the hill states rebelled and proclaimed the end of British rule. John Lawrence, who was the eommissioner in the Jalandhar Doab, used reluctant Sikh troops to quell the insurgency.

To retain his confidence in the loyalty of the Sikh Sirdar Sir Frederick Currie tried hard at Lahore. When September was over, some leading members of the Durbar were arrested for plotting. Those arrested were Ranjodh Singh Majithia and Sher Singh's brother. Grave suspicions were attached to the Sikh garrison of the strong fort of Govindgarh near Amritsar. In Govindgarh, apart from 2 guns known other guns found included eighteen mounted, and 52 buried, with the obvious intention that they should be put in order when the critical moment arrived.

The presence of the British sepoy regiments at Lahore, Amritsar and in the Jalandhar Doab, prevented any organised rising in the Majha region.

From the pessimistic British view the following was the situation: Peshawar had already fallen; Attock was being besieged; the siege of Multan was a standstill awaiting the Bombay contingent; the Bannu regiments had revolted, killed Fateh Khan Tiwana, and were on the march to join Sher Singh; the old Khalsa army were flocking to his standard; and the whole Sikh population north-west of the Chenab was in insurrection.

Sher Singh moved away from Multan on October 9 at such speed that the British troops could not follow him. The British army at Ferozepur was joined by a cavalry brigade, under Cureton. Sher Singh wanted to join his troops located at Bannu. In the meantime, Cureton, who had been joined by Campbell with two regiments of native infmtry, waited for the arrival of the main army.

In November the British army was complete on the 9th. Hugh Gough crossed the Sutlej, reaching Lahore on the 13th.

Second Siege of Multan

On September 14, 1848, Sher Singh went over to Mul Raj and the

British decided to await the reinforcements arrived from Bombay. On September 16, General Whish shifted his camp and retreated a mile and a half to command the two roads leading from Multan. In the intervening period of six weeks the Multan troops were busy occupying advanced positions, and creating barriers against the British lines. Mul Raj sent messengers to Bannu, to the Afghans and Pathans beyond the Indus. These places were not yet under the British. The move was a smart one; on the one hand there were prospects of getting material aid and on the other hand, the British interests could be seriously handicapped so far as their movement from the Majha region to Peshawar was concerned. The response was, however, lukewarm.

General Whish found Mul Raj's canal excavations a serious impediment for the British batteries. An attack on November 7 was planned and on the same Lord Gough's army was starting from Ferozepur. On November 6, en masse desertion of a Hindustani regiment of the Durbar occurred. They were known as the Katar Mukhi and occupied an advanced post under Van Cortlandt. They did not, however, attack their officers.

On the 7th when the attack was to begin, the Multanis had taken the initiative, and advanced to attack Edwardes' positions. The British repelled the Multani attack with some losses and Whish advanced, and attacked the left flank of Sikh position and in the end captured all their guns except three numbers. It had a silencing effect on the Sikhs.

On November 30, 1848, Colonel Cheape, the chief engineer of the army came in and his services for the battle at Multan were most necessary and on December 6, 16 and 18 he made site surveys. It was decided by the British to make a march through the city, beginning at its southern bastion. The Bombay detachments ultimately came on December 21. Two regiments of the British and five of the native infantry, with three regiments of cavalry, were thus added to the besieging force; the artillery count was now 67 siege guns and 80 field-guns.

On the plan of attack there were some changes made and plans of Majors Napier and Scott were adhered to in which the chief point of attack was the north-east angle of the fort. The whole force was required to drive away the Sikhs in the semi-circle from the south-west to the north-east on December 27.

The British formation was in three parts: the Bengal on the right; on their left, the Bombay Column, reaching the Wullee Mahomed Canal; and, on the left of that canal, Edwardes's Force, with the Bahawalpur men.

The British force to drive back the enemy, and Edwardes's troops were to cross the canal. The operations were most successful. During the following night and the next day (the 28th) breaching batteries started; on the 29th the right attack started and on the 30th the battery against the Khooni Burj started. The following day the centre battery breached the Delhi Gate. Other batteries joined in the attacking circle.

A big attack on Edwardes by a body of Sikhs was repelled. On the 30th, minor defences around the south face were destroyed. On January 2, 1849 the breaches in the city walls existed and attacks were made on them. The Khooni Burj was attacked by the Bombay Fusiliers, and two British columns, opened all the city gates in the south. Thus, the city was taken, but the fort remained in the hands of Mul Raj.

Mul Raj left his soldiers to fend for themselves and sealed the fort from within with his selected 500 odd men. The next day, both the Delhi Gate and the Dowlut Gate at the extreme north-east of the city were seized and all the city walls were under the British who could now survey and examine the fort or citadel defences.

The British planned that the best point for the attack was near the point called Bahawal Haq. Here, therefore, the sap, batteries and mines against the outer defence were caried forward. Other batteries succeeded in breaching the upper wall on the 20th. On the 21st, the route was decided for the assault.

But all this seemed to be unnecessary. On January 22, 1849 the siege was terminated by Mul Raj, as he and his men surrendered and the entire garrison laying down their arms and becoming prisoners of war. Mul Raj got the one thing which Edwardes had told his emissary he might count on; 'a fair trial'. He was taken to Lahore and was charged with the complicity in the murder of Agnew and Anderson, and found guilty.

British and Indian soldiers resorted to uncontrolled looting in the town. Mul Raj's treasury was worth three million pounds, a huge sum in those days. With the fall of Multan, General Whish's army could reinforce Sir Hugh Gough's main Bengal Army force.

As he awaited his trial, Mulraj was kept under the custody of John Spencer Login who told his wife that Mulraj seemed not to be the bloodthirsty despot.

Mul Raj was cleared of premeditated murder and although he was initially sentenced to death, the sentence was later commuted to exile for life. He was to be banished to Singapore but was instead jailed at Fort William in Bengal as he suffered a bout of dysentery.

He was to be shifted later to Benares but he died on August 11, 1851 en route to Buxar jail after a short illness. His loyal servants cremated Diwan Mul Raj Chopra on the banks of the Ganges river.

Battle of Ramnagar

Crossing of the Chenab by the British: November-December 4, 1848

As General Whish waited in Multan for the Bombay Column; two months before the actual assault on Multan the troops under General Hugh Gough's command entered Majha territory and advanced, to give a decisive blow to Sher Singh. Gough's troops were joined by Heaney's Irregulars and these did not include the troops at various points in the Majha district, and the Jalandhar Doab or those in Multan.

Table 2.5 Battle of Ramnagar (Rasool Nagar), Gujranwala, Pakistan

	Sikh Empire	*East India Company*
Generals	Sher Singh Attariwala	Hugh Gough
Strength (men)	10,000	15,000
Guns	20	50
Killed	Unknown	26
Wounded	Unknown	59
Result	Victory	Defeat

General Cureton was sent 15 days back to guard Lahore as Sher Singh marched from Multan to Ramnagar. Sher Singh with his army had taken position on the Western bank of the Chenab, opposite Ramnagar. Cureton and Brigadier Colin Campbell occupied positions about eight miles from Ramnagar, on the east side of the river. His cavalry was doing daily reconnaissance without fighting actually.

The river Chenab at that point was fairly wide and the river-bed was quite sandy with change in course all the time. At Ramnagar there was a fairly good ford and the Sikhs had established an outpost on the Eastern side i.e. on the side the British were located and they could easily communicate with their main body on the Western side. For the British, it was necessary to move to the opposite side to give the Sikhs a good fight.

On November 21, Lord Gough with the main army ahead and his artillery way behind made a rather amateurish decision to 'test' the strength of the Sikhs; a step which can be said equivalent to Harakiri.

Accordingly, in the moming on the 22nd, the British advanced to Ramnagar and the Sikhs, were getting ready to face them on the opposite bank, excited to meet their foes once again. The Sikh artillery stronger than the British one, opened a heavy fire; while numbers of Sikh soldiers forded the Chenab river to chase the British on their own side of the bank.

The Commander-in-Chief, 'Lord' Hugh Gough was a terrified man now and had no intention of indulging in a direct fight. Perhaps he wanted to show the British strength to the Sikhs by false manoeuvres to cow them down into surrender as they had done in Multan. Or maybe he wanted to overthrow the Sikh posts on his side of the river.

As the 1st Light Dragoons moved forward the Sikh cavalry came up very fast and drove Brigadier White and his men back who retreated meekly. The 8th Light cavalry of the British marched forward but were beaten back by the Sikhs. Now the Sikhs became greatly excited, and they marched forward. Once White had reached the non-sandy ground, he halted, turned, and now charged, causing some commotion among the Sikhs in front but the British again got stuck when uneven ground was reached.

The British could achieve only some fulfilment of their objective which was to gauge the strength of the Sikhs. The British cavalry continued to flee from the battle scene and during their retreat, 'an unfortunate incident' as per a British author occurred. A gun sent as a cover for cavalry and some wagons got stuck in the sandy base and these would not move any further. Seeing this, the Sikhs fired and planned to march on the British once again. The gun could not be retrieved and its abandonment was the only solution for the British.

There was another strong Sikh position near which Lord Hugh Gough wanted to camp. Some Sikh Ghorcharras or irregular cavalry, had crossed the Chenab, unperturbed by the heavy British presence on the eastern side and their presence was seen by the British who wanted to chase them away. The British troops and their leaders were aware of the heavy sandy base of the river bed with every possibility to get stuck and immobilised. Lt. Colonel Havelock, with the 14th Light Dragoons went on to attack the Sikhs and clear the ground, as instructed by Hugh Gough and at the same time take precautions that they did not get stuck in heavy ground.

The 5th Light Cavalry supported Wlliam Havelock's forces and repelled the Ghorchurras in front of them. But soon he saw that the dry broken ground ahead was full of Sikh infantry who were somehow not seen by the British. Such was the British ineffective planning! Despite showing great courage externally, the British knew they were trapped and Havelock's call for charging the Sikhs and encouraging his own soldiers was going to be fruitless. The opportunity seemed irresistible.

Brigadier-General Charles Robert Cureton (b: 1789) who realised the danger came running from Commander-in-Chiefs to restrain Havelock and advise him to retreat but a bullet struck him in the chest. Instead of applying his presence of mind to retreat, Havelock had made the second charge, and the horses began to get trapped in the sandy river-bed. The Sikhs swarmed down on them; and though the brigade succeeded in resisting the Sikhs, Havelock was a victim. Heavily wounded, after eleven of his troopers had been killed beside him, he was left for dead on the field. The lives of Cureton (who was 59), of Havelock himself (he was 55), and fifty soldiers, were a heavy price to pay for a reckless charge under the poor leadership of the Commander-in-Chief, Hugh Gough, whose bravado ended so many lives and yet the Britich gained nothing at Ramnagar.

The 14th Dragoons lost their Colonel, Captains Fitzgerald and MacMahon and Cornet Chetwynd. Captain Gall was severely wounded. The 5th also suffered considerable casualties and all this was due to the charge in the river-bed and bad judgment about the fighting capability of the Sikhs.

Dejected, the Commander-in-Chief, Hugh Gough encamped near the village, opposite the Sikh army, introspecting and watching the position of the Sikhs and examining fords across the Chenab and analyse the ways to cross it.

The various fords available were: at Ghurriki seven miles above Ramnagar held by a detachment of 4000 Sikhs; another higher up at Runniki also guarded; and a third, higher still, at Ali-Sher-ke-Chuk, which was unguarded, but it was dangerous as the strength of the stream was too much.

Then there was Wazirabad, 22 miles above and to travel 22 miles up and cross river and come down again 22 miles was too much for any army, considering the river banks were sandy. Also, the entire Army could not be moved or else Sher Singh could march to Lahore with the backing of the Sirdars. So, it was thought by the British to march their troops with the Chenab at their backs, with the Sikhs driven up to the Jhelum, to hold them more easily in check. Ultimately, the British took a division to cross the Chenab, above Runniki somehow with the strongest possible division available.

Sir Joseph Thackwell (67 years old) was in command and was joined by White and Colin Campbell; besides 30 field-guns and 2 heavy guns. The artillery had come up with the main British body and the force was to re-assemble at midnight on November 30, 1848.

The night happened to be extremely dark, and chaos followed. The start itself was delayed for two hours and some of the infantry lost their route! So much was said for British professionalism. Then the beleaguered army somehow reached Runniki at 11 o'clock. A halt of three long hours was made to examine the fords here and at Ali-Sher-ke-Chuk to decide whether to cross the river or not. Then a decision was taken to cross the river at Wazirabad and the whole force moved on to Wazirabad. John Nicholson, collected every boat on the river available, by the time the division arrived at about sunset. Almost one day had passed.

By noon the whole British force was ensconced on the west of the Chenab, and messages were passed on to Hugh Gough about the same. At two o'clock Joseph Thackwell commenced his march along the banks of the Chenab till his army and the Sikhs were separated by 9 miles. There the British encamped. The Sikh outpost at Ghurriki was unguarded, and communication with Lord Gough at Ramnagar was established. On December 1 and 2, Lord Gough concentrated on drawing Sher Singh's attention to empty threats of impending attacks. In fact, the British were scared.

On the morning of December 3, Sir Joseph moved forward with the intention of attacking the Sikh flank and it was planned that Lord Gough would engage the Sikhs from Ramnagar. But a message informed him about the reinforcements to join him from the Ghurriki ford. Joseph was confused and thought he was told to wait and not to attack till the reinforcements arrived, he stood actionless at Sadulapore, and sent a regiment to guard Ghurriki.

Hugh Gough, it seems had a mental block to take a decision and his indecisiveness can be gauged from his lack of making any concrete decision and total lack of coordination at the crucial time and place. He left everything to Joseph Thackwell's wisdom: to act or not to! Such was the pathetic state of the British command.

The consequences of this lack of communication and indecisiveness was adverse for the British. Sher Singh, finding Thackwell so near, marched against him from Ramnagar with a major part of his troops, and the British were surpised at about two o'clock by the sudden commencement of artillery fire. The British ran back some 200 yards, to avoid the fire and then the Sikhs did not press harder and still occupied a strong defensive position which they wanted to hold with stubbornness.

Even though Colin Campbell wanted to reply to the Sikh attack, Thackwell was numb and stood still, waiting for reinforcements. The day was coming to an end and still the old war horse named Hugh Gough could not pass on a direct command to initiate action. The ghost of Pherushah was still haunting the British who suffered heavily when they undertook the risk of storming Sikh entrenchment as the darkness fell. Here, they were scared of taking the same risk again and the Sikhs were given all the time at night to retreat to the place of their preference.

Sher Singh left Chenab for the Jhelum; from a rich country to a jungle and his capacity to influence anybody in the Durbar was far reduced as the distance had increased. It was an intense relief to Lord Hugh Gough.

Still, the position now occupied by Sher Singh was quite strong and covered to a great extent by jungle. His troops greatly outnumbered Gough's, while his position was superior in artillery. The Commander-in-Chief was content with the status quo till the fall of Multan. The wait for General Whish proved to be almost eternal and, in the end, all we had in Ramnagar was the British inaction.

A month later, Attock fell into the hands of Chattar Singh and major allies. The Sikhs could now strengthen their own army on the Jhelum. So, Hugh Gough had to act quickly so that the Sikhs could not combine. He moved to Dinghi which was within 8 miles of the Sikh entrenchments, just beyond the village of Chillianwala.

The Battle of Chillianwala: December 4, 1848 – January 13, 1849

Lord Gough was in a confused state of mind and the month-long period which saw his worst indecisiveness took a further toll on his decision-making capability. Around Christmas, Lord Dalhousie gave instructions to Gough that he could attack the Sikhs, if he considered it prudent. The indecisiveness or fear seems to have percolated from the highest levels of the East India Company.

Whether Dalhousie himself pressed hard for the same is unknown but an indirect messaging via Major Mackeson, the political agent may have been resorted to. At long last, 'Lord' Hugh Gough decided to take action and made an advance on Chillianwala, and a victory or a defeat awaited him. The mobilisation of troops in zig-zag fashion had already cost the British heavily. Gough was aware that Chattar Singh Attariwala wanted to join his son Sher Singh soon and no further dilly-dallying was possible.

On January 12 the army went to Dinghi, east of Sher Singh position beyond Chillianwala. Joseph Thackwell was in command of the cavalry division in lieu of Cureton who was already killed by the Sikhs in Ramnagar. Colin Campbell was holding the command of his infantry division. The whole force was of about 14,000 men.

Table 2.6 Battle of Chillianwala

	Sikh Empire	*East India Company*
Generals	Sardar Sher Singh Attariwala	Sir Hugh Gough
Strength (men)	30,000	15,000
Guns	60	100
Killed	Unknown	757
Wounded	Unknown	1651
Result	Moral Victory	Moral Defeat

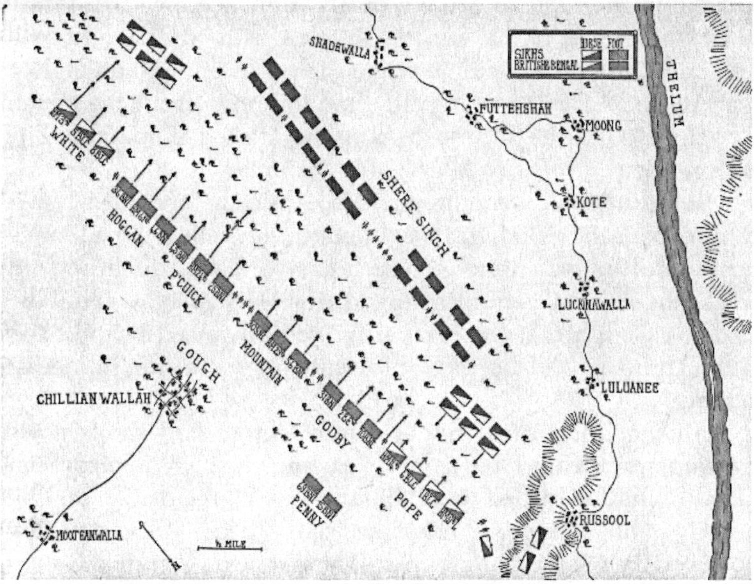

Fig 2.3 Battle Formation at Chillianwala; Credit John Fawkes

Sir Joseph Thackwell commanded the cavalry division. Brigadier M. White, Brigadier Pope, Major-General Sir Walter Gilbert, Brigadier Mountain, Brigadier Godby, Brigadier-General Colin Campbell, Brigadier Pennycuick, Brigadier Hoggan, Brigadier Penny, Brigadier Tennant and Brigadier Brookewere led the front with infantry, artillery and cavalry. The Foot Artillery was under Brigadier Huthwaite.

The Sikhs lay with the Jhelum behind them (please see the diagram above), occupying a group of villages covered by a jungle, with the Sikh formations' left touched a belt of hills near Russool. Chillianwalla was in advance of the line and had some outposts only. Lord Gough's intention again was enmeshed with confusion. He wanted to move from Dinghi to Chillianwalla and watch the situation, preferably waiting till the morning unless the circumstances demanded an immediate engagement with the Sikhs.

At 7 am on January 13, 1849, the British army advanced from Dinghi, in a line of contiguous columns. About twelve o'clock Chillianwalla and the Sikhs' entrenched position, stretching from Rusool on their left to Moong on the right were clearly visible. Lord Gough had two alternatives: one was to attack right away and pass through the jungle when there was enough daylight or wait till the next day, using the time to know about the terrain. Gough selected the second option and started preparations for encamping.

But the Sikhs were prepared to welcome the British with cannon balls. The Sikh guns opened fire revealing the advanced position of their batteries. Their homework was done perfectly which the more superior powered British lacked. Now it dawned on Lord Gough that the Sikh army had advanced beyond their entrenchments and he gave orders to 'prepare' for immediate action.

All that the British under Hugh Gough had thought that encampment would be as safe as one does in a picnic and 'delay' could be turned to advantage. In fact, the British bungled heavily in not sending an advanced party to know about the Sikh positions. In the first Anglo-Sikh War, the then Governor-General had himself gone on a round to do reconnaissance.

Now, there was no alternative but an immediate engagement. The advancement of Sikhs beyond the line of villages to force an engagement made the British 'delay' quite undesirable for the British. Their delay was in decision-making and the lethargic approach had taken them close to a disaster. To add to the agony, they had no cover over their heads. It must have been a pretty cold day in early January in Punjab. For one hour the battle was an artillery duel, in which the Sikhs had a vantage position and they also had the numerical superiority of the guns.

At 3 pm the advance by the British was made. On the flanks were the cavalry of Pope and White. Under Colin Campbell, Hoggan's Brigade was on the left of the line with Pennycuick's on the next. Under Gilbert were Mountain's, and Godby's brigades. Penny's Brigade (the third of Campbell's Division) was in reserve. For about six miles on the other side, the Sikh line extended, covered by thick jungle. The Sikhs' right flank considerably overlapped the British left.

As per plan, Campbell was to advance with the brigades of Hoggan and Pennycuick with the support of guns of his division. Accordingly, the Horse Artillery on the extreme left moved ahead, and came under fire from a powerful battery of Sikh guns. Three guns were ordered to go to the left to assist the Horse artillery and silence the guns of the Sikhs. The British Robertson left for about 500 yards and finding a considerable body of Sikh horsemen on his front, he dispersed them by quick fire.

Advancing again in the direction pointed out to him, that of the enemy's guns was made known to him by a shot or two crossing his front, timed apparently at the advancing infantry. Thereupon he brought up his right and took action against the Sikhs and re-joined his brigade by marking the track on which treaded the British infantry.

However, the British infantry brigades were making a disjointed march forward under Pennycuick and Hoggan and the former's brigade advanced too quickly and Robertson was unable to extend any support. This infantry brigade was carried in front of the battery at the very commencement of the action.

Campbell's primary function was to lead both the brigades of Pennycuick and Hoggan but he thought that the nature of the jungle would not permit it and he informed Pennycuick that he would take the lead of the left brigade, leaving the other to Pennycuick. In the end, the lack of coordination between the brigades proved to be disastrous for Pennycuick. On the other hand, Gilbert, with same difficulty marshalled his resources and troops more effectively.

Pennycuick was 59 years old then. He advanced fast but lost

the support of his artillery as he soon landed in thick and thorny bushes which obstructed his advance and his company got converted into columns. After marching a few hundred yards, the right brigade came under a volley of fire and the formidable Sikhs were invisible to the British. Chaos followed in the British camp and the troops seemed to have lost their way. Officers and men of the British Army began to fall in rising numbers but there was no escape. It was a dire strait for the British.

The troops continued their march forward despite the difficulties of the jungle. Had it been like Ramnagar, they might have retreated. At last they came too close and could view the Sikhs' guns in front of them. The British troops' agony mounted and there was no sign of relief at all. A swamp or pond partially filled lay ahead and crossing it would be another hurdle; they thought. Space narrowed down and the centre and left of the regiment came close to the muzzles of the guns in huge numbers and in much disorder.

The Sikhs once again welcomed them with a tremendous discharge of grape and musketry. Brigadier Pennycuick alongwith many officers and men fell as they closed on the enemy on a suicidal march. Lt. Colonel Brookes was seen cheering his men on.

The Sikh fire was quite heavy and the Grenadiers were forced back; but their Captain Travers, again advanced to the charge but was cut down by a Sikh's sword. The whole regiment now were hotly engaged and numbers fell on both sides. Close to the guns Colonel Brookes was seen to fall.

The British were now totally exhausted and this column which advanced readily wholly unsupported could proceed no further. The regiment needed to re-organise themselves outside the Jungle. Apart from the loss of British officers, the casualties of the British included: 231 men killed and 266 wounded. Apart from the British H.M.'s 24th, the 25th regiment Native Infantry on the right and the 45th on the left met the same fate, suffering serious losses and retreated along with the retreat of the 24th.

Several parties of both regiments quickly rallied and by their fire drove the Sikh horsemen away who were chasing the British brigade away. This party of British troops now moved with White's Cavalry Brigade and subsequently joined Hoggan's Infantry Brigade.

The 25th regiment lost 112 men and 92 were wounded. The 45th lost 20 non-commissioned officers and 59 were wounded. Hoggan's Brigade on the left was led personally by Colin Campbell but despite the jungle in front, good gun support was achieved by him. Mowatt's battery also covered it on the right.

Hoggan's brigade under Campbell reached almost 700 or 800 yards in front of the Sikhs at an unsuitable position and his men were urged forward another 300 yards to clearer ground, where Campbell saw a crowd of Sikhs, distant about 450 yards, their guns visible despite the smoke. After firing persistently at the Sikhs for 20 minutes, the Sikh fire began to melt away.

He saw Hoggan emerge from the jungle and go after the Sikhs, keeping up a heavy fire at the same time. Campbell combined well with his troops during the advance, despite the ground causing frequent breaks but he did not have to face such an adverse situation as faced by Pennycuick. Soon he met the Sikhs with four guns who created havoc in the British camp. The Sikh cavalry was dispersed but the regular Sikh troops fell on the British flank; Campbell, however, wheeled around and captured two Sikh guns. Mowatt attacked the opposite infantry and it was a brave action against the very tough Sikhs who were very well led by their chiefs and they once again withdrew to the jungles.

The British brigade concentrated on the right flank and their left flank of the 46th regiment was once again attacked by the Sikh cavalry in sizeable numbers. Major Tudor had to face this onslaught. At that critical moment for the British, the Sikhs brought up more guns and fresh infantry against the British right.

The British had to effect the change of front and that too very rapidly. The whole brigade advanced to the attack and the Sikhs retreated repeatedly, only to come back and attack once more using their cavalry, who followed up, compelling General Campbell often to halt, face his troops and drive them on. Thus, Campbell defeated and dispersed a part of the Sikh army which had inflicted so terrible a punishment upon Pennycuick's Brigade. Campbell now heard from Colonel Brookes about the disaster which happened to his right brigade. Campbell himself received a sword wound to his right hand.

Away on the left, White's Cavalry Brigade advanced towards

Campbell's Division. But the ground was quite impracticable for the cavalry and owing to the smoky environment and very heavy firing by the Sikhs, visibility for the British was a serious handicap. Sir Thackwell ordered the Grey squadron of the 3rd Light Dragoons and the 5th Light Cavalry to charge. The 5th Light Cavalry immediately came under the fire of the valiant Sikhs and were scattered in the thick and scrubby jungle. The 3rd Light Dragoons, coming on a smaller body met the same fate.

Now the Sikh horsemen followed up, and, falling upon those who were isolated and separated, killed many British soldiers. It had a sobering effect on Sir Joseph Thackwell who was now not attempting any further offensive movements, and he was obliged to content himself with affording such protection as he could with was left of Campbell's Division.

He now combined with the main British body, following Campbell's movements. The cavalry crossed the line by which Pennycuick's Brigade had advanced, and the battle field was littered with the bodies of the British and Indian soldiers fighting under the 'East India Company'.

From the disastrous campaign by the British on the left flank, one may see their performance on the right and right centre. Soon after the beginning of Campbell's movement Sir Walter Gilbert was getting ready to march forward. Pope's Cavalry Brigade was on the extreme right and the 3 troops of the Horse Artillery was under Colonel Grant. Then there were was Godby's Infantry Brigade and that of Mountain's and Dawes's battery was placed between them.

On the left, as we have seen, the British cavalry manoeuvres had yielded marginal results in the battle; on the right it was no better. Pope's Brigade performed rather painfully for the British and floundered against the mighty Sikhs and were held responsible for the results of Chillianwalla, by the British. But no amount of credit can be taken away from the valiant Sikhs.

A great number of the Sikhs threatened the British right flank alike on their left. Pope saw a considerable body of Sikh horsemen on the slopes towards *Russool* and to protect the flank, he detached a wing of the 1st and 6th Light Cavalry, and the 9th Lancers with some guns, under the command of Colonel Lane.

Then, advancing in line with the infantry brigades, he

encountered the Sikh horsemen immediately to his front. The guns were advanced but before these could be fired, Pope with his cavalry came in front of them, thus making firing impossible. There was total confusion among the British. His 9 squadrons were without any support and soon encountered the Sikhs but the guns fired very slowly and the British infantry was at the total mercy of the Sikhs. In front of Pope's axis of advance, soon another body of Sikh cavalry appeared. The best branch of the British—the Bengal Horse artillery was immediately deployed into action to engage these Sikhs.

The Sikh horsemen led by Jawahir Singh Nalwa, the bold and dashing son of Sardar Hari Singh Nalwa now realising that poor execution and bad terrain had brought Pope's weak cavalry charge to an absolute halt now counter-charged. Through the wild Doab jungle, Jawahir Singh with his band of horsemen emerged, once again and charged Pope's force, in the process of which some Sikh horsemen physically attacked Brigadier Pope, cutting him across the head with his sword, and wounding him. The British soldiers ran helter-skelter and something rare in the annals of British cavalry occurred. Some terrified officers gave the order to turn back and run fast! Some of his men turned and ran to the rear and it resulted in a panic; the whole brigade galloped in a reckless stampede to the rear. What a disgrace!

A body of Sikhs chased them and cut down many of the men, severely wounded Major Christie and occupied four guns and two waggons. The cavalry could not be stopped till they had completely left the battlefield. The panic which engulfed Pope's troops was incomprehensible if it was not the fear of the Sikhs.

When the advance by the British cavalry was to be made through the jungle it caused the troops to separate out and cohesion might have been lost and therefore adequate support for cohesion and command was necessary. Yet Pope's soldiers' flight left the right flank of the advancing infantry division open for the Sikhs to attack further.

Although the number of the British killings was not very high but the Sikhs carried off 53 horses and 4 guns, and rendered 6 more guns useless. Not a bad performance by the Sikhs.

Gilbert was leading his division to the attack with Dawes and his battery in line with the attackers in front. Mountain's Brigade came upon a strong battery of the Sikhs in front of the village of Lullianee carrying the entire guns at the point of the bayonet. This attack was followed by Godby's Brigade.

Godby's flank was unguarded by the movement of Pope's Brigade which was taken advantage of by the Sikhs who almost surrounded him. Mountain's Brigade met with the same brave resistance by the Sikhs and were compelled to turn around totally, to run away or repulse the enemy; but luckily for the British, Colin Campbell, with Brigade and White's cavalry, and the entire artillery of the left, moved up and joined them.

In the meantime, survivors of Penny's Brigade, came almost on the front and right of Godby and here Penny in turn attacked in front, right and rear, till the ubiquitous and inevitable Dawes came to the rescue with his gang, and drove the enemy away.

By this time Campbell had joined on to Mountain's Brigade, the whole of the artillery was brought up, and fire was opened upon the Sikhs who were in retreat. Colonel Lane, detached on the right related, virtually took no part in the main engagement and knew nothing of what was going on.

When Godby and Mountain had already stemmed the counter-attack of the enemy, Lane fired upon the Sikhs who were now retiring. But by this time the approach of darkness made it impossible to follow up the retreat, and the engagement was over. The Sikhs had gone to Tupai, and the British fell to Chillianwalla. However, during the night, the Sikhs succeeded in recovering and carrying their own guns which were left on the deserted battlefield.

The total losses (as per Sir Charles John Stanley Gough) of the British force were 22 officers, 16 native officers, and 561 killed, and 98 men mixing, who may be added to the number; 67 officers, 27 native officers, and 1,547 men wounded. Grand total, 2,338 men.

The casualties that the British suffered were relatively much larger in proportion as compared to any battle that they fought later or earlier at least as far as unit averages were concerned. There are many aspects of this issue. Firstly, native casualties as compared with the British unit casualties proved that the natives fought as well as the British despite no national motivation to do so. Secondly, most British casualties especially those of HM 24th

Foot occurred due to tactical ineptitude. Thirdly, the casualties suffered were much higher. Brigadier White's brigade had the vast bulk of cavalry casualties.

After Chillianwala: January 14–February 21, 1849

The Sikhs did not directly assemble at Russool where their strength was enormous but they assembled in Tupai. The British were quite overcome with fatigue and humiliation and were in no position to pursue the Sikhs any further. Had the British again continued their pursuit which was quite unlikely, they might have achieved some success but the chances of losing a substantial number of soldiers was always very high, considering their immediate experience with the Sikhs.

For two days after the battle torrential and unseasonal rain set in and it rendered any movement impossible and the soil in the neighbourhood of Tupai was quite soft and wet. The Sikhs got a chance to re-assemble at Russool. The British fight against the Sikhs at Chillianwalla proved to be ineffective. On January 19, 1849 Elahi Buksh of the Sikh artillery came and told the British that the morale of the Sikhs was quite low and it was now boosted by the presence of Chattar Singh Attariwala and they were now thinking about a victory over the British.

Public opinion in the English Isles demanded a scapegoat and who could have been a better prospect than the person of the Commander-in-Chief, Lord Hugh Gough? His recall was decided upon but all was not yet lost for the British or Gough.

Gough had to face many demands from different places as the political agents had urged him to send a brigade here, and a brigade there; to run heavy risks; to undertake a series of minor expeditions. Without arrival of reinforcements from Multan he had refused to advance against Chillianwalla until he buckled under strong pressure. At Chillianwalla, the British had sufficient force and they wanted to prevent the imminent junction between Sher Singh and big father.

Lord Gough's artillery was not markedly inferior to that of the Sikhs but the latter defended themselves well by better unity, cohesion, planning and execution of these with valour.

The British have mentioned the cruelty shown by the Sikhs when they mutilated the slain in the cover of darkness, but not many were left to die in the field, in the first place. Two men belonging to the 9th Lancers, who were caught straying in the jungle and taken captive were sent back by Sher Singh to the British camp. This is opposite to the cruelty charges by the British against the Sikhs. And Chattar Singh permitted George Lawrence to go to Lahore on parole. He also allowed Lieutenant Bowie who had been taken in the Derajat to visit Lord Gough on parole. The remarkable fact is that the Sikh chiefs were generous enough to give them the benefit of that confidence.

During the three days of heavy rain, large reinforcements were received by the Sikhs, who had now been joined by Chattar Singh. The British thought that the engagements with the Sikhs would be unwise. Lord Gough reverted to his determination to wait for the fall of Multan, and on the 26th the news about the fall of Multan was received and it was decided that the final conflict would not be long deferred. Some uncertainty persisted regarding the motive of the Sikhs, who removed part of their forces to Pooran, lying slightly to the north, without discarding Russool altogether.

In February, Sher Singh brought a part of his army down to Khoree threatening Dinghi. On February 5 it was ascertained that a part of the Russool entrenchment had been evacuated.

Lord Gough maintained a patient approach even though Sher Singh enticed him into a battle by exuberance approaching so near as Nur Jemal. The Multan Division of the British was on its way, though the Bombay column moved rather slowly. Gough thought he could intercept any attempt Sher Singh might make to circumvent him. The fords of the Chenab were kept under watch by the British. The British also thought that Sher Singh was in fact, not prepared to attack them where he lay; nor could he venture march southwards, since he would then be caught between Whish's advancing division in front, and Lord Gough's army on his rear.

On February 14, 1849 the Sikh army left its encampments for Gujarat, and the next day Lord Gough moved to Lusoorie and pushed forward a column to Wazirabad. Whish had already despatched a detachment, under Colonel Byrne. Gough moved on the 16th to Pukee Nuggar and Sadulapore. From February 17-19 the forces from Multan were joining, the army being completed in its full strength on the 20th. During these days the Commander-in-Chief made very short marches by Ishera and Tricca to Shadiwal, moving always in order of battle, contemplating the final attack.

Battle of Gujarat: February 21, 1849

The End of the Campaign

Instead of launching a counter-attack against Gough, Sher Singh wanted to join forces with the troops under his father, Sardar Chattar Singh Attariwalla. Muslim irregulars under British officers confined Chattar Singh's army in the Hazara region for several months. Amir Dost Mohammed Khan of Afghanistan had sided with the rebellious Sikhs at the start of 1849. His aim was to recover the area around Peshawar, which had been conquered by Ranjit Singh and his support was half-hearted. Chattar Singh moved out of Hazara and linked up with Sher Singh near Rawalpindi.

Gough was almost immediately superseded once the news of Chillianwala reached Britain, General Charles James Napier, his replacement would require several weeks to travel from England. The Siege of Multan had begun in the meantime. Gough knew about his dismissal but he remained in command till formally relieved of his charge.

Table 2.7 Battle of Gujarat

	Sikh Empire	*East India Company*
Generals	Sardar Sher Singh Attariwala	Sir Hugh Gough
Strength (men)	25,000 + 1,500 afghans	24,000
Guns	60	96+
Killed	Unknown	96
Wounded	Unknown	682
Result	Total Defeat	Total Victory

Sher Singh, who commanded the combined Sikh forces, had limited strategic options. Food and logistics for his large army was a major problem. Any move to obtain supplies in the neighbourhood would involve abandoning the main Sikh-populated area of the Punjab and moving into potentially hostile

Muslim areas. Against Gough he therefore tried an audacious outflanking manoeuvre. Intending to cross the Chenab his army moved east and then moved south before crossing the river again to attack Gough from the rear. To their dismay, they found the river had swollen by heavy rains, and the few fords were defended by irregular Muslim cavalry under British officers, later reinforced by some of the troops marching up from Multan.

On February 20, the arrival of the army boosted Hugh Gough's morale which was at an all-time low till a few days back. The artillery was reassuring to Gough and he now dreamt of overcoming the Sikhs who had held the British power at bay with such stubbornness hitherto unparalleled in Indian history. It can be recalled that Bengal was the first province to fall to the British, almost 92 years ago.

The British artillery had now 96 guns, 18 being of heavy calibre. The morning of February 21st broke in splendour over the open field of young corn which separated the opposing armies. The Sikh entrenchment was shaped roughly like a crescent stretching southward. Their right as well as left flank ran close to deep dry nullahs or water-courses.

The cavalry of the Sikhs was being managed by Afghan horsemen extending and crossing both the nullahs. Between the two nullahs, the Sikhs had occupied and fortified, the villages of Burra Kalra and Chota Kalra (Great and Little) in a skilled manner.

The British faced them, looking north, with their brigades and division, ably supported by the cavalry on the flanks. Gilbert's Division was on the right and on its left was the heavy battery of 18 guns; Whish upfront was supported by three troops of Horse Artillery.

On the left of the nullah, Campbell's Division was placed. As soon as the British troops made a move, its position was exposed and their guns' range was also estimated by the Sikhs. These guns were not reaching their targets. So, it was another British blunder but somehow the advancing troops were halted and the guns were instead moved upwards under the cover of the infantrymen, i.e. towards the Sikhs.

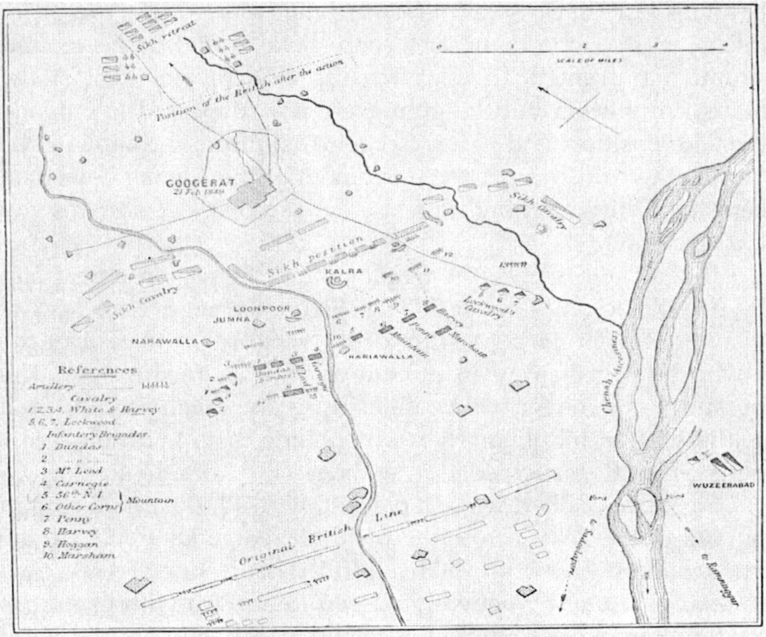

THE BATTLE OF GOOGERAT.

The troops and batteries of Artillery in the above Plan were commanded by the following officers:—

1. Huish. 2. Duncan. 3. Blood. 4. Ludlow. 5. Robertson. 6. Lane (previously 14). 7. Day. 8. Dawes. 9. Horsford. 10. Fordyce. 11. Anderson. 12. Mackenzie. 13. Warner. 14. See No. 6. 15. Kinleside. 16. Shakspeare.

Fig. 2.4 The Battle of Gujarat

At nine o'clock the long line of guns, at last, were in a position which was about 800 yards from the Sikhs, and then the storm began in earnest. For two and a half hours the British batteries fired incessantly upon the defending Sikhs. The British had assembled almost all the hardware they had in 'Hindustan' to silence the Sikhs. There was tremendous damage to the Sikhs no doubt, but the British artillery suffered heavily in the duel.

At 11:30, a general advance of the line was done with the artillery in front. Despite all they had suffered, the gallant Sikhs were still determined to fight to the end. From the village of Burra Kalra, they fired fiercely on the British advance party, who thought it was deserted. A similar charge was made on the British from Chota Kalra and the Sikhs not only stemmed the British advance, they also tried to push into the British lines.

The Afghan horsemen of the Sikhs tried to turn the British

left flank but Thackwell sent forward the Horse Artillery to begin intensive fire upon them, and send them to flight. The ground situation prevented Thackwell to use the cavalry against the Sikhs, any further but the guns were now deployed to enfilade the Sikh position, and hastened their flight from the battlefield.

On the British right, the movement of the Afghan horsemen kept the British alert but no real conflict took place nor was any damage done.

By half put twelve, the whole Sikh army was in retreat and by one o'clock, Gujarat itself, the Sikh's baggage, and most of their guns, were in possession of the victors. On the left of the town, the British were in pursuit as well as on the right. The pursuit was done for twelve miles using the cavalry till the Sikh soldiers fell or hid themselves, compelling them to drop the few guns which they succeeded in withdrawing from the field.

Sir Walter Gilbert was despatched with 12,000 armed men in pursuit of the Sikhs across the Jhelum. George Lawrence, to the intense admiration of the Sikhs, fulfilled his pledge and returned to their camp, and frequently passed to and fro with proposals for terms from Sher Singh. But to the British, the only proposal acceptable was 'unconditional surrender'.

The Sikhs had fought so relentlessly against the British in the Muslim-dominated areas where they always had food and shelter constraints that they had no chance of rest, so far. Their ammunition was exhausted.

On March 6, 1849 they restored all the prisoners and on the 12th, surrendered at discretion. The Sikh chiefs were not in a disgraceful defeat and had fought valiantly. This won the British admiration who thought about the Sikhs as the worthy foe and in days to come, they were to prove themselves worthy comrades in arms.

A few days later, the last remnant of opposition was ended with the surrender of Peshawar, and the flight of the Afghans across the border.

3

Punjab After British Annexation: Fate of Duleep Singh and Rani Jindan

Duleep Singh and Maharani Jind Kaur

The nobles, recalling the events following Sher Singh's assassination a few years ago, anointed the five-year-old Duleep Singh as Maharaja of Punjab on September 18, 1843 hoping to have found a puppet king. But the twenty-six-year-old Rani Jindan or Jind Kaur was a powerful and ambitious lady. She was too modern in that age and giving up the purdah of the women's quarters, she declared that she would govern Punjab herself in her boy's name.

With the Koh-i-Noor strapped to his arm as it was done by Ranjit Singh, Duleep sat in his mother's lap while she ruled. Her brother Jawahar Singh was the new vizier who was one of the most detested men having no commendable quality about him. But he loved his sister and set about destroying any challenge to her authority.

His intrigues were tolerated for a while. But on September 11, 1845, just two years into his nephew's reign, Jawahar on the pretext of escorting a disgruntled Prince Pashaura back to his home, separated him from his soldiers and had him strangled to death. In the eyes of the nobles, he had crossed the line by killing a prince of the royal blood. On September 21, now back in Lahore, he was summoned to a meeting of the Sikh Khalsa, where he went riding out on the Maharaja's own elephant, with Duleep on his lap.

The Khalsa soldiers reached up to pull the infant Maharaja away from Jawahar's arms. Jawahar was thrown to the ground and hacked to death. Duleep saw his uncle's blood and every brutal blow, and the experience would haunt him throughout his life. All the while, Rani Jindan was forced by durbar courtiers to watch the ghastly scene. Jindan seemed to drown in her grief for some time but her retreat was only temporary, and after a few weeks, she re-emerged as a regent. Her dignity masked her inner grief and turmoil as she was surrounded by the very men who had got her brother murdered.

The British East India Company watched events with interest. East India Company troops began to build up south of the Sutlej in 1843, the year that Duleep was anointed. British agents tentatively approached Jindan and also made overtures to the court's Sikh chiefs.

Thus, Rani Jindan and Maharaja Duleep Singh were surrounded by ambitious men, and some of the most senior ones proved remarkably easy to turn.

After the First Anglo-Sikh War the British sun was on the rise in Punjab. The British vowed after signing the *Treaty of Lahore* with the child Duleep on March 9, 1846 that when Duleep turned sixteen, he would be mature enough to govern for himself, and the British would part as friends. But the British started to garrison their soldiers in Lahore; ostensibly the British troops were protecting the boy king, and Duleep was, in effect, paying an occupying force to infiltrate his kingdom. The aristocrats of the court continued in their positions and Duleep remained on his throne. Rani Jindan could see through the game the British were planning. She threw her bangles at the court's Sirdars, challenging their masculinity.

Jindan begged her nobles to see the amendments to the original agreement as these were being pressed on her young son. The traitorous, General Tej Singh, a Brahmin initially from Saharanpur, was granted the Jagir of Sialkot, Jindan could stand it no more: all revenues from the district would go to him. Needless to say, Tej Singh was purchased by the British. As instructed by his mother, Duleep Singh refused to place a mark of saffron and vermilion on his forehead, despite great British persuasion. This insulted Tej Singh and infuriated the British in equal measure.

Letters were sent by Sir Henry Lawrence, the new resident of Lahore, to deal with Rani Jindan and he complained about her 'anti-English' behaviour and the 'scandalous profligacy of her conduct'. The British decided to remove Rani Jindan from Lahore and from Duleep in all respects. The British gave inadequate excuses for this horrendous decision.

When the Maharaja was barely nine years old in December 1847, he was sent to the Shalimar Gardens. Meanwhile, Jindan was removed screaming from her palace, resisting as she was dragged away, begging the Sikh men around her to wake up and fight. Not one man bothered to help her. Duleep Singh, Rani Jindan's son was sent away for playing at that time to prevent any uncomfortable scene. In Lahore fort, Rani Jindan was imprisoned for ten days and then moved to a fortress in Sheikhupura. From her prison cell, she begged the British for the return of her only child:

> Why take my kingdom by underhand means? Why do you not do it openly? ... You have been very cruel to me! .... In the name of God .... restore my son to me. I cannot bear the pain of this separation. Instead you should put me to death ...

She appealed to Henry Lawrence's humanity:

> My son is very young. He is incapable of doing anything. I have left the kingdom. .... I will accept what you say. There is no one with my son. He has no sister, no brother. He has no uncle, senior or junior. His father he has lost. To whose care has he been entrusted?

Lawrence was quite uneasy at this child and mother's forced separation but his boss Hardinge, had no such misgivings:

> *'We must expect these letters in various shapes,'* he wrote to Lawrence, *'which a woman of her strong mind and passions will assume as best suited either to gratify her vengeance or obtain her ends ...'*

Lawrence was decidedly uneasy; keeping a child from his mother. Sir Henry Hardinge, his superior, had no such emotions. In 1848, Lord Dalhousie was the new Governor-General. He sealed the fate of the Maharaja and his entire kingdom. Sir Frederick Currie was appointed as the new resident at the Sikh durbar by Dalhousie. He raised taxes to refill the depleted British coffers. The outlying areas of Punjab were hit hardest by the increasing demands and this measure proved to be unpopular.

Rani Jindan's role in the court was thus highly marginalised and she was not allowed much opportunity of seeing her son.

But her continuing presence in Punjab made the Resident uncomfortable.

After the Second Anglo-Sikh War and loss of thousands of lives, total surrender took place on March 12, 1849. Mulraj and other rebel leaders were rounded up and made to await trial.

On March 29, 1849, a new legal document was imposed upon Duleep Singh, laying out stricter terms for surrender. The young Maharaja already terrified by the recent fighting, separated from his mother and surrounded by foreigners and weak courtiers was told to sign over his kingdom, his fortune and his future. The British demanded nothing less than his complete acquiescence. The ten-year-old Duleep Singh obediently signed on the document, agreeing to all its terms.

> His Highness ... shall resign .... from the sovereignty of the Punjab. ...
>
> All the property of the State ...shall be confiscated to the Honourable East India Company, in part payment to the British Government of the debt due by the State of Lahore and of the expenses of the war.
>
> The ....to the Queen of England ....Koh-i-Noor... shall be surrendered.
>
> His Highness Duleep Singh shall receive for the support of himself, his relatives and the servants, a pension of not less than four and not more than five lakhs of the Company's rupees per annum.
>
> His Highness shall ....retain the title of Maharajah Duleep Singh .... to receive .... pension as may be allotted to himself personally....

Punjab was now unquestionably a British territory with the signing of the final Treaty of Lahore; the British owned the Koh-i-Noor; Maharaja Duleep Singh was a British problem. When Dalhousie came to know that Duleep had signed the terms of surrender in 1849, he reacted with jubilation. *'I had now caught my hare'*, he wrote to a friend and he declared that the seizure of the Koh-i-Noor was as important as the annexation of the region.

Duleep's fate was now entirely in Dalhousie's hands even though the fate of the diamond was settled and it was already decided to send him away from Punjab, far from everything he had ever known. For Duleep's banishment, the Fategarh Hill Fort in the Farrukhabad district of Uttar Pradesh was chosen, and a Scottish doctor, John Spencer Login and his wife Lena were his de facto parents who were to raise him till he reached maturity.

Because of Lord Dalhousie, the Koh-i-Noor was destined for England and India would never see its jewel again. Punjab would lose its king. John Login was given the keys to the *toshakhana*. Login catalogued the Sikh Empire's treasures in the vaults, including the Koh-i-Noor. He recorded descriptions, took measurements and estimated values for the East India Company, while being surrounded by gold.

When Dalhousie made it clear that every valuable item was to be sent back to England, Login wondered whether Dalhousie had any legal or moral justification to start the second Anglo-Sikh War in the first place.

Login also had to take charge of Duleep and he resolved to treat him with kindness. He believed that an innocent boy was being punished. Sir Henry Lawrence might have overlooked the pleading letters from Rani Jindan earlier but he too was touched by Duleep Singh's plight. Henry Lawrence and Hardinge never wanted to annex the Punjab and as opposed to the military campaign from the start, they would have preferred to forge a mutually beneficial alliance with Duleep Singh on the throne. But Dalhousie was an over-ambitious and expansionist Scot who wanted to expand British territory at any cost. He had no thought for human values or sentiments. Lack of compassion was his trait from childhood when he almost drowned a classmate by dunking him repetitively. He was not a bright student either. Though he was placed in the fourth class of honours for Michaelmas 1833, he entered for a pass degree.

The decision to annex the kingdom was a sore grief to the generous-hearted Resident, Henry Lawrence. His brother John Lawrence was subsequently preferred by Dalhousie. The British press crowed over the annexation and had no words of sympathy, painting the boy king Duleep as the author of his own misfortune. Dalhousie had little sympathy for him. The Governor General tried to denigrate the boy and cast doubt on his legitimacy and his conduct towards a minor was loathsome. Dalhousie went so far as to argue that the loss of the Koh-i-Noor would have little effect on Duleep Singh who would in future be grateful for what the British had done for him. At the entire mercy of the British were now Duleep and his diamond.

Passage to England

Duleep's new life began on April 6, 1849, the day he was formally introduced to Dr. Login who described Duleep Singh as 'very lovable' and eager to please. Duleep had inherited his mother's fine features. He loved to paint and read books. His passion for Persian poetry and hunting with hawks was indeed regal. Duleep would at times retreat into himself, loving his own solitude. Login avoided the sensitive topic of his mother or the Koh-i-Noor.

Login decided to throw a large and colourful party on Duleep's eleventh birthday. *'I should like to see as many children as possible, on the little fellow's account'*; Login wrote. The request for a few token trinkets was granted by the uncompassionate Dalhousie and the Maharaja was duly presented with an assortment of gems; these were in any case the Maharaja's a few weeks back. On his birthday he looked like a Maharaja. But Duleep had not forgotten his mother or the Koh-i-Noor. He remarked, of course innocently that on his last birthday he had worn the Koh-i-noor on his arm.

After the birthday party a few weeks had passed and rumours were afloat that the Queen had declined to accept the Koh-i-noor as a gift. Soon, Login's hopes were dashed. The Queen never refused to accept the diamond, nor was she against the Maharaja's 'adoption' by the Logins. There was a remote chance that Duleep might be restored to his mother.

Meanwhile, the British tried to massacre the reputation of Rani Jindan by painting her as a sexual predator who needed to be kept imprisoned. Dalhousie, the mean Governor-General then attacked her telling Queen Victoria that Jindan was a cruel mother, who was used to beating her own son every day.

Queen Victoria wanted regular updates on the Maharaja's welfare and progress. Duleep was almost the same age as Victoria's eldest son and she could feel for Duleep. While Login was planning Duleep's birthday party, Rani Jindan was now behind bars for 16 months. As if her banishment from Lahore to Sheikhupura was not enough, Resident Currie ordered in July 1848 to transfer Rani Jindan to a cell in Chunnar Fort, in the Mirzapur district of Uttar Pradesh.

From her prison, the lonely Rani Jindan awaited eagerly for any information about her son. It was one of the saddests moment of her life which could break her totally when she heard of the annexation of Punjab and the seizure of the Koh-i-Noor. Rani Jindan escaped from Chunnar Fort by exchanging her clothes with a seamstress just a few days after Duleep had signed the treaty, on April 19, 1849.

What a woman Rani Jindan was. Her desire to survive and fight the mighty British for her rights, her kingdom and her son is highly commendable. She took a circuitous route of almost 1,280 kilometres to reach the Kingdom of Nepal. She was now at the mercy of the ruler Jung Bahadur. Unknown to her, British envoys had reached the ruler and had advised him to offer Rani Jindan sanctuary under stated conditions. He was to stop her from setting foot in India again. She must not attempt to contact her son nor attempt to stage an uprising in Punjab or challenge British rule. The Rani was to be kept in an Indian prison from which she would never escape again in case there was failure to comply with the rules laid by the British for her captivity in Nepal. Rani Jindan had no option but to accept.

While Jindan wasted away in Nepal, in early February 1850 the residents of Lahore watched as their Maharaja's caravan left Punjab for the very last time for Fategarh where Login lived. His wife Lena and children would join them in Fategarh.

The young Maharaja was beginning to be fascinated by England, enquiring routinely about its people, culture and queen.

Koh-i-Noor

The British press was very enthusiastic about the Koh-i-Noor but showed no concern about Duleep Singh. However, *Lloyd's Weekly*, was less pleased the way Dalhousie had done its confiscation.

> .... is a mockery; the lad [Duleep Singh] did exactly what he was bid, ... He signed the paper placed before him quite regardless of its contents; and the responsibility of its terms rest [sic] entirely with the Governor General ...

Dalhousie was an over-ambitious person bypassing the social norms, even for his pettiest gains. He was depicted as an arrogant man, and the paper went on to charge Dalhousie with betraying the EIC and overstepping his mandate in India. Dalhousie behaved as if he were the man presenting the diamond to the queen when he had no legal right to do so. The diamond, like the annexed Punjab, belonged to the East India Company.

John Lawrence was chosen to guard the Koh-i-Noor till its passage to England could be arranged. The diamond was now in John's custody; he removed it from its casket, placed it in his waistcoat and promptly forgot all about it. To send the great diamond to England and to Queen Victoria, a message arrived on January 12, 1850. The Governor General, Lord Dalhousie, took a ludicrous decision to carry the Koh-i-Noor himself, all the way to Bombay and chose Captain James Ramsay as his companion. He was Dalhousie's nephew.

At a small ceremony in Lahore on December 7, 1849, with John Lawrence, Henry Lawrence and Mansel in attendance, Dalhousie signed a receipt for the Koh-i-Noor and left Lahore for Bombay.

On February 1, 1850, after nearly two months, the Koh-i-Noor finally reached Bombay. On April 6, 1850, the Koh-i-Noor was finally taken aboard HMS Medea and it reached Plymouth on June 30, 1850. The officers of the 22nd Foot, and a private secretary to the chairman of the East India Company, accompanied by an exhausted Ramsay and Mackeson, took it to the headquarters of the EIC when Medea finally reached Portsmouth a day later. The Company's chairman, John Shepherd accepted it on behalf of his queen. The Koh-i-Noor, at least, was yanked from a boy Maharaja and it was on the British soil, at last.

The Koh-i-Noor had finally landed in the queen's lap. May 1, 1851 was to mark the most anticipated event in Victoria's reign when the Koh-i-Noor, and other treasures, were to be revealed to the world. The Koh-i-Noor sat on a bolt of rich red velvet inside a gilded iron cage for public viewing. Despite all attempts to show it as a big artefact, audience for the Koh-i-Noor remained lukewarm. More tinkering was needed.

A new and dramatic display was revealed to the public on June 14. The celebrated changes drew fresh crowds but the enthusiasm quickly waked, thanks to the unbearable temperatures inside the cabin. The display into a sauna, thanks to the gas lamps, mirrors and heavy fabric, caused visitors to swoon after only a few minutes.

The Koh-i-Noor was finally taken back to the vaults once the Great Exhibition ended in October.

Duleep Singh in England

Duleep Singh had lived for almost seven years as an English aristocrat, invited to the parties that mattered, and befriended by the most powerful men in the realm. When he turned twenty-one, i.e. in 1859, Duleep's thoughts drifted towards his real mother. His mother Rani Jindan was twenty-one when Duleep was born. Now at 42, she was in a Nepalese prison, and the years had taken a terrible toll on her. She had aged dramatically and had lost weight, and had been progressively losing her sight. Despite all the attempts by the British to stop any news about Rani Jindan's failing health reaching the Maharaja, in 1860 the worrying rumours reached him.

In the meantime, Lord Dalhousie who mastered the annexation of Punjab and snatched the Koh-i-Noor from the young Maharaja died in Dalhousie castle on December 19, 1860; he was buried in the old churchyard of Cockpen.

Duleep sent a letter to his mother in secret via a trusted servant. When they intercepted the letter, the British were in a fix. On what grounds could they block the son from speaking to his mother? Duleep Singh was given permission to travel to India to meet his mother for the first time since she had been confined. The authorities selected a place far away from Punjab at *Spence's* Hotel in Calcutta and it was there that Duleep waited for his mother on January 16, 1861.

When the Rani was brought in to see him, she ran her hands all over her son's face. With her fading eyesight, she relied on her fingertips to check her son's features and as Jindan felt for the hair on Duleep's head, she cried out in agony. With his shorn hair, Duleep Singh was no longer a practising Sikh.

Rani Jindan knew that the British had taken away his kingdom and his Koh-i-Noor but she never thought that Duleep would give up or renounce Sikhism. When Rani Jindan finally calmed herself, she turned to Duleep's British escort and declared she would never leave her son alone. This meant she would travel to England.

Duleep wrote to the Logins about his mother's wishes, and his agreeing to her idea that he might as well go along with the idea. The British told the queen that she should be allowed to come to England. They thought that Rani Jindan on British soil could not get involved in any insurrection back in India and a close watch on her could be kept.

With his mother beside him, Duleep slowly changed, turning from an obedient Maharaja of the British to one who dared to question its diktats. Duleep's friends gossiped about his mother but could not create a wall between the two. Unaccustomed to the clothers worn by elderly Punjabi women, the British aristocratic ladies despised and ridiculed Rani Jindan.

Duleep decided to purchase a house for his mother in an exclusive part of London, opposite Hyde Park, at 1 Lancaster Gate. Duleep himself lived just around the corner. The terms of the settlement which he was compelled to sign years ago were now being questioned by the Maharaja, much to the dismay of the highest levels.

Login had a discussion with Sir Phipps regarding the marriage prospects of Duleep Singh to wean him away from his influential mother. A country estate far away from London was being earmarked by the India Office so that the Maharaja could start his new life. The British planned to somehow lock up Rani Jindan again after sending her back to Asia. Rani Jindan died peacefully at her home in London on August 1, 1863. She was only forty-six.

Before her death, Rani Jindan had really influenced her son's mind against the exploitative British. On June 7, 1864, Duleep married Bamba Müller. The notorious British press said:

> *His choice, though, was bizarre to say the least. She was a beautiful 16-year-old, little educated, illegitimate daughter of a German merchant and an Abyssinian slave. She had lived in the cloistered environment of a Christian mission in Cairo from the moment she was born, and spoke not one word of English.*

Duleep Singh purchased an attractive estate on the Norfolk–Suffolk border close to the Sandringham home of his close friend, the Prince of Wales. Over the next five years, Duleep tore down the existing mansion and rebuilt it into a magnificent shape.

Duleep Singh liked his drink and led the life of a British aristocrat. By 1874, he was the father of six children. His daughter Sophia would make a name for herself, later on. The Maharaja was spending heavily on his hobbies and he had developed those luxurious habits by a thorough pampering of the British who tried to legitimise every illegitimate act they had performed, be it the annexation of Punjab or be it the looting of the Koh-i-Noor. Also, it may be kept in mind that Duleep was the son of Maharaja Ranjit Singh, the most powerful monarch of Punjab in the last few centuries.

By 1877, the British government almost stopped funding the Maharaja and he was now close to bankruptcy and ruin. Duleep continued to spend as he had done and challenged the India Office to return almost half a million pounds worth of family jewels, which were looted from his family and were not a part of any treaty. He also demanded over a million pounds' worth of ancestral lands. Though he appeared unaffected, the stress was taking its toll. The once beautiful young man had gained a lot of weight and was drinking too much.

In the early months of 1880, the British government offered Duleep £57,000 to clear his debts. But there was a catch; his abode Elveden would have to be sold upon his death and all proceeds paid back to the British government. The Maharaja was shocked as it would leave nothing as savings for his heirs. Duleep had only one option left and he wrote directly to Queen Victoria and pleaded with her to let him keep Elveden. Queen Victoria's reply offered little.

The situation was going to get much worse for Duleep Singh and his family. The Maharaja turned to his influential friends but they abandoned him. Duleep then turned to the press, requesting the British people to put pressure on their government. Though the newspapers published his letters, they ridiculed him at the same time. He suggested to Queen Victoria that he might renounce Christianity.

To her courtiers he warned he might try and forge an alliance with Britain's old foe, Russia, and go to war, with an army of avenging Sikhs behind him.

The Maharaja put the Elveden Hall up for auction in January 1886 to use the money raised from the sale at Elveden to buy tickets for him and his family to return to India. Duleep and his family were arrested on April 21, 1886 at Port Said, Egypt before their ship could reach the Suez Canal. His obsession had consumed him although he would eventually be released. It wrecked his family and broke his health.

On October 21, 1893 Duleep Singh died penniless and alone in a hotel in Paris. He was fifty-three. None of his children would ever be heirs in the years to come. A tragedy indeed for the Punjabis in general and the Khalsa in particular.

Administration in Punjab from 1849 Onwards

Before analysing the administrative changes in Punjab from 1849 onwards, the system of government followed by Ranjit Singh can be examined. Most of the state resources were used for war and military equipment. The collection of the taxes was an area which was accorded the highest attention by all his officials. Ranjit Singh used all known sources of taxation. The revenue of remote provinces was delegated to men of wealth and influence who faced no interference. Military chiefs, who enjoyed the revenue of jagirs and were responsible for supplying troops, also exercised unlimited authority. The local agents, or *Kardars* worked under these farmers and jagirdars and the pay of these local tax-gatherers varied.

The auditing of the accounts for many years was defective and towards the close of the Maharaja's reign, a semblance of sanity prevailed. This accounting system could not stop embezzlement. Ranjit Singh knew this.

There were no regular courts of justice. However, there was a judicial officer, termed *adalati.* Under the direction of local authorities, private arbitration was done and the arbitrators were often selected according to their respective faiths. The *Qazis* and *Qanungos* exercised the functions continuing from the Mughal times. The former solemnised the marriage ceremonies, to register testaments and attest deeds; the latter to declare recorded facts and expound local customs. The Maharaja constantly toured his dominions, heard all complaints and any Governor in whose province grievances were numerous had to face the angry Maharaja's rebukes.

Imprisonment was almost unknown and capital punishment was rare. Mutilation of body parts was sometimes ordered and most of the time, punishments could be commuted by payment of fines. The Maharaja himself gave punishments in many cases.

Being an accuser, judge and jury, the Maharaja took just five minutes as the longest period to decide a case. The duty of the local police officers was to check local disturbances and to assist the movement of troops.

Ranjit Singh had built schools and done some work towards the welfare of subjects. His armies were constantly on the move from one place to another and roads and bridges must certainly have been kept in usable condition. This is in sharp contrast to what Thorburn said later. However, due to constant war-like scenarios, the towns remained poor collections of huts. Barring the Sikhs, the other communities lived generally in clusters of hovels.

Condition of Punjab After Ranjit Singh's Death

For about forty years Ranjit Singh ruled happily over Punjab which was free from religious bigotry. The army had become very powerful and it directed the affairs of the state and established their panchayats. Soon came the demand for the increase in pay and dismissal of all officers disliked by them; some were murdered and then they plundered Lahore. The European officers fled and there was anarchy for some time.

Due to this instability, the province's trade declined. Robberies along the roads, exploitative nature of duties and tolls, interruptions in the development of manufactures and the flight of capital hampered mercantile transactions.

After the First Sikh War (1845) the remedies were attempted by the Council of Regency during its existence from 1846 to 1849. The army was downsized and the discharged soldiers were paid off. The troops were disciplined and the finances were scrutinised. Efforts were made to strengthen the economy. In the fiscal department, the demand on the people and the remuneration of the revenue officers were limited. Liberal salaries were allowed to the Kardars once summary settlements of the land revenue were made. The indirect and miscellaneous taxes regime was simplified. The revenue was restricted to a few fixed duties and relief was given to the people without any compromise to the state interests.

For appointments separately as administrators of civil and criminal justice separately, people of integrity were selected. The penal code was made more humane but severe. The Council of Regency tackled the issues related to the heinous crimes. Hearing of appeals from all the local chiefs was done routinely. European officers were deputed to visit the outlying districts. All the intelligence chiefs were summoned to Lahore for framing the rules and regulations for the future. Plans were formed for the construction of new canals, the repair of old ones, the re-opening of ruined wells and relocating the people of deserted villages. An engineer of rank and experience was appointed from the British service and Rs. 3,00,000 were earmarked by the Council for public improvements. These welfare plans were interrupted by the Second Anglo-Sikh War which resulted in the annexation of Punjab.

Let us now go to 1849 when Punjab was annexed finally by the British.

Punjab Under the British: 1849-1853

On March 29, 1849, Sir Henry Elliot, the foreign secretary held a Durbar at Lahore to inform about the decision by the Government of India. Duleep Singh occupied the throne for one last time. All the Sikh chiefs were present. The proclamation of annexation was made in English, Persian and Hindustani. The traitor Tej Singh handed over a paper to Duleep Singh to sign. He did it as asked. Elliot then rose and left the hall.

Punjab was lost to the British. The British flag was hoisted on the ramparts of the Lahore citadel and the Kingdom of Lahore had ceased to exist.

The British were masters of manipulation and literary jugglery. Thus, the instrument by which the Punjab was declared annexed was supposed to be a 'treaty' between the Maharaja and the EIC, and ratified by the Governor-General. On April 5, 1849. It was a dishonest amendment to the original terms of the annexation.

The Durbar believed in the good offices of the British government when a treaty was signed on December 16, 1846 which was to *'have effect during the minority of ... Maharaja Duleep ....and terminate on His Highness attaining 16 years....on the September 4, 1854'*. But 5 years and 5 months before the due date, the Maharaja being still a minor, being eleven years of age only,

Lord Dalhousie, a man of doubtful integrity, blinded by power broke his faithful commitment, so unlike a British honourable person and cheated Duleep Singh of everything, including the Koh-i-Noor.

The Board of Administration (1849-53)

On the March 12, 1849, Sardar Chattar Singh, Raja Sher Singh and thirty-five chiefs surrendered before General Gilbert anal laid down their arms.

After the British annexation decided on by Lord Dalhousie the administration of the Punjab was placed in the hands of a Board as shown below:

Table 3.1

Board of Administration for Punjab		
Sl	*Name*	*Designation*
1	Henry Lawrence (1806-57)	President
2	John Lawrence (1811-79)	Member
3	Charles Mansel (1806-86)	Member

This combination was known as *'the triumvirate'*. Under them were many young British civil and military officers selected by Dalhousie. Henry Lawrence was already well acquainted with the Punjab and its Sardars and soldiers as he had commanded the Sikh troops who had accompanied General Pollock's force to Kabul earlier. Earlier, Sir Henry Lawrence was a British resident in the Punjab before its annexation. Sir Henry had already had many short brushes with Lord Dalhousie and there was some uneasiness between the two and they knew about it and despite that, Henry was made the president of the board. So, credit goes to Dalhousie who rose above his personal prejudice as well as Henry Lawrence who rose to deservedly occupy that post.

Henry Lawrence was the best man for the job. He was a political assistant, first at Ludhiana, and then at Ferozepur. He understood the Sikhs' strengths and weaknesses very well. Since March 1846, he ensured the implementation of the Anglo-Sikh treaty and resisted Hardinge's desire to interfere. A kind of moderation was followed by him while dealing with the Sikhs, whose fiery nationalism he was aware of and also their pride. He did not reduce the Durbar's nominal authority, but enforced his decisions judiciously. His newly formed Council had a number of portfolios. It comprised 6 Sikhs, 1 Hindu and 1 Muslim. The army was split up into regular and irregular forces; a Public Works Department was created. Bhai Nidhan Singh oversaw a Sikh ecclesiastical portfolio.

John Lawrence

He was 6 years younger than his brother Henry. He attended Haileybury College where he picked up Bengali. John knew Persian and Hindustani also and was a district officer in Delhi, Panipat and Etawah. His knowledge about the Sikhs was far less as compared with his brother Henry. In other matters like financial skill, general civil administration and capacity to go into details, he was far ahead of his elder brother. Lionel Trotter wrote about Henry's sympathies on the side of the aristocracy while John was protective about the masses who toiled hard with their own hands and brains.

While posted at Panipat, John showed his mettle from 1834-37, when equipped with a gun, dog and horse, he secured the countryside of Panipat. Earlier the armed bands routinely snatched local power from one another. John was accessible to the people of his district and was never above his work far removed from his flatterers.

Lawrence is credited to have halted the despicable practice of killing infant girls by the Bedi clans.

Charles Mansel

He was another member of the board and was a civilian like John who did his apprenticeship in the North-West. Mansel was a balancing factor between the two brothers.

Other Officers

Some officers were selected to work under the board. George Christian, the Secretary, was selected by John Lawrance and Meelvil was specially appointed by Lord Dalhousie to the post of Assistant-Secretary. There were to be four Commissioners for the four divisions of the new province Lahore, Jhelum, Multan and Leia; while under them, fifty-two Deputy and Assistant Commissioners were selected, from the civil and military services.

The start of British Punjab is characterised by two events: Firstly, the happiness of the province's Muslims regarding the end of the Sikh rule. Muslims were now free to make a call to public prayer from the minarets of their mosques. Ranjit Singh was not anti-Muslim but the fact was that the leading Muslim families like the Chatthas and Bhattis were against the Sikhs and they supported the British against the Sikhs in the Anglo-Sikh wars. Second was the fact that the Sikh chiefs saw in Henry Lawrence, a person who was willing to erase the humiliation of their defeat and remove their bitterness. John Lawrence also recognised Sikh valour.

The Punjab after annexation along with the part the British were already ruling, was split into six administrative divisions: Lahore, Multan, and Jhelum, Leiah, Jalandhar Doab and Ambala. Later the Jhelum and Leiah divisions were merged to form the Rawalpindi division.

Achievements of the Board

The administration began to suffer from the difference between the two Lawrence brothers and Dalhousie tried to ease the situation by appointing Montgomery in place of Mansel to act as a sort of umpire between them.

Peace in the Punjab

The greater portion of the Khalsa army recognised the British supremacy, after the battle of Gujarat. They had returned to the plough. The old and invalid among them were pensioned off. The remainder obtained their long arrears of pay, and permission was given to many to re-enter the British service. It was due partly to the tactful handling of Henry Lawrence and largely due to the political sagacity of the Sikhs themselves.

General Disarmament

The Sikh army was disbanded. About six weeks after the annexation a proclamation ordering general disarmament was circulated everywhere and was obeyed. All types of weapons of every size and species including the bows and arrows were surrendered. The people of Hazara and trans-Indus frontier were allowed to retain their arms as they faced danger from their neighbours across the border.

Raising of the Frontier Force

To guard the frontiers, raising of 10 regiments—5 of cavalry and 5 of infantry—was planned to be raised and Hindustanis, Sikhs and Muslims responded cheerfully to the British call.

The Irregular Regiments

Within a year several of the Punjab irregular regiments saw action in the British service against the Afridis, the Swattis, and other turbulent tribes beyond the border. Three field batteries, a camel corps at Dera Ismail Khan and the reputed Guide Corps were the movable defences of the frontier.

The 'Guide Corps'

It was a brain-child of Henry Lawrence and the idea was mooted at the close of the First Sikh War. The Guide Corps had 750 men, horse and foot and contained representatives of almost every race, place, language and religion from the North/North-West of India. It contained men of every shade of moral-character, and also of no character at all like the cunning trackers, the notorious cattle-lifters, the daring freebooters. They got good pay and soon they were found to be prepared 'to go anywhere or do anything'.

The Intelligence Department

The Guides formed the *'Intelligence Department of the Punjab.'* These guides knew the local terrain and the language. They could tell about the hostile encampments. These were the men for a daring reconnaissance. Raised first by Lieutenant Harry Lumsden they rendered commendable service in border fighting and in the Second Sikh War, They were soon to serve under Sir Colin Campbell against the Muslims.

Protecting Frontiers

The whole frontier force reported directly to the board under the command of Brigadier-General Hodgson. At Peshawar valley, one part was kept in reserve to assist the regular troops, such was the panic in Dalhousie's mind about the Afghans. With the fords of the Indus, the best passage into India, directly in its rear, was to be guarded by a force of men, nearly 3,000 of them Europeans.

The Board thought that the dangerous parts, from Hazara to Dera Ismail Khan should be defended by forts of considerable size, capable of standing a siege. Below those, again, from the Tonk Valley down to Sindh, a chain of smaller fortified posts at intervals of 12 miles apart were to be built. The whole should he connected together by a good military road, with branches going towards the hostile mountains, and also towards the friendly river. There was no serious threats to the peace of the Punjab.

War on Crimes

Adequate measures for Detection and Prevention of Crime were taken. Two large bodies of police were created:

Preventive, with a military organisation and were 8,000 in number, horse and foot, many among whom had done good service to the late Durbar, and had remained faithful to the British in the Second Sikh War. The Military police had two sections the a) infantry, and b) the cavalry. It had 10 Battalions and not only did it do the escort work for civil officers and treasure, and duty at the jails, they also aided in garrison duty at Kohat, Bannu and Hazara on the Frontier.

Sir John Lawrence remarked in the Administration report for 1852-53, that 'in the force and vigour of its Police—the Punjab may challenge comparison with any province in India.' During the terrible outbreak of 1857, the Military Police guarded jails and police posts but in many cases they were transferred to cantonments for regular military duty.

The Detective Police numbering 7,000 men, and divided amongst 230 police districts (*thanahs*) were deployed for a) detection of crime, b) in the guarding of ferries, and c) for the passage of the rivers, collecting of troops' supplies or of boats. A complete system of diaries and record was maintained.

The Board gave large powers to the native revenue collectors, called *tehsildars* for organising and controlling the police. Even the village watchman was also carefully maintained by officers. Precautions were required in the criminally infested districts. The Peshawar-Valley was a nest of assassins. The centres of the Doabs having miles of jungle and long grass had been a place of cattle lifters and often the spoils included whole herds of oxen driven away from the richer lands.

Around Peshawar, huge cordons of police posts were thrown. They filled in the ravines and hollows and connected adjoining districts with a network of roads. In the Doabs, mounted patrols of police were sent along them.

Professional Trackers were introduced who were men of amazing skill John Lawrence had himself used in the pursuit of criminals at Delhi, Panipat, and Gurgaon. They were men with extraordinary senses.

Dacoity or Robbery had been in practice over Punjab's entire history. It had grown with the growth of the Sikhs. Often, the most successful gang robber after amassing huge quantities of money or of cattle under the sword, captured big estates or principalities. The leader of a band was least ashamed of his occupation. The districts of Lahore and Amritsar began to swarm with them till severe action against them checked this evil. The evil was checked by the deploying of strong precautions and severity. During the first year, 37 dacoits were condemned to death in Amritsar district alone and in a few years more crime ceased to exist throughout the Punjab.

The *Thaggi* (Cheating) was an evil more in India proper but it was there in Punjab as well, the severity might have been less. The Punjab thugs nonetheless practised this dreadful crime but were not that expert. The initiator of this crime was straightway hung from the neck by Maharaja Ranjit Singh. The successors often made up for their want of skill in the use of the handkerchief by hacking their victim to pieces with their swords, and left the corpses carelessly to rot by the wayside.

The *Anti-Infanticide Movement* was started by the Board and since the Board's Report (August 1852) a complete inquiry was made. It was found from the districts and divisions of the Punjab, that this practice extended more widely than had been previously supposed, especially among the Rajput tribe. Prevalence of the crime was found among Sadazai Pathans, Khatris and the Mohmands of Multan. Getting a suitable groom for the girl child was cited as the principal reason for their murder. In 1852 meetings were held with Bedis and Khatris and the causes, progress, extent and possible eradication of this crime was prepared by Major H.B. Edwards, the Deputy Commissioner of Jalandhar.

A grand meeting was held in Amritsar and the participants were the Sikh Chiefs, Hill Chieftains, the commercial millionaires, the Muslim Nawabs and Hindu priests. From the British side were present: The Judicial and Financial Commissioners, the Commissioners from Trans and Cis Sutlej areas and the district officers. Rules were outlined for intermarrying between various sub-castes or sub-divisions of the same tribe and reduction of the marriage expenses. The rules were fixed by the Committees and received wide publicity.

For the *Reformation of Criminals,* the Board introduced reforms in the system. The criminals were well-fed, clothed and housed and were given a chance for educating themselves. Twenty-five jails of different sizes and models were erected in the different districts of the Punjab. The great Central Jail at Lahore was built as per the latest design. John Lawrence was able, with the help of Dr. Charles Hathaway, Inspector of Prisons, to carry out the improvements in the system.

The Legislation

The prevailing native customs were taken as the basis of English Law. Those customs which were absolutely pernicious and incapable of adopting were rejected. Those related to marriage, divorce, and tending to the degradation of the female sex, were modified before adopting and those related to inheritance and adoption, were incorporated at once. Each village or a group retained a court of their own and the tehsildar played an important role.

The land tax was a varying share of the products from soil claimed by the government. Under the earlier governments, it was generally paid in kind. Earlier the officials were somewhat exploitative but under the English, a low average of the product of the district was taken on the returns of several years. The money value of the share of the government was calculated at a low average of the current prices. It was a win-win situation for all, especially the farmer. The land-tax now amounted to half or to a quarter of what it had been before.

The state did not suffer much due to remissions as the revenues of Multan and those of other outlying parts flowed into the government treasury, rather freely.

The *trade policy* was liberalised. On January 1, 1850, all town and transit dues, all export and import duties, were abolished by the Board. Excise was levied on spirits to offset that. Stamp duties were started; tolls at chief ferries over large rivers were authorised. A controversial tax on salt was being planned now. The vast stores of the salt range came under the British control. Importing of salt from other districts was banned. The people did not oppose it as they did not find it a burden.

The Public Works Department (PWD) underwent an appreciable change in 1854. Since that year, the Engineering Works whether civil, Military or Public had been placed under one department, headed by a Chief Engineer. The overall financial and other supervision was placed under the authority of the chief commissioner.

Colonel R. Napier was a reputed engineer who was well aware of Punjab's needs and had earlier worked under Henry Lawrence when the latter was a resident at Lahore. His ideas were translated into physical things which became the pride of the Punjab.

Roads and canals were the first to be modernised and Napier had an efficient staff with him. During the Sikh rule the Punjab Army had been modernised but the roads and canals and other infrastructures like colleges, schools, hospitals, municipality and civil administration were far behind Europe. EIC was not changing Punjab into Europe either but they wanted to upgrade its infrastructure to rule more efficiently and more productivity in agriculture was their goal too.

Any development work needs funds which were fairly provided to Napier and special grants were needed for very big tasks like upgradation of the Grand Trunk Road and the digging of great canals. During the first three years the progress of road buildings was as under:

1. 1,349 miles of road, had been cleared and constructed;
2. 853 miles were under construction;
3. 2,487 miles had been traced; and
4. 5,272 miles surveyed and exclusive minor cross and branch roads.

The Grand Trunk Road had been traced between 1849 and 1851, surveyed and put in progress. Operations were started;

however, it was not opened to the public with full access. Rebuilding this highway had military connotations and principally it stood for the safety of the Empire. But indirectly, it benefited the Punjabis as many arterial roads connected with it and made communication faster for import and export trade between India, Central Asia and the West. G.T. Road held together all the British great northern cantonments and maintained communication with Peshawar, their greatest frontier station. It connected Hazara and Kashmir with Punjab which was suffice for military exigencies.

The canals need a special mention. Before the British annexation, in the north of Bari Doab, a canal known as the Husli or Shah-i-Nahar, travelled a distance of 110 miles to Lahore. It was undoubtedly a major achievement but it served no villages and merely supplied the royal water works, conservatories and fountains of the palaces.

The Board proposed another great canal which was planned to start from the same point in the Ravi, as the earlier channel. It was to pass the whole length of the Bari Doab, channelling from the upper part of its course, three branches into districts each sixty to eighty miles long. These were planned to replenish the water in the empty reservoirs and the disused watercourses of the great southern waste, calling into existence new villages everywhere.

The British had another problem. The types of *coins* in usage were too many and these needed standardisations. The common man must have suffered, and only the money-changers, and possibly, the Sardars, would have flourished. Here was a case for prompt action to be taken by the government. New coins stamped with the mark of the English Queen were circulated.

There were many *languages* in the Punjab. In the two western Doabs, Persian or dialects derived from it were in use officially; in the eastern part Punjabi. In one of the Indus districts, Pashto was spoken; in another Baloch. The difficulty of establishing a settled government and administering justice amidst these languages was great. Ultimately it was decided that Urdu should be the official language of the eastern Punjab and Persian of the western half of the Punjab.

The work done by the Board in its first three years relating to Education was mainly preparatory in nature. Montgomery found that throughout the Punjab there were elementary schools for all communities: Sikh, Muslim and Hindu. Students from artisan classes also were to be found in sizeable numbers along with those of higher castes like Rajputs, Brahmins or Khatris. Female education was encouraged by Ranjit Singh and in Lahore only there were sixteen schools for girls. In fact, there was a general desire for education even though the standard at those schools, if compared with the British ones was not high. However, it taught writing and arithmetic which was sufficient, at all events, to enable students to do compound interest calculations with accuracy.

Punjab Under John Lawrence (1853-59)

The Board of Administration could not be prolonged enough. Sir Henry Lawrence was inclined to favour the Sikh Chiefs and Sardars and tried their material improvements only but John Lawrence had more sympathy with the peasants than the Sikh Chiefs whom he regarded as parasitic growths who put a heavy financial strain on the state exchequer.

The two brothers held strongly divergent opinions on the important subject whether to give continued patronage to the Sardars or not. Henry wanted to secure for the Sikh Sardars an honourable position. To his chagrin, he saw that his brother was determined to thwart him in the policy he intended to follow. Other issues such as collecting land-tax or the plans to be followed in the Public Works Department, he had not contested but the benefits of the Sikh Sardars were in his radar. Henry wanted to pursue a liberal treatment for the vanquished Sikhs. John's insistence was more pragmatic for the British as he concentrated on the financial aspects of the question and his refusal to recognise the Sikh aristocracy, spelt the ruin of the class which Henry so persistently wished to preserve.

Board is Abolished

The differences between the brothers proved a serious handicap for the administration. In early 1853, the two brothers agreed that it would be better for one of them to go. Dalhousie removed the elder brother Henry, to his deep chagrin, to Rajputana as an agent for the Governor-General. Dalhousie explained to Henry that he needed a civilian to look after the affairs of Punjab. The officials, chiefs and people of Punjab were equally disappointed at Henry Lawrence's removal. The Board was abolished and John Lawrence was made Chief Commissioner of the Punjab.

Punjab on the Road to Progress

Major projects calculated to ameliorate the condition of the masses were launched. John Lawrence had no big problems at hand and Punjab undoubtedly was a peaceful place. John Lawrence inherited all the powers of the Board of Administration and he enjoyed total control over all departments and support services. He also had to take care of the defence and management of the whole trans-Indus area. John was to be assisted by two Commissioners for Financial and Judicial work respectively. The new administration was to be regulatory shackle-free and in an unbroken chain of subordination, the delegation of power went down.

Divisions, Districts and Tehsils

Punjab was divided into Divisions, Districts and Tehsils. The province was divided into seven divisions. Each division was in turn sub-divided into small districts, so that intimate contact between the people and deputy commissioner was possible. Usually, a district was headed by a deputy commissioner in later years as well. Again, the district was divided into Tehsils looked after by Tehsildars. Half the selected men were civilians and half were from the military.

The Divisions were:

(1) Cis-Sutlej States Division (2) Trans-Sutlej States Division (3) Lahore (4) Jhelum (5) Multan (6) Leia, (7) Peshawar.

The Deputy Commissioners and their assistants carried out the work of judges, revenue collectors, conservancy officers, and sometimes sergeants and chaplains. They were instructed to move among the people and develop personal contacts. John Lawrence did not want his officers to be cut off from the main currents of popular feeling. The multifarious duties made them mini-dictators but Punjab now saw the period of successful development.

North-West Frontier Policy

The North-Western Frontier of India always drew the attention of

John Lawrence. The tribal raids could not be completely halted by the Guide Corps and the Punjab Frontier Force. Lord Dalhousie wanted to play safe and he desired to limit his boundaries to the limits reached by the erstwhile Sikh state as going beyond that would not only attract trouble but also those tribal areas would have been hard to control. He maintained the status quo and respected the independence of the trans-frontier tracts. In any case, the tribesmen soon proved to be dangerous.

Two different lines of policy regarding to the tribal areas:

> This recommended that the tribal belt should be annexed to the Punjab and the frontier be extended beyond the existing boundary. This was the *'forward school of thought'* which even advocated dangerous thoughts of Trans-Khyber conquests and extending the British domain somewhere in Afghanistan.

The other school advocated non-advancement of British frontiers and suggested strengthening the Indus frontier. It was thought that the inhospitable nature of the trans-frontier territory and the ferocious tribesmen formed a natural barrier against Russia. John Lawrence and Herbert Edwardes belonged to the second school of thought. John Lawrence believed in a punitive expedition followed by a withdrawal. He maintained the conciliatory method of the Board.

Crimes Controlled

In 1856, John Lawrence recorded that the attachment of the people to their own jury system was unabated; crime was mild and rare. Thugs were well controlled and were unable to commit crimes very freely. But still, 400 of them were at large.

Education

The existing system of education was back-dated and the teachers were very poorly paid. The schools were a sort of religious kindergarten level teaching in Gurmukhi, Hindi, Arabic and Persian sentences from their several scriptures. Lawrence planned to open 30 schools at district headquarters, 100 village schools in rural tracts, four normal schools and a central college at Lahore. These were to be supervised by one director and two inspectors of schools, and the cost was to be £30,000 plus £1500 as grants in-aid to missionary and other private schools.

John introduced the system of teaching of elements of English and funds for the purpose were to be obtained from the 1 per cent education cess on the revenue. But sadly, the peasants had to pay that tax but they were unable to send their wards to school whereas the traders and moneylenders who paid no taxes, they sent their wards to school. John's idea had failed.

Vernaculars were made the medium of instruction and had he introduced English compulsorily, his endeavour of schooling would have backfired.

Land-Tax

John Lawrence analysed 'land-tax' in detail and saw that it provided three-quarters of the state resources and that was paid by agriculturists who were three-quarters of the population. He thought that on the whole the reduction of taxation allowed by the British Government on its first occupation of the country was not less than Rs. 5 million at the minimum.

Overall the peasantry largely benefited. John was charged by the Sikh Sardars and others that in his desire to benefit the cultivators, he had sacrificed income to which landlords and jagirdars were entitled. John Lawrence justified lower tax and demonstrated by figures that by lapses of fiefs and resumption of jagirs, he had recouped to the state all that he had given up for the benefit of the people.

John Lawrence further explained that his policy 'to tax the agriculturists lightly' had been due to a fall in prices by 50 per cent nearly but in fact the relaxation in taxes between 1852-56 were not proportional with the fall in prices.

John expected agriculture to remain the sole occupation of Punjabis, and that without facilities for export, land revenue could suffer. So, he laid emphasis on road building in all the Doabs. He wanted to assist peasantry with an outlet for their surplus produce, estimated by him at 0.78 million tons annually. He was convinced that the valley of the Indus must become the great highway for the export trade of the Punjab.

Undoubtedly the British system of administration was beneficial to village moneylenders, and enhanced facilities for recovering their loans from the landholders but John thought that the money system had become more efficient, that both benefited:

lender and the borrower. In reality, a new class of moneylenders became much more powerful and exploited the peasants.

Seventy-five per cent of the population of the Punjab was engaged in agriculture. The change in payment methodology, i.e. payment of land-tax in money rather than grain distressed the farmers as the procurement price of grain was already low. To meet the situation remissions of land-tax were granted.

Judicial Administration

Small courts were introduced and these proved to be very popular with the people. Thus, justice was being brought close to the peasant's door. There were now 104 such courts, besides 11 regular courts. In these courts nearly two-thirds of the judicial business was conducted. These were so located that a petitioner need not travel from his home more than 14 miles.

The procedure was very quick and the average period of a suit in 1854 was 28 days which came down to 23 days in 1855. No fees were charged by the courts and it was rare that a pleader was employed.

The Census

The Census was taken during the night of December 31, 1854, with the help of the people themselves, a fact proving the confidence and good understanding existing between the subjects and the Government. The population of British possessions in the Punjab was found to be nearly 13 million which was about three million more than the rough estimates of 1849. The number of villages was returned as 26,000; 4 cities had population more than 50,000.

Table 3.2

Sl	*City*	*Population*
1.	Amritsar	1,22,000
2.	Lahore	94,000
3.	Multan	56,000
4.	Peshawar	53,000

Of the total population, 7.5 million were Muslims and 5.5 were Hindus (Sikhs included). The Sikh identity often merged with the Hindu identity and they were not clearly identified. In the Lahore Division, they were numbered as a meagre 2,00,000 out of 3 million total population, despite their founding the Sikh Empire.

Extension of the Telegraph System

Dalhousie had always wanted to extend the telegraph system to the Punjab and development in this regard was really great. By 1857 he had given the country 400 miles of instantaneous communications, including an excellently equipped line from Calcutta to Peshawar.

* * * * * * *

In the summer of 1855, Dalhousie had made up his mind to annex the territory of Oudh even though it supplied most of the soldiers for the Bengal Army and even though by signing a treaty in 1837, it had committed itself not to annex it. John Lawrence approved the annexation of Oudh.

John Lawrence and the Governor-General met for the last time in Calcutta in 1856. In March 1856, John Lawrence became Sir John Lawrence. Dalhousie was replaced by Lord Canning in Calcutta on February 28, 1856. Canning was born in the same year as Dalhousie, i.e. 1812 CE. Like Dalhousie, Charles Canning had also served in the cabinet before coming to Calcutta. Trouble was brewing in India's west. Persia had claimed Herat and had Russia's backing. The British announced in July 1856 that any attack on Herat would be an attack on the Empire. Dost Muhammad had asked for British help, in any case. The British decided to mount a naval show of strength on Persia's shores. Canning asked John Lawrence for the commander for the force and the latter recommended his brother Henry's name. However, James Outram was chosen by Her Majesty's Government in London.

Canning asked John Lawrence to sign a new treaty with Dost Muhammad to reaffirm British support and recommended that a large British presence in Afghanistan was to be avoided to reduce costs. On January 7, 1857, an agreement was signed. The Anglo-Persian war began in November 1856 and many soldiers of the Bengal Army took part in it and it ended in April 1857. The British victory ensured that Persia withdrew its claim on Herat, which was returned to Afghanistan.

4

From Mutiny Till the End of the Century

Mutiny of 1857 and the Punjab

In the spring of 1857, there was discontent among the Bengal Army's Hindustani sepoys over greased cartridges for the new 'Enfield' rifle. They believed these to be greased with cow-fat or pig-fat and even the Punjab-based sepoys refused to touch it. Lawrence thought that the 1,000-yard range of the rifles would motivate them to use these.

The repercussions were severe and two regiments in the Calcutta area had to be disarmed in March and April, sepoy Mangal Pandey was hanged at Barrackpore (27 kilometres from Calcutta). He had disobeyed British officers and tried to kill them. John Lawrence thought and got satisfied that Calcutta was far and Punjab was safe, in any case. In early May, John Lawrence took his wife and child to Rawalpindi on the way to Murree hills to escape the severe summer of May.

On May 11, a telegram was typed for him and relayed via Ambala and it reached Lawrence on May 12. It said that *Sowars* from Meerut were burning houses and killing Britons in the Mughal Capital. Information was also sent to Lahore where Robert Montgomery was in charge and also to Peshawar where Edwardes was the commissioner. It was shocking news for Lawrence and the British in Punjab heard of the Delhi killings and Meerut Mutiny before such news could reach the Punjab-based troops, thanks to the telegraph.

There were 36,000 sepoys of different 'native' regiments of the Bengal Army, stationed in Punjab. Twelve 'European' regiments having 11,000 British soldiers were positioned in Punjab in Peshawar and Ambala, i.e. two extreme ends. The

Punjab Irregular force with Guides comprised 14,000 men who were Pashtuns and Punjabis and were positioned mainly in the trans-Indus region. Also, there were 15,000 native military policemen in Punjab.

Indian soldiers outnumbered the whites in Lahore, Rawalpindi, Ferozepur, Jalandhar and Hoshiarpur and by a greater number in Amritsar, Gurdaspur, Sialkot, Jhelum and Multan.

The telegraph line between Lahore and Rawalpindi was down and therefore the acting chief commissioner, Montgomery and his colleagues in Lahore acted on their own. Edwardes and Nicholson in Peshawar did the same. A disturbed John Lawrence pondered on how Delhi might be recovered and he sent a telegram to the Bengal Army's commander-in-chief, General George Anson, asking him to descend from Shimla on Delhi with a force, and another to Governor-General Canning in Calcutta to get China-bound British troops diverted to India.

Lawrence also wrote to the EIC chairman asking that a large body of European infantry be despatched to India urgently. In Punjab, Hindustani regiments were disarmed in one station after another facilitated by the ownership of heavy guns in the hands of the British. On May 12 in Lahore, a Brahmin informer cautioned the British about the impending danger from the Hindustani sepoys. Immediately, the British officers were persuaded to disarm the native soldiers positioned at Mian Mir suburb. The Hindustani sepoys surrendered their arms as instructed. How much the danger really lurked is a controversial matter.

After Mian Mir, the same process was repeated at barrack after barrack in Punjab in the days to follow. Usually it was the DC, acting on his own or under orders from Lawrence and passing advice to a Major or Colonel to accomplish the disarming.

All the places where the troops were stationed, i.e. from Lahore to Amritsar, Govindgarh fort, Ferozepur to Multan, were all secured. Even Kangra was not spared. Through messengers and where possible through the telegraph, Lawrence and Montgomery instructed officers in Punjab to secure the treasure and send it to the nearest military station. Punjabi police were to escort it and the Hindustani guards were to be distrusted.

Though Ferozepur had been alerted, the Native Infantry

rebelled and joined the rebels in Delhi. In June, three native regiments revolted in Jalandhar and reached Delhi. Lawrence was at his wit's end. Regiments of Sialkot, Jhelum and Rawalpindi also revolted.

In Multan, where sixty British artillery men were stationed, 35,000 native soldiers were disarmed by Major Chamberlain.

In Peshawar, Herbert Edwardes received the telegram about Delhi on May 11, a day before Lawrence in Rawalpindi and expected Dost Muhammad to provide help to the British. John Nicholson, DC, was also present in Peshawar in May. On May 13, Edwardes, Nicholson, an old major-general (Thomas Reed) and brigadiers Sydney Cotton and Neville Chamberlain held a five-man 'council of war' in Peshawar. It was decided that Chamberlain would lead a column of troops to Delhi, suppressing rebellions on the way. It was planned to raise new PIF units around Peshawar.

Reed, Chamberlain and Nicholson rode to Rawalpindi to meet Lawrence and decided that Delhi ought to be retaken. In the meantime, Reed and Chamberlain were called to Delhi and Nicholson was asked to lead the column to Delhi on its dangerous mission. Before leaving Peshawar, Nicholson disarmed three native regiments, executing quite a few native troops. After the disarming, many frontier men turned up to join the new units of PIF. He chased the Mardan-based Hindustani troops.

Those who escaped Nicholson were chased and killed by pro-British tribesmen. Lawrence proposed moving most of the British troops from the Peshawar region to the Delhi front. But this idea was not acceptable to Edwardes, Nicholson or the Governor-General.

On May 11, the rebel soldiers coerced the old Bahadur Shah Zafar to declare himself as the Emperor of Hindustan, once again. Many Europeans and Indian Christians were murdered in the city during the day. British women and children who had taken refuge in the Fort were killed. though not with Zafar's consent. In the days to follow, Hindustani regiments of the Bengal Army from the Ganga-Yamuna Doab reached Delhi. They did what the sepoys of Meerut did earlier. But Meerut like Agra was still under British control.

A British force from Meerut was stopped by the rebels at Hindan, twelve miles east of Delhi. The bigger British force left

Ambala on the night of May 24, but it was plagued by desertions, shortage of transporting animals and illnesses. Many succumbed to cholera but at last the Delhi Frontier Force (DFF) reached the ridge overlooking Delhi on June 8, after enforcements had arrived from Hindan. A furious fight ensued but the ridge was captured by the British.

Earlier, in Karnal, the DFF was joined by Delhi's magistrate, Theo Metcalfe who had escaped from the Delhi killings of May 11 and was returning with a vengeance to recapture it.

The British had suffered major reverses in Awadh's capital, Lucknow, and also in Kanpur, fifty-five miles southwest of Lucknow and the army-cum-transport town on Awadh's outskirts. Awadh's chief commissioner was Henry Lawrence whom Canning had brought in from Rajputana to head the freshly-annexed Awadh.

On May 30, rebel sepoys and loyalists of Awadh's deposed nawab forced the new chief commissioner along with all the Europeans of Lucknow, and about 700 Indian loyalists inside a few buildings within the so-called Residency part, and locked them in. This had the tacit approval of Lucknow's population. Henry Lawrence had already readied the Residency for its inmates' survival.

On June 5, a week after Lucknow was in the rebels' grip, Kanpur was captured by four native regiments with the British watching in dismay from a distance. The British shelled Delhi's walls continuously. On July 2, the men on the ridge heard of the arrival of five more rebel regiments along with heavy guns.

Zafar, on the other hand, did not have enough money to pay the sepoys who looted their needed articles from the merchants. The city and the Ridge were plagued by shortages, sickness and deaths. The British had asked for the 1st Madras Fusiliers who under Colonel Neil reached Allahabad on June 9. Another column was brought in by Henry Havelock. Seven Hundred more men of the 5th Fusiliers arrived in Calcutta instead of going to China. Now both Neil and Havelock marched towards Kanpur and Lucknow and once near Allahabad, they killed the locals indiscriminately. The British column was still far from Kanpur and on June 25, General Wheeler sought peace and surrendered before Nana Sahib (a giant of a figure from the Indian nationalism perspective). Despite promised a safe passage, Wheeler and many other British people were either shot or detained. There was an infamous *Bibighar Massacre* in which the imprisoned were all slaughtered and it included women and children.

On July 4, Henry Lawrence was killed inside the Lucknow Residency by a rebel-fired shell which exploded near him. He was fifty-one years old. Thus the life of an extraordinary person ended, far from Punjab and the Punjabis whom he loved from the bottom of his heart.

Meanwhile in Punjab, John Lawrence knew about the Sikh soldiery's disdain for the Hindustanis, but he also knew that Sikhs and Hindus had been close during Sikh rule, and that made him somewhat wary. A new regiment raised in Mian Mir on June 8, the 25th Punjabis comprised Punjabi Muslims, Sikhs and Dogras. Lawrence could freely arm the Sikhs and Muslims believing that they would not use them against the British but against their own Purbiyas.

By the end of the revolt, the army and military police in Punjab and present-day KPK was thus constituted:

Table 4.1 Army and Police Demographics

Communities	*No. of Men*
Europeans	11,000
Muslims	24,000
Sikhs	13,000
Hindus	8,000
Dogras	2,000

Lawrence had adopted the proverbial 'Divide and Rule' policy for the composition of Army and police with encouraging results for the British. John Lawrence functioned, in the eyes of most Britons west and north of Delhi, and even in some rebel eyes as the de facto Governor-General and the de facto C-in-C. To take Delhi, he was prepared to transfer his resources from Punjab. He continued monitoring the situation in the Ridge. He had a Sikh advisor named Nihal Singh Chachi at the crucial moment. Lawrence was shocked when he came to know that Amritsar's DC, Frederick Cooper had captured 303 out of 400 disarmed rebels. About 237 rebels were shot and thrown into a well in Ajnala, Amritsar and the remaining 66 were asked to be produced before him. Forty-five had already choked to death in the small place they were kept captive. Only twenty-one were only alive.

Two months before the Ajnala killings, a similar cruel end awaited the 120 deserters who were blown apart by heavy guns by none other than Edwardes and Nicholson.

While Punjab's Sikhs did not desire Mughal rule, Punjabi Muslims did not want Sikh rule again and the British rule was an acceptable alternative to most Punjabis. On a broader perspective, the Punjabis were aloof from the revolt of 1857, some instances of sympathy for the rebels notwithstanding. On June 9, Jalandhar's Delhi-bound rebel sepoys released prisoners and looted government houses in Ludhiana, joined by many Muslims of Ludhiana. Abdul Qadir Ludhianvi, one of the city's leading Arains joined the rebels.

In Sialkot on July 9, Hindu and Muslim Hindustanis, revolted and marched to Gurdaspur and were joined by hundreds from adjacent villages. On July 12, near Gurdaspur, John Nicholson and his column faced them. The jail in Sialkot had been unlocked on July 9 by the rebels and some Europeans were murdered, but the majority including women, children and the elderly, military officers too were spared. Later, the faithful servants in Sialkot protected the lives of the city's Europeans but 'the Europeans' houses and the Parsis' shops were completely gutted.

On the morning of July 10, Sikh levies helped MacMahon, a young Briton in clearing Sialkot's cantonment of looters killing 24 men. Jail officers and other Indian employees who connived in the revolt in Sialkot were hanged after a quick trial.

The defiance in Jhelum (July 7-8) was a response to the sepoys' glimpse of European troops arriving to disarm them. In the battle that ensued, 40 British and many times more Hindustani sepoys were killed. However, the local population did not support the rebels.

A native regiment was disarmed on July 7 in Rawalpindi in John Lawrence's presence and the sepoys found no local backing. Forty sepoys who were deserters in Rawalpindi were shot or captured. Ferozepur's disarmed 10th Native Cavalry, consisting mostly of Hindustani Muslims, ran all the way via Hansi to Delhi along with many horses. They were sympathetic to the Mughal Emperor.

The Peshawar-based 51st Native Infantry which had already been disarmed was less fortunate. A rumour that the regiment's men had obtained arms and hidden them triggered a search. Facing guns, they ran towards Jamrud, near the Khyber. All 870 were killed in pursuit or, later by a firing squad. The whole regiment was decimated.

On September 1, 1857, men of 300 villages of Dhund tribesmen attacked Murree but were repelled by the British who had prior information about the same.

The Gogera rebellion is a well-known Punjabi part of the 1857 revolt. Ahmed Khan Kharal roused all the important tribes of the region on the Ravi side of the district known as Sahiwal. The rebellion was joined by Wattos, Joyas, Fatianas and Sials. The idea of restoring Mughal rule appealed to Ahmed Khan. The Sikh Cavalry, a company of British infantry and three heavy guns were taken to attack Ahmed Khan and his supporters. Reinforcements were brought in from Multan, Jhang and Gurdaspur. Ahmed Khan and his son were killed.

On July 19, John Lawrence was back in Lahore. Command at the Ridge awaited help from Punjab urgently as other troops were far from Delhi. Nicholson was asked by him on July 22 to hasten towards Delhi with the movable Column which was now 4,000-strong. Needing no persuading, Nicholson commandeered batteries and gunners for his Column.

Rejoining his Column before it neared Delhi, Nicholson led its entry onto the Ridge on August 14. His Column had 4,200 men, of whom 1,300 were Europeans. The Sikhs comprised a majority of the rest, but Punjabi Muslims, Pashtuns and Dogras were also among them. The British were fortunate to be perched on the Ridge, as realised by Nicholson who assumed charge of difficult operations while he and everyone else eagerly awaited the arrival of a 'long train of heavy guns pulled by elephants and of bullock wagons loaded with shot, shells, and of all kind'.

On July 24, Nicholson got information that rebels in large numbers with heavy guns had marched towards Najafgarh to harass the train expected from the rear and disrupted its passage. As it rained, Nicholson with 16 guns and 2,500 men made a pre-emptive attack. His soldiers were Punjabi Sikhs, Muslims, Dogras and Europeans. It was July 25. The rebels were beaten and killed in scores. Then Nicholson returned to the ridge with captured guns. Four of his officers and 91 of his men were killed.

Najafgarh was a big setback for the rebels, who wanted to discuss a truce but they were rebuffed. On September 4, elephants of the siege-train carried the batteries which would breach the Delhi walls. Men brought in from Punjab started to erect batteries near Delhi despite intermittent firing by the rebels. By September 7, batteries were ready.

John Lawrence had sent all 1,000 European soldiers, many of whom were sick. Ultimately despite some initial indecision, on September 14, 4 columns of British troops marched forward through breaches in northern and western sides but found the rebels, ready to fight, lurking from every corner.

As the men slowed down at the Lahori Gate side, Nicholson urged them to march forward and then he was hit by a bullet from the back. Nicholson was brave to the point of insanity. He had thrown caution to the winds such was his keen desire to succeed; at any cost. A sepoy called Kaleh Khan had shot him. Nicholson was taken to the field hospital in the afternoon. Many other Britons were either wounded or killed. Casualties continued to mount. Another person injured was Charles Nicholson, the brother of John.

Between the end of May and September, about 4,000 from the British side died and it included many Indians also but Delhi was recaptured by the British. On the first day 8 officers and 265 men were killed in action. It included 103 Indians. Of the wounded, 52 were officers, 822 were men including 310 Indians.

Major General Wilson became the military ruler in the Diwan-i-Khas on September 20. Zafar and his sons had fled from their palace. The king was discovered in Humayun's Tomb by William Hodson. finding espionage first from the Ridge and now from Delhi, Hodson brought Zafar, his wife Zeenat and their son Jawan Bakht back to the fort promising to spare them their lives. They were imprisoned on September 21.

The following day, three other Mughal princes also hiding in Humayun's tomb Mirza Mughal, Mirza Khizr Sultan and Mirza Abu Baler, surrendered to Hodson. En route to the city, Hodson shot the three princes with his own hand.

Soon, twenty-one Mughal scions were hanged, and thus the whole dynasty was almost wiped out in 1857. Charles Nicholson recovered but John Nicholson could not. He died on September 23, 1857.

The British killed many civilians who were often unarmed. The Sikh and Muslim soldiers complied with the British orders with glee. In an incident outside the fort, 400 mutineers were hanged one after another and the British watched the scene and sipped their whiskies with sodas.

After Delhi was in British control, the British sent their Sikh and Muslim troops under Colin Campbell and Havelock after the mutineers to Awadh and the Rohilla country.

In September 1857, Colonel Neill was dead and two months later Havelock was no more; he died of dysentery. In March 1858, Campbell's soldiers had made Lucknow safe, assisted by the Sikh soldiers on rampage. Hodson was also in Lucknow and looking for booty, he marched into a Begum Palace, only to be shot in the abdomen. He died a few hours later.

By the summer of 1858, Rohilkhand and Awadh were back in British hands, thanks to the Punjabi soldiers. In June, the Rani of Jhansi was killed in Gwalior. Nana Sahib and Begum Hazrat Mahal had to leave India.

In London, Parliament abolished the Company rule and asked Queen Victoria to take up the governance of India and the Governor-General would henceforth be called Viceroy as well. In November 1858 a proclamation by the Queen assured native princes that their rights and dignity would be protected.

Delhi was formally ceded to Punjab in February 1859 becoming one of its districts. Punjab's head would now be called lieutenant-governor rather than chief commissioner. Robert Montgomery became Punjab's first lieutenant-governor, with jurisdiction over Delhi as well, for forty-seven-year-old John Lawrence had decided that it was time for him to return to England. He left India in February. He was created a baronet, granted a GCB, made a Privy Councillor for his service in the mutiny and he received an annual pension from the East India Company of £2,000. Canning declared in July 1859 'War is at an end'.

After the Mutiny

In Punjab and across India decades of imperialist success followed the mutiny of 1857. The British learnt lessons from the Revolt but it cannot be said for the Punjabis and other Indians. One unique feature of the mutiny was the Hindu-Muslim unity against the British. The divide between the elite and the common people was another feature which caused the failure of the mutiny. The Revolt's principal leaders lacked good cohesion with the peasants. The Empire cleverly continued its strategy of keeping Punjab's Muslims, Hindus and Sikhs divided based on their religious affiliations.

After the mutiny of 1857, the British decided, not to proselytise and recognise the sensitivities of India's chiefs and aristocrats. The British thought of providing Punjabis and other Indians a better quality of life by building roads and canals, railway lines, post and telegraph offices, schools, hospitals, colleges, universities and law courts. They wanted to encourage farming and also recruit new soldiers for the Empire's armies from rural Punjab but keep the Indians away from big weapons. The soldier was an agent of the British Empire in his village.

Peace was now being maintained in the Punjab from 1860 onwards. Canals built between 1860 and 1920 brought close to 10 million acres of new land under agriculture. Ownership of land went in a large share from village or tribe to an individual farmer and the same was recorded in the books. The rate of land revenue was lowered and as the agricultural output soared, the government's revenue increased proportionately. The exports of cotton, wheat and oilseeds from Punjab were being handled by the British banks, ships and agencies. The British Empire manipulated Punjab's growing wealth to fill its coffers.

Trade expanded in Punjab and land was monetised and agriculture became commercialised. The moneylending business prospered and this was mostly in the hands of Hindus and Sikhs. Indian banks were started but they were doing more business in cities rather than villages where the peasant depended on the ubiquitous moneylender. Mortgaging land was common.

Cities grew and there was a rise in urbanisation. Tree-lined avenues emerged in the 'civil lines' of Lahore, Amritsar,

Rawalpindi, Multan and Ludhiana, where British rulers and their immediate Indian juniors lived. The cantonments lodged soldiers and their officers. In Rawalpindi alone, 5000 British soldiers were quartered.

Started by the Christian missionaries and the government, new schools expanded literacy. Higher education opened up. Lahore's Government College started in 1864 and the University of the Punjab on January 1, 1882; also, in Lahore. A medical college had opened in 1860 in the city, Forman Christian college (a Presbyterian institution) in 1866, and a law college in 1870.

Although G.W. Leitner, an education administrator in the province tried to revive Arabic, Persian and Sanskrit, his wish was not fulfilled; Urdu rather than Punjabi became the medium of instruction up to the matriculation level.

A new small Indian middle-class emerged, educated in English and entering government service or professions like teaching, medicine and the law. In the bureaucracy and also in the professions, Punjab's Hindus—chiefly Khatris, Aroras, Brahmins and Banias advanced far more rapidly than the province's vast majority of Muslims.

Punjab During 1859-71

Sir Robert Montgomery 1859-65

Sir Robert Montgomery (1808-1887) was born in 1808. He was appointed the member of the Punjab Board of Administration after Charles Grenville Mansel in 1850. When the Board of Administration was dissolved in 1853, he was appointed Judicial Commissioner. His duties included the superintendence of education, road, police and municipalities. During the mutiny of 1857, he disarmed the sepoys at Lahore on May 13, 1857.

On February 26, 1859, he was appointed Lieutenant Governor of the Punjab, and held that post till 1865, when he resigned and returned to England on pension.

It was during his time that the Penal Code was extended to the Punjab in 1862. Compared to the former years, the Sessions cases were far fewer. A very large number of cases were disposed of by the District Magistrates.

The powers of the financial commissioners were enhanced in 1865 for the purpose of hearing appeals or suits regarding land, or the rent, revenue or produce 0f land, until the establishment of a Chief Court, with two or more judges. This act was passed to reduce the burden of the Judicial Commissioner, whose office was abolished, and a Chief Court consisting of two judges, was created in Lahore with final appellate authority in civil and criminal cases.

The Court of Judicature Act IV of 1866, was a re-enactment of the provisions of Act XXVII of 1865. This act was generally known to amend the constitution of the Chief Court of Judicature in the Punjab and its dependencies. In addition to the above acts, Acts of the Legislature were extended to the Punjab such as the pleader's, Mukhtiar's and Revenue Agent's Act.

At the end of 1869, there were 540 tribunals of various kinds for disposal of criminal Civil or Revenue cases, i.e. one tribunal to every 32,400 personnel. These were apart from the settlement courts.

The Chief Court, consisting of three Judges (one of them a Barrister), the final appellate authority in civil and criminal cases.

The Court of the Financial Commissioner.

12 Divisional Courts of Sessions and Appeal.

32 Courts of District Officers.

119 Courts of Assistants to District Officers, Native and European.

8 District Small Cause Courts.

8 Cantonment Courts.

7 Boards of Honorary Magistrates in towns.

216 Courts of Tehsildars and Naib-Tehsildars.

22 District Honorary Magistrates

Mr. Princep became Settlement Commissioner in 1863. He undertook the revised Settlements of Amritsar, Gurdaspur and Sialkot and his assistants looked after the revised Settlements of Lahore, Gujranwala, Gujrat and Montgomery. Revision of the rights of Kangra was effected by Mr. J.B. Lyall.

The Punjab government was strongly in favour of a very lenient assessment as it was on the verge of a great development of trade and a big rise in agricultural produce. The British wanted to keep Punjab in peace and encourage the rapid rise in agricultural activities. The policy of making permanent settlements in well-developed tracts was under discussion, and had been accepted in-principle by the orders issued by the Secretary of State in 1862 CE.

Famines

The first *famine* in the Punjab, as per records available occurred in 1783-84 CE. It was acute in the neighbourhood of Delhi. The Eastern Punjab was severely affected by this *Chalisa* famine (it corresponded to the year 1840 of the Bikrami calendar). In 1869, 300,000 cattle died in Hissar only and a few years later, Rohtak lost 37 per cent of its stock.

The cultivator had no rights to trade with, and had not much concern beyond raising and harvesting his crops. The harvest fulfilled his immediate requirements—food and warmth—which were easily satisfied by soil and climate. There was hardly any pressure or incentive to produce more. Beyond production, other activities were managed for him by the state farmer or revenue officer or the village headman as the village was subservient to the local authorities.

Under such conditions, progress lagged and the generation of wealth was slow. Bumper harvests caused a surplus which replenished the stores but the community's economic upliftment was not achieved by it.

Immense economic loss on the other hand was caused by a severe drought. The former could not counterbalance the latter. The trading community could not use the market dynamics by absorbing losses of drought using the profits gained during the boom period. The more efficient organisation of commerce and communications was lacking, in this regard.

Famines occurred at long intervals and a development of trade and communications in that area was not stimulated enough to deal with food-grains and other goods. No province could generate asurplus unless there were rewards commensurate with the labour expended.

Only the districts between the Jamuna and the Sutlej were affected by the famine of 1860-61. This resulted from the Mutiny in part and in part due to the deficient rainfall over two years followed by a failed monsoon in 1860. The principles adopted in 1833-34 were again followed. The relief mainly in the form of cooked food was provided. Practically the same tract was again affected in 1868-69, but the great influx of famine-stricken immigrants from Rajasthan exhausted the private charity resources.

The government acknowledged its responsibility to supplement aid by charitable organisations and about Rs. 3,00,000 of revenue was remitted in the Punjab.

Amritsar during Famine

During the years 1868-69, the city of Amritsar was affected and distressed persons from British and other territories depended wholly upon charity. Relief works were started on which labour was paid for at famine rates, such as roads from Taran Tarn to Jandiala, Vairowal, and Hari-ke-ghat, and from the city of Amritsar to Ajnala.

The poor were fed from designated houses in Amritsar city and at the tehsil's headquarters. The work of filling in the great ditch which was a fruitful source of disease, was begun using nearly three thousand labourers a day. The work was brought to a close in April, 1869, after the rain had removed the main fear of famine, but had to be re-opened in August, when the usual rains again failed. The Ahluwalia Dhab, a morass in the centre of the city, was next taken up and nearly 1,00,000 labourers were employed to fill it up.

The Great Famine 1877-97

The great famine of 1877-78 hardly affected Punjab and only scarcity existed. Fazilka and the Districts of the Delhi division, were the worst affected. From 1878 onwards, despite short harvests, the Punjab had a respite till 1896-97. The monsoon was deficient in 1895 as it weakened in August itself and it resulted in a poor autumn harvest which was followed by a deficient spring crop in 1896.

The Lahore and Rawalpindi Divisions were affected in parts. The monsoon failed again in 1898 and 1899, and it supervened in the same tracts. A high rate of mortality among cattle was caused by the scarcity of fodder and the human suffering knew no bounds. Relief was provided in terms of 52 million day-units at a cost of Rs. 4.8 million. To alleviate the sufferings of the peasants, the government decided to forego Rs. 4.4 million of land revenue and as soon as favourable rain fell in the autumn of 1900, Rs 1.9 million was granted for the purchase of seeds and cattle.

The effects of scarcity on the population of the Province was practically negligible. The famine of 1899-1900, the most severe since the annexation of the Punjab, affected the health of the people but there were no mass deaths.

Despite the two famines of the decade 1891-1900, the population in Hissar and Rohtak Districts, as per the Census of 1901 showed an increase of 5,711 since 1891 in the former, and an increase of nearly 10 per cent in the latter.

Practically no deaths from actual starvation were recorded in the province in the famines. The cholera was most to be feared; but when famine ceased, after a plentiful monsoon, malaria killed hundreds of people.

The government decided to take protective measures: a) extension of railway and (b) irrigation. As to the former, from the point of view of famine protection, the province was as a whole well off and further plans were being made to channellise the enormous surplus being generated by the large canal colonies. Regarding irrigation, much was done and much more was in the pipeline. The Chenab and Jhelum canals, by rendering cultivable a vast area of waste, had been of incalculable help in reducing the pressure in thickly populated districts. The insecure tracts were to be rendered productive by the extension to them of irrigation to rule out any famine.

The Ambela Campaign 1861-68

In 1824, one Sayyid Ahmad Shah, the Pindari, along with about forty followers among the Yusufzai tribes settled on the Peshawar border. He sought refuge in Swat in 1827, after being driven by the Sikhs, went to Buner and eventually he seized Peshawar. His Pathan disciples, tired of his attempted reforms, drove him across the Indus to Balkot in Hazara. There he was attacked by the Sikhs under Maharaja Sher Singh and was defeated and slain.

Sayyid Akbar Shah, his surviving disciple sought refuge at Sittana, a village of the Utamanzai Yusufzai. Here under Sayyid Akbar Shah, spiritual chief of Swat, the Hindustanis built a fort and established a colony. It was a good place to hide and soon political refugees, escaped criminals, and deserters from British India began coming here. In 1853 an invasion of the territory of the Khan of Ambela British feudatory, necessitated a punitive expedition. The fanatics made an attack on the camp of the British Assistant Commissioner of Mardan in 1858. It demanded action. The tribes settled on the northern side of the Mahaban mountain and used to kidnap Hindu traders from Hazara, and in 1863 they reoccupied Sittana.

Two British columns, one from Peshawar and the other from Hazara, were organised. The 9,000 strong former column under Sir Neville Chamberlain, occupied the Ambela Pass fulfilling the initial task of marching through the Chamla valley and attacking Sittana. After an uprising en masse, the tribes of Buner and Swat made repeated attacks on the British. However, the march to Chamla valley continued and the British lost 20 officers. But the Hindustanis holed up at Malka were silenced. Their stronghold was destroyed by the people of Buner, as a condition for their surrender.

After the departure of Montgomery in 1865, Montgomery Hall was built; financed by the Chiefs of Punjab. It was built close to Lawrence Hall in Lahore in 1866.

Punjab Under Sir Donald McLeod (1810-72)

Sir Donald McLeod, an Indian administrator was born at Fort William, Calcutta on May 6, 1810 and he was the son of Lieutenant-General Duncan McLeod (1780-1856). In 1826 he entered Haileybury, where he became a friend of Sir John Lawrence, and on December 10, 1828 reached Calcutta. He was posted at Monghyr in Bengal for some time but in 1831 spent a short time on the special service created by Lord William Bentinck for the suppression of the 'thugs' and dacoits. In 1849 he succeeded Sir John Lawrence as Commissioner of Jalandhar, and the trans-Sutlej states. He became the Financial Commissioner of the Punjab in 1854.

He remained at Lahore throughout the Mutiny and in 1859 he returned to England. But he was back at Lahore the following year. He was President of the Famine Relief Committee in 1861 and in 1865 he became Lieutenant-Governor of the Punjab, and was made KCSI in 1866, and retired in 1870. He is credited to have established the Lahore Museum and incorporated the Punjab Murderous Outrages Act 1867.

McLeod was a sincerely religious man but somewhat slow in business matters. Very few administrators had managed, as McLeod, to gain the esteem of both natives and Europeans.

Punjab University, Lahore

A proposal to the Supreme Government was submitted in 1858 by the Punjab Government to establish a University at Lahore. The Government sanctioned the establishment of an institution after a detailed correspondence, to be styled as the Lahore University College, which was to have a governing body or senate, consisting of the Lieutenant-Governor of the Punjab on the ground of their being eminent benefactors and original promoters of the institution, or persons distinguished or attainments in literature or science.

The Senate so constituted was empowered to expand the income, deciding fellowships and scholarships; make grants to educational institution; give rewards for vernacular translation of European standard works, higher studies of Oriental Literature, issue certificates of proficiency after examinations, etc.

Further the Senate was responsible with the educational officers of government, the 'Council of Education', or consulting body, in matters relating to education for the province. Equivalent of subscriptions and endowments up to Rs. 21,000 per annum were granted by the government.

Lastly, while disallowing for the present, the title of 'University' and declining to grant power to confer degrees, the government promised it to upgrade from institution to university, if it proved its worth.

The idea of the improvement and extension of vernacular literature generally and of the encouragement of Eastern classical language and literature was initiated by McLeod who addressed the Director of Public Instructions. He expressed his view for the development of the scheme. The Director communicated this for Punjab-i-Anjuman, a society at Lahore for the diffusion of useful knowledge under the presidency of Dr. Leitner.

McLeod's scheme became a university movement getting encouragement from greats, Sir Charles Aitchison and Sir James

Lyall. An oriental school and college was established by the senate at Lahore and also began lectureships, literary scholarships and conducted examinations.

In January 1870, McLeod's term expired but he was asked to continue for another six months.

On February 9, 1870 the Duke of Edinburgh and second son of Queen Victoria visited Lahore. A ball was arranged in the Montgomery Hall and an inspection of troops was held at Mian Mir. A conversation took place at Government House and he left for Amritsar on February 12.

Sir Henry Marion Durand (1870-71)

Durand left Britain for India in 1829, after training at the East India Company's Military Seminary at Addiscombe (1827–8) and he arrived in May 1830. Initially, he served as a Second Lieutenant in the Bengal Engineers. He rose to the rank of Major-General, and served in the First Anglo-Afghan War (1839–42), and the Second Anglo-Sikh War (1848–49). Appointed as the Resident of Gwalior (1849–52), he was also the acting Resident of Baroda (March 1852–March 1854). He served as a military commander in Western Malwa during the Indian Rebellion (1857–58). He was finally posted as Lieutenant-Governor of the Punjab on June 1, 1870.

In making a tour of the North-West Frontier of his province Durand arrived on the last day of 1870, his 'howdah' was crushed against the roof of the gateway and he was thrown to the ground, his head striking against a wall. He became senseless and though he recovered consciousness, he died peacefully on January 1, 1871.

Durand was a man of warm affection and great ability, gentle and courteous of manner and deeply against religious bigotry.

Communal-Relations in 1850s

In 1853-54, before the Revolt, a judicial commission who interviewed Muslims. Hindus and Sikhs regarding to the vernacular schools found harmony among these communities. The Sikhs, Muslims as well as the Hindus seemed to be shedding their religious bigotry or extremism.

But after the Revolt, the emphasis now was on purity and not harmony. Some Sikhs concluded, looking back, that their losing the kingdom was due to the corruption of pure Khalsa and they thought that the Hindu rites had been unnecessarily pushed and projected in the kingdom's ceremonies. Ranjit Singh's kingship and his court were not what the Sikh Gurus had preached.

Muslims also rued the abating of the purity of Islam and thought this ruined the Mughal Empire for more than 50 years now. In their view, the 1857 bid to resuscitate the Mughal Empire by a morally corrupted Muslim like Zafar was destined to fail. They thought that if they remained under the British, the cleaner version of Islam could be preserved

Even more willing than the Muslims and Sikhs to accept the Raj and embrace its schools, and relieved that the British rule ended Muslim supremacy in India, Punjab's Hindus gained maximum so far as capturing the new openings in trade, government service and the professions were concerned. But some of them looking for a purer Hinduism also jumped on the British bandwagon.

The British were cautious with respect to the propagation of Christianity, which was being advocated in Punjab in the 1850s and missionaries were acting from Ludhiana, Lahore, Amritsar and Sialkot. In 1853, Maharaja Duleep Singh, then fifteen, had accepted Christianity and so also one Harnam Singh Ahluwalia, a Kapurthala prince with lineage going back to Jassa Singh Ahluwalia.

In Amritsar, a maulvi named Imamuddin and Rallia Ram, a Hindu prominent Khatri became Christians in the 1850s. A person of the Churrah caste named Ditt of village Marali near Sialkot became the first of numerous Christian converts from his local community.

This upsurge of Christianity required the Muslims and Sikhs to introspect their lack of so-called purity. Muslims also faced the rise of Hindus' prosperity as they became a part of the British working machinery.

The Badshahi Masjid had been recently restored to Muslims. A few Muslims in Lahore established the Anjuman-i-Islamia in 1869. Four years later, Amritsar saw the emergence of its own Anjuman-i-Islamia. Both bodies attempted to popularise education and to make the British aware of the aspirations of Punjabi Muslims.

Soon there were similar Anjumans in more than a dozen towns in Punjab. Another association, the Anjuman-i-Himayat-i-Islam, came into being in Lahore in 1884 and was also replicated elsewhere in Punjab. This association aspired to save Muslim boys and girls from the ill-effects of 'the teachings of other religions' and also to 'acquaint the Muslims with the benefits of loyalty to the government'. This killing of two birds with one stone was pursued by all three communities, Muslims, Sikhs and Hindus, i.e. keeping their purity intact and becoming close to the British at the same time.

One of the first to chastise the Sikhs for a supposed compromise was old Baba Dayal, a Malhotra Khatri from Rawalpindi. He spoke in 1853 of the 'shortcomings of the mighty' and discouraged 'rites and observances' of the Hindu religion. Like other Sikhs, he discouraged the worship of images and insisted on returning to a formless god advocated by Guru Nanak. Baba Dayal caused a scare among the Christians but later he himself formed an off-shoot of Sikhism and led an altogether different course, leading a movement known as the Nirankaris.

Punjab During 1871-82

Sir Robert Henry Davies was appointed as the new Lt. Governor of Punjab in 1871. He was born in 1824 and educated at Charter House and Halleybury. He became a clerk in the Bengal civil service in 1844 and was an official under the East India Company and the British Raj for the rest of his career.

To the Commissioner of the Sutlej states he served as assistant, and later became the settlement officer of the Lahore division. Transferred to Oudh State, he became a Chief Commissioner there from 1868 till 1871 and then became Lieutenant Governor of the Punjab in 1871, serving till 1877.

Davies was made a KCSI in 1874, and appointed a Companion of the Order of the Indian Empire (CIE) in 1877. His tenure saw the following:

Murree made summer capital in 1873
Singh Sabha Movement
Mayo School of Industrial Arts's establishment
Opening of Lahore Zoo
Simla made summer capital in 1876

Delhi Durbar of 1877

He was a member of the Council of India, based in London after his return to the United Kingdom, from 1885 till 1895, when he retired.

Sir Robert Eyles Egerton became the Lt. Governor of Punjab after Davies in 1877. He was the youngest son of William Egerton. Born in 1827, he attended Haileybury between 1847-49.

Working as an aide to Sir Henry Davies the lieutenant governor of the Punjab Province, he later got himself appointed to the position himself in 1877. In 1857, during the mutiny, he was the Deputy Commissioner of Lahore. He was a Commissioner (acting) of Nagpur in 1869 and came back to Punjab in 1871. He worked as a member of the Governor-General's legislative council, from 1871 to 1874.

The Kuka Movement 1871-72

Early History of Namdharis

The Namdhari sect was founded by Balak Singh (1797-1862) of village Hazru of KPK, Pakistan. He was inspired by Jawahar Mal, known as Sain Sahib. Balak Singh emphasised living a simple life and shunning religious ritualism other than repeating God's name or Naam (hence Namdhari). Before he died, he chose one of his most ardent disciples, Ram Singh as his successor. The headquarters of the Namdharis shifted from Hazru to Ram Singh's village Bhaini in Ludhiana disrict.

Baba Ram Singh's (1816-85) first twenty years of life were spent at his native place, attending to the family business. When he was about 20, he was enlisted in the Khalsa army. He entered the military service of Maharaja Ranjit Singh in 1836 and remained in that position till 1845. He was attached to a regiment of Prince Nau Nihal Singh, a grandson of Ranjit Singh.

He had ample time in the army for his religious pursuits. In the First Anglo-Sikh war, Baba Ram Singh fought against the English at Mudki. After the occupation of Lahore, he gave up service. Baba Ram Singh saw the prevailing moral degeneration amongst the Khalsa. Drinking, plural wives, keeping mistresses, leading a life of luxury on the pattern of Muslim Amirs was the real character of the prosperous Sardars. The Sikh religion had been gripped by practices in contravention with Nanak's teachings. The social evils of Sati, child marriage and infanticide plagued the society.

He established the missionary as well as political foundation. Bands of musicians (*Ragi Jathas*) were sent from Bhaini Sahib for the propagation of the Sikh religion and social up-lifting; these bands were to sing only the hymns of the Holy Granth.

Baba Ram Singh had separate gurdwaras built for his followers and he appointed *subas* who collected funds. He arranged for training of young men in the use of weapons and built a paramilitary organisation. He abolished all distinction of caste among Sikhs; advocated indiscriminate marriages of all classes, etc. He advocated a sort of dress code for his followers who wore a different style of turban. Baba Ram Singh's religious discourses began to have a political fervour. When he administered *pahul*, he condemned wickedness of the Sikh princes and landowners; of many Hindu practices creeping in.

Kukas even avoided use of the post offices established by the British and depended upon their own arrangement of postal communication.

In early 1867, Baba Ram Singh requested the British government to allow him to visit Muktsar on the sacred day of Maghi but this was refused by the government. On the occasion of Holi he sought permission to hold a fair in his own village. The British wanted to restrict the number of visitors to be allowed. At Anandpur Sahib, Baba Ram Singh decided to hold the festival where Sikhs gathered for this purpose from all over the province. The Lieutenant Governor gave him the permission. Mahant Singh of Keshgarh gurdwara did not want the Kukas to be admitted into the precincts of Anandpur. Later the Kukas were allowed to enter the gurdwara proper under certain conditions.

Some of the Kukas joined the armies of the Indian princes and it did not go down well with the British. They feared armed rebellions by them once they returned to the Punjab. The Kukas visited Maharaja Ranbir Singh of Kashmir in 1869 and offered to join the state forces. The Maharaja's new regimcnt enlisted about 150 but the force was disbanded under pressure of the British.

In 1863, Baba Ram Singh wanted to go to Amritsar for Baisakhi celebrations and it alarmed the cautious British once again. But he was allowed to attend. After all, 1857 had happened just six year ago. When the Kukas announced two months later that a meeting would be held at Ferozepur district, prohibitors' orders were issued and all Kuka meetings were banned. Ram Singh was being monitored and was asked to limit his activities within Bhaini.

He arrived in Amritsar during Dussehra in 1867 with 3,500 followers and was allowed to baptise 2,000 Sikhs including those from well-to-do families. It was also during this period that many of the Kukas were found digging up graves and other superstitious places. Such desecration was done in Ludhiana, Amritsar, Jalandhar, Gurdaspur, Gujranwala, and Sialkot.

A band of ten Kukas started to destroy the butchers of Amritsar. On June 15, 1871, a murderous attack was made on the butchers in the slaughter-house, situated outside the Lahori Gate of Amritsar city. While four butchers were killed, three were badly wounded. Four of the accused–Fateh Singh, Beela Singh, Hakim Singh and Lehna Singh were hanged on September 15, 1871. It was alleged that the Kukas who murdered the Muslim butchers were led by Baba Ram Singh. Butchers at Raikot were murdered on July 15, 1871. In 1856, the slaughterhouse at Raikot, was started near a gurdwara. The vultures carried the bones from the slaughter-house and perched themselves on the temple walls to devocer the carrion. The Sikh priests narrated it to some of the Kukas who were on a visit to this gurudwara. To butchers were killed and seven were injured. Eight Kukas were hanged for it.

Baba Ram Singh was again restricted to his village and assembly of Kukas, anywhere in the Punjab was forbidden. On the Maghi festival of 1872, they assembled at Bhaini and passionate speeches were made. Some of the Kukas thought of attacking Malerkotla where they disapproved of the cow slaughtering. The Kukas were angry that one of their comrades Giani Rattan Singh had been hanged under false charges.

On January 13, 1872, the Kukas assembled at Bhaini and the religious fervour made 250 of them extremely agitated. They wanted to take revenge on some Muslim officers of Malerkotla who had the British patronage. Baba Ram Singh informed the police about the possible trouble. These men went to Pael, Patiala and then arrived near Malaud, the seat of Sardar Badan Singh and secured some arms. They next proceeded to Malerkotla which is nine miles from Malaud, and on the morning of the 15th, made a sudden attack on the palace of the Nawab and treasury of the state, but they were driven back. At Malaud and Malerkotla they had killed 10 men and wounded 17, while their own loss had been 9 killed and 38 wounded. On getting news of the attacks, the DC of Ludhiana started. Mr. Cowan came and by blowing by guns at Malerkotla, killed 49 of the captured Namdharis and the others were tried by the Commissioner and executed next day. It was a harsh decision by the British and for the manner of killing, the British removed Cowan from service and Forsyth from Punjab.

The Kuka outbreak of 1872 thus ended. The doctrines of Baba Ram Singh were responsible for what happened. He had become a danger to the British and was at once deported to Rangoon and remained a state prisoner there till his death in 1885.

The Namdhari fervour reached its peak in 1885 when its leader died and Maharaja Duleep Singh expressed his desire to return to Punjab. However, in 1890 Duleep Singh became loyal to the British once again.

Singh Sabha Movement

In 1873 in Amritsar, the first Singh Sabha was founded as a response to what were identified as three main threats:

- From Christian missionary activities who attempted to draw people from the Sikh community;
- From the 'reverse-proselytising' of the Arya Samaj, which denigrated Sikhs or claimed them as a minor Hindu sect;
- The possibility of losing British patronage owing to the disruptive actions of groups like the Namdharis.

The British felt comfortable with this movement which began when four Sikh students of Amritsar mission school expressed their desire to renounce their faith. A group of Sikhs meeting in Amritsar founded it. They included Thakur Singh Sandhanwalia, Baba Khem Singh Bedi and Bikrama Singh. Their aim was to take Sikhism to its pristine purity, publishing religious and historical books, recovering apostates and involving Englishmen in their activities.

It propagated messages in Punjabi and this movement became

quite popular in the 1880s and 1890s. They used the soldiers very effectively to reach out to the peasantry with the reformist ideology. A choir of reciters from a regiment was ready to visit the villages during the congregations and sing sacred hymns.

Arya Samaj

While the Sikhs and the Muslims were searching for means to become 'purer', Hindus were not left behind. They thought that Swami Dayanand Saraswati (1824-83) of Gujarat would be the perfect foil for this purpose. Swami visited Punjab in 1877. He opposed idol worship and other pernicious rituals but encouraged the *Havana Ceremony*. His *Satyarth Prakash* was published in 1875 and urged Hindus to revert to pure monotheism going back to the days of Vedas. The controversial book criticised Christianty, Islam, Sikhism and idolatrous Hinduism.

The Swami advocated a woman's right to read scripture and get educated. He despised untouchability and observed that Indians should learn from European achievements. The Swami's Arya Samaj quickly attracted a following among Puniabi Hindus. Arya Samajis set up 'Anglo-Vedic' schools and colleges in different parts of Punjab to promote education and they promoted the idea that Vedic beliefs could coexist with European modern thought.

When he came to the Punjab in 1877, he was at once acclaimed as a saviour of the ancient Aryan culture and civilisation. He attracted quite a few admirers, mainly from the ranks of the local Brahmo Samaj. Many devoted young men, like Lala Pandit Gurudatta, Hans Raj and Lala Lajpat Rai came under the fold of the new Samaj in a few years and they lent strength to it. He opened a branch of the Arya Samaj at Lahore. The Arya Samaj gained many Hindu and Sikh adherents via proselytisation (*Shudhi*—purification) which was an important part of its activities.

College at Lahore

His followers in the Punjab decided to found a college to serve the double purpose of perpetuating the memory of the great reformer and as a means of reviving and resuscitating the Vedic religion. A modest beginning was made with a High School which developed into the well-known Dayanand Anglo-Vedic College of Lahore. Lala Hans Raj became the Honorary Principal and served with devotion for 25 years.

Like the Fergusson College, requests were made to the university graduates to serve the institution on an ordinary allowance. It worked on the model of Aligarh, imparting religious education along with the normal curriculum at the DAV College. Inspiration also came from the Fergusson College of Poona (now Pune).

Division of the Samaj

In 1892 the Arya community got divided into two groups. One was the College or 'Cultured' party and the other Vegetarian or 'Mahatma' party. The former was progressive while the latter were similar to orthodox Hindus who advocated the ancient Hindu education.

Dayanand Anglo-Vedic (DAV) College's objectives were to encourage and enforce the study of:

(a) Hindi literature;

(b) Classical Sanskrit and the Vedas; and

(c) Sciences, both theoretical and applied and English literature

Furthermore, this college was to provide means of imparting technical education. According to Dayanand, everything worth knowing, even the latest inventions of modern science, were alluded to in the Vedas.

The Arya Samaj Reform Movement propagated abolition of caste, which had taken roots among the educated Hindus in the Punjab, and Dayanand Saraswati believed that this defect impeded the political advancement of the Hindus and started proselytising work to bring the lower castes and outcasts into their fold. He even tried to win back by the purification process those Hindus who had drifted to Islam and Sikhism under the very controversial *'Shuddhi Movement'*.

To the orthodox Hindus, the caste system was even dearer than the Vedas, and the violent hostility of militant Islam.

At the Samaj Anniversary in Lahore on November 30, 1907, , Prof. Lala Sain Das, M.A., gave an address. He urged the assembly to realise how little they were working compared with Christian Missions, how weak their spirituality was and how impotent socially through the caste system. He added:

> In India two new forces are now at work (1) English education, and (2) Christian evangelisation. The first a weakness to the Hindu society, is now in Arya Samaj, a source of strength. Superstition yielded to the scientific education. In order, therefore, to fully avail ourselves of the former and to nullify the effect of the latter, we should open as many schools ....where latest in science should be taught and education on modern lines was to be imparted to a number of students as the funds permitted.

Qadianis

The Muslim community was blessed with Mirza Ghulam Ahmed (1835-1908). Born in Qadian, northeast of Batala, Mirza Ahmad founded the Ahmadiyya sect in 1889. He was a proselytiser of high order. His forefathers had settled in Qadian in the sixteenth century and his family was conferred the family's title to Qadian and 5 nearby villages by Maharaja Ranjit Singh.

Ghulam Ahmad's writings and speeches aimed at proving Islam's superiority over Christianity, Hinduism and Sikhism, made him famous all over Punjab in the 1870s and 1880s. He also attracted a wide following in the province and had his roots in Punjab. In 1890, he claimed that he was the messiah who had communicated with the Prophet. Suddenly, he was at the receiving end and he became a leader of the heterodox sect.

Often Ahmed, the Christian missionaries, Arya Samajis and the Singh Sabha members entered into animated religio-political debates. As many new journals were there in the market in English, Urdu and Punjabi—the debate was carried to all corners of the Punjab. The British took comfort from the fact that Muslims, Hindus and Sikhs were not coming together or thinking of a common platform.

The religio-political controversies marking Punjab in the last quarter of the nineteenth century did not merely divide Muslims, Hindus and Sikhs from one another. They also produced schisms within each of Punjab's Muslim, Hindu and Sikh worlds.

Punjab's Arya-Samajis were boosted by Swami Saraswati but the acrimony in Punjab increased as many Hindus were unwilling to give up *Sanatan Dharam* or the typical conservative Hinduism. The Singh Sabhas were successful like the Muslim Anjumans and the Hindu Arya Samajis but there were offshoots like the Nirankaris and the Namdharis.

The perceptible threat to the Hindus, Muslims and Sikhs was common: Christianity. But Christianity did not expand as suspected but the unity of the Muslims, Sikhs and Hindus suffered a great deal.

Another dimension was added when at the end of the nineteenth century, a text appeared. It was titled *Ham Hindu Nahin* and was first published in 1898. It pressed its claim vehemently and vigorously to the distinction of the Sikh identity and religion and the author gave a versified note describing the characteristics of the Khalsa.

Bhai Kahn Singh Nabha wrote this book in order to clarify and answer the misconceptions and questions raised on the different identity of the Sikh religion. Writers discussed in detail the differences between Hinduism and Sikhism, as religions, in this book. Many letters were received by the writer from various Sikh scholars and prominent Sikh shrines, in favour of this book. The book did a deep analysis along with references to religious texts and historical incidents.

The Singh reformers felt a threat from the Arya Samaj more than the threat of Islam and Christianity. Some years back in 1888, Dayanand Saraswati got away by criticising the Sikhs in *Satyarth Prakash* but the times were changing fast, even though some Sikhs even at the start of the twentieth century stood behind orthodox Hinduism. These types of Sikhs were fast losing ground to the Singh Sabha.

Ganga Ram the Great

Sir Ganga Ram (1851-1927) was born to a police sub-inspector in Mangtanwala, a village 40 miles south-west of Lahore. Lahore city was transformed into the symbol of the colonial state. He had migrated to the city for better economic opportunities after acquiring a degree in engineering.

The colonial state, in the aftermath of the war of 1857, redeemedg and defined itself. The British tried to present continuity between former empires of India and the new British Empire.

Architecture played an important role in his constructions and led to the emergence of the Indo-Saracenic tradition. Under this architectural approach, the colonial state endeavoured to incorporate traditional structural techniques with colonial architecture. The British wanted to depict the British symbols of authority in traditional visual forms for the local people to appreciate these.

So, architecture was used as a powerful propaganda tool by the colonial state. Lahore, along with other major cities of British India, served as the template to be replicated in other places.

The Museum, Post Office Building, Aitchison College, Lahore High Court, the Anglican Cathedral, and National College of Arts stand as a testimony in Lahore to the brilliance of Sir Ganga Ram. Using a mixed or hybrid tradition, these buildings were constructed.

In such buildings we have balconies, columns and watchtowers which interact with domes, chattris (canopies), arches and screens. By raising such buildings of iconic status the glory of the British Empire got reflected. Sir Ganga Ram, thus, transformed the landscape of Lahore city. Thus, a new city, more glorious than the former, was raised from the debris of its past.

Lahore's Ganga Ram Hospital, later replicated in Delhi, was only one of the institutions he created as a philanthropist. He died in 1927 in London.

Rudyard Kipling

Also, part of the Lahore scene in the 1880s was a creator of another type. Rudyard Kipling (1865-1936) lived there for five years, from 1882 to 1887, as an assistant editor on the *Civil & Military Gazette.*

Scores of Kipling's short stories were written mainly in Simla and appeared in the Gazette. His *Kim* and *Jungle Book* and the famous poems were written later and outside India, but their spirits had been sourced from Punjab. Gunga Din was written four years after he left Lahore and reveal the Empire's uglier side.

Press

The newspapers and journals printed in Punjab were 263 in number by 1905 and they did the opposite of harmony. Most, including Hindu-owned ones, were published in Urdu, a few in English, and some in the Gurmukhi script. In the eastern districts, some started to appear in Hindi in Nagari characters.

The Vernacular Press Act, 1878 was enacted to restrict the

freedom of the Indian press and prevent the criticism of the British policies. It was proposed by the then Viceroy of India: Lord Lytton. So, *The Tribune* of Lahore came out in English and *The Hindu* from Madras. When the Vernacular Press Act was passed, there were 35 vernacular papers in Bengal, including the *Amrita Bazar Patrika*. *The Tribune* was brought out by a trust founded by Dyal Singh Majithia who was a sympathiser of the Brahmo Samaj. Many Muslims and Sikhs saw *The Tribune* as a Hindu publicity paper.

In response to the act, some vernacular papers in Calcutta became English-language ones. Lord Ripon, a liberal and recent Catholic repealed the hated Vernacular Press Act in January 1882.

Language Issue

The communities were greatly divided over the language issue as it assisted one for a government job. Competence in English was essential for getting a certain class of jobs. The use of Persian in West Punjab was discarded even though it had been used for official work for centuries.

The British were in a dilemma over choosing between Urdu, Punjabi and Hindi. In the North Indian areas ruled by them before 1849, Hindustani was favoured and orders were issued in UP to replace Persian with Hindustani in the Persian script. Some speakers of the language borrowed heavily from Sanskrit whereas the others borrowed from Arabic and Persian and the product was called Urdu.

This Urdu or Hindustani was used already by several of the Raj's officers who had learned it already before their posting in Punjab. This became a decisive factor for the use of Urdu in Punjab and not Punjabi.

Moreover, the British officers desired a pan-Indian or a link language. To them Urdu seemed the answer and in comparison, Punjabi and Pashto seemed 'barbarous'.

Not written widely in Punjab, Punjabi may have been a handicap. Punjab was plagued by Muslim-Sikh rivalry and the Gurmukhi script was related to the Sikhs' sacred texts and was unacceptable to Punjabi Muslims. G.W. Leitner and a few others underlined Punjabis' claims and it was pointed out that hundreds of Punjabi-language books existed, most of them in Gurmukhi but many also in the Shahmukhi (Persian) script, including several on the fine arts, and that powerful poetry had been composed in Punjab which was romantic and mystical.

The DC of Shahpur district was J. Wilson who proposed in 1894 that a Roman script based on Punjabi should be for both primary education and running of government. But it was early days for such a revolutionary idea in those days. *[Punjabi users of Social Media now use this Romanised Punjabi while communicating with each other in India, in Pakistan, around the world wherever a Punjabi is settled – author]*

The pro-Urdu lobby was quite strong and the British wanted to rule India with ease and for them the priority of a local language like Punjabi had no meaning. The British got ample support from bodies like Anjuman-i-Islamia and the Islamic preachers in mosques. The preachers never wanted the Muslim masses to become literate quickly which Punjabi could have helped and instead the preachers preferred Urdu.

In UP, the advancement of Hindi along with English and Urdu did not go down well with the Muslim leaders in Punjab and Hindi was bracketed with Punjabi as the languages of non-Muslims and this phenomenon did no good to Punjabi or Gurmukhi.

In the 1880s, in Ludhiana, many Muslim and Hindu girls along with Sikh girls learnt Punjabi in the Gurmukhi script in schools or in Devnagari and Persian script at home. Even though the viewpoint of the Muslims in Lahore, Rawalpindi and Multan was different than what was practised in Ludhiana, the girls of these areas would write in Gurmukhi script; if they wrote at all in Punjabi. This was a continuing process from the days of the great Maharaja who had opened schools for the girls.

Ultimately Urdu joined English as the language of the administration in Punjab and became the medium of instruction in schools. Hindi had to wait till 1917 to be added to the curriculum. One Bengali person P.C. Chatterji made a failed attempt in 1909 to make Punjabi the language of instruction even after securing the support of Governor Louis Dane.

Muslim newspapers warned that Punjabi was being used to block Urdu. It was alleged by the Muslim intelligentsia that the Hindus had rejected Urdu in UP and were now forcing the Muslims in Punjab to learn Punjabi.

Although it was expected that a language spoken by all Punjabis might unite them but instead the issue created so much bitterness that people started to talk of two Punjabs: one Muslim and the other Hindu.

In the 1880s and 1890s riots between Hindus and Muslims occurred in Multan, Mianwali, Dera Ghazi Khan, Ludhiana, Rohtak and Delhi. The rural Punjab, however, remained peaceful. Often there was an urge to tease the other community with the minds of the people already poisoned over the years of acrimonious propaganda. To some extent, the prosperity of the Hindus and Sikhs caused resentment among the Muslims who could not encash the benefits under the Raj. The cow-slaughter often triggered riots.

Often the disturbances died down quickly and normalcy was restored. The British often took a non-partisan attitude and did not create religious animosities.

The press in Punjab contributed to the occurring of riots. Papers like the *Tribune* or the Muslim-owned papers like *Rafiq-i-Hindi, Rahbar-i-Hind, Chaudwin Sadi* and *Paisa Akhbar* were guilty of fanning the fire of communal hatred, *Akhbat-i-Aam* was appreciated for its conciliatory approach and admitting to its past indulgence in publishing 'hate material'.

Changing Communal Relations

Despite all this, it seems that the Muslims, Hindus and Sikhs lived peacefully with each other whether in the village or the town, at work and at a fair. The festivals were celebrated together. Hindus and Sikhs visited the Sufi shrines.

In the last quarter of the nineteenth century, the indigenous faiths were challenged by colonialism and missionary activity which caused rapid growth in the number of native Christian converts. This resulted in the launching of religious reform movements in North India and resulted in religious and sectarian revivalism. The number of Punjabis who embraced Christianity were 3,912 in 1881 and the number became over 19,000 in 1891 and by 1901 it was close to 38,000. John Oman wrote in 1908 *'The .... aggressiveness of Christian missionaries has forced the Hindus...to reconsider the foundations of their faith....'.*

Writers have argued that such activities of nineteenth century religious reformers magnified the blurred religious differences in colonial Punjab. Punjab has been marked as the centre by Ayesha Jalal from which Muslim separatist and Hindu nationalist discourses radiated to the rest of North India. This was a period of growing communalism in the region. Because of the strong presence of Christian missions, sectarian educational institutions and printing presses, the urban area became an important centre for these burgeoning social and religious societies and the growing organisational strength of, and the rivalry among the religious strengthened existing communal divisions. This process of reinterpreting the past and presenting a new sceptical vision of the future badly and forever changed relations among the communities who had lived in harmony for generations.

In March 1897, 40-year-old Pandit Lekh Ram, a prominent Arya Samajist was killed by stabbing and this worsened Punjab's communal atmosphere. He had taken part in debate contests with Mirza Ghulam Ahmed, the Qadiani. It was alleged that some of his writings offended the Muslims. His death resulted in the trade boycott between the Hindus and Muslims in many towns. His funeral was attended by 8,000 people. Members of the Arya Samaj planned revenge. Rawalpindi was chosen this time as a city for revenge where a Hindu, dressed as a Muslim, presented poisoned sweets to the Muslims after a prayer in the mosque. Fourteen Muslims were taken ill and two died.

Hindu-Muslim rivalry took another turn for the worse when James Lyall was said to be formulating a policy to appease the Muslims by giving them a quota in government jobs to reach the desired ratio of Hindu and Muslim bureaucrats.

Now a strange phenomenon was taking place. The upcoming Punjabis were not identifying themselves merely as Punjabis but with an identity which was of their religious communities.

Founded in 1875, the Arya Samaj's membership rose to nearly 1,00,000 in 1901, and during the next four decades the Samaj founded in North India more than 150 schools and colleges, generally called Dayanand Anglo-Vedic (DAV) institutions. The role of the Arya Samaj in the growth of communalism in Punjab has been well-debated. DAV College of Lahore came up in 1888.

Islamia College followed in Lahore in 1892 and Khalsa College started in Amritsar in the same year.

The first Hindu Conference was hosted in Lahore on October 21-22, 1909 and in it 800 delegates came to participate from all over Punjab. Lala Lajpat Rai was among the many prominent leaders. The Muslim-Hindu relations were well expressed in his speech on October 21. He said:

> The relations between the two communities are more strained today than they were in 1880 or before, while the Muslims have gained in unity and solidarity....the Hindus have lost ground in every direction.

British Army

Till the 1880s, the Raj's primary military concern was to prevent another rebellion and Indians in the British army were required merely for internal security. In 1858, when the Empire's Peel Commission was trying to formulate a military policy in India, the three-man Punjab team comprising John Lawrence, Herbert Edwardes and Neville Chamberlain emphasised that the Indian soldiers be stationed in their own provinces only to rule out any All-Indian network.

The second recommendation of the three men was the ethnic mix of a native regiment which was suggested to be of a mixed nature. For example a regiment based in Punjab could have Sikh Jats, Hindu Jats (or Dogras), Punjabi Muslims, and Pashtuns. the three armies of Bengal, Bombay and Madras were to remain, therefore, segregated at Pan-India-level and minimal interaction between any two regiments was encouraged so that if one regiment rebelled, the other regiment would be ready to counter it. The ideas were implemented and the armies remained separate.

The Bengal Army stationed in the North had fewer Poorbias but more Punjabis and Gorkhas. Different groups were mixed in a regiment so that they just followed the orders from British officers and were not to be from the same stock so as to rule out any mutiny like situation. In 1870, Punjab supplied 35 per cent of the Bengal Army's soldiers.

The situation changed in 1890 when Frederick Roberts took charge of the Bengal Army. He did not believe in mixing the various people to balance each other in the army and instead believed that to increase the efficiency what was needed was the recruitment of 'martial races' in adequate numbers. He was not the first to suggest this point but recommended it strongly and the Empire acted upon it. The specific races in question were:

- The Sikh Jats from Central Punjab
- Muslim Gakhars, Janjuas, Awans, Tiwanas and Khattar Jats from North-Western Punjab
- Hindu Jats from Hissar and Rohtak
- Hindu Dogras from Jammu and Kangra
- Pashtun Tribes from Frontiers
- Gorkhas of Nepal

After this, there was slow abandonment of mixed regiments and support for 'mono' regiments started which seemed simpler to organise and were deemed to be more efficient. Although divide-and-rule remained a British policy, it was not deployed at the regimental level. No attempt was made by the British to bring the Sikhs and Pashtuns closer in the army, or the Sikhs and Punjabi Muslims. Instead the Raj wanted the Khalsa to be purer, i.e. Sikh troops to be strictly turbaned and bearded.

Muslim conservatism was demanded from the 'martial' Muslim tribes providing recruits: Tiwana, Gakhar, Janjua and Khattar Jat. For the British, it made strategic sense to encourage Sikh and Muslim fundamentalism to keep them one against the other and at the same time ensuring that they were pro-Empire in this period.

Recruitment was now increasingly confined to a few locations and a few castes or tribes. In the town of Rawalpindi, officers recruited Punjabi Muslims of the Salt Range—Gakhars, Janjuas, Awans, Khattars and Tiwanas. Jat Sikhs were taken into the army from Amritsar. Hindu Jats were taken from Rohtak, Hissar, Gurgaon and Western UP. For Dogras, the centre was Jalandhar town. The Pathans were absorbed by the recruitment centre at Peshawar.

Ahirs, Gujjars and the Awadh groups who joined the Bengal army in sizeable numbers were losing out to the said 'martial races.' The rural community's social structure was often replicated in a company or regiment, where the subedar major was likely also to be an elder in his village.

The Punjabi percentage in the Indian army steadily rose.

By the year 1900, Punjab supplied more than 50 per cent of the combatants of the entire Indian Army.

After providing estimates in 1855 and 1868, India's British rulers conducted a comprehensive census in 1881 and every ten years thereafter. If essential for governance, the census also fitted perfectly into imperial strategy.

Condition of the Muslim Agriculturists of the Western Punjab in the Nineteenth Century

The Punjab was annexed in 1849. The Muslim tribes of its Western half were now owners and cultivators of the soil. The opportunity for introducing the best possible revenue and land laws based on the British experience of Bombay, Bengal, and the North-Western Frontier were supposed to do the best possible welfare for the people of the Punjab. Easy credit was being offered against the market valuation of land. Fixed cash assessment of the farmers was replaced by fluctuating kind payments. Both these changes were supposed to give people double benefit.

Unfortunately, in the Punjab area under consideration, a good production was never certain and these two factors along with a complicated system of civil law and procedure always risked the farmers becoming serfs to their creditors. A glance at their economic condition is necessary, because the highest administrators, from official optimism and their luxurious remoteness from rural facts, still believed in the general prosperity of the Punjab agriculturists.

The indebtedness of the agricultural classes was on the increase as revealed by the inquiries of 1870. In 1859 the number of civil suits rose enormously and the new law forced creditors into the courts every third year when they failed to get their debtors to sign their bonds with interest and compound interest added. Thus, the civil courts were soon clogged with so many backlog cases.

In 1866 the Chief Court the Punjab was established at Lahore. The Judicial Commissioner was superseded and Act VIII of 1859 which was the Civil Procedure Code of the Regulation Provinces was extended to the Punjab.

The number of cases rose steadily and reached 1,65,520 in 1866 and 2,05,606 in 1870 which meant that there was one suit for eighteen heads of families. It was too high a figure. The figure became 2,71,375 in 1871.

The Lieutenant-Governor commented that the British officers who recommended some relief to the peasants to come out of debt were 'taking a gloomy view of the financial position of the peasantry' and 'the state of the peasantry is .... prosperous!'

Five years later this opinion was emphatically endorsed by Sir Richard Temple and he felt that 'in the Punjab the condition of the peasant proprietors was eminently creditable to British rule' and that the peasants were under no seriòus financial burden. But there was this rising flood of petty litigation, in which agriculturists were chiefly the defendants and Banias the plaintiffs and the claims on 'money due' was constantly rising.

To reduce the number of pending cases, in 1874-75, two new posts were created: Munsiffs and Judicial Assistants. This alteration helped the disposal of suits and it was well appreciated by the moneylenders and village shopkeepers but not by the people at large who felt that the Banias were being granted a big favour.

Despite the optimism shown by the British officers in describing the state of the peasants which was the official narrative, it must be said in their enthusiasm to implement the British like judicial system and law, it was the bania who gained the most at the cost of the peasant.

The state of peasants in 14 districts of the pre-NWFP days can be discussed to analyse this Bania vs Peasant deadlock. The conclusion to which the Famine Commission came in 1880 was, in their words:

> ....about one-third of the land-holding classes are deeply in debt and the same proportion is in debt from where they can recover themselves.... the most eligible customers of the moneylenders. The classes which have the best security to offer are

A Commission, then, of unbiased experts, after carefully considering the best obtainable evidence, gave a verdict directly contrary to that of the Punjab Government and Sir R. Temple. Of the 14 districts of the Western Punjab in 1880, five only were quiet rural districts, namely Gujrat, Shahpur, Jhang, Muzaffargarh and Montgomery. The headquarters of the other nine had large garrisons.

Gujrat and Shahpur were settled in around 1860 and the other three districts Montgomery, Muzaffargarh, and Jhang—were settled between 1868 and 1880. These districts lie together south of the Salt Range, in the great arid plain. The opinions of the Settlement Officers on the condition of the peasantry in them, may be accepted as absolutely correct.

Jhang

In 1880, it was reported that from 40 to 50 per cent of owners, and 60 to 70 per cent of tenants-at-will, were in debt. In the case of owners, their average indebtedness was about 25 per cent of their income, and in the case of tenants, 50 per cent due to improvident expenditure on marriages and funerals, or to failures of harvests. Debt was impossible to be paid off as the interest charged was abnormally high. When the peasant and owner of a good well or a fat piece of *sailab* dealt with a Bania who was always eager to hold some land in mortgage, he found that his credit was unlimited and he could have whatever he wanted and whenever he wished. At harvest time the Bania was paid back a few payments in grain for four to five years, or often longer. Now the peasant got into the Bania's debt trap who insisted upon a registered bond for the amount due on the mortgage. The debtor often took his chance of a law-suit but invariably lost the case and he made over a share in his property on a verbal *lekha-mukhi* contract to his creditor. This was the very worst thing he could do and the zemindar could never generate enough revenue to buy back his portion of land.

Muzaffargarh

Mr. O'Brien has given us details of peasantry in Muzaffargarh of 1879. The average area owned by proprietors was five acres and that by tenants was thirteen acres. Each harvest barely sufficed for the wants of the half year, and was regularly forestalled by borrowing. The Muslims were five times the number of the Hindus and 70 per cent of Muslim proprietors were in debt, whereas only 30 per cent of the Hindu proprietors were in debt. The amount borrowed yearly was equal to 30 per cent average yearly income. The highest estimate gives the debts as 80 per cent of the yearly income.

Forty per cent of Muslim tenants and 20 per cent Hindu tenants were in debt. The yearly debts of the tenants were equal to 20 per cent of their yearly income. The Muslims were nearly always uneducated; Hindus were always more or less educated. Muslims had only agriculture as the source of income whereas the Hindus always combined moneylending and trade with agriculture. Hindus acquired land as payment for debts. Muslims generally borrowed money to buy land.

Multan and Dera Ghazi Khan

In the neighbouring districts of Multan and Dera-Ghazi-Khan, the general condition of the peasantry was slightly better than it was in Muzaffargarh. In Multan, the peasants were fairly well off and some were affluent. Of the Muslims, 50 per cent were in debt, many only temporarily. The 50 per cent, of the debtors was thus sub-divided:

Table 4.2 Multan and Dera Ghazi Khan – State of Indebtedness

(i)	Those so involved that they could not free themselves without selling all or a part of their land	10.0
(ii)	Those who were solvent, but could not pay immediately	25.0
(iii)	Those who could pay immediately	15.0

Debts were due to two main causes: (a) ostentation and profligacy, (b) litigation. Of the Hindu proprietors, only some 15 per cent were in debt. Of these, about half were petty Kirar zemindars, who were probably insolvent. Some 20 per cent of occupancy tenants were in debt, but their debts were small.

Let us examine the demographic situation of Multan in those times. The vast majority of the people was Muslim Jats, the descendants of Hindus and might have come from Rajputana and Sindh, while others were in Punjab before the time of Alexander. Afghans in a superior position gained their lands with the Nawabs of Multan. During the Sikh rule a considerable number of Hindu Kirars may have been brought by Sawan Mal into nearly all the villages. Many of the better-off amongst the Jats, managed their estates most successfully. But the bulk of the smaller zemindars were ignorant and careless, not even attempting to look at the loan documents as long as the moneylender gave them money and on the day of settlement they found themselves in a hopeless situation and then they started to blame the *Kirar* instead. Now they would look to the District Officer to cancel their debts and reduce their assessments.

Hindu Kirars were thrifty and hardworking, and most of those who owned land did no moneylending. Most of the leading Afghans and Jats indulged in extravagance and it led to a very serious level of indebtedness.

In Dera-Ghazi-Khan two-thirds of the Muslim land-owners were said to be indebted but the government empowered the position of the Baluch tribal chiefs; even disapproving the acquisition of rights in land by Banias. In 1879 a person named Chiman Lal, who had served for about 20 years in the district reported to the Famine Commission that whether occupancy or tenants-at-will, two-thirds of the Muslim landowners and half the tenants, were involved in debt. The Muslims, with the exception of the best of the great Biluch tribal chiefs were as depressed as their brethren in Cis-Indus Muzaffargarh.

Bannu

In the Bannu district the peasantry in two tracts in Marwat (Trans-Indus) and in the Mianwali up-lands (Cis-lndus) were in a difficult situation. In both a very light land assessment tax was imposed. Here the average annual rainfall was only about 9 inches and very uncertainly distributed resulting in frequent drought and crops would fail in some years.

The large majority of the land-owning classes were self-cultivating peasants of small means and frugal habits and were all fairly prosperous. Then there are *Marwat* and *Bannuchis*, whose holdings were small and gave bare subsistence. Once a debt of the class known as *ghara* (neck) was incurred, in a few years the debtor had no alternative but to sell his land. Thus a debtor either agreed to pay as interest a certain portion of his earnings to the creditor, or a certain measure of grain each harvest, crop or no crop. The cause of the smallness of the holdings was over-population, and the Bannuchis were such a poor caste or tribe that they had marginal political account.

The landlord class—the *sufaid-poshes*—did not cultivate with their own hands. They were neither frugal nor prosperous but were a better peasant proprietary class. Twenty per cent, of them were deeply in debt, and a large minority habitually lived beyond their income. A few of course, say 10 per cent were shrewd and their holdings and incomes were growing.

Due to a foolish pride the head of the house thought he must maintain a high order of hospitality which was considered to be one of the top qualities amongst Pathans, and to maintain it, he mortgaged and borrowed freely. His sons continued the pernicious tradition and were brought up in idleness and married early, and never worked with their own hands.

Dera Ismail Khan

In the Dera-IsmaiI-Khan district the small Muslim peasants would end up losing all their proprietary rights and end as mere tillers of the soil, with enough to live upon, but no credit to pledge and evidently no property to lose. The worst part of the change from their original position under the previous Sikh government was not much better than this. Over the heads of a naturally dominant Muslim population, the small Muslim proprietors were doomed to sink beneath the superior thrift of the despised Hindu moneylender who lorded over those Muslims.

S.S. Thorburn served in D.I. Khan from 1882 to 1884 as Deputy Commissioner, and latterly as Divisional Judge, and collected substantial information on agricultural indebtedness. In June, 1884, he reported that excluding the 5,00,000 to 8,00,000 of petty debts most of which could be easily paid off after any average harvest, the debts owed by Muslims to Hindus in this district, amounted to between Rs. 1.2 and 1.4 million. Taking the lower figure of Rs. 1.2 million, the annual interest on it was not less than on the average 18 per cent, or Rs. 2,16,000. The true state of the indebtedness of the agricultural population of this district was yet to be evaluated. He proposed the following table:

Table 4.3 Dera Ismail Khan – State of Indebtedness

State of Indebtedness, if Any	*Percentage of Muslims*
Already ruined	13
Irretrievably involved	10

Seriously, but retrievably involved	28
Would be free with two good crops and a slight thrift	26
Owing nothing, or if anything, under Rs. 50, and easily able to pay it	23

During the Sikh rule, in years of drought the Muslim cultivator could easily save himself and cattle by migrating elsewhere, but now through the increase of population and the recording of rights, arrested his freedom of movement, and prevented him from freely selecting even a temporary piece of land.

Shahpur

It was settled in 1866 and till 1880 there were no large bankers in the district, but every village had a petty moneylender, generally of the Khatri caste *[The roots of the differences between Muslims and Hindus leading to ultimate partition of India can be traced to this period, i.e. the late nineteenth century— Author]*, to whom the people were largely indebted. The peasantry was in general in debt. This was due to successive seasons of drought, as well as extravagant habits of the agricultural classes during marriages. Also the high interest obtained by moneylenders for loans, for which the rate without security was often as high as Rs. 6-4 per cent per mensem, or Rs. 75-12 per annum. On mortgages the rate varied with the nature of the security, from one to two per cent per mensem.

Montgomery

There were very few villagers who were not seriously in debt. So long as the Kirar did not try to oust the proprietors and get the land into his own hands the matter was of minimal business importance. Incidentally, except in the canal villages, a *Kirar* made a great deal as a creditor that made people very bitter about their exactions and made unpleasant comparisons between now and the good old Sikh times.

Thus, there was a consensus that in the late nineteenth century, most of the agriculturists south of the Salt Range were in debt; a large proportion not less than 25 per cent was in a hopeless situation. Except for some good years (agriculturally), the rights in land were passing from them to the moneylending class, in an annually increasing rate mainly for two reasons: 1) Some characteristics common to all ignorant Muslims; 2) mainly due to the British system which gave a facility to borrow from market selling the land.

In the districts *north* of the Salt Range, we find that in sub-montane tracts, the amount and periodicity of the rainfall varied in the nineteenth century as in these days. In the south of Himalayas over a band of 48 to 80 kilometres there was on an average 30 inches of rainfall and the peasant had a substantial harvest like the canalised land. Further south the rainfall gradually diminished.

Hazara, Peshawar and Kohat

The spirit of the tribes occupying the land, coupled with the rarity of failure of crop and lightness of the revenue assessments restrained the all earth-hunger of the Banias except in the vicinity of cantonments and towns. A Bania was usually shrewd enough to know which land to grab and the tough Pathans kept them at an arm's length. Fear and prudence in combination make the Bania fight shy of the status of mortgagee or proprietor.

Colonel Hastings reported that debts were increasing in Peshawar. For the Hazara district it was reported that although more borrowing than before took place, there was less real indebtedness. This statement was relevant for the cultivating classes only and the bigger zamindars were prone to extravagance during marriages and other social events and tended to borrow heavily. Almost all the landed gentry of the district was deeply in debt. Hazara was generally prosperous. The cultivators were under less burden and embarrassment of debt as compared to the landlord classes. Although there was more borrowing in the 1880s compared to the earlier times, there was less real indebtedness amongst the agriculturists of the district than in Sikh times. However, all the leading men, except five, were more or less in debt.

There was a custom in the northern part of the Hazara district, by which the village banker would take at every harvest from the agriculturist as interest an *odi* (four seers) of grain for every rupee due to him. On non-payment of the interest, the cash value of the grain due was added to the account. There were cases when a man's entire harvest was confiscated against the cumulative interest payable.

For the Kohat district the wildest Pathans always kept the lands secure in their hands.

In Peshawar, the people were not extricating themselves from debt although they were better off than under former rulers. Due to the custom of vying with each other in expenditure at marriages and deaths, debts mounted. Spending more money and gambling which was becoming rampant, contributed to the indebtedness of certain classes. Cash loans were obtainable between the rates of 1 and 3 per cent, interest per mensem; seed-loans, from half a seer to one seer per maund *[1 maund = 40 seers]* was paid as interest. Money could be received on a deposit of jewels at Re. 1-9 per cent, per mensem. Sometimes the land was mortgaged to two persons, the proprietary right to one and the cultivating right to another.

In the other districts of the *northern table-land* the people were generally believed to be quite prosperous. In the outlying southern tracts where the rainfall was less in quantity landlords cultivated their lands through tenants. No revision of settlement took place in Gujrat since 1867-68. The Jhelum settlement of 1880 was moderate and the revision of the Rawalpindi settlement of 1860-61 was underway. However, the cesses were being raised by nearly 40 per cent. Thus, in the northern table-land, the people had been far lighter assessed, considering their fair prospect of an annual crop compared with the rainless districts south of the Salt Range.

Such exemption had just ceased for Rawalpindi and the same was expected in Gujrat. In Jhelum the revised settlement in 1880 was 19 per cent. The effect of the increased demand was still to be felt as there have been no bad years since then.

Rawalpindi

The prosperity of the district rose as the peasantry was rapidly extricating themselves from debt. Under Sikh rule, 50 per cent peasants were said to have been in debt, but in the 1880s not more than 10 per cent, of the cultivating classes were in debt.

The rate of interest now for a cash loan was a deduction of one anna in the rupee at the time the money was paid and 2 per cent, per mensem on the full amount afterwards. In loans of grain the interest was often 50, never less than 25 per cent.

Advances could be had against deposit of jewels, at a rate of 1 per cent, per mensem, and where land is mortgaged as security, interest is rarely paid in money.

Jhelum

The agriculturists gave all their grain to the Banias at harvest time. It was the custom to charge two annas in the rupee for lending money and therefore when a man signed a bond for Rs. 100, he only received Rs. 87-88. He was then charged interest on the Rs. 100 at two annas (12.5 per cent) per harvest; the unpaid interest being added at each harvest to the principal. In the Sikh days, the land could not be sold at all and the new British system added to peasants' woes.

Gujrat

As the settlement operations advanced it gave a false indication that the debts had increased. But the people felt that the debts had not really increased. The attendance of the borrowing classes at the Settlement was an opportunity for the moneylenders to get all debts duly recorded in statements and signed. Despite the apparently prosperous condition of the district, the people were undoubtedly much in debt, and the registration of bonds had largely increased in 1867.

Gujranwala

In this Muslim-dominated district, it is estimated that 80 per cent, of the owners, 20 per cent of the occupancy tenants, and 10 per cent of the tenants-at-will were indebted. Another estimate was that the average indebtedness of the owners was about 30 per cent, on their average yearly income; while based on similar calculation, the average indebtedness of the occupancy-tenants was estimated at 12 per cent, and that of the tenants-at will at 5 per cent.

The North West State Railway work completed in 1882 and covered the whole width of all the districts of the northern table-land, except Hazara and Kohat, for a length of 250 miles, put hundreds of thousands of rupees into the pockets of the peasants every year. The Kabul War (1878-80) also brought wealth to people as well as the Banias. The comparative freedom from serious debt of the peasants north of the Salt Range could not have continued indefinitely as the sources of profits and savings open to them between 1870 and 1885 were closing one by one.

It can be said that the condition of the peasants in eight districts south of the range or in the south Western plain including the range itself was gloomy. These eight districts were: *Shahpur, Montgomery, Muzaffargarh, Jhang, Multan, Bannu, Dera Ismail Khan and Dera Ghazi Khan*. But that throughout the northern table-land—wherever the crops were fairly good and certain—the peasantry was reasonably prosperous if they desisted from extravagance.

Thus, the peasantry are generally free from serious indebtedness in the sub-montane zone, more involved as the Salt Range is approached, and south of it almost universally so.

People and Demographics

The population of Punjab was 17.6 million in 1855 and rose to 20.8 million in 1881 and to 25.1 million in 1921. The most populous areas were around Lahore, Amritsar, Gurdaspur and Sialkot and the Jalandhar Doab. The population density dropped to the west of this fertile base, in the Charnba and Kangra, in Bahawalpur principality and a somewhat less sharply in Hissar.

The number of towns in Punjab rose from 168 in 1881 to 185 in 1921, with an average population of around 18,000 in a town. In 1921 Lahore was twice its size of 1881.

In the countryside, census figures confirmed that fertile lands close to rivers contained more Jats and Rajputs (whether Sikh, Muslim or Hindu) than members of other rural communities. The Muslim percentage in Punjab rose from 47.6 in 1881 to 51.1 in 1921. The Hindu percentage declined from 43.8 to 35.1 whereas the Sikh percentage rose from 8.2 to 12.4 per cent, and the Christian from 0.1 to 1.3 per cent. Many people previously calling themselves Hindu, now reported as Sikhs.

While in 1881 among all the Hindu and Sikh Jats, less than 54 per cent described themselves as Sikhs, in 1921 the percentage went up to 80.

The British found every district as a mixture of castes. Gujjar (who were Muslim and Hindu), Jats or Jatts and Rajputs (both as Muslims, Hindus and Sikhs), Awans and Arains (almost all of them Muslim), and Khatris and Aroras (almost all Hindus or Sikhs) lived in significant numbers in some districts. Clans like Gakhars, Janjuas and Ghebas (almost all Muslims) were concentrated in the Rawalpindi division. Throughout the province 'menial or 'low' castes were noticed.

The Western Punjab had a much higher Muslim percentage, a larger stock of Pashtun and Baloch people, and a higher percentage of people doing pastoral work or living as nomads than in central or Eastern Punjab. It also had a more egalitarian culture, a lower population density, and fewer towns. This part had a lower influence of casteism and showed more tribal propensities. The Sikhs were numerically strongest in the middle of the province but not in an absolute majority in any entire district.

Many Muslims had retained pre-Muslim or clan names and great many Punjabi Muslims like a Noon, Tiwana, Minhas, Wattoo or Bhatti did not claim to be descendants of the Prophet and did not feel ashamed to say that they were Rajputs, Jats etc. They were even proud of it.

The population of the Punjab, as per the census of 1881 exclusive of its dependencies was 1,88,50,437. The distribution is shown below:

Table 4.4

Division	*Muslims*	*%*	*Hindus*	*%*	*Sikhs*	*%*	*Total*	*%*
Eastern	11,41,145	22.73	37,69,786	75.08	1,10,120	2.19	50,21,051	100.0
Central	36,99,736	51.71	25,74,174	35.70	9,36,740	12.99	72,10,650	100.0
Western								
(a) Northern Table Land and Salt Range	23,29,386	90.24	2,16,103	8.37	35,692	1.38	25,81,181	100.0
(b) South-Western Plain	33,52,535	84.71	5,67,426	14.34	37,708	0.95	39,57,669	100.0
+ (b)	56,81,921	86.89	7,83,529	11.98	73,400	1.12	65,38,850	
	1,05,22,802	56.06	71,27,489	37.97	11,20,260	5.97	**1,87,70,551**	

In the Eastern Punjab 85 per cent of the inhabitants were rural. This was the great agricultural Eastern Punjab. Tribes were Jats and Rajputs who lived in the 1880s the way they did hundreds of years ago. In the plains, after the Muslim conquest of Upper India many Hindus adopted the faith of their masters but socially and politically, Hindus and Muslims lived as one people; ancient ties of blood were stronger than the separatist teachings of a half-learnt religion. We are talking of the late nineteenth century.

Regarding the agriculturists of the nine central districts which were the stronghold of Sikhism but the Muslims considerably outnumbered both Hindus and Sikhs put together and like the eight districts further east, the central Muslims were mostly the descendants of Hindu Jats, Rajputs, and minor agricultural tribes who were converted during the reign of Aurangzeb. The whole rural population of the Punjab east of the Jhelum, whether Hindus or Muslims, could be considered, for all administrative purposes, as one people.

The Muslim tribes occupying the Western Punjab needs some discussion. The total population of the tract is, as we have seen, nearly six and a half millions, thus distributed: Muslims 86.89 per cent, Hindus 11.98 per cent and the Sikhs 1.12 per cent.

In the Western Punjab the following dominant tribes constituted the lion's share:

Table 4.3 Muslim Tribes in Western Punjab in 1881

Sl	*Name*	*Number*	*%*
1	Pathans (Afghans)	7,45,000	19
2	Baluch	2,79,000	7
3	Jats	10,82,000	27
4	Rajputs	6,00,000	15
5	Syeds, Shaikhs and Ulemas	2,72,000	7
6	Awans	4,85,000	12
7	Gujars	2,15,000	5
8	Gakhars	26,000	1
9	Mughals and Turks	68,000	2
10	Arains including Bhagwans	1,34,000	3

11	Miscellaneous	94,000	2
Total		40,00,000	100

The rest of the Muslims belonged to a variety of tribes and castes, interspersed with the general population. Many were cultivators, dependent on agriculture for their livelihood. Refugees from neighbouring states included Kashmiris numbering a hundred thousand, and chiefly concentrated in Rawalpindi, Shahpur, and Ludhiana.

Every rural community had the menial and artisan classes such as scavengers, carpenters, workers in leather, and blacksmiths, who received for their services fixed grain-payments at harvest time. Every village also had a number of professionals like the barbers, weavers, potters, oil-pressers, dyers and washers, butchers, all useful members who apart from practising their hereditary profession, also worked as field labourers or cultivators. The number of the village menial and professional classes numbered 1.25 million. Watermen numbered 2,25,000; workers in metals 45,000; and Muslim traders known as Khojahs and Pirachas—mostly recent converts from Hinduism—30,000. A miscellaneous assortment of other castes doing menial tasks, nomads, and beggars, many of whom do field work at harvest time, were the rest.

British Attempts to Improve Agriculture

The British introduced several policies for the development of agriculture in the Punjab. The Board of Administration sanctioned advance for the repair of old wells, for the sinking of new ones and for the excavation of water courses. Since 1851 people were being made aware of new methods of agriculture, scientific basis for the same and using improved seeds. The digging of canals and reclamation of lands began all over Punjab.

The agriculture of Punjab was to be developed on scientific lines as the British believed. The iron-based agricultural implements were now being made in large quantities and in November 1863, an exhibition was held in Lahore displaying agricultural and horticultural implements to make people aware of new technological equipment.

Cultivation of Gram, Vegetables, Pulses and Grain

In 1871, the Department of Revenue became the Department of Agriculture. During the year 1877-78, the experimental sowing of the French gram was introduced in Punjab. The season of 1877-78 remained very unfavourable for the local gram; in most places the yield was poor but the experiments with white French gram also met the same fate.

The cultivation of champion potato was experimented with in 1882 and at Lyallpur in the Chenab Colony an experimental farm of 55 acres was set up in 1901.

The year 1881-82 was a landmark period in the development of wheat trade in India and it boomed throughout the 1880s. By the year 1883, the Punjab had seven million acres under wheat cultivation and the yield was equal to that of the United Kingdom. Earlier, in 1881-82, six million quintals of the Punjab wheat were exported to France via Sind amounting to Rs. 30,33,961.

The wheat price had been fluctuating in Punjab.

Table 4.5 Area in Punjab Under Wheat Crop

Year	*Area Under Crop in Acres*	*Percentage*
1880-81	2,19,98,379	17.7
1892-93	2,67,32,864	21.5

The export of wheat in the earlier years (1874-75 to 1877-78) from the Punjab via the Indus route remained as follows:

Table 4.6 Export from Punjab via the Indus Route

Year	*Exports*
1874-75	3,03,911
1875-76	4,23,853
1876-77	5,95,153
1877-78	13,05,675

Cultivation in the Punjab

Punjab cultivation had two harvests: spring harvest and autumn harvest, known locally as *rabi* and *kharif* respectively. The following were grown in the spring harvest: wheat, barley, pulses, oilseeds, vegetables and sugarcane. The main autumn crops: millets, maize, rice, cotton and hemp. There were numerous varieties of crops like wheat and sugarcane.

Development of Canal Colonies

With the exception of the Salt Range Tract the Punjab plains consisted of one vast unbroken territory. The low hills of chiniot and Kirana in Jhang district and the narrow sub-montane zone covering parts of the districts of Ambala, Hoshiarpur, Gurdaspur, Sialkot and Gujarat broke the uniformity of the surface of the land.

The slope of the Punjab plains was generally south-west wards and these were rarely over 1,000 feet high from sea-level. The lowest contour ran in two branches in northern and southern directions. The combined result of these two slopes was a fall of two or three feet per mile. The British engineers found the Punjab well-suited for canal irrigation on a large scale.

Thus the plans for the dual processes of *canalisation* and *colonisation* began. It was essential to identify the lawful claimants who claimed rights to the soil and who were liable to pay the land revenue.

In the 1880s, the government desired to make an optimum utilisation of its dry and arid Western plains as the prospects of agricultural growth were high there. Now the British embarked upon an extensive irrigation system in order to lay a number of irrigational canals for the said agricultural improvement. They all aimed at colonising nearly 10 million acres of tracts of uplands of the Chaj, Rachna and Bari Doab area.

The government's colonial policy comprised three phases:

- reduce the pressure of population in the highly congested districts where the agricultural limits had been reached;
- to create villages of a superior type. Thus, the capitalists who would constitute a healthy agricultural community appeared on the scene; and
- the government intended to combine the requirements of the army and allotted land for the camel, mule and select cattle breeding and plantations.

Compared to the north-eastern Punjab canal irrigation was more significant in the south-western Punjab and the canals were either *perennial* or *inundation*. The former worked almost throughout the year and were managed by the state. In the Upper Bari and Rachna Doabs, irrigation from them was concentrated. The perennial canals were the following: Hansli Canal and the Western-Jamuna Canal.

Most of the canals, however, were inundation canals, which worked only during the rainy season when the rivers had enough water. These canals took their supply from the Sutlej, Ravi, Chenab, and Indus rivers and were simple to construct.

The development of the canal colonies was undertaken in Punjab by the British Government to (i) increase the agricultural output and (ii) to create a loyal political base for the British. Those who helped the British in suppressing the revolt of 1857, were given the land grants and those who had served in the British Army were also given the land grants.

The major canals either newly constructed or renovated and expanded by the British government between 1850-1900 were, Western Jamuna Canal (1820- renovated in 1878), Upper Bari Doab Canal (1859), Sirhind Canal (1882), Swat River Canal (1885), Lower Sohag and Para Canal (remodelled in 1885-86), Sidhnai Canal (1886) and lower Chenab Colony (1892).

A successful attempt was made in the 1870s to harness the waters of the sacred Jamuna and it was capable of irrigating 5,00,000 acres in the year 1870. By reason, however, of its faulty alignment, this canal although a very profitable work, caused loss to the country by waterlogging and could not be extended due to insecurity of supply. In 1870, it was decided that the canal should be remodelled. In 1873, the old alignment of the canal was improved.

The first work in the Eastern plains in the early years of the British rule was the construction of the Upper Bari Doab Canal from a branch of river Ravi at Madhopur. It irrigated an area of 89,756 acres in 1860-61.

The Bari Doab Canal between 1865 and 1867 delivered on an average 1,400 cusecs against a design of 3,000 cusecs. The extension of the Bari Doab Canal enhanced the price of land in the Amritsar area.

The Sirhind Canal was constructed to irrigate the tract between the rivers Sutlej and Ghaggar. The work of its construction began in 1876 and irrigation started from 1885.

To irrigate the plains lying between Swat and Kabul rivers the Swat River Canal was constructed. This canal proved to be a highly remunerative work for the British Government.

To irrigate certain tracts which could not be covered by the Sidhnai Canal three small canals in Multan district were constructed in 1888-89. In 1882 three projects were undertaken: 1) the Sidhnai canal from the Ravi, 2) the Lower Sohag and Para Canal from the Sutlej and 3) Ram Nagar Canal, later named the Chenab Canal from the Chenab. The Upper Sohag Canal was taken over by the irrigation department in 1855, whereas the Lower Sohag Canal was improved, remodelled and opened in 1885-86.

The new colonisation scheme was designed to reduce the pressure on those areas where agriculture had reached the maximum limit. The new areas were to be populated with highly-skilled and motivated peasants having their own holdings and the peasant class formed 75 per cent of the people of the colony.

Now the cultivators were dependent on towns and cities to buy implements and could sell the growing surplus produce in the city. This was a paradigm change from the past when the peasant produced primarily for his own subsistence.

The villages thus got integrated with the markets within and outside the Punjab. In the Punjab, the standard of living of the peasantry improved.

Impact of Canal Colonies on the Lives of People

Expansion of irrigation led to transition from the traditional to modern agriculture where the new implements made of iron like plough, sugarcane crusher, Persian wheel, chaff-cutter, harrow and drill were used. Thus, some mechanisation of agriculture took place. New methods of cultivation and crop rotation were evolved.

Many new varieties of seeds suiting the soil of the Punjab were introduced. The growth of irrigation, means of transport and communications, and the new technology yielded surplus and the commercialisation of agriculture greatly benefited the cultivators.

Three meals were consumed in most of the province where two meals a day was common. The chief staple food of the Punjab was now wheat. There was the greater use of vegetables like cabbage, cauliflower, potatoes and peas. Pucca houses were built by many and people clothed themselves better.

The greatest change was in the canal colonies where the British Government also worked for providing better facilities. Dispensaries had been established by the year 1897. The British sought to develop canal irrigation to remove the extreme reliance on rainfall.

The colonisation also led to urbanisation and urban centres like Lyallpur and Multan became famous and specialised goods were being sent for national and international markets. New towns mostly developed along the railway lines. The railway stations developed as grain markets like an urban centre. The crowding of large towns was mainly due to the development of industries in the canal colonies.

The tracts once described as poorest now came to be regarded as one of the richest parts of the Punjab. The richness led to a higher standard of living, higher culture and civilisation. The people once described as pastoral, had become industrious agriculturists and residents of well-planned houses.

Lastly, the construction of the Chenab canal was the chief factor in the growth of the area covered by the Chenab colony. The district of Lyallpur became the model for the advancement of agriculture and civilisation.

Effect of Canal Colonies

From the late 1880s, population density rose greatly in the districts of Montgomery (afterwards Sahiwal), Multan, Lyallpur (later called Faisalabad), Jhang and Muzaffargarh, all in the Multan division, and in the district of Shahpur in Rawalpindi division. The migrants came mainly from seven heavily-populated districts: Amritsar, Gurdaspur and Sialkot (Lahore division); Jalandhar, Hoshiarpur and Ludhiana. In Jalandhar division and Ambala, the population density, in fact, declined.

Muslim, Sikh and Hindu Jats comprised two-thirds of the canal colony migrants and the rest included Arains, Sainis, Kambohs and Rajputs who were equally diligent but did not have big holdings like the Jats. Canal colonies also drew Muslim farmers from adjacent dry areas of Dera Ghazi Khan, Mianwali and Jhelum districts.

Entrepreneurs, mostly Hindus and Sikhs, established small industries on colony plots. The Empire got revenue from everything the colonies raised and produced.

Eight canal colonies were launched between 1886 and 1916. The first was established in the district of Multan, the second in Montgomery district, and the third in Chunian in Lahore district. The fourth (and the largest), called the Lower Chenab colony, covered parts of four districts (Jhang, Lyallpur, Gujranwala and Lahore). Its creation yielded a new administrative district, Sheikhupura, made up of the 'colony' portions of Gujranwala and Lahore. The fifth, and almost equally large, canal colony was the Lower Jhelum cutting across two districts, Shahpur and Jhang. The Lower Bari Doab colony in the districts of Montgomery and Multan was the sixth, followed by the Upper Chenab and Upper Jhelum colonies, the former situated in parts of three districts (Sheikhupura, Gujranwala and Sialkot) and the latter Gujrat district.

In practice, while farmers tilling small farms in their home districts indeed comprised a majority of the canal colony grantees, a number of men from other classes were also allotted one or more 'squares' of colony land, each square approximating to 25 acres. Thus, the man with the biggest grant in the second canal colony, Sohag Para of Montgomery district was Baba Khem Singh Bedi of Rawalpindi district, related to Guru Nanak and he got 7,798 acres.

Settled between 1892 and 1905, the Lower Chenab colony was populated by grantees described as *abadkar* (peasants). The military element became dominant in the Lower Jhelum colony (straddling the districts of Shahpur and Jhang), which was settled between 1902 and 1906. As the horses and mules were needed for the army, 54.4 per cent of this colony's land was allotted for horse-breeding. But land was grabbed by prominent landlord families of north-Western Punjab.

Prince of Wales Visited Lahore: 1876

In January 1876, the Prince of Wales visited Lahore. The Prince drove round the city and visited the Lahore fort. In the armoury, at the fort, the Prince inspected the weapons employed by the Sikhs. His attention was attracted by a tiny cannon, mounted on a revolving frame, which was used as a toy by Maharaja Duleep Singh when he was young. At the desire of the Prince of Wales, that tiny cannon was sent to England.

Congress Party is formed

A Scot, Allan Octavian Hume (1829-1912), who had resigned in 1879 from the ICS formed in 1885, the Indian National Congress as he wanted to allow Indians a say in their governance. In 1885 the Indian National Congress held its first session in Bombay, under the presidentship of Calcutta's Womesh Chandra Bonnerji. Hume served as the INC 's active secretary till his departure for England in 1892. Hoping to bring India's religious, linguistic and provincial elements under a single platform and resolving to convene annually in different parts of India, the INC met in Calcutta in 1886 and in Madras the following year. In 1893, the body gathered in Lahore, under the presidentship of the eminent Parsi from Bombay, Dadabhai Naoroji.

Punjab's Muslims were getting their inspiration from Syed Ahmed Khan (1817-98), the first Muslim to be nominated to the Imperial Legislative Council and the founder of Aligarh's Mohammedan Anglo-Oriental College (MAO) in 1875 *[It became Aligarh Muslim University in 1920 – Author]*. He was a scion of Delhi's Mughal nobility and a former judicial officer for the East India Company.

The fear of Hindus lording it over Muslims was a stronger sentiment in the MAO founder. Suspicious of the INC, Sayyid Ahmed opposed its pleas for adding elected members to the Raj's local or provincial councils and for wider openings for Indians in the civil service and asked India's Muslims to stay clear of the INC. It was better for them to ally with the English, some Muslims disagreed, including the talented Bombay lawyer Badruddin Tyabji, who chaired, in Madras, the INC's third annual session, but Syed Ahmed's reach was more extensive. He was knighted in 1888.

In Punjab, the *Anjumans* supported Sir Syed Ahmed Khan in his attitude towards the Indian National Congress. Sir Syed Ahmed Khan had innumerable followers among the Punjabi Muslims, who provided enthusiastic help to the Aligarh movement. Anjumans all over the Punjab met to condole his death in 1898 paying tributes and raising money for MAO.

Punjab Between 1882 and 1892

Sir Charles Aitchison (1832-96)

Lieutenant Governor of the Punjab, was born in Edinburgh and he was the son of Hugh Aitchison of that city and he took the degree of MA on April 23, 1853.

As an Under-Secretary in the Political Department he joined the Secretariat of the Government of India in 1859 and served there until 1865. Then he undertook administrative work in the Punjab at the instance of Sir John Lawrence, then Governor-General, serving first as a Deputy Commissioner and subsequently as Commissioner of Lahore. In 1868 he re-joined the Secretariat as Foreign Secretary, and remained the same until 1878.

He became Lieutenant-Governor of the Punjab on April 4, 1882 and staunchly advocated the policy of advancing natives of India in the public service as they proved their fitness for higher posts and for more responsible duties. He advocated measures even more liberal than Lord Ripon. His tenure ended in 1887 but he came back at the request of Lord Dufferin to join the Governor-General for special duties.

A Religious Man and a Great Administrator

He was a consistent supporter of Christianity and after his superannuation, he was an active member of the Committee of the Church Missionary Society. His service record dated back to the Mutiny year, and he was one of the most outstanding civilians of his generation. But he did not get the full support of his colleagues who thought his ideas of reforms, heavily borrowed from Lord Ripon, to be premature. There was this feeling that the Secretariat was gaining an under influence and that the test of efficiency and eligibility for promotion had more to do with the skill in minute writing rather than capacity to run administration.

He will be remembered for doing the following work:

1. Start of the Sidhnai and Sohag Para Colonies
2. Establishing Aitchison College, University of the Punjab and University of Veterinary and Animal Sciences
3. Creation of the Lahore Bar Association
4. Opening of the Punjab Public Library

Sir James Broadwood Lyall (1887-92)

Born in 1838 James Lyall was the son of Alfred Lyall and Mary Drummond. At Eton college, he was first educated and then he studied at the Haileybury College.

In 1857, he joined the Bengal Civil Service the following year. He served with the Punjab Commission until the end of 1859 and went on to serve as the financial commissioner of the Punjab since 1879.

He was the University of Punjab's first vice-chancellor, a post to which he was appointed in October 1882. He was appointed as a Knight Commander of the Order of the Star of India in 1888 and GCSI in 1892.

The decade long period of 1882-92 was very important for Punjab. The Weir at Khanki or the supply for the Lower Chenab Canal was finished in 1892. Founding and developing of many of the canal colonies throughout the Punjab was done by Lieutenant-Governor, Lyall. It was an ambitious plan to harness the rivers of the region and transform a big desert of about 60,00,000 acres (24,00,000 ha) into agricultural land. He was also instrumental in establishing Lyallpur, one of the first planned cities in British India. It was named in his honour.

The following important events occurred during his governorship:

1. Starting of the construction of the Chenab Colony
2. Founding of Lyallpur
3. Ahmadiyya movement

He died in Eastry, Kent on December 4, 1916 and is buried in the local churchyard.

Acts Passed Specially for the Punjab

In the year 1883-84, the district Boards Act XX of 1883 superceded the old Local Rates Act of 1878.

The Punjab Municipal Act, XIII of 1884 and the Punjab Courts Act, XVIII of 1884 were passed.

The Punjab Tenancy Act XVI and Land Revenue Act XVII of 1887 came into being. The former was enacted to overcome some oversights and shortcomings of the Act of 1868. It was also meant to improve the relations between the landlords and tenants, especially in Sirsa and Hoshiarpur. The Revenue Act replaced an incomplete earlier act which was deficient in village record-keeping. The Act also continued the provision about 'excess waste,' which had usually found place in Revenue Acts (cf Section V7, Act X1X of 1873, and p. 37).

Colonisation of Waste Tracts

Even after the allotment, there were districts was which great tracts of land could still be disposed of by the state; and these were not in demand, as without rainfall cultivation was not possible, and the land was so near the 'bar' that wells could not profitably be sunk.

The soil was good. The Chenab Canal had made the cultivation of a large tract of its kind in the Rechna Doab (Gujranwala and Jhang Districts) possible, and the recently-constructed Sidhnai Canal (from the Ravi) benefited the northern part of the Multan district. The same success was achieved with the Lower Sohag Canals in the Montgomery district.

It had become the duty of the land-revenue administration to manage the allotment and colonisation of these new canal lands.

The government leased, and did not sell the land, charging a low rate of land-revenue and also took a rent (for malikana), which amounted to one-fourth of the revenue. No lease was allowed without the sanction of the government, except in eight districts (Montgomery, Jhang, Multan, Shahpur, the two Derajat districts, Muzaffargarh and Bannu).

Panjdeh Incident 1884

The chief dispute centred round Panjdeh, a village and district, one hundred miles due south of Merv where the Murghab and Kushak rivers unite their waters. The whole position was complicated and difficult. Neither the Government of India nor the Russian Governor-General of Turkistan had direct control over the Commissioners who reported to higher-ups at the Foreign Offices of London and St. Peterburg respectively.

Between the border with Turkmenistan and the Afghan city of Herat, it was an area of northern Afghanistan. Suppressing the Afghans further south, the Russians occupied the Panjdeh oasis and the person who aggressively protected the Russian interests in the region was the Russian General Alexander Komarov. All the Afghans were indeed killed in the battle as per the reports.

The British felt that the Russian penetration so far south clashed with their interests. Lord Dufferin, the Viceroy was assured by the Afghan Emir that it was only a border skirmish. But in London caution was urged.

Finally, the war was avoided by diplomatic means. Viceroy Lord Dufferin made an agreement with the Russians that the Panjdeh oasis would remain a part of the Russian Empire, but Russia would respect the territorial integrity of Afghanistan in future.

The shrewd common-sense of the Amir helped in avoiding the war. He declared that he was not sure whether Panjdeh belonged to him or not and he was also not very particular of keeping the same in his possession. The Amir further declared willingness to give up his claim to Panjdeh if he was given lands anywhere else.

A meeting was held at Rawalpindi where Lord Dufferin's personal charm and tact influenced the Amir but he just wanted to eject all the British troops from Afghanistan.

The Boundary Line was to be demarcated between the British and the Russians. Sir West Ridgeway, after discussions with the Amir at Kabul and Lord Dufferin at Simla, went to England. After prolonged negotiations between Kabul, Simla, London, and St. Peterburg, an agreement delineating the border was settled at St. Petersburg in July 1887. The Amir did not lose anything because of the new boundary. The settlement of the frontier up to the line of the Oxus restricted Russian advance in the direction of Herat, which was the key of India. But, in the direction of the Pamirs the Russian forward movement still continued till another Anglo-Russian convention was signed in 1895.

A British agent was posted at Gilgit and the importance of Gilgit was that it gave direct communication with Chitral, a small state with mountaineer tribes.

The British Forward Policy

In the 1890s, starting from 1878 onwards, the districts of the North West Frontier were quite disturbed because of:

1. The forward policy adopted by Lord Lansdowne and Lord Elgin
2. The intrigues of the Amir in Afghanistan

By 1889, the British control had extended over Bori and Zhob Valleys, in the south of the Gomal pass. From a military, political and commercial perspective, the occupation of Zhob was quite important. It shortened the British line of defence and effected better control over the outlaws who had a tendency to escape into Afghanistan, after committing crimes. The Gomal trade route also got the necessary protection. In 1890, the boundary between the Punjab frontier zone and Baluchistan was delineated with the Gomal river stretch from Domandi to Zhob stream serving as a border. NWFP (KPK) was yet to be formed.

The Anglo-Afghan relations deteriorated dramatically in the 1890s and the reasons were not just minor. The ever-expansionist policy of the British was the root of the problem. It had scant regard for the territorial limits of the smaller and neighbouring states. The British undertook punitive expeditions against the Shirani tribes, Orakzai clans, the Isazai tribes and the smaller chiefs of Hunza. Then there was this silent acquisition of Kurram valley. The situation was so pervasive that the Anglo-Afghan war seemed inevitable.

Before despatch of the Durand Mission to Kabul, in 1893, it had been rumoured that the British wanted of a more exact delimitation of the Indo-Afghan Frontier and Abdur Rahman Khan had to write a letter to the Viceroy warning Lord Lansdowne of the results of a more-forward policy.

Durand Line

The Western ends of the Khyber Pass and the Kurram valley were marked as a border between British India and Afghanistan, but on the north and south of these routes no boundary was fixed. Historically, the strong tribes in Afghanistan and frontier like the Afridis, and Mohmands, used to get allowances from Amir Abdur Rahman for keeping the passes open. They had been living independently for ages.

Sher Ali, the amir of Afghanistan went to the Russian territory, but he died in 1879 while on the way. Yakub Khan, his son agreed to the Treaty of Gandmak 1880 and the Afghani foreign relations policy was compromised and he allowed a British Mission, with European members, to reside in Kabul. The British got the jurisdiction over the Korram and Pishin valleys, the Sibi district, and the Khybar pass. A telegraph line between Kabul and British India was proposed under the terms of the treaty. Yaqub Khan was promised an annual subsidy of Rs. 6,00,000.

The eastern half of the old sub-province of Kandhar was added to the Indian Empire as per the boundary line fixed in 1880. In 1894, the modified Frontier line along the top hills of the Suleiman range of mountains was now known as the *Durand Line*. Under the British sphere of influence now came the tribesmen living in the Khyber, and Mohmand Tirah, Kurram, and Waziristan. Subsequently the eastern slopes of the Suleiman mountains came within British control.

A sort of formalisation of boundaries was agreed upon by the Amir in 1893 and a mission, under Sir Mortimer Durand, proceeded to Kabul to discuss the matter. An agreement was signed definitely fixing the line with the Government of India and the Amir had agreed to finalise the border of Afghanistan from Chandak to the Persian border. To demarcate the boundary commissions were issued and the final demarcation was carried out in 1895.

The Durand Line demarcation in 1894, under which the Amir of Kabul ceased to exercise any control of the independent tribes of the border, the British Government assumed a responsibility over the tribal territory spread over the five districts of the North-West Frontier and the border of Afghanistan.

The three agencies of Malakand, Tochi and Warta were developed in 1895-96. The Tochi and Warta agencies were left in charge of the Punjab Government working through its Commissioners. The Malakand agency was placed under the direct control of the Government of India. The British Government had assumed control under the treaty with the Amir of Afghanistan over the independent territory of Tirah, Waziristan and the rest but these were in any case held by the various tribal laws. The British control was confined to various roads driven up the different passes in Khyber, Kurram, Tochi, and Gomal for defence purposes.

The demarcation was not based on sound topographical data. There were many places which were marked on the Durand map but in reality, these did not exist. Parts of Waziristan, peopled by Darwesh Khel Wazir was handed over to the Amir of the Barmal;

this was one of the many ethnic inconsistencies perpetrated. Worst of all was that the boundary cut the Mohmand tribal area into two separate parts. There was no evidence that the tribesmen were consulted and it is hard to comprehend what prompted the Amir to sign this agreement. It might have been that he was bribed into acquiescence.

A mission was sent to Chitral as the Mehtar there had changed and the mission was led by Dr. Robertson. Lord Lansdowne issued instructions in 1893 to withdraw the political officer from Chitral provided there was no further trouble. In 1895, Mehtar got murdered and Umra Khan proclaimed a 'Jihad' in the areas of Dir, Swat and Bajaur and Robertson got besieged in the fort of Chitral; Chitralis and Pathans being the attackers.

The six-week siege that followed included an unsuccessful attempt on March 3, 1895, when the British-led forces took heavy losses. When a relief force, under Colonel Kelly, arrived and dispersed the armed tribesmen the siege was over on April 19.

Punjab During 1892-1902

Sir Dennis Fitzpatrick GCSI (1837–1920)

An Irish barrister and member of the ICS became Lieutenant-Governor of the Punjab 1892–1897. He was born in Dublin in 1837, the son of a physician and was educated at Trinity College, Dublin.

In 1859 he joined the Punjab Commission and worked in the Delhi territory as a magistrate until called for special duties.

He became a deputy-secretary in the Legislative Department and a Judge of the Chief Court in Lahore in 1876. Later he became Secretary of the Legislative Department and at the end of 1885 he became Resident in Mysore and for a few months Chief Commissioner of Coorg.

He returned to the Punjab as Lieutenant-Governor in March 1892 and remained so till 1897 when he returned to the United Kingdom to join the London-based Council of India. Fitzpatrick retired from the Council in 1907. He was made a Knight Grand Commander in 1911.

The following events took place during his reign:

1 Chunian Colony commencement

2 Khalsa College, Amritsar and School of Medicine for the Christian Women's establishment

Fitzpatrick died in London on May 20, 1920.

Plague in 1897

It came from China and it first broke out in Bombay in 1896 and in the coming years it assumed an epidemic form in the Punjab and the local outbreaks severely used the resources of the Punjab government. Young faced the situation with grim courage.

The first outbreak of plague occurred in October 1897 and the affected village was Khatkal Kalan in the Jalandhar district. The infection, in fact had been sourced from Hardwar in May 1896. The disease in the intervening period was totally confined to the adjacent parts of Jalandhar and Hoshiarpur districts.

Chitral Scenario

Chitral was a state in the Dir, Swat and Chitral Agency of the North-West Fronticr Province and comprised the whole of Tirich valley. In 1885-86, Chitral was visited by the Lockhart mission and in 1889, after a political agency was established, Aman-ul-Mulk received a subsidy of Rs. 6,000 per annum from the British and in 1891, this was increased to Rs. 12,000 on the condition that he accepted the advice of the government in all matters connected with foreign policy and defence.

In 1892, Aman-ul-Mulk died and his second son Afzal Mulk was seated on the throne. His uncle Sher Afzal, who had been a refugee in Afghanistan, returned and the Chitral fort was opened to him where Aman-ul-Mulk had taken refuge and Afzal Mulk was murdered. Sher Afzal pronounced himself Mehtar. Nizam-ul-Mulk, a brother of Afzal Mulk was then allowed to re-enter Chitral from Gilgit and he ascended the throne. In January 1895 the Nizam was murdered and it was a scheme of his half-brother Amir-ul-Mulk. Amir seized the fort.

The political agent at Gilgit had been sent to Chitral to report the situation. In the meantime, the rurn of events so happened that a young boy of 14, was provisionally recognised as Mehtar.

The garrison of the fort was besieged from March 3 till April 19, 1895, During the siege, two successes were gained elsewhere by the locals. The first was the capture at Buni of two British officers, the destruction of their following, and the seizure of 40,000 rounds of ammunition. The two officers kept as prisoners by Umra Khan for a month were released on the approach of the relief force.

The other success was the practical annihilation near Rashtung of a detachment of 100 men of the 14th Sikhs under Captain Ross. A week later the advance guard of the main relief force captured Sher Afzal and Umra Khan fled to Afghan territory. The selection of Shuja-ul-Mulk as Mehtar was confirmed and Sher Afzal, Amir-ul-Mulk, and their leading followers were deported to India.

Since then Chitral enjoyed an unwanted peace. Cultivation was extended and the Mehtar's mental horizon was much enlarged by his visits to Calcutta in 1900, to the Delhi Durbar in 1903, and to Peshawar in 1904. Chitral levies were raised in 1899 for the defence of Lower Chitral to provide a irregular force for the defence of the country in case of invasion.

Battle of Saragarhi

The Battle of Saragarhi was fought before the Tirah Campaign and the battle took place on September 12, 1897. The fight was between the Empire of the British in India and the rejuvenated Afghan tribesmen. It occurred in the present-day Khyber Pakhtunkhwa, Pakistan. The Sikh soldiers of the British Indian Army fought against the Pashtun Orakzai tribesmen in this battle.

Twenty-one Jat Sikh soldiers of the 36th Sikhs (now the 4th battalion of the Sikh Regiment) were deployed in this Sikh contingent created on April 20, 1894. It was stationed at an army post and attacked by 10,000 to 12,000 Afghans. The Sikhs, led by Havildar Ishar Singh, chose to fight to the end. Some military historians consider it as one of history's greatest last stands. Another British Indian contingent recaptured the post after two days.

Background

Situated on the Samana Range, in present-day Pakistan, Saragarhi was a small village in the border district of Kohat. Under Lieutenant Colonel John Haughton five companies of the 36th Sikhs were sent in August 1897 to the North-West Frontier of British India (modern-day Khyber Pakhtunkhwa) and were stationed at Kurag, Sangar, Samana Hills, Sahtop Dhar and Saragarhi.

A number of forts originally built by Ranjit Singh were consolidated. Two of the forts were *Fort Lockhart* and *Fort Gulistan* situated a few kilometres apart. Saragarhi was created midway as a communication post as the forts were not visible to each other, and it was on a rocky ridge.

The Afghans began in 1897, and between August and September many attempts by the Pashtuns to capture the forts failed; thanks to the resistance by the 36th Sikhs. Afridi tribesmen along with the Afghans, attacked Fort Gulistan twice at the beginning of September but on each occasion, they were pushed back. A relief column from Fort Lockhart reinforced Saragarhi comprising three non-commissioned officers (NCOs) and eighteen other ranks (ORs), i.e. 21 men in all.

Table 4.7 Battle of Saragarhi

	Afghan Tribesmen	*British Army*
Led By	Gul Badshah	Havildar Isher Singh
Strength (men)	6,000-10,000	21
Killed/Wounded	180/Much More	21/-

The Battle

The details of the Battle of Saragarhi are accurately documented as Gurmukh Singh signalled events to Fort Lockhart by heliograph as they occurred.

Around 9 am on September 12, 1897, approximately 6,000–10,000 Afghans reached the signalling post at Saragarhi. No immediate help was possible to be sent to Saragarhi. The soldiers in Saragarhi decided to fight till the end to prevent the enemy from reaching the forts. Sepoy Bhagwan Singh was the first soldier to be martyred and Naik Lal Singh was seriously wounded. The Afghans broke a portion of the wall of the picket. Haughton estimated that between 10,000 and 14,000 Pashtuns were attacking Saragarhi.

The leaders of the Pashtun forces reportedly persuaded the Sikhs to surrender. Two determined and failed attempts were made to rush open the gate. The wall was breached subsequently and one of the fiercest hand-to-hand fighting occurred. Displaying outstanding chivalry, Havildar Ishar Singh ordered his men to go into the inner layer, while he himself remained to fight. All the defending Sikh soldiers were killed not before killing quite a substantial number of Pashtuns.

Sepoy Gurmukh Singh, who was signalling messages now asked for permission to close the heliograph and take up his rifle. It is said that he alone killed 20 Afghans before the Pashtuns set fire to the post to kill him.

The Afghans had been engaged too long before they turned their attention to Fort Gulistan and the British reinforcements arrived there on the night of September 13–14, before the fort could be captured. The Pashtun death toll as per their own admission was about 180 killed and many more wounded. But when the relief party arrived, some 600 bodies are said to have been seen around the ruined post. This is the combined figure of the Pashtuns killed in the Battle of Saragarhi as well as by the use of intensive British artillery fire.

In the entire campaign, including the Battle of Saragarhi, the total casualties numbered around 4,800.

Tirah Campaign

The Afridi tribe had an agreement with the British for safeguarding Khyber Pass for sixteen years and they got some financial benefit in return. A local regiment entirely composed of Afridis was thus stationed in the pass. However, there was a tribal revolt and these tribesmen captured all the posts in the Khyber held by the Afridis and attacked the forts near the city of Peshawar. The Battle of Saragarhi occurred on September 12 at this stage. The British authorities were engaged with the Mohmand rising north-west of the Khyber Pass.

General Sir William Lockhart was commanding the Punjab Army Corps, having 34,882 British and Indian men, in addition to 20,000 followers and on October 18, the fighting ensued. Without much opposition, the Dargai heights were captured but due to lack of water, these were abandoned. On October 20 the same was recaptured but with a loss of 199 of the British casualties. On October 29 at the Sampagha Pass leading to the Mastura valley, there was a tough fight between the British and the Afghans and on October 31 at the Arhanga Pass from the Mastura to the Tirah valley.

The British force in the Tirah district destroyed the walled and fortified hamlets of the Afridis. The two divisions consisted of nearly 20,000 men and a force of about 3,200 troops under Richard Westmacott attacked Saran Sar but while withdrawing the troops suffered 64 casualties. On November 11, Saran Sar was attacked again and the casualties were only three.

On November 13 a third division visited the Waran valley not much difficulty was experienced and several villages were destroyed; but 72 British casualties happened as the retreating rear-guard was attacked all day along. Almost daily the Afridis waged guerrilla warfare, and troops were engaged in fighting them. On November 21, a brigade under Brigadier-General Westmacott was detached to visit the Rajgal valley. The mission was successful but with 23 casualties during the retirement and it was the initiative of Brigadier-General Gaselee who collaborated effectively with the Kurram movable column to punish the Chamkannis, Mamuzais, and Massozais. The Chamkannis offered resistance on December 1 and 2 causing about 30 British casualties even though the Mamuzais, and Massozais surrendered.

The Kurram column returned to its camp, and Lockhart decided to evacuate Tirah. He sent his two divisions by separate routes: the first via the Mastura valley, destroying the forts on the route and to join at Bara, close to Peshawar; the second division to move along the Bara valley. The target was to transfer from Kohat to Peshawar. The retreat started on December 9 under severe cold conditions but the first division completed its journey practically unopposed, but the second division faced great hostility from the Pashtuns over the stretch of 40 miles which it covered suffering 140 casualties.

On December 14 the two columns met finally. Without opposition, the first division, aided by the Peshawar column, took possession of the Khyber forts.

Treaty

Negotiations for peace began with the Afridis. On April 4, 1898, the expeditionary force was broken up. The presence in the fighting line of the Imperial Service native troops under their own officers was a unique feature of this campaign.

Waziristan Campaign

It was a political agency in the north-west with Kohat in the north and Bannu on the east and on its south was the Khaktu stream from the point where it entered Shuidar. Separated by high barren hills, it comprised four large and fertile valleys.

The people of Northern Waziristan, except the Daurs of the Daur valley, all belonged to the Darwesh Khel branch of the Wazirs consisting of the Utmanzai and the Ahmadzai tribes. Both these were subdivided into numerous clans. The incessant raids on the Daurs by Darwesh Khel who were the least tractable of the Pathan tribes compelled the former in 1894 to petition the British Government for protection.

Daur was taken over and was put under a form of direct administration, while the wazirs were merely under political control. Under the agreement made with the Amir of Afghanistan in 1893, the boundary was delineated in 1894-95 with minimal resistance from Darwesh Khel. Raids in the British zones continued and in 1897 the British troops were deployed from Datta Khel to enforce the collection of fines from village Maizar. The British force was attacked by the villagers and five British officers were killed and to punish the latter, their lands were laid waste by a military expedition. The Afghans submitted and desisted from further uprisings in the frontier.

For quite a few years, the landmass between Thal and the Tochi on the lower Kurram valley was a safe haven for the Kabul Khel section of Utmanzai and a number of outlaws took refuge there. In 1902, at last, troops reached here from Tochi, Bannu and Thal. The tribesmen at Gumatti who were a gang of outlaws made a desperate fight but when all their towers were blown up and their rebuilding was not permitted, a large number of outlaws, about 250 surrendered. The country was since then open to the passage of troops and British officers. Roads were laid from Thal to Tochi and to Bannu.

The necessity for maintaining peace between the British and the trans-border tribes dawned on the British. A special political agency for the Khyber was started in 1878 to keep the pass open. The cession of Kurram in 1879 by the Afghan Government led to a similar agency creation for the Kurram area in 1892.

Heads of the Punjab (1849-1947)

Sl	*Name*	*Took Charge*	*Left office*
	President of Board of Administration		
1	Sir Henry Montgomery Lawrence (1806-57)	1 Apr 1849	17 Jan 1853
	Chief Commissioners		
1	John Laird Mair Lawrence (1811-79)	18 Jan 1853	31 Dec 1858
	Lieutenant-Governors		
1	Sir John Laird Mair Lawrence, (1811-79)	1 Jan 1859	25 Feb 1859
2	Robert Montgomery (1809-87)	25 Feb 1859	10 Jan 1865
3	Donald Friell McLeod (1810-72)	10 Jan 1865	1 Jun 1870
4	Sir Henry Marion Durand (1812-71)	1 Jun 1870	20 Jan 1871
5	Robert Henry Davies (1824-1902)	20 Jan 1871	2 Apr 1877
6	Robert Eyles Egerton (1857-1912)	2 Apr 1877	3 Apr 1882
7	Sir Charles U Aitchinson (1832-96)	3 Apr 1882	2 Apr 1887
8	James Broadwood Lyall (1845-1920)	2 Apr 1887	5 Mar 1892
9	Sir Dennis Fitzpatrick (1827-1920)	5 Mar 1892	6 Mar 1897
10	William Mackworth Young (1840-1924)	6 Mar 1897	6 Mar 1902
11	Sir Charles Montgomery Rivaz (1845-1926)	6 Mar 1902	6 Mar 1907
12	Sir Denzil Charles J Ibbetson (1847-1908)	6 Mar 1907	26 May 1907
13	Thomas Gordon Walker (1849-1917)	26 May 1907	12 Aug 1907
-	Sir Denzil Charles J Ibbetson (1847-1908)	12 Aug 1907	22 Jan 1908
-	Thomas Gordon Walker (1849-1917)	22 Jan 1908	25 May 1908
14	Sir Louis William Dane (1856-1948)	25 May 1908	28 Apr 1911
15	James McCrone Douie (1854-1935)	28 Apr 1911	4 Aug 1911
-	Sir Louis William Dane (1856-1948)	4 Aug 1911	26 May 1913

16	Sir Michael Francis O' Dwyer (1864-1940)	26 May 1913	26 May 1919
17	Sir Edward Douglas Maclagan (1864-1952)	26 May 1919	3 Jan 1921
	Governors		
1	Sir Edward Douglas Maclagan (1864-1952)	3 Jan 1921	31 May 1924
2	Sir William Malcolm Hailey (1872-1969)	31 May 1924	9 Aug 1928
3	Sir Geoffrey F. de Montmorency (1876-1955)	9 Aug 1928	19 Jul 1932
	Sikandar Hayat Khan (1892-1942)	19 Jul 1932	19 Oct 1932
	Sir Geoffrey F. de Montmorency (1876-1955)	19 Oct 1932	12 Apr 1933
4	Sir Herbert William Emerson (1881-1962)	12 Apr 1933	1 Feb 1934
	Sir Sikandar Hayat Khan (1892-1942)	15 Feb 1934	9 Jun 1934
	Sir Herbert William Emerson (1881-1962)	9 Jun 1934	4 Apr 1938
5	Sir Henry Duffield Craik, Bt (1876-1955)	4 Apr 1938	7 Apr 1941
6	Sir Bertrand James Glancy (1882-1953)	7 Apr 1941	8 Apr 1946
7	Sir Evan Meredith Jenkins (1896-1985)	8 Apr 1946	15 Aug 1947

5

The Punjab from 1900 to 1918

Plague in Punjab

After the plague had hit Jalandhar and its adjoining areas in 1897, it affected Gurdaspur in November 1900 and soon spread to Sialkot. In 1901, the plague outbreak occurred in several districts and spread rapidly. Till 1901 about 21,000 deaths were reported and in 1902 it was ten times higher. The epidemic was still in full strength. The deaths in 1905 were close to 4,00,000 which was 15.8 per cent per thousand of the population.

Steps were taken for restricting outbreaks like the isolation of plague patients and the segregation of persons exposed to infection, the evacuation of houses and villages and the disinfection of houses and effects.

Treatment and anti-plague inoculation were sadly not availed of by the people who preferred *Yunani* and *Ayurvedic* medicines, and avoided inoculation. The scheme did not prove successful.

Plague reached Hoshiarpur District from Jalandhar in 1897 and despite considerable opposition strict measures were taken for three years and the results were inspiring.

The human agency was not the means of infection; even though the disease might have been conveyed in bundles of clothes, but in the great majority of instances it was found that some persons had come from an infected village and brought the disease with them.

Rats were found to be the agents of infection. The disease increased at a rapid rate and when it was found that it was not attacking distant villages widely, it was held that rats must in many cases have been the infecting agents. In several instances men had broken the cordon to go and condole with friends in other villages, bringing back from it food and clothes and the persons did not catch plague themselves, but infected other members of their household on their return.

People's ignorance was also a cause of this epidemic.

Punjab Land Alienation Act, 1900

The marketability of farmland and the concomitant increase in its value would have made the farmer happy but the rise in revenue was not that much and it encouraged the propensity to give the land on mortgage or on borrowing. The wasteful social expenditures increased and often the peasants fell into debt traps of the moneylenders who were often Hindus and Sikhs. This caused land alienation and the British government had to do something about it.

In the 1880s, the area of land being grabbed by moneylenders who were mostly urban was close to half a million acres every year. The percentage of Muslim peasants who were in the debt trap varied from 70 to 90 depending on the location in the province. This undoubtedly caused communal tension, and in the decades to come, this acrimony would rise further.

Advocates of market economics were engaged by the British to find a solution and the debate resulted in the Punjab Land Alienation Act. It came into operation in 1901 and the Act prevented the sale of agricultural land to persons of non-agricultural tribes. Thus, this act categorised Punjabi castes into agriculturist and non-agriculturist. The power and influence of the rural agricultural castes and classes was thus consolidated over the Punjab. They in return helped supply soldiers to the army from their villages. The Punjab supplied nearly half the soldiers to the Indian Army.

Many feared that a ban on buying land by the non-agricultural castes would harm Punjab's economy but Lord Curzon would have none of it.

The moneylending castes of Baniyas, Khatris and Aroras in meetings across Punjab led an unsuccessful agitation. Both the Hindu-owned newspapers as well as INC criticised it.

S.S. Thorburn was one of the first to support such a law and he had published a book *Musalmans and Moneylenders in the Punjab* in 1886, which influenced opinion in Calcutta and

London. Muhammad Hayat of Wah was another great supporter of this act. He was a big landowner, a member of the Punjab legislative council. Hayat, a Khattar Jat, asserted that he was a truer representative of the Punjabi farmer than the pro-Congress Harnam Singh, a Christian from the Kapurthala family.

The ban on urban Punjabis buying rural lands did not, in any way, affect Punjab's economy. But this act could not stop moneylending, indebtedness and consequent alienation of land. Often the moneylending classes would use a middleman in the village to buy land on their behalf and the exploitation continued as before. The bigger landholding Jats of Eastern Punjab and their Muslim counterparts in the Punjab along with other big landlords exploited the situation to their advantage and increased their landholdings considerably.

British Policy of Dividing Provinces: NWFP Creation

Lord Curzon (1859-1925)

The Viceroy who had got the Land Alienation Act passed was always wary of Russia and he wanted it to be far removed from India as he felt that the British colonialism could be challenged by the expansionism of Russia. The revolt by Afridis and Pashtuns in 1897 was a very near memory and he felt that the governance structure needed to undergo change.

In 1901, a new province called the North-West Frontier Province was carved out of Punjab. It was created for the Pashto-speaking frontier places and including the districts of Hazara, Peshawar and Kohat and the trans-Indus portions of Bannu and Dera Ismail Khan. The frontier was to be managed directly from Calcutta, with no controls from Lahore. The hard feelings this caused among the Raj's officers in Punjab was much milder than Lord Curzon's decision to divide Bengal in 1905.

Opposition vas expressed through a boycott of British goods and campaigns for swadeshi. The 1905 defeat of Russia by Japan generated a feeling that the Asians could defeat Europe. The INC asked for the division to be annulled. Lala Lajpat Rai, who had participated in the Congress's 1900 session in Lahore, Bal Gangadhar Tilak (1856-1920) from Poona and Bipin Chandra Pal (1858-1932) comprised the famous pan-Indian 'Lal-Bal-Pal' trio.

Some years back Bankim Chatterjee had written Anandamath

which first showcased *'Bande Mataram'* and had anti-Muslim innuendos. Then the Muslims did not protest but now when Bengal in the East had a Muslim majority, they found that the Hindus were protesting. Muslims did not protest Bengal's division. Though in east Bengal men like A.K. Fazlul Huq and Nibaran Chandra Das preached non-communal ideas but a serious Hindu-Muslim dialogue, was not taking place at this juncture, whether by Muslims or Hindus. Punjabis or Bengalis failed to bridge the gap between their different religious communities.

A pivotal meeting in Simla between a large and influential Muslim deputation and Curzon's successor as India's Viceroy, Lord Minto took place.

Punjab Governors During 1902-13

Sir Charles Montgomery Rivaz

He was born in Essex, on March 11, 1845 and entered the Indian Civil Service in 1864, and was immediately appointed to the Punjab. After working for six years at district level; from 1871 to 1876 Rivaz was in the Provincial Secretariat. Then he became the Superintendent of the former Kapurthala State as the Maharaja Jagatjit Singh was a minor from 1876-85. He received the CSI in 1885. After two years in 1887 when he was in the Kangra district he was made Commissioner of Lahore where he worked till 1892, and was a Financial Commissioner of the Punjab from 1892-97. In October 1897 Rivaz was appointed to the Executive Council of the Governor-General where he served as a member of the Home Department, Revenue and Agricultural Departments. He initiated the treatment of landed indebtedness in the Punjab. The alarming appropriation of the peasants by the commercial classes led him and Ibbetson, then revenue secretary to launch the Punjab Land Alienation Act, 1900. Rivaz was promoted as KCSI in 1901, and early in 1902 left the Governor-General's Council in order to become Lieutenant-Governor of the Punjab. He held this post till March 1907. He was indefatigable in visiting every place of interest, in his province and he did much to improve the appearance and amenities of its capital, Lahore. During his term of office, the Punjab developed steadily. Large irrigation schemes were carried through and the bold experiment of colonising the newly irrigated wastes of province proved eminently successful.

He was succeeded by Sir Denzil Ibbetson in 1905.

During his governorship, the following events occurred:

- In 1903 the Delhi Durbar was held
- Sargodha was founded
- Punjab Agricultural College and Research Institute was started
- Passing of Colonisation Bill, 1906
- Punjab unrest of 1907

He died in London on October 7, 1926.

2. Sir Denzil E.J. Ibbetson

Born on August 30, 1847, at Gainsborough in Lincolshire Sir Denzil Ibbetson came from a branch of the Yorkshire family. He was educated at St. Peters College, Adelaide, and then at St. John's College, Cambridge. In 1868 he qualified for the Civil Service of India and joined the Punjab Commission at the end of 1870. He was appointed an Assistant Settlement Officer in 1871 at Karnal. His report made the writer's name popular. His treatment of the Punjab Census 1881 displayed the highest qualities and it was a sort of data mine which is referred to even now, more than 139 years after it. His report detailed castes, customs, and religions and it was of high anthropological value. He afterwards quarried his outline of Punjab Ethnography. He undertook compilation of the *Punjab Gazetteer* in 1883.

Ibbetson introduced many educational reforms and, at the end of 1888, he was entrusted with the conduct of British relations with the erstwhile Kapurthala state.

In 1896 as Secretary to the Government of India in the Revenue Department, he became Lord Elgin's main man in handling agricultural problems and prepared the ground for the Punjab Land Alienation Act. He was made CSI in 1896. To take charge of the Central Provinces as Chief Commissioner he was sent there in 1898. He joined the Council of Lord Curzon in 1902. In 1903 he was promoted as KCSI. On the retirement of Sir Charles Rivaz, on March 6, 1905 he became the Lieutenant-Governor of the Punjab. The rise of revolutionaries, ravaging of Punjab by famine and plague made the lives of the peasantry miserable. Even bringing three million acres under canal irrigation was going against the Government. With prompt action Ibbetson repressed the disturbances in the Canal colonies owing to higher taxes. He secured the authority of the Supreme Government for the deportation of Lala Lajpat Rai and Sardar Ajit Singh without trial. He resigned from the office and was succeeded by Sir Thomas Gordon Walker in 1907. But as Walker's tenure was short, he became Lt. Governor again on May 16, 1907.

He saw the creation of the Punjab Muslim League in 1906.

3. Sir Thomas Gordon Walker 1907-08

Sir Thomas Gordon Walker, GCSI and CSI was born on September 14, 1849. He was the son of Rev. Henry Walker of Urquhart and was educated at the Aberdeen University and entered the Indian Civil Service in 1872. He worked as Settlement Officer, Ludhiana from 1872 to 1884 and as a registrar, chief court from 1884 to 1888. In 1896 he was appointed a DC and in 1898 a Judge of the Chief Court. From 1901-07, he worked as Commissioner of the Delhi Division. From 1903 to 1907 he was made the member of the Viceroy's and Provincial Legislative Councils. He succeeded Sir Denzil Ibbetson in 1907, as the Lieutenant-Governor of the Punjab and again in 1908. He had two short tenures. Sir Louis William Dane succeeded him in 1908.

4. Sir Louis William Dane 1908-13

Sir Louis William Dane, Indian Civil Servant, was born on March 21, 1856 at Chechester and after passing the examination of the Indian Civil Service in 1874, he was posted in 1876 to the Punjab. In 1879 he became Private Secretary to the Lieutenant-Governor of the Punjab and in 1898 he was appointed Chief Secretary to the Punjab Government in 1898. In March 1903 he was foreign secretary in the Government of India. Thanks to his efforts, a treaty with Afghanistan was signed in March 1905. In 1908 Dane became Lieutenant-Governor of the Punjab. He laid the foundations of the Provinces' Industrial Development, and he especially encouraged the growth of the Canal Colonies.

The growth of population which the rapid development of the agricultural resources of the province would have taken place throughout his period of administration was completely halted by the plague. The unrest which came to a head in 1907 was mainly caused by it. A terrible earthquake, centred in Kangra, occurred in 1905 and more than 20,000 people had perished under the ruins of their houses there.

By the passing of the Cooperative Credit Societies Act in 1903 and the organisation of a Provincial Agricultural Department in 1905, the welfare of the rural population was taken care of. At the Coronation Durbar on December 12, 1911, the King announced the transfer of the capital of India to Delhi. Consequently, the city and its suburbs were separated from the Punjab province after 53 years. It had been made a district of the Punjab in 1858 after the mutiny. In 1913 Sir Michael O'Dwyer succeeded Sir Louis Dane.

The following events occurred during his term:

1 Anand Marriage Act, 1909
2 Delhi Durbar of 1911
3 From Punjab Delhi transferred and made the capital of British India
4 Kinnaird College for Women started at Lahore
5 Colonisation of Government Lands Act, 1912

Earthquake

On April 4, 1905, the Shivalik Hill country round about Kangra was devastated by a disastrous earthquake, levelling 700 square miles, and in which 20,000 people died. Both the towns of Kangra and Dharmshala were reduced to ruins. The shocks were also felt severely all over the Punjab causing serious damage to houses and public buildings at Lahore, Amritsar, Sialkot and other important towns [*Author's ancestral house in Othian, Ajnala, Dist. Amritsar was damaged too; though only partially*].

The loss of human life was much heavier as the earthquake occurred in the early hours. Several social and religious reform associations of the Punjab promptly organised relief parties and rendered much needed help to the survivors. The survivors began the task of extricating and relieving the living and they performed the last rites of the dead. Pushing up relief parties from the plains was done without delay, and in a week, at five centres, medical relief stations had been started; in two weeks the treasuries were opened, and the machinery of government was active once again.

Grants of timber for the rebuilding of houses and liberal advances of money were made: and the private charity contributed over Rs. 1.35 million for relief work.

Heavy Casualties

This earthquake has been ranked as one of the severest in modern times as 20,000 human beings perished. The loss of life occurred principally in the Kangra Valley, Dharmshala, Mandi, and Kullu, but the shock was perceptible to the unaided sense throughout an area of some 16,25,000 square miles. Although this must have been one of the most damaging earthquakes, those which occurred in the Province in 1803, 1827, 1842 and 1865 were severe too.

Simla Meeting of 1906

Indians were demanding for a long time a role in the Raj's councils and despite Curzon's reservations, it could not be withheld. The British knew that involving Indians would mean Hindu-Muslim fights but it was still better, as they thought, rather than the India-Britain fight.

The Simla interaction was scheduled on October 1, 1906. From the Muslim side the following were present: MAO's honorary secretary, Mohsin-ul-Mulk who assembled the Muslim deputation, Sir Sultan Mahomed Shah Aga Khan, leader of the 35-men deputation of prominent Muslims from all over India with five from Punjab at least: Umar Hayat Tiwana, the Punjab legislative council member, Mian Muhammad Shah Din and Mian Muhammad Shafi, both barristers from Lahore, Khwaja Yusuf Shah and Shaikh Ghulam Sadiq of Amritsar.

Sayyid Hussain Bilgrami with Mohsin-ul-Mulk prepared the address for the Aga Khan to read out the same. Their agenda focused on Muslim representation in any future council, be it municipal, provincial or national, and in the Raj's services. They conveyed that it was just not the question of only the strength of their numbers but also their political importance and the services rendered in the defence of the Empire and their owning the Mughal Empire till a century ago. He went on to say that the Muslim community should not be placed at the mercy of an unsympathetic majority and that the Indian Muslims were a distinct community.

The Aga Khan said he wanted that in every case the local

authority should declare the number of Hindus and Muslims entitled to seats on Municipal and District Boards and each community should be allowed to return [its] own representatives as was done in many towns in the Punjab

The Viceroy had received an advance copy of the text and gave an assurance that the Muslims' 'political rights and interests as a community would be safeguarded' in any new political arrangements. Articulated on October 1, 1906, this historic commitment for separate electorates had evidently been thought through and decided upon by the Viceroy and his advisors a few days before that date.

Even as the INC and most politically-conscious Hindus across India were busy demanding Bengal's reunification, the Empire had enabled Syed Ahmed's ideological successors to walk off with the prize of a separate Muslim electorate in India as a whole and lead to the division of India, 41 years later.

Muslim League is Formed in 1906

Later, Minto's biographer made a sensational observation that *'the Viceroy's words were accepted as a charter of Islamic Rights'*. Before the Simla meeting took place, the newspaper *Bengali* of Calcutta, appealed for a united Muslim-Hindu front before the British Government but the belated appeal got no positive response from the Muslim brethren.

Despite efforts by the pioneers of the Congress to attract Muslims the majority of the Muslim leadership, such as Sir Syed Ahmed Khan and Syed Ameer Ali did not accept the theory that INC truly represented the two distinct communities.

The Muhammadan Educational Conference was founded by Sir Syed in 1886. Later the new awareness of Muslim needs for an expansion of educational upliftment known as the Aligarh Movement helped stimulate a political consciousness among Muslim elites, who went on to form the All-India Muslim League.

By 1901, the formation of a Muslim political party at the national level was seen as an essential step for the Muslims. The meeting held at Lucknow in September 1906, with representatives coming in from all over India was the first step towards its formation. The issue was reconsidered by the Simla Deputation in October 1906 and decided to frame the objectives of the party during the annual meeting of the Educational Conference, scheduled to be held in Dhaka. A detailed scheme was prepared by Nawab Salimullah Khan and he suggested that the party should be named All-India Muslim Confederacy.

The All-India Muhammadan Educational Conference's annual meeting was held in Dhaka from December 27-30, 1906. Three thousand delegates attended, headed by both Nawab Waqar-ul-Mulk and Nawab Muhasan-ul-Mulk (the Secretary of the Muhammaden Educational Conference). The objectives were detailed and the unity of Muslims under the banner of an association was emphasised. The formal proposal was made by Nawab Salimullah Khan which was supported by Zafar Ali Khan, Syed Nabiullah, a barrister from Lucknow, Hakim Ajmal Khan, Maulana Muhammad Ali Jauhar, and Syed Zahur Ahmad, a prominent lawyer.

Punjab Colonisation Bill

When Bengal passed through an unprecedented upheaval over the Partition of the Province, Punjab was stirred to its very depths by government measures, unwise and provocative to the extreme.

Punjab's agricultural production and revenue had increased but the social equitable scenario was far off. Many people with no experience in farming had arrived in colonies simply because they had served the Raj or were influential. The Punjabi bureaucrats involved with the colony schemes became grantees as well and there were very few who were associated with the Montgomery colony and yet had not claimed a tract of land for himself.

The Raj wanted to stop this malpractice and so it introduced the Colonisation Bill of 1906 and it empowered the provincial government to act without initiating civil court proceedings.

The excessive land-tax with a further addition of irrigation and other rates accompanied by rules and regulations of the most exasperating kind made the life of the peasants difficult. The officers of the Canal Colony tried to dominate two million people cultivating three million acres as if they were dealing with a village.

The bill attempted to alter the very basis of land relationship in the Punjab and attempted to deprive the farmer who had been called from the central Punjab districts to dig canals and irrigate the barren, but extensive wastelands of West Punjab. Once the area became one of the most fertile regions in India, the government of Punjab, with an excuse of introducing uniformity, tried to modify the tenure system. It was alleged that the government was desirous to convert these lands into plantations as done in Assam and thereby reducing the farmers from owners to cultivators. The settlements at Rawalpindi took place at higher rates and the water coming in from Bari Doab was levied at a much higher cost thereby agitating the farmers even more. By March 1907, the atmosphere was quite charged. The students of Khalsa College gave a hostile demonstration during the farewell of the outgoing Lt. Governor Rivaz.

The Bill provided for transfer of property of a person after his death to the government if he had no heirs. His property could be sold by the government to any public or private developer. This was completely against the social norms and was summarily rejected by all the sides.

The whole of Punjab was in a turmoil. The Bill touched the cultivator most vitally. One provision debarred them from cutting down trees standing on their own lands without the previous written permission of the authorities. The new colonies were mostly inhabited by the Sikh Jats from the Central Punjab, and Muslim cultivators from the western districts of Punjab and excitement ran high.

Thus, the land revenue collected by the government was not a tax but the landlords' share of the yield of the land. By March 1907 the situation was very tense. A new song was on the lips of the people *'Pagri-Sambhal 0 Jatta'*.

Protest meetings in bigger cities were organised by the Arya Samaj. Lala Lajpat Rai, Sardar Ajit Singh of the 'Bharat Mata Society', Sufi Amba Prasad and Pindi Das, editor of *Young India* took the leading part.

In the Chenab colony the first protests erupted since this area was reportedly worst affected by this bill. The first protest saw various organisations submitting memoranda to the government to redress their grievances, but the government ignored these. It was followed by a protest at Lyallpur. With the support of Lala Lajpat Rai, a secret society named *Anjuman-i-Muhibhan-i- Watan* was formed by Ajit Singh, a Jat Sikh. The working class in the railways also protested in Rawalpindi during the same period.

Ajit Singh made a brave attack on the rise of land assessment and said that *'the peasants were the real rulers of the country, that Rajahs were their Kamins and the Deputy Commissioner, Superintendent of Police and the Chief Officers and Government were their servants.'* He asked the peasants to stop the cultivation till the rates of taxes were brought down. He asked the Hindus and Muslims to unite fearlessly. The DC served a notice on Ajit Singh for his seditious speech and asked him to attend a public enquiry on May 2 at 11 am. In the protests, out of 68 persons, 6 were arrested.

The Punjab government, on June 18, described the situation in the Punjab as very serious and explosive; thanks to Lala Lajpat Rai and his 'agent' Ajit Singh. The latter had addressed many meetings at Bradlaugh Hall, Lahore and he was an excellent orator. Ajit Singh's close associate was Sufi Amba Prasad who was originally from Moradabad. He worked as a sub-editor of *Hindustan* and later as editor of *Bharat Mata*. The government identified him as a dangerous man capable of fomenting big trouble and he was thought of as the brain behind the disturbances. On the other hand, Lala Lajpat Rai was viewed as the 'moving spirit of the whole movement, even though his personal character was thought to be above reproach'.

It was alleged that Lala made inflammatory speeches, asked peasants not to pay water tax and paid Rs. 100 every month to Ajit Singh. Two letters written by Lala and sent to Parmanand in London were also produced to confirm his hand in these activities.

The period was full of mass agitations which ended after the deportation of both Rai and Ajit Singh. Lala was deported on May 9 and Ajit Singh on June 3, 1907. The editor of *Punjabee* was also arrested. The deportation of Lala Lajpat Rai and Ajit Singh led to violent demonstrations throughout the Punjab and the atmosphere was full of hatred towards the British and even a 10-year-old lad was arrested for insulting a British officer.

They were released on November 14, 1907.

In the Lyallpur district where the martial classes lived and supplied the best recruits to the Indian army, big meetings were held and thousands of peasants attended it.

Umar Hayat Khan Tiwana, a member of the Punjab legislative council also joined the protests. Apart from serving on the

Legislative Council, Umar Hayat was running one of the large stud farms in the lower Jhelum colony. His loyalty to the British throne was without any doubt. The Punjab officials dominated the council and they ensured the passage of the Colonisation Bill. However. the Viceroy vetoed it. The British needed the support of men like Umar Hayat. Also, the reports of the stir affecting Sikh sepoys who might cause a revolt made the British think about the bill once again. Lala Lajpat Rai and Ajit Singh were released and allowed to go home.

The settlers accused the government of breach of faith as this unjust legislation was to affect the proprietary rights of the agricultural population in their lands.

The Punjab Government, with Sir Denzil Ibbetson as the new head, saw the seeds of rebellion and the British officials believed that but for the finances and determination of Sir Denzil Ibbetson, the efforts of Lala Lajpat Rai and Sardar Ajit Singh would have resulted in another Mutiny.

In 1918, Ajit Singh (Sandhu) came into close contact with the Ghadar Party in San Francisco. In 1939, he returned to Europe and later helped Netaji in his mission in Italy. In 1946, Ajit Singh Sandhu came back to India at the invitation of Pandit Nehru. He stayed in Delhi for a while before he went to Dalhousie where he died on August 15, 1947. 'Thank God, my mission is fulfilled', he said as he died.

The Bill is Amended

The agrarian movement in the Punjab dispelled the British notion that the Punjabis would be loyal to them, come what may. There was more disappointment for the British as the Sikhs also joined the agitation, rather led it in a big way. The Sikhs proved their loyalty to the national cause as the subsequent turn of events would show. Bipin Chandra Pal expressed satisfaction at the involvement of the Sikhs while he was in London in 1908.

The trouble in the Punjab was mainly agrarian and confined to the areas affected by the proposed legislation or enhanced revenue demands of the government. The amended Bill was passed by the Punjab Government. The Government of India vetoed the amended Act and restored the status quo.

Ramsay MacDonald, Keir Hardie and others came running to

India to review the situation and due to their active interest, the peace was restored soon. Lala Lajpat Rai went to an unknown destination. Sardar Ajit Singh was also 'wanted' and was arrested a few months later and deported to Mandalay where Lala Lajpat Rai had already preceded him.

Infused by the Bengal Agitation

The ferment in Bengal infected the minds of the redoubtable Punjabis and tales of assault, of boycotting and general lawlessness from East Bengal reached Punjab and the newspapers there duly reported them. Signs of unrest were visible more in the urban areas than in a rural area as in Rawalpindi, Sialkot and Lyallpur. Seditious speeches were openly delivered, rioting broke out and measures were adopted to strengthen the hands of the agitators in the Chenab Canal Colony and Bari Doab.

Attempts were made to arouse the passions of the Jat Sikhs, and the Police were advised to quit the service of the government, while the invitation was addressed to the Indian soldiers. Some Indian leaders endeavoured to kick the British out of the country either by force or by sustained resistance of the people.

A strong feeling of radical hatred in the barracks of soldiers was another target and the military authorities viewed the matter very seriously and Lord Kitchener intervened for the repeal of the Colonisation Bill.

There was a reduction in the Land Tax and the water rate. Returns of water tax were significant. The capital of 7 million sterling was invested in the Punjab canals yielded in 1906-07, a handsome net profit of 101 per cent. But in the case of the Chenab Canal Colonies the returns were nearly 22 per cent and it was here that the agitation was the strongest.

The arrested and deported Punjab leaders returned home after six months in Burma. The Rawalpindi lawyers who were arrested and kept in jail for five months were released on bail. They were acquitted by the Judge a few days later.

Revolutionary Activities in the Early Stage

Once Ajit Singh Sandhu was released, he continued along with his fellow revolutionaries in their so-called 'seditious' activities. Some pamphlets like *Kumar Singh* and *In Memoriam* were circulated among the people of the Punjab. The pamphlets paid glorious tributes to the Martyrs of the Freedom Struggle of 1857: Tantia Tope, Kumar Singh, Lakshmi Bai and others.

A weekly publication from Berlin named *Talwar* advocated revolution and appealed to the Hindus and the Muslims to rise against the British in the spirit of 1857. From Europe itself, another journal titled *Maro Feringhi Ko* appeared with the basic purpose of arousing anti-British sentiments. Zia-ul-Haq wrote *Akhiri Awaz Suno* in a Peshwar Newspaper in 1909. The author was persecuted and sent for five years of deportation. The government was angry and launched a search on various presses and publication agencies.

Search was made at the houses of Ajit Singh's father as well as father-in-law and many books were seized. Kishan Singh, the brother of Ajit Singh was the main distributor of the literature. Many authors and publishers were arrested but Ajit Singh and Sufi Amba Prasad were in the Persian Gulf at that time. Kishan Singh, Nand Lal, Ishwari Prasad and Munshi Ram were sentenced for long terms of imprisonment.

It was felt in 1907-09 that only that revolution could yield results which had the blessing of all the communities of Punjab and affected all of them. The common element was peasantry: Hindus in East Punjab (present-day Haryana), Sikh and Muslim peasantry in Central and Western Punjab.

It is a paradox that when the Hindu nationalist leaders gave a call for the Swadeshi movement after the division of Bengal, a substantial percentage of Muslims became sceptical of it. The Muslims were indeed looking forward to the British for some advantages and reservations.

In 1906, the demand for 'Separate Electorates' had been made by the Muslim deputation and Muslim League had been created. Although the Muslim peasantry had participated in the agitation against the British once the Colonisation Bill was proposed, the Muslim leadership nevertheless almost condemned the Swadeshi movement and appealed to the Muslims not to be a part of it. Instead, a *Swajati* movement was started to unite the Muslims.

The movement in the Punjab had roots in the economic crisis for the peasants but it was not standalone type. It had links with other radical movements within and outside the country in Europe, Japan and America. Those who studied abroad were also learning the trade of making arms and using them. When too many restrictions were placed within India, the revolutionaries shifted base to outside India.

Famine 1908

In some parts of India including Punjab the monsoons were deficient in 1907 and the Viceroy made an appeal for funds to combat the distress. According to him the famine affected some parts of the Punjab, Bengal, the Central Provinces and even Bombay. More than 1,50,000 persons were in receipt of famine relief in British India at the end of the first quarter of the year. In March and April 1908 the Government of India advanced about Rs. 2 crores as *takavi* loans. The revenue suspensions sanctioned in two years was Rs. 3.5 crores and a sum of Rs. 1.32 crores was provided for famine relief during the following year.

Minto-Morley Reforms-1909

The limited representation with indirect elections was brought in by the Indian Councils Act of 1892. Lord Curzon had earned the ire of Indians already by creating the partition of Bengal. The government suppressed the extremists and at the same time tried to soothe the moderates. In 1908 Gopal Krishna Gokhale went to England to meet Mr. Morley, the Secretary of State for India. Both the Viceroy and the Secretary of State for India decided to reform the legislative councils. So the name came up. This culminated in the Indian Councils Act 1909. At both the levels viz. central as well as provincial, the expansion of legislative councils was done.

Salient Provisions

Expansion of the Legislative Councils

The expansion of the both the central and provincial legislative council was undertaken. The Central Legislative Council's number of members was raised from 16 to 60. However, in the provincial legislative council the number of members was not uniform. The number of members in each of the legislative councils of Bengal, Bombay and Madras was increased to 50. It was decided that the provincial legislature of UP would have 50 members, whereas

Assam, Burma and Punjab would have 30 each.

Communal Representation

The Indian Councils act for the first time recognised the elective principle for the appointment of non-official members to the councils. On the basis of class and community, the electorate was decided. A provision of three categories was made for the provincial councils, viz. general, special and chambers of commerce. However, a fourth category—Muslims was added to the central council. This was for the first time that *on the basis of religion for Muslims*, the seats in the legislative bodies were reserved. Separate constituencies were marked for the Muslim citizens and only they were given the right to elect their representatives.

On India's polity, the separate electorate for Muslims had a long-lasting impact. It recognised the Muslim community as a separate distinct community in India and triggered the Hindu-Muslim differences which ultimately culminated in the partition.

Under the separate electorates, in constituencies specially reserved for them, the Muslims could vote exclusively for the Muslim candidates. That the political, economic and cultural interests of the Hindus and Muslims were distinct, was being emphasised by this action.

Other Features

It empowered the members to discuss the budget and before it was approved finally resolutions could be moved.

To discuss matters of the public interest, the members were given rights.

On any subject not within the legislative competence of the particular legislature, no discussion was permitted.

Analysis of the Act

The Minto-Morley Reforms of 1909 was not up to the expectations of the Indians. What the people expected was responsible government in the country but they got instead 'benevolent despotism' and an attempt to create a 'constitutional autocracy'.

There was no real majority of those who represented the people and although the non-official majority was given in the

Provincial Councils, it got nullified by the fact that it included nominated members.

The real political solution lay in complete self-rule by the Indians. Here the position of the Governor-General remained unchanged and so also his veto power. The narrow franchises, indirect elections, limited powers of the Legislative Councils resulted in the government with little accountability.

The Act rather created political complexity with the introduction of the separate electorate system. No link between the supposed primary voter and his representative on the Legislative Council existed. Therefore, the political participation, awareness and education remained an illusion. The 1909 Act was 'the shadow rather than the substance'.

Merits of Minto-Morley Reforms

They were a step towards the growth of representative institution, and also towards the responsible association of elected Indians with the administration. It gave recognition to the elective principle for the composition of the legislative council for the first time thus giving Indians a chance to express their grievances, criticise the executives and suggest steps for improving the administration. The demand of complete Indianisation of the legislature was furthered by the enlargement of the legislatures.

Delhi is Raj's Capital in 1911

George V, then Emperor of India, along with Queen Mary, his consort, made the announcement at the Delhi Durbar on December 12, 1911, that the capital of the Raj was going to be shifted from Calcutta to Delhi. He had come to lay the foundation stone for the Viceroy's residence in the Coronation Park, Kingsway Camp. King George V and Queen Mary laid the foundation stone of New Delhi at the site of the Delhi Durbar at Kingsway Camp on December 15, 1911, during their imperial visit.

Hindu-Muslims Aspirations in Bengal and Punjab

In December 1911, King George announced that Eastern Bengal would be absorbed into the Bengal Presidency and the Districts, where Bengali was spoken, were once again unified and the non-Bengali speaking parts like Assam, Bihar and Orissa were separated out.

Muslims were shocked because, despite the Bengali terrorism which was mainly Hindu in character, they saw a Muslim majority Eastern Bengal as a safeguard of interests, by the British. They saw the unification as if their interests had been compromised just for the Hindu protests and administrative convenience.

In 1905, when Bengal was partitioned, the Muslims leaders did not support it but once the Muslim majority province of Eastern Bengal and Assam came into being, prominent Muslims saw it as advantageous. Muslims, especially in Eastern Bengal, had been quite backward, compared to the Hindus, in the period of United Bengal. The subsequent Hindu protest against the partition was seen by the Muslims as detrimental to their interest. With the capital moving to a Mughal site, the British thought, rather wrongly, that Bengali Muslims would be appeased.

Already disturbed by the European attacks on Muslim power in Turkey, Indian Muslims now had a new reason for being upset.

The chasm between the elites of the Hindus and Muslims continued in Punjab. Hindu-owned Urdu papers like *Hindustan, Punjabi, Jhang Sial and Akash* attacked the Muslims, whereas the Muslim-owned papers like *Watan* and *Paisa Akhbar* attacked the Hindus.

Occasionally an appeal for sanity was made, as in 1909, Lahore's Hindu-owned *Akhhar-i-Aam* cautioned Arya Samajists who targeted Muslim journals and the latter also did the same. Mahboob Alam, the editor of *Paisa Akhbar*, professed 'Indian nationality' among Punjab's different communities, but that the British rule should remain.

INC again met in Lahore at the end of 1909 but its popularity was not rising in Punjab and they had to face Arya Samajists having a hostile mindset towards the Congress. The major INC split in 1907 did it no good. Now the two Maharashtra stalwarts, Tilak and Gokhale, where in opposite camps, with the Moderates managing to oust Extremists or 'Nationalists' like Tilak and his allies.

Initially, the Minto-Morley package was disliked by many Hindu Punjabis. They saw the INC as having failed to prevent a separate Muslim electorate. In the opinion of Lahore's *Hindustan*, the separate electorate would *'permanendy cripple the notion of a common Indian nationality'* and was worse than Bengal's partition. The journal asked Punjab's Hindus to abandon the INC and support the Punjab Hindu Sabha, started in 1907.

Soon, the Hindus and Sikhs of Punjab realised that separate electorates and weightage formula could be deployed in Punjab to their advantage since as minorities in their province, they were entitled to the same.

In the field of education, Punjab's Muslims were laggards. Although they numbered about 53 per cent in the Punjab province in 1911-12, they made up only 24 per cent of Punjab's college enrolments and 24 per cent again in the schools.

Some Prominent Personalities of India

Muhammad Ali Jinnah, the legendary leader and the new prophet of the Muslims was born in 1876. Jinnah (in Arabic means 'wing' of a bird or army) was born a Shia Muslim Khoja of the Ismaili sect. Disciples of Ismaili Aga Khan in thousands fled from Persia as they faced persecution between the tenth and sixteenth centuries CE. The exact year of the flight of Jinnah's ancestors to India is unknown. He, like his parents, was a Gujarati-speaking person and trained in law in London. He joined the INC in 1906.

He was quite young and was not a part of the Muslim delegation which met in 1906 in Simla and nor was he present in Dhaka during the formation of the Muslim League, the same year. Jinnah served as Dadabhai Naoroji's private secretary when the latter, INC president-elect asked for 'Swaraj' at the session held in Calcutta towards the end of 1906.

In 1908, Jinnah failed to defend Tilak in a Bombay court for sedition and the latter was sentenced to jail for 6 years and he served this term in Burma. Jinnah was closest to Gopal Krishna Gokhale who thought of Jinnah as the 'best ambassador of Hindu-Muslim unity'.

By 1909, Jinnah entered the Imperial Legislative Council by winning Bombay's Muslim seat. Jinnah addressed the annual meeting of the Muslim League in December 1912 even though he was not yet a member. He joined the Muslim League in 1913, although he remained a member of the Congress as well. On behalf of the Congress, in April 1913, he again went to Britain, with Gokhale, to meet officials.

Another delegation of the Congress was led by Jinnah to

London in 1914 but as the First World War had begun, he found officials cold shouldering him regarding the Indian reforms.

Mohandas Karamchand Gandhi had become well known for advocating satyagraha, non-violent non-cooperation, while in South Africa as a lawyer. Both Gandhi and Jinnah, later on became political rivals but this time Jinnah who like Gandhi was in London, attended a reception for Gandhi, and returned home to India in January 1915.

By 1915, both Pheroz Shah Mehta and Gopal Krishna Gokhale were dead and this resulted in a setback to the moderate faction in the Congress; Jinnah was still a part of the Congress Party. Naoroji was in London where he died. Jinnah felt isolated. Jinnah worked earnestly to bring the rival parties the Congress and League together. Hoping that the Indians would be rewarded with political freedom, Jinnah supported the British war effort and in 1916, along with Tilak and Annie Besant, he contributed greatly to the founding of the All India Home Rule League.

In 1916 Jinnah was the president of the Muslim League and INC and Muslim League signed the Lucknow Pact, setting quotas for Muslim and Hindu representation in the various provinces. This pact doubled the Muslim representation in the provinces where they were in a minority but reduced their representation in Punjab (and Bengal) where they were in a majority. So, in Punjab despite having a population of 55 per cent, their representation was limited to 50 per cent. Even though the pact could not be implemented in full, its signing led to a period of cooperation between the Congress and the League. In Punjab, this pact was not welcomed by any Muslim leader. For the first time since 1857, Muslims and Hindus had asked for the same thing jointly.

In Punjab, Maulana Zafar Ali (1873-1956), owner and editor of Lahore's *Zamindar* was a new champion of Turkey's cause and was warm towards the INC and the idea of Muslim-Hindu unity. He supported the 1907 stir against the Colonisation Bill; he also sought 'worldwide Muslim unity'. Under his editorship, the newspaper *Zamindar* attained a circulation of over 20,000 during the Balkan wars to became Punjab's foremost Urdu daily.

Equally passionate about the Muslim cause was Muhammad Ali (1878-1931), born in Najibabad, UP. He wrote in his English newspaper *Comrade* and the Urdu *Hamdard.* Matching them was Abul Kalam Azad (1888-1958) whose *Al Hilal* was printed in Calcutta.

These three authors stirred the Muslims of India from 1911 onwards on the question of Turkey and the Empire's attitude to it. Punjab's celebrated poet, Muhammad Iqbal (1876-1938) was far removed from the issue over Turkey. He was born in Sialkot in a tailor's house and in his twenties wrote powerful Indian nationalist poetry like *Saare Jahaan Se Achcha,* and rebuked, in *Naya Shiwala,* both the Brahmin and the Mullah for spreading venom. He urged the Hindus and Muslims to raise a new temple of unity in India.

But the time he stayed in Europe from 1905 to 1908 changed lqbal's thought process. The temple of unity named 'India' was now erased from his mind and he thought in a global perspective about all the Muslims of the world.

Secondly, he asked India's Muslims to learn about dynamism from modern Europe. Yet he asked the Muslims to desist from nationalistic competition since he thought all Muslims of the world needed to unite for a better world for them.

He noted that Europe's first advance was guided by the intellectual culture of Islam which spread from Spain and Italy. Slowly, Iqbal who used Urdu and Persian became a poet of Islam and the unity of India was far from his mind. He mesmerised Lahore's Muslims with his rendition of his poems. He did not however ostracise Raj over its role in Turkey.

He remained a poet of the Muslims and their intellectuals and distanced himself from the peasant class of all communities including Muslims. He was too Persianised even though his roots were from Sialkot. The question of opposing the colonial powers and siding with the peasants was unthinkable for him.

Then there was Fazl-i-Hussain (1877-1936) whose forefathers were on the rolls of Maharaja Ranjit Singh. He was a Bhatti Rajput educated at Cambridge. He did his graduation from the famous Government College, Lahore and Iqbal was one of his classmates.

Interestingly, Fazl-i-Hussain joined the INC in 1905 when he moved to Lahore and Bengal was partitioned. He went to Dhaka in 1906 when the Muslim League was launched. A different and more loyal provincial unit of the League was launched by Mian Muhammad Shafi, an Arain from the famous *Mian* family of Lahore whose forefathers had worked for Maharaja Ranjit Singh and he was in Dhaka too.

Fazl-i-Hussain tried to strengthen the Islamia College by joining the Anjuman-i-Himayat-i-Islam and in 1913 he jumped into politics vigorously, possibly influenced by the Balkan Wars.

In 1915, Fazl tried to enter the provincial legislative council from the 'general' Punjab University constituency where the Hindus formed a majority. His rival was Kapurthala's Raja Harnam Singh. Despite being a Congress candidate, Fazl headed for defeat but the disqualification of Harnam Singh ensured his victory. Fazl-i-Hussain learnt a lesson: separate Muslim electorates could be always advantageous for the Muslim candidates.

Towards the end of 1916 when assemblies were held at Lucknow in the presence of such luminaries as Tilak, Jinnah, Annie Besant and a few others who were 'the authors of the Congress-League Pact'. The separate electorates were accepted by both the parties. It was the famous *Lucknow Pact* and 10 months later in October 1917, a Punjab Political Conference under Fazl-i-Hussain ratified it.

The conference tried to awaken Punjab which was called a 'politically lethargic' province. Interestingly, Fazl was the president of INC in Punjab and also the general secretary of the Muslim League's provincial branch. Shafi's faction was disaffiliated and that of Fazl was accredited.

1913-19

This was the period of political awakening and has been of great political awakening in the history of the Punjab. Punjabis including the Sikhs had to face stern tests by the British Government. The movements which cannot escape attention are:

The Ghadar Movement,
the Komagata Maru or Nanak Jahaz,
the Jallianwalla Bagh Massacre and
other political events which occurred under the Governorship of Sir Micheal O'Dwyer.

Sir Michael O'Dwyer

Sir Michael Francis O'Dwyer, (1864-1940) was Punjab's Lieutenant Governor from 1913 to 1919 and was certainly one of the most controversial ones. He was the sixth son in a family of fourteen and his father was John O'Dwyer, of Barronstown, Tipperary. He was educated at St. Stanislaus College, Tullamore, and passed the open competition for the Indian Civil Service in 1882 and the final examination in 1884. Like many other Britishers from the 1850s, he was an Irishman. Unlike John Nicholson and the Lawrence brothers, he was a Catholic.

He was first posted in Shahpur and after distinguishing himself in the Land Revenue Settlement he was made Director of Land Records and Agriculture in the Punjab in 1886. He was later selected by Lord Curzon for a prominent part in the new NWFP and its separation from the Punjab. He was Revenue Commissioner from 1901 to 1908 and in December 1912, he was appointed as the Lieutenant Governor of the Punjab and he occupied this post until 1919.

In a book written by him and named *India as I Knew it*, he wrote how the Punjab narrowly escaped from widespread disturbances after the return of the Sikh emigrants from America, Canada and the Far East, in the first few months of the First World War of 1914-18, and how he turned the Punjab into a loyal recruitment centre for the war. His appointment as GCIE in 1917 was a testimony of his services to the British empire.

He claimed that for the interest of the rural masses, he was opposed to political reforms. He felt that the Indian masses neither understood nor desired the representative government. He felt that Punjabis who belonged to cities and had political aspirations were 'untrustworthy'. He believed that any revolt needed to be suppressed immediately. He could not tolerate any agitation which could bring the Hindus and Muslims together.

The tragedy of Jallianwala Bagh followed the passing of the *Anarchical and Revolutionary Crimes Act* in March 1919. The shooting was directed by a military officer, Brigadier General Reginald E.H. Dyer but the action was, no doubt, approved by O'Dwyer. O'Dwyer was later shot dead by Sardar Udham Singh at the Royal Central Asian Society in London on March 13, 1940.

The period from 1913 to 1919 was a time of political awakening in Punjab. Many tests of sacrifices and endurance were given by the Punjabis like the Ghadar Movement, Komagata Maru, Jallianwala Bagh Killings and other political events which took place during the reign of Sir O'Dwyer.

Martial Races and Their Appeasement

The First World War was on and the British needed Indian troops. Out of nearly 6,83,000 recruits to the army, nearly 60 per cent or 3,50,000 were from Punjab. Germany had Turkey on its side and the oil wells of the Middle East became vulnerable. So, the Indian soldiers were to be sent not only to Europe but also to the Middle East, Egypt and Africa. There was a large scale decimation of the Indian troops in Baghdad and early in France. Half of the Lahore Division was dead in a few weeks and this could pose a serious problem for fresh recruitment.

To keep the recruitment on, new castes and races were added to the list of so-called 'Martial Races'. Men from all the districts of Punjab were now suitable for the job. The DC of the district was empowered to recruit principally. Every civil functionary was given the task of recruitment and he was given a target. A Zaildar was a head who consulted Lambardars of villages for this recruitment process.

Any Punjabi with clout was considered a suitable recruiter —Landlords, Pirs and Sajjda Nashins in the Western Punjab, wealthy Sikh farmers in central districts and Hindu Jats of Eastern Punjab. The carrot followed the Stick. About 1,80,000 acres of land were earmarked for the officers and men doing duty and another 15,000 acres who were most efficient at providing cannon fodder in flesh and blood.

Another lure was the awarding of titles like—Knighthood, Rai Sahib, Rai Bahadur, Khan Sahib, Khan Bahadur. Then some got swords of honour and grants of money or land.

So, the Punjabis rushed manpower for the War as never before.

Dilemma of Muslim Punjabis

It was a dilemma for Muslims whether to fight for the British Empire against Turkey which was an Islamic country. British government shrewdly declared Germany as their principal foe and Turkey had just joined a wrong country and that they (the

British) were not against Turkey or Islam.

Earlier the Ali brothers Muhammad Ali (1878-1931) and Shaukat Ali (1873-1938) who were leading the Khilafat movement, had written to the Sultan of Turkey not to remain neutral but their request went abegging. Neither the Ali brothers nor Zafar Ali and Maulana Azad supported the Empire on this issue. Their efforts were not rewarded but it created goodwill for them in the Punjab.

Muhammad Ali was even made the president of the Punjab Muslim League in 1917. Punjab's Muslim chiefs, however, overcame their own reluctance and accepted the Raj's assurance and offers and sent soldiers in thousands to the war front, mainly from the Western Punjab.

The British received help from Maulana Ahmed Raza Khan Barelvi having the largest Punjabi Muslims followers who issued a *fatwa* which claimed that since the Ottoman did not belong to the Quraish tribe of the Prophet (PBUH), they were not Islam's caliphs. This fatwa made the task of many Pirs of Punjab much easier.

The Raj met the demands of the Empire's war manpower supply successfully but the Punjab civil military balance was disturbed. The civil-military merger for recruiting soldiers resulted in the militarisation of the bureaucracy. Also the involvement of zamindars and land owners in the recruitment resulted in the unwanted closeness between rural and military people to create a lobby in Punjab's large villages.

The Ghadar Movement 1914-15

The Khalsa Diwan Society

In 1907 the Khalsa Diwan Society was organised in Vancouver and built a Sikh Temple in Vancouver in 1909. Another temple was erected in Victoria in 1912, and the Khalsa Diwan Society of the United States of America built a gurdwara at Stockton. The Diwan mainly concentrated on religious, educational, and philanthropic activities but problems of the immigrants and cases of racial discrimination were undertaken by them as well.

To safeguard the economic interests of Indian workers and to fight cases against immigration authorities these organisations also came up (1) The United India League in Vancouver (2) The

Hindustani Association.

Indians met at gurudwaras which became centres of political activities. The Indian organisations began to publish papers in Gurmukhi, Urdu, and English. Punjabis who had a very high percentage of Sikhs were disillusioned with the Raj despite their committed loyalty towards the British and these people were ex-soldiers or policemen. Now words like 'gora' and 'gore-shahi' were coined and they got drawn towards the radical groups led by men like Lala Lajpat Rai who visited them in Canada and the United States.

Now new leaders emerged, e.g. a lecturer at Stanford University in California, Hardayal of Delhi, became the political mentor of the immigrants. Abroad, the effective control remained in the hands of the largely illiterate Sikh workers of peasant stock. Jwala Singh and Hardayal formed a body named 'The Hindustani Workers of the Pacific Coast' at Stockton (California). Sohan Singh Bhakna (1870-1968) of Oregon and Hardayal were elected President and Secretary respectively. Jwala Singh remained behind the scene providing funds to the prospective Indian students. The party began publishing a weekly paper called *Ghadr* (revolution) in Urdu from San Francisco and later in Gurmukhi and other languages. And soon the *Ghadar* paper was being read by Indians in Canada, Japan. the Philippines, Hong Kong, China, Malaya, British Guyana, Singapore, Trinidad, the Honduras, South and East Africa, and other countries.

Events Leading to the Komagata Maru Tragedy

Attempts were being made by young Indian men abroad to overthrow the British by subversive activities and also to generate opinion against the colonial rule, worldwide. Thereafter were formed, the Indian Independence League in the USA, the Indian Association of the Pacific Coast, the Indian Independence Committee and the Berlin Committee in Germany.

The Indian Independence League was formed in 1908 by a few young men who had arrived in Berkeley, California, in 1907 for studying. Simultaneously, there was great discontent among the Punjabis including Sikhs in Canada and USA due to hardships faced due to their Indian nationality.

Quite a few Sikhs had concentrated in Portland and it served the purpose of sowing the seeds of hatred against the British. The arrival of Vishnu Ganesh Pingley and Hardayal in San Francisco in April 1911 provided a good boost to the work of 'the league'. Hardayal with his speaking prowess boosted the morale of the revolutionaries. The first issue of the *Ghadar* was published on November 1, 1913 from a press called Jugantar Ashram in San Francisco.

The same year, three Sikh delegates of the Ghadar Party visited Punjab and talked about the adverse situation being faced by the Indians abroad. The Ghadar Party organised many meetings in USA and it was even attended by senior German officials.

The Sikhs landed in a series of conflicts with the British; possibly they had not yet forgotten that 60 years ago, they were their own masters in Punjab. A caustic comment by one Major Hill about a Sikh engineer at Khalsa College generated many protests and 75 Sikh associations condemned his statement.

There was unrest in Punjab and violence often broke out and this was facilitated by the revolutionaries who had for some time been in Canada or USA. The loyal peasants and soldiers of cantonments were approached to be a part of the Ghadar Party and the response was positive for the freedom-fighters.

In the meantime, the Canadian government was alarmed and it passed an order for Indians to leave Canada and to migrate to the British Honduras but the Indians did not take it easily and reacted.

Under the Immigration Act, 1910 of Canada, the list of prohibited immigrants was expanded and the federal cabinet was given enhanced authority to make indiscriminate judgements regarding admissibility and deportation. Under a new provision the Governor-in-Council could arbitrarily prohibit the landing of any immigrant considered 'unsuited to the climate or requirements of Canada.' Now every prospective immigrant had to satisfy the Canadian Government that he possessed 200 dollars and had travelled making a journey without stopovers on a through ticket from his country of origin to Canada.

The Komagata Maru

Two Societies, viz., the United India League and the Khalsa Dewan Society, Vancouver, were formed on December 15, 1911, a year after the passing of the Immigration Act, 1910. These organisations' deputation met thc authorities but it proved inconsequential.

Gurdit Singh was a rich and well-connected contractor in Singapore and Malaya who went over to Hong Kong in 1913 looking for a new destiny and chartered a Japanese ship, the *Komagata Maru,* on behalf of the Guru Nanak Navigation Company. On April 4, 1914 this ship started from Hong Kong and picked up passengers at Shanghai, Moji and Yokohama. With 376 passengers it reached Victoria on May 21 and Vancouver on May 23. During the voyage, Barkatullah and Bhagwaan Singh Giani, the Indian nationalist revolutionaries met the passengers. Bhagwan was the head priest of the gurdwara in Vancouver and had been one of three delegates sent to represent the case of Indians in Canada. *Ghadarite* literature was distributed and political meetings took place on board. The ship was cordoned off by armed men of the Canadian Government and all but 22, who had been returning to Canada, were not allowed to land on the Canadian soil.

In nearly two months the essential facilities were badly under stress with the food and water in the ship being exhausted. The situation became very critical as the Indians were ravenously hungry and very thirsty. The Japanese passengers were allowed to bring water far from the shore and fights for it became frequent. The tension was running high and on July 19, 1914, the ship was ordered to leave the port. The passengers were not prepared to budge; determined to die at Vancouver after a struggle rather than meet a certain death on the high seas by starvation. The passengers could not establish any contact with any one on the land.

As a next step the government decided to force the ship to leave the port. A large steam boat, the Sea Lion, was sent near the Komagata Maru with scores of armed policemen in it. On July 19, a fight ensued between the heavily armed Canadians and Indians with improvised weapons and both sides suffered injuries of varying degrees. The news of the fight spread and the crown of England asked force to be used and ordered warship *Rainbow* and another to be sent to evacuate Komagata Maru.

Meanwhile, the Indians on the shores watched the drama unfold as mute spectators. Now, some provisions were supplied and the Komagata Maru left Vancouver (on the west coast of Canada) on July 23, 1914 for Yokohama after nearly two months. Now, the Hong Kong authorities refused permission for the passengers to land. The ship left Yokohama on August 18 for Kobe where it reached on August 21, 1914 and new difficulties cropped up. The Hong Kong chapter was closed and the British Government in India prepared itself to bear the expenses of diverting the ship from Kobe to India.

On September 16 the Komagata Maru reached Singapore and it was kept eight kilometres from the coast. Nobody was allowed to disembark. Near Kulpi on September 26, it reduced its speed and some European officers boarded it to do a thorough checking. It was near Budge Budge on September 22, 1914 and its fateful journey was coming to an end. There was a special train waiting for the Punjabis to take them back to Punjab straightway.

About 60 passengers including all Muslims boarded the train but the remaining 300 started to march towards Calcutta (now Kolkata). Their march was stopped by a strong military force and in the melee that followed 18 Sikhs were killed. Many ran in various directions but most were caught. About 30 Sikhs including their leader Gurdit Singh, however, escaped. An executive enquiry was held but most of the arrested men except for 31 were released since the most dangerous ones had either been killed or had run away.

This incident provided a powerful stimulus to the *Ghadar* propaganda and it displayed the returning Sikhs' defiant and highly explosive temper.

S.S. Tasu Maru

Carrying mostly Sikhs from America, Japan, Manila, and Shanghai the Japanese S.S. Tasu Maru arrived at Calcutta on October 28 bringing 173 Indian passengers. Most of the Ghadar leaders were among them out to cause rebellion in the Punjab, and had been allotted separate circles in the Sikh populated districts. After hearing of the strict search for arms, the Ghadarites discarded their weapons and ammunition before reaching Calcutta.

The Punjab Government sent a strong force of Punjabi Policemen to bring them to the Punjab, to investigate their antecedents. Seventy-three men were identified as less dangerous and released but out of them, six were afterwards hanged for participation in the subsequent Ghadar outrages, six were transported for life. The other six strongly suspected in the same connection were re-arrested and interned, and two, who were among the chief leaders in the subsequent campaign became informers and helped the government to reveal the conspiracy.

From October 1914, thousands of Punjabi Sikhs from abroad were coming back and the Ingress ordinance was used to deal with them. On the basis of enquiry, it was decided whether he should be: 1) Interned in jail, if really dangerous 2) Restricted to his village, if less dangerous and 3) Discharged with a warning if believed to be free from the Ghadar view.

Out of 8,000 who returned in the first two years of war, 400 were jailed, 2,500 were released. The government got the information about the planning of seditious activities and the organisation of Punjabi gangs and attempts to influence British Indian troops.

Between October 1914 and September 1915, there were a series of explosions, Punjab policemen were getting murdered and people loyal to the government were getting killed too. Robberies to raise funds was a common phenomenon now. Attempts were made to derail trains. Guns and revolvers were being requisitioned by the Ghadarites.

Military pickets were being attacked now and an attack was made on the Indian military picket close to Amritsar and their rifles were taken. Plans for seizing the arsenal at Ferozepur and the magazines at Lahore were being made and attempts met with some success too.

Rashbihari Bose and N.G. Pingley moved into Punjab to take charge of the operations. Rashbihari was a link between Bengal and Punjab. N.G. Pingley, a Maharashtrian had returned from America with the Sikh revolutionaries. It was tried that the troops returning to India should be persuaded to become a part of the Ghadar movement and accordingly maps were prepared showing the centres at which the work would continue. Pingley was arrested on March 23, 1915, with explosive bombs while he visited sepoys in the barrack at Meerut. He was assisted by Kartar Singh and Harnam Singh who approached soldiers' barracks to join them in the *Ghadar.*

Unfortunately for the revolutionaries, the general mass remained loyal to the British government. On November 27, 1914 15 Ghadar Sikhs gathered at Ferozepur awaiting orders from headquarters for an attack at Ferozepur arsenal. They decided to loot the government treasury at Moga which had only a small police guard. They shot dead a Sub-Inspector and a Sikh Zaildar but were hotly pursued by the Sikh villagers and a few policemen. Two of the revolutionaries were killed and seven were captured, who were tried, convicted and hanged within two months of the incident. The six who escaped were all arrested later and punished.

Meanwhile, Ghadar outbreaks became more alarming in the early months of 1915. Forty-five serious outrages had been committed up to February 1915, by the revolutionaries, who were recruiting the lawless elements in the population. The Lieutenant Governor of Punjab informed the government about two startling developments of an extremely serious nature: The abortive attempt at rebellion in the Province on February 19, and the agrarian rising of the Muslim peasantry in the south-west Punjab, directed mainly against their Hindu creditors, which broke out early in March.

These two outbreaks, though simultaneous but unrelated, showed how seriously the public security was disturbed in a province which was the cannon-fodder for the British.

In the meantime, the government got the information that a general rising had been planned for the night of February 21, 1915, when certain troops would mutiny in the cantonments of Northern India, murder their British officers and assisted by the Ghadarites would seize the arms and ammunition, and cause a general rising.

But on the morning of February 19, 1915, information was received that Rash Behari and Pingley had moved their headquarters to Lahore and they had advanced the date of the uprising to the night of the 19th, and had sent messages to the various selected centres and cantonments accordingly. The government was fully alert.

First Lahore Conspiracy Trial, 1915

The four separate houses at Lahore housing the revolutionaries were raided by the police that afternoon and thirteen of the most determined revolutionaries were captured with all the paraphernalia of the conspiracy, explosives, literature and flags. Rashbihari and Pingley were not among those captured. The government unleashed a reign of terror and the conspirators were hunted and given very severe punishments. The case was known as the first Lahore Conspiracy Case. Seven were sentenced to death and the rest were given varying terms of imprisonment.

Those who were hanged were: Kartar Singh of Sarabha (Ludhiana), Bakshish Singh of Gilwali (Amritsar), Jagat Singh of Sur Singh (Lahore), Surain Singh I of Gilwali (Amritsar), Surain Singh(II) of Gilwali (Amritsar); and Bhai Harnam Singh of Bhatti Gurrava (Gurdaspur). Several other similar trials were held in India.

Pingley was arrested at Meerut on March 23, 1915 in the lines of the 12th Cavalry at Meerut with a large cache of bombs brought up from Bengal. He and Bhai Parmanand were among those tried. They were convicted and sentenced to death in the first Lahore conspiracy case by the Special Tribunal under the Defence of India Act. A few months later, Pingley was hanged while Bhai Parmanand's sentence was later commuted to one of transportation for life. He was imprisoned in the Andaman Islands until 1920 and had to do hard labour. Bhai Parmanand went on hunger strike for two months in protest against harsh treatment of political prisoners. As the result of a general amnesty order, the King-Emperor, George V, released him in 1920. Later, Parmanand died on December 8, 1947 of a heart attack.

The events foiled the plans for a general uprising on February 19. All the nearby cantonments Sialkot, Ferozepur, Rawalpindi were immediately informed by telegraphic messages so that the necessary pre-emptive steps could be taken by the government. Finding an adverse situation, the Ghadarites slipped away. The Ferozepur Depot was removed to a distant station.

Now, one after another Ghadar leaders in the Punjab were being captured. To save their skins several of them gave information which gradually provided the organisational details and methods. The Special tribunals of three Judges exhibited an ostensible sense of justice and gave stern punishment to the guilty.

It was decided by the government in March 1915 that committees of the local Sikh magnates should be established in the districts in which the conspiracy was most active. The task of such committees was to keep a watch upon the returned emigrants and their supporters. and to advise the Deputy Commissioners as to the action to be taken under ordinance, if necessary. The Administration got valuable inputs from these Sikh committees.

In retaliation, one loyal Sikh Sardar Chanda Singh was murdered in Hoshiarpur and two returned emigrants were convicted for it and hanged. In June, one Sikh magnate of Amritsar, Sardar Achar Singh was murdered by two returned emigrants and these two were quickly caught, convicted and hanged. Another government informer Kapur Singh met the same fate as he was murdered outside his house. The assassins escaped but were later apprehended and hanged.

To plan a seize of the state magazine a meeting of revolutionaries was held in Kapurthala state in early June. A gang of eight men attacked a military picket near Amritsar and seized rifles and ammunition. The people of the country-side were loyal to the British and they lost no time in chasing the rebels who were well inside the Kapurthala state now. The revolutionaries had shot a ferryman and killed one of the chasing party. Five of the rebels were captured with the help of police, tried by the Tribunal and hanged. Two others escaped; one turned approver and another was caught later and hanged.

By August 1915, i.e. within 9 months of the first outbreak, the Ghadar rebellion was crushed. Almost all the leaders and most of the highly active comrades were awaiting trial or were brought to justice later. The internal order was restored and sadly the Sikh community was used as a loyal tool by the British to eliminate the Punjabi freedom fighters.

Agrarian Rising in 1915

The Muslim peasantry of the south-west Punjab were a simple lot heavily under debt to Hindu moneylenders and had to endure the high prices and freeze in credit due to the war. The epidemic of plague drove many of the Hindus to the towns. Towards the end of February 1915, when the Ghadar troubles were at their worst and the anti-British Pan-Islamic movement inspired the Lahore students to go to Kabul, the British Government was quite worried about this sudden rising of the Muslim peasantry in Multan, Muzaffargarh and Jhang districts of the south-west Punjab.

This was unrelated to the Pan-Islamist or the Ghadar Movement but the propaganda against the British Government regarding their apparent defeat in the First World War spread far and wide. The peasantry organised themselves in bands, and between February and March 1915, committed no less than 50 gang robberies on the Hindus.

But soon the British forces swung into action and the outlaws were brought under control. Some 4,000 of these criminals were arrested and housed in some sort of concentration camps in Multan.

Soon the Defence of India Act was passed and special Tribunals were set up. In a few months, the Multan tribunal dealt with 800 of the main accused, convicted 500 of them and punished them. In the disturbed areas strong contingents of police were posted to reduce serious crime to a very low level. There was bitterness, especially among the Hindus who had suffered so heavily and under Muslim officers, Conciliation Committees were established to restore good feeling.

Here it can be mentioned that the moneylending profession would become one of the reasons of bitter relations between the Hindus (and Sikhs) and Muslims in the decades to come and would become one of the reasons for the 'Pakistan' demand.

Lieutenant-Governor Michael O' Dwyer in a tour six months later clarified that he would get the heavy sentences imposed on the raiders reduced by the Courts and would withdraw the punitive police, once cordial relations were restored. Slowly the local people came to an amicable settlement.

Gurdwara Reforms Between 1849-1921

Looking Back

After the death of Guru Gobind Singh, Adi Granth and gurdwaras became the centres where the Sikhs congregated. Gurdwaras were meant for propagating the social and spiritual message of the Gurus. As the Sikhs gained power, some importance began to be attached to the external signs of glitter and show at the gurdwaras and large estates were attached to the more important gurdwaras in Maharaja Ranjit Singh's time, though some jagirs had also been granted by the Mughal emperors. Ranjit Singh got the beautification of the gurdwaras done.

Before the British annexation, the 'Sangat (followers)' was supposedly in charge of the gurdwaras. The Jathedars of the gurdwaras were held in high esteem by the Sikhs and the former exercised great influence in the community.

After the death of Maharaja Ranjit Singh, chaos prevailed and the 'Pujaris' in charge of the gurdwaras ignored the indifferent *Sangat* and the conducting of affairs of the holy places by '*Gurmata* (Guru's intention)' fell into disuse.

During the British Rule

After the British annexation of the Punjab in 1849 the situation became worse; the defeated Khalsa lost much of their interest in the sacred places of worship and everything drifted into a state of chaos. The 'Mahants' and the 'Sadhus' in charge of the gurdwaras assumed an arrogant attitude towards the 'Sangats' and considered the shrines as their own property. Vices crept in; idol worship was encouraged in many shrines to get offerings from the orthodox Hindus. Even in some of the most important gurdwaras corruption and debauchery were common phenomena. Taking advantage of the prevailing situation, the British Government took over the control of the Sikh holy places like the Golden Temple with the Akal Takht as well as some of the other important gurdwaras.

An outside authority began to control and manage the affairs of the Golden Temple. Sardar Lehna Singh was selected as the manager of the Golden Temple by Sir Henry Lawrence and the former had to take his orders about everything from the Agent.

Just after the mutiny, disputes arose now and again among the 'pujaris' of the Golden Temple, the Akal Takht and the attached shrines over the distribution of money donated by the followers. In 1859, a committee of Sikh Sardars was formed to manage the affairs of the temple and also to settle some old disputes of the

'Jagirs' regarding their dues. The committee appointed a Manager to look after the temple and he was to report to the Deputy Commissioner who was his boss. The committee constituted had nine Sardars and they were some sort of trustees for the same. This committee controlled the administration, money spending and keeping the establishment under strict discipline.

A *Sarbarah* or agent was appointed in 1883 and the committee was quietly dropped. The Sarbarah was now directly controlled by the Deputy Commissioner. Corruption spread to every activity of the temple. The articles offered to the temple were auctioned by the Sarbarah or appropriated by the priests.

During the British rule after the annexation, the aristocratic Sikh families had lost their pride and had assimilated into the common mass of Sikhs and the ranks of the community had drastically thinned. The Khalsa had lost its pride and the religious border between Sikhism and orthodox Hinduism was not that impregnable for reversal from Sikhism to Hinduism.

British Help Revives Sikhism

The British enforced the rigid following of rites and ordinances of the orthodox Sikh faith among its enrolled Sikh soldiers. The recruiting officers were instructed to pay special attention to enlist men who observed all the rituals and rites of Sikhism. These Sikhs were encouraged to go to the gurdwaras attached to their regiments and were expected to behave as regular practising Sikhs. A necessary accompaniment of a Sikh regiment was the Granth Sahib under the charge of a priest. The exemplary services rendered by the Sikh soldiers in containing the mutiny went a long way to restore the Sikh community's pride to its previously lost position.

The landed aristocracy of the Khalsa got strengthened upon receiving the grants for their services during the mutiny of 1857.

Formation of the Singh Sabha

All the communities started their own associations to remove the social and religious prejudices as a number of colleges and schools were established once the universities were in place.

Although the Namdhari Movement had protested against the gurdwara's corrupt priests it failed to rouse the Sikh community as a whole. The Singh Sabha which followed it impressed the whole community's consciousness. A society named *Singh Sabha* was formed, in 1873, which undertook:

1. To restore Sikhism to its pristine purity;
2. To edit and publish historical and religious books;
3. Using Punjabi as the medium to propagate current knowledge; start magazines and newspapers in Punjabi;
4. To reform and bring back into the Sikh fold the apostates; and
5. To look after the educational programme of the Sikhs by involving the highly placed Englishmen.

This first Singh Sabha was set up and backed by a faction of Khatri Sanatan Sikhs, Gianis, and Granthis who rejected Khalsa practices like the *Khande di Pahul*. They were concerned about their caste status (all Sikh Gurus were Khatris) and promoted even idol worship which is against the basic tenet of Sikhism i.e. monotheism. They called themselves 'Sanatan Sikhs'. The Sanatan Sikhs detested inclusion of Jats who formed the majority Khalsa group. These Sanatan Sikhs regarded themselves as the natural leaders of the Panth during and after the end of Sikh rule. They regained their social prominence in the eighteenth and nineteenth centuries by taking over the main gurdwaras and other Sikh institutions while the Khalsa Sikhs were fighting for their survival against the Mughals, Pathans and the British. The Sanatan schools had many sects like Nirmala, Udasi, and Giani which were strongly influenced by Brahmanical philosophy and therefore the Sanatan Sikhs tried to align Sikh tradition with the Brahmanical order and caste ideology; they wanted to retain their status somehow.

These groups like the one headed by Khem Singh Bedi, leader of the Sanatan Sikhs, believed the principle of authority of Sikh tradition was in living gurus and not in the Guru Granth Sahib, which was upheld by the dominant Khalsa tradition. This ideology invited stiff opposition and the Khalsa followers formed the *Tat Khalsa* faction, or 'true Khalsa,' in 1879, headed by Gurmukh Singh. The Tat Khalsa promoted monotheism, icono-clastic sentiments, egalitarian social values and notion of a standardised Sikh identity unlike the polytheism, idol worship, caste distinctions, and diversity of rites practised by the Sanatan faction.

The Tat Khalsa, quickly gained ascendancy in the Singh Sabha movement, challenging the Sanatan faction as early as the early 1880s, and soon the term 'Singh Sabha' became synonymous with the Khalsa faction. Many other Singh Sabhas were formed in every town but Tat Khalsa actions and views ultimately prevailed. Once the Singh Sabha movement started, the rivalry of the Lahore and the Amritsar units was intense.

Sikh public leaders, despite this rivalry formed a central committee and a General Sabha in 1880. This General Sabha evolved into Khalsa Diwan Amritsar on April 11 1883 and had 37 affiliated local Singh Sabha chapters. It was opposed by the other Singh Sabhas and there were also internal dissensions. No agreement on its constitution or its leadership structure could be arrived at by the Singh Sabha chapters, ultimately leading to a split into Khalsa Diwan Lahore with about 30 chapters and Khalsa Diwan Amritsar with about 7 chapters. On October 30, 1902, the Chief Khalsa Diwan of Amritsar was formed and another group called Panch Khalsa Diwan was established by Babu Teja Singh at the village of Bhasaur in 1906. The sponsors of the Chief Khalsa Diwan founded in 1908 the Sikh Educational Conference to propagate Sikh education and it gained wide support in the community. The said conference encouraged furthering the cause of the study of Punjabi language and literature and consistently endeavoured to have Punjabi introduced in government schools and offices.

The Singh Sabha rejuvenated the Sikhs and had a profound moral effect upon them. Sikhism was in a debilitated state before the Singh Sabha's birth and the priests were ruling supreme with their rituals, superstitions and corrupt practices. The Singh Sabha awakened the Sikhs by touching the very basic elements of Sikhism and revived the Sikh beliefs and their practice. It effected the intellectual upliftment of the Sikhs to cope with the changing times and protested against the exclusion of Sikhs of untouchable castes and the performance of idolatrous rituals in the bigger shrines.

Hindu idols were removed from the precincts of the Golden Temple in 1905 as a result of pressure by the Singh Sabha which pressed upon the Deputy Commissioner after the death of the manager the need to consult representatives of the Sikh community in the appointment of a successor.

The Singh Sabha leaders were loyal to the government leaders who believed in doing no more than making representations to officials or instituting suits. More drastic action was needed to halt the misuse of gurdwara property and the situation worsened in 1912, when, the government acquired land attached to Gurdwara Rakab Ganj in Delhi.

In 1914, a dispute arose when the British brought down a part of the boundary wall of the gurudwara for straightening a passage to the Viceregal building. When the Sikhs protested and agitated, the government yielded in 1918 and the boundary wall was rebuilt at public expense.

The atmosphere was once again agitated in the autumn of 1918. Disappointment over the Montague-Chelmsford constitutional proposals, followed by large-scale oppression by the martial law administration, made the Sikh masses critical of the government.

The Central Sikh-league was formed in the winter of 1919 at Amritsar by the nationalistic view holding Sikhs who wanted to break the hold of the Singh Sabha over the Sikhs. At Lahore, the League passed a resolution of non-cooperation with the British and decided to send volunteers to take forcible occupation of Rakab Ganj land acquired by the government. The Central Sikh League demanded control of the Khalsa College, Amritsar be given to a Sikh Committee rather than under the government hands.

Montagu-Chelmsford Reforms

Britain had claimed during the First World War that Britain and her allies were fighting the war for the freedom of nations. It was believed by many Indian leaders that after the war, India would be given Swaraj. The British government however had other ideas and did not want to concede the demands of the Indian people. As a result of the Montagu-Chelmsford Reforms, called the Government of India Act, 1919, changes were introduced in the administrative system.

However, the reform provided only a terminological change at the centre and it turned the Imperial Legislative Council into the Central Legislative Assembly.

The Provincial legislatures were to be formed under a restricted franchise with only 10 per cent of India's adult males eligible to vote and would have limited powers; the actual power was with the Raj's Provincial governor and his nominated executive council. Each province was to be under some sort of Dyarchy with two power centres: (a) an elected ministry and (b) unelected council enjoying more powers. These reforms enabled the Indians to gain access to the ICS and Military Officer corps with less difficulty.

The demand for separate electorates for Muslims and Sikhs was a part of the Muslim League and Congress demands and this aspect was addressed by the Montford reforms. The British policy was to allow separate electorates and thereby prevent a national front to emerge against them.

In fact, the 1919 act did not live up to the Sikh expectations of a guaranteed share of 33 per cent in the elected bodies in Punjab. Ninety-three members would comprise the Provincial Legislative Council and 15 were to be Sikhs to be elected through separate electorate. In the Central Assembly and council of states, their representation was even more minuscule; 3/145 and 1/60. Sardar Sundar Singh Majithia, Secretary of the Chief Khalsa Diwan wanted an equitable and fair treatment for Sikhs. He appealed to the British:

> ....The other communities have a majority in one province or the other....they can counteract each other's activity....Sikhs have a large number of gurdwaras which need protection. We are a military community. We have fought for the Empire ....in Africa and the Great War.... No minority should be at the mercy of the majority .... to be tyrannised over.

Minorities including Sikhs were asking for representation for themselves in the Punjab in much more percentage vis-à-vis their actual percentage in the Province, e.g. Sikhs were 13.2 per cent of the population of the province but demanded 30 per cent representation (on the same grounds as the Muslims—that they served in the Indian Army and Police in disproportionately greater numbers than their percentage of the population). The Congress as well as the Punjabi Muslims opposed the Sikh demands. Both Sir Shafi and Sir Fazl-i-Hussain were opposed to the Muslim representation being less than what the Muslim percentage of population warranted.

For the first time, bicameralism and direct elections in the country were introduced. A bicameral legislature consisting of an Upper House (Council of State) and a Lower House (Legislative Assembly), therefore, replaced the Indian Legislative Council. By direct election, the majority of members of both the Houses were chosen.

Further, three of the six members of the Viceroy's Executive Council (other than the commander-in-chief) were to be Indian.

Also taken care was the weightage for minorities and distinction was made between urban and rural seats. Rural seats were reserved for clearly defined agricultural communities. This enabled the landowning rural groups and other dependable groups to corner most of the franchise.

In the cities, those paying Rs. 2,000 as annual income tax or Rs 50 as municipal tax were allowed to vote. Loyalty to the British was another factor for the selection of voters, particularly in the rural area. All *jagirdars, zaildars, lambardars* and *safedposhes* and those farmers who paid more than Rs. 25 annually as land revenue were allowed to vote and so were the commissioned and non-commissioned officers. No wonder these restrictions limited the percentage of population which could vote.

Sl	*Community of Voters*	*Village to City Ratio of Number of Voters*
1	Hindus	3:1
2	Muslims	7:1
3	Sikhs	20:1

The 1919 Government of India Act and the Punjab

British response to the growing dissatisfaction of Indians to their rule was in the shape of another set of reforms.

a) The voting rights were expanded but remained narrow based on property, tax payment and education.

b) The system of Dyarchy was introduced at the provincial level. The key subjects remained with the British Governor but some subjects were given to elected members of the provincial legislatures.

Gandhi and Punjab During 1915 to 1919

Mahatma Gandhi had returned to India from South Africa in 1915 at the age of 46. A fair amount of success by using 'Satyagraha (*Satya* means truth; *agraha* means polite insistence and Satyagraha is a combination of these two words)' had been achieved by the Indians under his leadership in South Africa in 1913.

In 1917, two years after his arrival in India, he took up the cudgels on behalf of the Indigo planters in Bihar's Champaran district. Champaran Satyagraha was the first popular satyagraha championed by Gandhi and it gave direction to India's youth and freedom struggle, which vacillated between moderates and the extremists from Bengal; while the former wanted Indian participation in the British colonial system, the latter asked for the use of violent methods to topple the British colonialists in India. Relief was obtained for Bihar's farmers.

Next year, in 1918, textile workers in Ahmedabad and farmers of Kheda district in Gujarat obtained relief using Satyagraha.

A conflict between mill owners and workers of the Gujarat Mills took place in February 1918.

As the plague epidemic subsided in January 1918 the textile mill-owners announced their intent to discontinue the 'plague bonuses'; during the times of wartime inflation the workers demanded 'dearness allowances' of 50 per cent over their wages on the July salaries in order to sustain their livelihood.

For help in fighting for economic justice, the hapless workers of the mill turned to Anusuyya Sarabhai, a social worker who was also the sister of the president of the Ahmedabad Mill Owners' Association. Gandhiji was urged by the lady to intervene and help resolve the impasse between the workers and the employers.

The mill owners staged a lock-out of the mills on February 22, 1918 and called back the workers who had accepted the 20 per cent increase in wages.

Gandhi opined that a 35 per cent rise in wages was a just demand that the industry could also economically support. This was rejected initially by the mill-owners but later accepted by them.

To support peasants who were unable to pay the high taxes levied by the British due to crop failure and a plague epidemic, Gandhi organised the Kheda movement.

His chief lieutenant was Sardar Vallabhbhai Patel who along with his colleagues organised a major tax revolt and the peasants of Kheda signed a petition calling for the tax for this year to be scrapped. The government in Bombay threatened the peasants with confiscation of their lands and properties and arrests unless they paid up their dues. None of the villages flinched and the government finally agreed for an honourable agreement for both parties. It was agreed that the tax for the year in question, and the next would be suspended.

The Punjabis did not know much about South Africa, Champaran, Ahmedabad or Kheda in 1919 but two thoughts of Gandhi appealed to them: 1) Non-violence to protest against an unjust law; and 2) Muslims and Hindus needed to come together against the British Raj. The Lucknow Pact of 1916 had brought the Hindus and Muslims close. In Punjab, Fazl-i-Hussain was the head of both the parties in 1919 and Gandhi was looking for still stronger bonding between the Hindus and Muslims.

To bolster the Lucknow Pact, Gandhi attended the League's annual session at the end of 1917 in Calcutta where the President Chaudhary Muhammad Ali was represented by his portrait since he and his elder brother Shaukat Ali were detained by the British.

This information was available to the Punjabis and when the Rowlatt Bill was imposed, Gandhi asked Hindus and Muslims to behave as if they were the children of the same parents.

In Lahore, the Rowlatt Bill was already being criticised in the first week of February. Barrister Duni Chand had formed Lahore's Indian Association and at a meeting the speakers who denounced this bill included: 42-year-old Fazl-i-Hussain, 41-year-old rising barrister Gokul Chand Narang, lawyer and 53-year-old Brahmin Arya Samajist Rambhuj Dutt Chaudhari, 53-year-old businessman Lala Harkishen Lal who controlled *The Tribune* and Duni Chand himself.

The meeting did not draw a big crowd but when Gandhiji participated in the next meeting conducted by the Indian Association on March 9, the crowd was large and intensive and it compelled Fazl-i-Hussain to agree to be part of the passive resistance being envisaged against the Rowlatt Act.

6

The Punjab from 1919 to 1929

Rowlatt Act and the Jallianwala Bagh Massacre

The people had expected changes at the end of the war as promised by Montagu-Chelmsford but the ultimate offer was nowhere near the Swaraj that the people dreamed of. There was widespread discontent throughout the country. The government resorted to new measures of repression in the midst of this discontent. On March 18, 1919, the *Anarchical and Revolutionary Crimes Act*, popularly known as the *Rowlatt Act* was passed which was based on the report of the Rowlatt Commission. Disorder ensued after passing of the Act. The government wanted to supplement the ordinary criminal law and for the exercise of emergency powers by the government. This Act had provisions for the arrest and confinement without assigning any reason and speedy rough and ready trial with no right to appeal.

In protest many leaders who were assembly members, resigned. Writing in his letter of resignation, Mohammad Ali Jinnah observed that a government that passes or sanctions such a law in times of peace forfeits its claims to be called a civilised government. The passing of this act generated new measures of repression which were condemned as Black Acts.

Gandhiji asked the Indians to observe March 30 as the *Hartal* day which was postponed to April 6, 1919. Gandhiji asked the people to observe a day's fast on that day. People in Punjab were not used to the idea of fasting and participating in the hartal together.

From Bombay, Gandihiji started on April 9 for Delhi. On April 10, he was served with a notice forbidding him to enter Punjab. He was told not to enter Delhi and the Punjab. Gandhiji disobeyed and he was arrested and ordered to remain in Bombay and not to go anywhere else. A few front-rank Punjab leaders were arrested on the same day.

Gandhi called for a country-wide protest. April 6, 1919 was observed throughout the country, as a national humiliation day. All over the country there were demonstrations and hartals. Business throughout the country came to a grinding halt. This united protest had never been seen in India before. The government resorted to brutal means to quell the agitation by resorting to lathi-charges and firings at a number of places.

Protests Against the Rowlatt Bill in Punjab

Earlier, a meeting was held on February 6, 1919 to protest against the bill and speakers from Lahore came down on February 9, 1919 at Amritsar. There was a mass meeting of Muslims on February 13 and 21 which were addressed by Dr. Kitchlew and Dr. Satyapal respectively. The leaders did not take the challenge posed by the passing of the bill lightly which was declared as 'highly inexpedient and injurious to the best interests of the country.' Gandhi resorted to a 24 hours' fast in protest and it was decided to observe March 30, as a day of mourning.

To add fuel to the fire, the government on March 29, 1919 passed an order under the Defence of India Rules forbidding Dr. Satyapal to speak in public. The Hartal on March 30 was observed successfully and the whole business of Amritsar city came to a halt but no disorder resulted. Next day the news of the riots at Delhi was received.

On April 4 orders were served on Dr. Kitchlew, Dina Nath. Swami Annubhava and Pandit Kotu Mal not to speak in public, in Amritsar. In Lahore, the local Congress Committee, responding to Gandhi's call and supported by the Indian Association, declared the proposed *hartal* on April 6. It was agreed to by Lahore DC Fyson and some senior leaders of the city that no coercion would be resorted to and the protestors and administration would be restrained. Lahore's markets were quiet that day and any untoward incident was avoided through the good offices of the senior citizens and a large number of mostly Hindu College students along-with poor Muslims who marched towards the Bradlaugh Hall.

The successful rally of Bradlaugh Hall did not go down well

with O'Dwyer who warned that the people organising protests would be held 'accountable'.

The District Magistrate was assured by a meeting at the chief citizens on April 5 that it would not take place but in the end, it was decided to proceed with the hartal plan which was to be held on April 6 and no untoward incidents were reported. To consider the continuation of the hartal, a private meeting was held on April 7.

The *Ram Navami* Festival in that fateful year was celebrated on April 9 by Hindus and Muslims alike. In Lahore, 20,000 people came out in a procession with a substantial number of Muslims. Hindus and Muslims drank water from the same cups. Chaudhari emphasised the 'Hindu-Muslim unity as the supreme need of the hour'. Amazingly, the Hindu leaders Harkishen Lal and Rambhuj Dutt Chaudhari were allowed to address the Muslim crowds from the pulpit of the Badshahi mosque.

In Amritsar, the hartal was observed on March 30 and 30,000 people attended the rally, fasted and accepted Gandhi's satyagraha as a weapon. In Amritsar, the crowds shouted for Hindu-Muslim unity and for Mahatma Gandhi; without showing any hostility or discourtesy towards the Europeans. On April 6, a second rally was held in Amritsar. The Punjab Government was wary of the effect of the speeches of Dr. Kitchlew and Dr. Satyapal. Therefore under the Defence of India Rules they decided on their internment and conveyed orders to this effect to the District Magistrate. The British held them responsible for *'Conspiracy having as its object the dissemination of sedition.'* In the majority of towns in the Punjab like Ambala, Ludhiana, Jalandhar, Sialkot, Batala, Hafizabad, Gujranwala and Rawalpindi, there had been a hartal on April 6, and no disorder had followed.

The Punjab police observed that two things were common: 1) Reverence of Gandhi and hatred for the Rowlatt Act and 2) Punjab's Hindus, Sikhs and Muslims were united as never before and there were some local factors in play. The economic grievances of Hindu traders and grain merchants combined with pro-Turkey sentiments of Lahore's Muslims. The situation was perfect for Gandhi's call for a united *satyagraha* against Rowlatt.

Drs. Satyapal, Kitchlew and Rambhuj Dutt Chaudhari realised that for better understanding of Satyagraha, it was pertinent for

Gandhi to visit Punjab. But O'Dwyer had him arrested on April 9, near Delhi.

Tension Builds in Amritsar

There was admittedly a state of tension but the situation was under control. The internment of Dr Kitchlew and Satyapal had not prevented them from continuing to direct the agitation.

On April 9, 1919, the DM did not anticipate any local disturbance other than a possible demonstration in the Civil Lines and it was decided to prevent them from crossing the railway line.

It was believed that the peace of the city would be safeguarded by a force of 75 armed police under an Indian DSP in the Central Police Station. Drs. Kitchlew and Satyapal were brought to the District Magistrate's house on 10th April morning and at 10:30 am were sent off to Dharmsala in motor cars. Around noon crowds began to collect in the city.

The removal of Gandhi, Drs. Satyapal and Kitchlew angered the people of Lahore and Amritsar who declared a hartal that very day and came out on the streets to show their protest. The size of the procession overwhelmed the British. The British were panicked and they mobilized cavalry as well as artillery and remembered the days of 1857 and the governor told the police '*...there was to be no firing in the air*'.

Crowd Turns violent

The crowd passed several Europeans in Amritsar but did not harm them. On finding itself checked at the Hall Gate Bridge, the crowd was angrily opposed by the small picquet stationed there. The picquet was stoned and the mounted police held the crowd back for some time. The DM went to fetch military assistance and the mounted troops were again heavily stoned, in his absence. The troops opened fire to stop the crowd from crossing the picquet at the railway station and it resulted in the killing of a small number of rioters and some of them were wounded. The crowd was driven back on the railway line, but not before the infantry had opened fire again.

The retreating crowd attacked the telegraph office and destroyed the telephone exchange, and a detachment at the

Railway picquet repulsed them. A section of the crowd turned to the goods yard where they did considerable damage. A guard named Robinson was brutally murdered. About 260 Gorkhas armed with *Khukhries* came to the aid of the Station Superintendent.

The crowd now went in many directions and between 1 and 2 pm led by two Hindus who were, reportedly the Lieutenants of Kitchlew and Satyapal, attacked the National Bank, murdered Mr. Stewart, Manager and Mr. Scott, Assistant Manager of the National Bank; sacked and burnt the bank, and looted the go-down having valuables to the value of several hundreds of thousands of rupees.

Next, the Chartered Bank was attacked, and the door and windows set alight, but the European Manager and his Assistant were rescued by the police. The Alliance Bank was also attacked, and the Manager was murdered.

The Religious Book Society's Depot and hall were set on fire but the inmates, native Christians, somehow escaped. The Sub-Post Offices at the Majithia Mandi, Golden Temple, and Dhab Basti Ram were looted.

The Zenana Hospital was entered and Mrs. Easdon, the lady doctor in charge, who was a potential target, however escaped.

Precautionary measures were taken on the morning of the April 11 to prevent any trouble over the burial of the rioters killed whom the leaders desired to bury in the Jallianwala Bagh. Any demonstration over them was forbidden to be made, and these orders were carried out. Further reinforcements arrived from Jalandhar and Indian officials and local notables were sent out to help maintain law and order in the villages. The District Magistrate informed respectable citizens that the troops had orders to restore order; people would be fired at if they assembled.

In Lahore, on the contrary, no Englishman was wounded or killed. Chaudhari's effort in keeping the protestors peaceful was successful. The total number of protestors killed or wounded on April 10 in Lahore and Amritsar was three dozen.

The British control was lost in Lahore between April 10 and 13. On Badshahi mosque, a huge rally on April 11 was attended by 35,000 Muslim, Hindu and Sikh leaders. The majority of the attending mass was Muslim. Chaudhari described this gathering as a 'success' and gave thumbs down to the Rowlatt Bill.

Sadly, Fazl-i-Hussain kept away from Lahore's protestors, fearing it would become violent. Mian Muhammad Shafi (who belonged to a leading Arain family of Baghbanpura would later become an iconic Muslim League leader) who in 1917 was a member of the Imperial Legislative Council and earlier a CIE in 1916, tried to mediate between the government's civilian officers and Lahore's top leaders.

But, O' Dwyer did not believe in diplomacy. On April 12, the protestors were fired upon in Lahore and 10 unarmed protestors were killed by army bullets near the Badshahi mosque. On April 14, Chaudhari, Harkishen Lal and Duni Chand were arrested in Lahore and the city was placed under Martial Law.

General Dyer

That evening the General Officer Commanding, Jalandhar Brigade, Brigadier General R.E. Dyer (his Irish father had a brewery in Murree) arrived to take charge of the military operations. The following day, he sent the military to Amritsar city to pre-empt any disturbance. The crowd was hostile and had cut the telegraph line between Chheharta and Khasa.

Meanwhile, in Lahore, disturbances of an alarming nature occurred and 4 Europeans were killed. The next afternoon when General Dyer marched through the streets, he was welcomed with slogans like 'Hindu-Mussalman ki Jai', 'Mahatma Gandhi ki Jai'. The General came to know about the cutting of telegraph lines and he declared a general emergency and declared all meetings as illegal.

The Congress had already given a call for meeting on April 13, 1919 which happened to be the auspicious day of Vaisakhi for the Sikhs. People had come from villages and gathered in Jallianwala Bagh. Most of them were unaware of any such proclamation banning any meeting.

General Dyer issued two notices under the authority given to him by the Commissioner:

1. Prohibition of all meetings and warning that damage to property or incitement to violence would be punishable by Martial Law.
2. Prohibition regarding leaving the city without a pass and any person found after 8 pm in the streets would be shot.

The Massacre

Martial Law had not been declared. There were times, he claimed, '*when one had to act without rules and regulations*'. He marched around the city in the forenoon of April 13 to issue a warning that no meetings were to be held.

To overfly the Bagh and estimate the size of the crowd Dyer arranged for an aeroplane and it was reported to be 6,000. The Hunter Commission's estimate of the crowd was 10,000 to 20,000 by the time of Dyer's arrival. Colonel Dyer and Irving, Deputy Commissioner for Amritsar, took no action to prevent the crowd assembling, or to peacefully disperse the crowds.

At the Bagh the meeting started as per the schedule at 16:30 hours and Colonel Dyer arrived after 1 hour at the Bagh with a group of ninety Sikh, Gorkha, Baloch and Rajput soldiers from the 2nd/9th Gorkha Rifles, the 54th Sikhs and the 59th Sind Rifles. 50 of them were armed with .303 Lee–Enfield bolt-action rifles. The two armoured cars which he had brought along were too wide for the narrow streets and he kept these outside. He took no machine gun and reached the Bagh, he found thousands of people there being addressed by a speaker on a raised platform.

Dyer and his troops blocked the main entrance behind them and took up position, a few feet higher than the general level, on a raised bank. He gave neither any warning nor did he order the crowd to disperse but opened fire on them for about ten minutes, directing their bullets mainly at some open gates through which people tried to escape, until the ammunition supply was almost exhausted. Some of the soldiers initially shot higher in the air, at which Dyer shouted: '*Fire low. What have you been brought here for?*' During the enquiry, he was not remorseful for having ordered his troops to shoot.

Dyer was predetermined and he ordered to open fire. The firing was directed where the crowd was the thickest and dispersal of the crowd was not his priority, rather he wanted to punish the Indians. Dyer stated in a report the following day that '*....between 200 and 300 of the crowd were killed. My party fired 1,650 rounds....*'.

About 400 people were killed including 41 children. Approximately 1,000 were injured. Curfew was imposed as soon as the firing ended. In Dyer's words, the city became 'absolutely quiet' with 'not a soul to be seen'. The dying and the dead spent the night with deadly dogs and vultures. However, Dyer had no evidence at all to justify his assumption that this was a seditious assembly.

Upon getting the news from Amritsar while he relaxed in Lahore, Lt. Governor O'Dwyer sent a message to Dyer *'Your action correct and Lieutenant Governor approves.'*

The attack was condemned by both former Prime Minister H.H. Asquith and Winston Churchill, Secretary of State for War. As 'a symbolic act of protest', Rabindranath Tagore decided to renounce his British knighthood

British Cruelty Continued

The Jallianwala Bagh Massacre shook the country and instead of bringing people under control, it infuriated them further. By April 15, Punjab was in a state of open rebellion. The British even used aeroplanes to bomb ordinary citizens and fire them with machine guns in Lahore. Gujranwala, Lahore and Amritsar were under Martial Law. People were not concerned about the consequences of violating the Martial Law. Under the air attack on April 14 and 15, 12 people were killed and 24 injured and on April 16, Martial Law was imposed in Gujranwala district and elsewhere in Punjab. It required the public to serve policemen and soldiers and also salute when an officer appeared.

In Lahore, students of 3 colleges were to report many times a day to military authorities at different assigned places. Sometimes, the distance to be covered was 17 miles a day during the sultry month of April.

Amritsar's water and electricity were cut off by Dyer and electric fans were taken away for the Englishmen. People were told to crawl on the lane where Miss Sherwood had been assaulted. This lane was 200 yards long. People were openly flogged with hands and legs tied together. Students were forced to walk long distances and hundreds of them along with teachers were arrested. Very young students aged between 5 and 7 were forced to attend parade and salute the Union Jack. People were forced to crawl at a spot in Amritsar and open cages were built and placed in central places where arrested men were confined like animals. Persons were handcuffed, tied together and kept in open trucks for 15 hours or more at a stretch in the hot Indian summer.

Punishments

The disorder following the massacre resulted in the British putting 62 cases in front of the Martial Law Commission in which there were 298 accused. Fifty-one people were sentenced to death and the rest for varying periods of jail.

More than 100 people were convicted for joining an unlawful assembly to loot Taran Taran Tehsil, for dishonestly receiving property belonging to the National Bank, with trespassing in post offices to commit offences, with damaging telegraph wire etc.

The only places where violence did take place before and after the Jallianwala Bagh Massacre were Lahore, Amritsar, Kasur, Gujranwala, Wazirabad, Nizamabad, Hafizabad, Moman, Dhaban Singh, Chuharkana, Khem Karan, Patti and Malakwal, having a population of about two and a half lakhs and only a small part of the population took part in the alleged disorders. The European lives lost were four.

Punjab crawled to normalcy once the 'non-existent' revolutionary plot had been dealt with by the Raj. Gandhi halted his satyagraha which failed to be non-violent in Punjab. Soon the unrepentant O'Dwyer and a similarly sounding Dyer returned to Britain. Rudyard Kipling defended Dyer and contributed to a fund for him; much to the chagrin of the Indians. Kipling called Dyer 'the man who saved India'.

Dyer was initially lauded as a hero in Britain by people like the members of the House of Lords who directly benefited from the British Raj. The House of Commons, however, widely criticised him and in July 1920, the committee of investigation censured him. As he was a soldier acting on orders, he could not be tried for murder. He was simply removed by the military from his current job, rejected his promotion, and barred him from taking any other employment in India. After retiring from the Army, Dyer returned to England. The House of Lords gave him a vote of approval and a fund of 20,000 was raised for him. He died unrepentant in 1927.

By 1921 O' Dwyer had been replaced as governor by Edward

Maclagan who was a Lt. Governor earlier. A British judge Lord Hunter was made a head of a committee to investigate the Punjab violence.

Punjab After the Jallianwala Bagh Massacre

The army openings still attracted the peasant youth in Punjab and the jobs for educated unemployed were available and as in earlier times, the titles for the rich were there for grabbing. In October 1919, Mian Muhammad Shafi joined the Viceroy's executive council.

The British Raj expected that by generation of competition for jobs, titles and jagirs, competition would increase between the Hindus and Muslims and it would automatically drive a wedge between their newly acquired unity. The provincial councils were an ideal place to fulfil personal as well as the community's ambitions and were a potential dividing source.

Gandhi was barred from visiting Punjab but he was not yet finished. After his failed satyagraha strategy in Punjab, he advocated a halt to defiance and advocated non-violence. In October 1919, he arrived in Lahore to gain first-hand knowledge about the province. Gandhi did not accept the Hunter Committee's report and ordered his own enquiry. He visited Amritsar, Lahore, Gujranwala, Kasur, Lyallpur and a dozen other places to mix and bond with the Punjabis. The Punjabis welcomed him in large numbers. He was honoured at the Golden Temple and people accepted him as well as Khadi and Charkha. Gandhi was struck by the plain-speaking Punjabis. Gandhi sought funds for a memorial for the victims of the Jallianwala Bagh massacre.

Gandhi in Punjab

The turn of events in Turkey greatly disturbed the Muslim leaders who invited Gandhi to attend their deliberations in Delhi in November 1919. The defeat of the Sultan was seen by them as the defeat of the Sunni Muslims including those in India. Muslims were worried that the control of Islam's holy places in Arabia and Iraq, now out of governance by Turkey, might go into the hands of non-Muslim victors.

The Muslims saw in Gandhi a friend of their community and asked him to suggest as to how to save their holy places. Gandhi spelled out a possible 'Non-Cooperation' if the Allies and the British played any tricks with Turkey. Indians could return the Raj's titles and honours and withhold cooperation even from the councils of the Reforms Act. The Delhi gathering were, however, intrigued.

The annual session of INC was held in Amritsar by December end, close to Jallianwala Bagh. All-India Muslim League headed by Ajmal Khan met there and the Central Khilafat Conference was also present.

To encourage the participation of the Indians in the new councils created by the Reforms Act, the British released the Ali brothers, Zafar Ali, Kitchlew and Satyapal. Most of the INC leaders were sceptical of the British intentions, considering the recent turn of events. The Muslim League and the Khilafatists were even more doubtful.

Gandhi was in favour of giving the councils a try and despite the protests of Tilak and C.R. Das but with the tacit approval of Jinnah. Mohammed Ali Jinnah was still in the Indian National Congress as well as Muslim League and he was an associate of Tilak who died in 1915. Jinnah then the ambassador of 'Hindu-Muslim unity', was a part of the historic *Lucknow Pact*. It was approved in Amritsar via a resolution to work the Reforms Act.

Gandhi's resolution on the Jallianwala Bagh massacre was being considered controversial as it condemned violence by all, including that by Indians. Peasants as well as women attended the Congress meetings. Gandhi was asked to undertake reorganisation of the INC hierarchy which was to include village-level communities. Shaukat Ali at the Muslim League session asked his Muslim brethren to continue to seek the Hindu support as they had done regarding to Turkey.

Following the end of the First World War, the British government decided that Mecca and Medina would be placed under a pro-British chieftain. France was to control Syria, Britain was to look after Iraq where Karbala and Najaf were, and also Palestine. Thus, all key Islamic sites were to be under the Christian countries.

This news angered the Muslims and the publishing of the Hunter Committee report on the Punjab events further infuriated the Punjabis. The rest of India also felt exploited by the Empire.

Gandhi sensed a golden opportunity to build a Hindu-Sikh-Muslim Alliance and strike for independence.

Jinnah Bids Farewell to the Congress

With the passing away of Mehta and Gokhale in 1915, the moderate faction of the Congress was undermined. Naoroji remained in London till his death in 1917. This further isolated Jinnah. However, Jinnah endeavoured to bring the Congress and League together. In 1916 the two organisations signed the Lucknow Pact with Jinnah as the president of the Muslim League. Quotas for Muslim and Hindu representatives were set in the various provinces. Even though the pact was never implemented as agreed upon nevertheless, it resulted in a phase of cooperation between the Congress and the League.

Jinnah, like other Indian moderates supported the war effort of the British in the belief that the Indians would be given political freedoms. The All India Home Rule League was formed in 1916 and Jinnah along-with Annie Besant and Tilak contributed to its formation demanding 'home rule' for India. It was envisaged to have the same status as that of a self-governing dominion in the Empire as in Canada, New Zealand and Australia. With the war on, Britain did not consider Indian constitutional reforms.

With the Indian people Gandhi's local style of leadership gained great popularity. However, Jinnah criticised Gandhi's Khilafat advocacy, which to his mind was the advocacy of religious zealotry. The proposed Satyagraha by Gandhi was regarded as 'political anarchy' by Jinnah who believed that self-government should be secured through constitutional means. He opposed Gandhi, but the Indian opinion was with Gandhi. At the 1920 session of the Congress in Nagpur, Jinnah was ignored by the delegates, who passed Gandhi's proposal, pledging Satyagraha until India was independent. He was literally shouted down.

Jinnah felt that such a movement would lead to violence of a high degree and *'Swaraj'* instead of *'Swaraj within the Empire'* was not acceptable to him. In Nagpur, the Muslim League's meeting was also being held but an upset Jinnah did not attend it which passed a similar resolution. As Gandhi's campaign was endorsed by the INC, Jinnah resigned from it, leaving all positions except in the Muslim League.

Jinnah was going to remain in the political wilderness till the year 1933 and the Muslim political revivalism took place after the Pakistan declaration of Muhammad Ali.

Non-Cooperation Movement, 1920

From May 1920 onwards, Gandhi presented 'Non-violent Non-cooperation' as a strategy to all the parties concerned: INC, Muslim League and the Khilafat Conference. In Punjab, the response was positive except from Allama Iqbal and Fazl-i-Hussain. Those who agreed were Swami Shraddhanand, Tilak (who died soon on August 1, 1920), Lajpat Rai, Ali Brothers, Abul Kalam Azad and none other than Jinnah.

Also, to support it was Zafar Ali, Kitchlew and Ataullah Shah Bukhari of Amritsar. Non-cooperation did not attract Iqbal and Fazl-i-Hussain who were busy in 1919 with the Khilafat movement, in any case.

Lala Lajpat Rai presided over the special session of INC in September 1920 in Calcutta and the Non-cooperation was endorsed. The Muslim League was with INC. A regular session of the INC was held in Nagpur, later in 1920 and there were now two dissenting voices: Madan Mohan Malaviya and Jinnah! Soon Jinnah left INC. At this session, Gandhi made the ascendancy.

Although Malaviya and Jinnah felt that some sort of a 'rule within an Empire' was the proper goal, most of the Indians felt that the British Empire was no longer indispensable.

In 1920 and 1921, the INC, the League and the Khilafatists suggested that the following points may be adhered to:

Staying clear of the new councils, returning the titles given by the Raj, quitting the Raj's colleges, quitting the Raj's law courts, resigning civilian posts with the government, leaving Police and Army and not paying the taxes.

Also, the INC would distribute 2 million charkhas, raise 1 crore rupees for the Tilak-Swaraj Fund and enrol 1 crore as INC members. Gandhiji believed that following the above, Swaraj would be a reality within a year. But the targets were not easy nor was the sticking to the non-violent path. Gandhiji advocated that the non-violence would be an integral part of the non-cooperation movement.

Many Muslims believed that *hijrat* or migration to Islamic

countries like Afghanistan would be an acceptable solution and so also inviting Afghanistan to attack British India. Gandhi felt that Non-Cooperation was a better tool than these methods.

From August 1920, titles were being surrendered. Students left colleges in thousands, hundreds of lawyers shunned courts and in November, prominent politicians boycotted the provincial council elections.

Town-dwellers moved into villages, people wore khadi and burnt foreign clothes. New charkhas in thousands were brought in, funds for Tilak reached the target and the INC enrolled 6 million members.

Towards the end of 1921, thousands of Indians non-violently disobeyed laws and entered the Raj's jails. Nobody feared the Raj any more. Motilal Nehru, C.R. Das, Hakim Ajmal Khan, M. A. Ansari and Lajpat Rai went to prison without any qualms.

The new leaders appeared on the horizon: Jawaharlal Nehru, Vallabhbhai Patel, Subhas Bose, Rajendra Prasad and Rajagopalachari, all of whom were jailed and people started to know about them. The Ali brothers, Abul Kalam Azad and Abdul Ghaffar Khan also went behind bars.

In Punjab, many prominent lawyers including Kitchlew, Duni Chand and Agha Safdar of Sialkot gave up their legal practice, peacefully violated the orders from the Raj and embraced imprisonment.

In December 1921, Agha Safdar was the Punjab Congress president and some time later, he was put behind the bars and Kharak Singh occupied that position. But he too was put behind bars. Sardar Sardul Singh Kavishar, secretary of the Sikh league and also of the Punjab Congress was among many others who served a prison term.

Punjabis and Gandhi's Non-Cooperation

Just in 1919, Hindus, Muslims and Sikhs walked hand in hand opposing the British but the situation was slowly changing in favour of the British Raj. Indians helped the Raj to turn the tides against the Indians. Slowly the Hindu-Sikh-Muslim vs Raj was becoming Hindu vs Muslim or Muslim vs Sikh affair. Two Punjabi Muslim giants who could have stopped the communities from creating walls between themselves, stayed out from the changing politico-social scenario. They were Allama Iqbal and Fazl-i-Hussain.

Zafar Ali and Kitchlew tried their best to make Non-cooperation workable for the Muslim majority in Punjab but that was not to be. In November 1920, a jolt was given by Fazl-i-Hussain, who headed the Punjab Congress and the Punjab League, just the previous year, now wanted to enter the new council. Perhaps he thought that instead of Gandhi's Non-Cooperation, British Cooperation would give better results for the Punjabi Muslims. The upliftment of Punjabi Muslims was always at the back of his mind for Fazl-i-Hussain who had left Congress in 1920. He was re-elected to the legislative council on a Muslim landowner seat and he was one of two ministers appointed by the Governor of the Punjab. The other person appointed was Lala Harkishan Lal. Fazl-i-Hussain became a spearhead of the rural Muslims, Hindus and Sikhs who dominated the council. But his rejection of Non-cooperation proved to be a boon for the British Raj.

The INC and Muslim League had failed to win over the Punjabi peasant; now the Raj's opponents were the advocates of the Raj. Lala Lajpat Rai was the biggest all-India figure in the Punjab. he was already 57 years old and was a staunch supporter of the Non-cooperation movement. He was respected by all Punjabi Hindus and Sikhs but Rai lacked a good Muslim following. In June 1920, he had cautioned Punjabi Muslims against harbouring the wishes for advancing an invitation to Afghans to invade India.

The love for the British titles and positions re-emerged among the rural landlords and the urbanites as well. The Non-violence advocated by Gandhi had fewer takers vis-à-vis the greater part of India. When Gandhi visited Punjab in 1920 and 1921, he found that his call for Non-cooperation did not go down well with the Punjabis and also the non-violence against the Raj was not adopted by the sturdy people of the Punjab. Punjabis were loathed to rejecting titles, as he found out.

Soon, the pro-government Muslims started to convince their anti-Raj co-religionists like Zafar Ali that Khilafat was a political and not a religious movement. Maulana Azad tried to caution the Punjabis against this pro-British stand but his speeches could not make a big impact; he was no Punjabi Muslim, after all.

The situation was changing in Turkey with Mustafa Kamal and the Turkish Sultan pitted against each other; much to the disappointment of the Khilafat conference. Hindus were upset by a careless comment of Muhammad Ali that he would support an invading Afghan army. The Viceroy of the Raj did not like it either. By these small happenings, the Hindu-Muslim rivalry increased and the mutual trust was diminishing. A fatwa in Punjab asked the Muslims to leave the police and Army of the Raj but the response to it was lukewarm. The Muslim percentage in the Punjab Police was as high as 75.

Then news came in 1921 from Malabar that the 'Moplahs' who spoke Malayalam rose against the government and then against their Hindu landlords. A large number of Moplahs were killed and this affected the Hindu-Muslim relations.

On February 5, 1922 the infamous Chauri Chaura occurred when a sizeable number of protesters, supporting the Non-cooperation movement, were fired upon by the police. Soon, the angry demonstrators set fire to a police station, in retaliation, killing all its occupants. As many as 22 policemen were killed compelling Mahatma Gandhi to halt the Non-cooperation movement on the national level on February 12, 1922, since he was opposed to the violence as a means to achieve freedom.

Even after 18 months of the movement, Swaraj was a distant dream but the Raj had been well-shaken. The Khilafat movement which brought Hindus and Muslims together was now a fast fading issue having little relevance to India. Consequently, the Ali brothers slowly moved away from Gandhi and the INC; Swami Shraddhanand and Lala Lajpat Rai also moved slightly away from Gandhi. Muslims and Hindus sought solace in the British arms individually and thought it better to move away from each other for their own gains.

Shiromani Gurdwara Prabandhak Committee (SGPC)

The Sikh gurdwaras were occupied by priests who were unfamiliar with the fundamental tenets of Sikhism. The Sikhs' central shrine, the Golden Temple at Amritsar, was under a *Sarbarah* or an agent who was controlled by the British DC. Idols were installed within the temple not allowing the lower caste people inside the Durbar Sahib before 9 o'clock in the morning. This was against the basic tenets of Sikhism.

The Akalis took the initiative of taking over their holy places from the Mahants. With a view to establishing a Central Committee of administration to look after the Harimandir Sahib Complex and other important historical gurdwaras; the new Jathedar of the Akal Takht called for an assembly of Sikhs on November 15, 1920. Each delegate was required to satisfy five conditions:

1 that he was a baptised Sikh;
2 that he read the hymns regularly;
3 that he subscribed to the Sikh forms;
4 that he was an early riser; and
5 that he gave regularly one-tenth (*Dasvand)* of his earnings for the Panthic cause.

Two days before the proposed conference, a committee was set up by the British government consisting of 36 Sikhs to manage the Harimandir Sahib. Sikhs elected a bigger committee consisting of 175 members and named it Shiromani Gurdwara Parbandhak Committee. The government appointed committee members were also included. The iconic Master Tara Singh was one of the 175 members elected to the committee. The formation of the Shiromani Gurdwara Parbandhak Committee was a turning point for the movement for the reformation of Sikh religious places. As the Committee began to take over management of gurdwaras one by one, it faced resistance from the incumbent mahants.

A large number of orders called *Jathas* came up in late 1920 whose main purpose was to gain control over local gurdwaras. A *Jatha* under a Jathedar was supposed to occupy a shrine and remove the current incumbents from its management. Sometimes the transfer went peacefully and on other occasions with the threat of force.

On December 12, 1920 the first session of the SGPC was held at Akal Takht Amritsar.

Sikhs unite

After the serious happenings at Nankana Sahib, Guru-ka-Bagh and elsewhere, obviously something was necessary to be done to sort out the serious disputes between the Mahants and the SGPC with the latter representing the whole community. The Sikh community was united in their claim that the management of their sacred shrines under the Mahants was far from satisfactory and action was called for, at the earliest, to place the control of the gurdwaras and their funds with the true representatives of the Sikh community, consistently with the teachings of the Sikh faith.

First Gurdwara Bill, 1922

On November 7, 1922, Sir Fazl-i-Hussein, as Minister for Education, introduced an official Gurdwara Bill in the Punjab Legislative Council. The Guru-ka-Bagh Morcha, which had been the cause of so much misery and pain to the Sikh Community and caused anxiety to the government, was still unresolved.

Sir Fazl-i-Hussein's Gurdwara Bill was destined to fail. On the *select committee* of the Bill 5 moderate Sikh MLCs were appointed. Four of them did not attend meetings while Bawa Hardit Singh Bedi, the fifth member, participated in some meetings of the committee. He was soon persuaded by other members not to participate and from November 5, 1922 he also refused to work on the Select Committee. By this time it had become quite clear that even the moderate Sikhs on the Legislative Council were against Hussein's measure as it had been framed without considering the aspirations of the whole community.

Second Gurdwara Bill, 1923

A further step was registered when, on March 8, 1923, Sir John Meynard said after Sir Henry Craik's amendment to S. Randhir Singh's resolution that the '*Government would be prepared to release all Guru-ka-Bagh prisoners if an agreement could be reached between the SGPC and ....the other parties ....on the common principles on which the proposed Gurdwara Legislation was based*'. That the Akalis had repudiated his proposal and had shown '*complete unwillingness even to listen to the suggestion*' was regretted by him.

SGPC Becomes the Powerful Body of Sikhs

The SGPC adopted a formal resolution at their general meeting on September 20, 1923, to field its own candidates for elections to the Indian Legislative Assembly and the Punjab Legislative Council. In this regard the Committee appealed to all the Sikh voters to extend their full support to the nominees of the Committee.

The SGPC guided and controlled the activities of the whole Akali Movement with its ratifications all over the province. The seven or eight men who were chiefly concerned with the conduct of the day-to-day and hour-to-hour business of the organisation were to be found wherever their immediate duties took them. They would return every now and then to the 'office' to give instructions to the volunteers (sewadars).

Holding of religious *Dewans* in all parts of the Province was the most essential part of the activities of the SGPC. Gutkhas consisting mostly of selections from the Sikh scriptures were sold by tens of thousands for private daily recitations at an exceedingly low price for mass usage.

Dewans became important centres for the recruitment of men for the Akali struggle for the control of the gurdwaras and for the revival of the Sikh faith as envisioned by the Gurus. There was no shortage of volunteers and they were enlisted from anywhere. These volunteers went to every corner of the country to hold Dewans.

Information and Publicity Bureau was the small office directly attached to the council of action from which the SGPC communiques were issued; at least one communique every morning, sometimes even two or more.

A member of the *confidential staff* was present too to prepare the required number of copies of the communique, and send these to their respective destinations like all the important nationalist papers in India and some Sikh and non-Sikh persons sympathetic to the Gurdwara Reform Movement. The communiques contained the Committee's own version of the facts and opinions and not even the Indian National Congress was so prompt in carrying out this part of their propaganda as the Akali Bureau.

Seeing the immense potential benefit from the journalistic propaganda, the SGPC took great pains in organising this department of their Publicity Bureau through their own daily journals in English, Urdu and Punjabi languages. As they had no English daily newspaper under their own control, on August 27, 1923, they took over *The Nation* of Lahore and soon 5,000 copies of it were being sold. Often the editor would be a dummy person like those of Russian revolutionary journals.

Sir E.D. MacLagan (1919-24)

Sir Edward MacLagan was appointed as Lieutenant-Governor on May 26, 1919 and he became the first Governor of the Punjab. Born in 1864 and educated at Winchester, New College, Oxford, he entered the ICS in 1885. He was appointed a Secretary of the Education Department to the Government of India from 1915 to 1918. He got the KCIE in 1913 and CSI in 1909.

As the Governor of the Punjab, he was given an Executive Council of two members. While the Hon'ble Sir John Maynard, KCSI; CSI was appointed as a Finance member, Sardar Bahadur Sunder Singh Majithia, CIE was appointed as Revenue Member. Fazl-i-Hussain and Lala Harkishan Lal were the two Ministers nominated from among the elected members of the Legislative Council for the Departments of Education and Agriculture respectively. The latter was later deported and imprisoned in 1919 in connection with the disturbances in the Punjab.

Sir E.D. MacLagan had a hard life during his regime in the Punjab. He had to witness quite a few problems related to the Sikhs. The Nankana Holocaust, the Jaito Massacre, the Babbar Akali Movement and many political movements shook the very foundation of the British Empire in India. These events are covered briefly in the following pages.

Nankana Holocaust February 20, 1921

Guru Nanak was born at Talwandi, later known as Nankana Sahib, in 1469 CE. It is a district in West Punjab, Pakistan. It is 48 kilometres to the south-west of Lahore. The area surrounding it in the 1880s was a jungle. The gurdwara had a huge area of about 77 square kilometres.

This historical shrine was under the custody of Mahant Narain Dass, an Udasi, infamous for corruption and vice. He enjoyed the income from the gurdwara. Local Sikhs threatened to eject him from the holy place. The attention of the authorities was attracted for intervention as the situation became very tense. The government had issued a press release on February 16, 1921 declaring the appointment of Shaikh Asghar Ali to preside over a conference of the Akalis while the mahants, saints and pujaris were represented by Lieutenant Kartar Singh Bedi.

Who Were the Udasis?

The word 'Udasi' denotes a person aloof from or disregardful of worldly attachments, a stoic, or a mendicant.' For each of the four preaching tours of Guru Nanak the term udasi has also been used in the Sikh tradition. Thus, udasi means a prolonged absence from home. Baba Sri Chand, Guru Nanak's son was the founder.

About a century ago, gurdwaras were managed by ascetic priests, known as mahants who were the virtual owners of the shrines. They did not have to get their accounts audited and their control over the assets was absolute.

They were dependent on the British rulers for the civic services and security, and therefore, they were loyal to them to the extent of being *chamchas* or sycophants. Police officers were accorded the red carpet treatment. This system suited the British rulers. The mahants had temporal authority over the masses, and so the Raj officers had to win the loyalty of a handful of 'godmen' to manage the vast number of people.

The mahants are said to have been ascetic. Most of them did not marry and chose their successors with the informal consent of the devotees. But over the years they became corrupt, unethical and in some cases, even immoral.

Dewan Scheduled at Nankana

Meetings of the SGPC were held on January 23, 1921, and again on February 6 and it was resolved that a big Diwan would be held at Nankana Sahib on the March 4-6, 1921. The goal was to devise ways and means to put an end to the corruption in the Nankana Sahib Gurdwara. The mahant was one named Narain Dass, a Brahmin. The Sikhs were also directed to observe complete non-violence on the occasion in spite of provocations. The SGPC knew that the mahant was well-equipped with weapons to be used in case the necessity arose.

Based on original and genuine religious feelings, the agitation for the reform of the Sikh shrines was started. The Sikh reformers alleged that the mahant, Narain Dass had a corrupt and evil lifestyle and had kept Muslim concubines. Right or wrong, the Sikhs decided to take forcible possession of Nankana Sahib and its surrounding properties.

Mahant's Apprehensions

An appeal to the authorities for special police to protect him was made by Narain Das Mahant of the gurdwara. The British rejected his appeal, and he decided to take his own measures of defence. He hired Pathan mercenaries and retired Sikh soldiers.

Sikhs Reach Nankana Sahib

The SGPC had arranged a Diwan a few miles from Nankana Sahib, on February 20, 1921. The Jathedar of this Diwan, Bhai Lachhman Singh, started early in the morning of February 20, 1921 and Mahant Narain Das suspected that Bhai Lachhman Singh was coming to Nankana Sahib with a huge number of Sikhs to capture the Janamsthan Gurdwara.

As Nankana Sahib lay on the way, Bhai Lachhman Singh told other Sikhs while on their way from Chuharkana that they should pay homage at the Nankana Sahib that day. He knew that the Mahant had collected a large number of mercenaries.

The Jatha had a bath in the sacred tank of Gurdwara Bal Lila near Nankana Sahib and they paid their homage. Then he and others went to the Janamsthan gurdwara. They were received with all courtesy but the evil designs of the Mahant were not known to the Jatha. Then, the doors of the Gurdwara were closed. The Akali Jatha, to their surprise, saw a large number of men, who had been sitting on the roof out of the view, started firing at them. The Akalis ran helter-skelter into the small rooms but the mercenaries shot at them through the holes in the doors. Several Sikhs were wounded while others were literally murdered.

A landlord and Secretary of the Sargodha Khalsa School named Sardar Dalip Singh of Sargodha was known to Mahant Narain Das and was supposed to have some influence with him. He was asked by other Sikhs to persuade the mahant that Lachhman Singh had come to the gurdwara only for 'darshan' and should not be molested. Dalip Singh saw the mahant on a murderous spree and shouted to him to desist but received a gun shot on the forehead and he fell dead.

The Sikhs who had come with S. Dalip Singh and staying back at an inn were done away with by the Pathan murderers. Thus, the gruesome drama led by Mahant Narain Das ended. Bhai Lachhman Singh was brought before the mahant who watched in glee as his head being severed before him. The Sikhs within the gurdwara who escaped bullets were killed by axes. Some of them were burnt alive. The hired ruffians murdered some Sikhs outside the gurdwara. The number of Sikhs killed were between 82 and 156.

Raj Officers Reach the spot

The DC of Gujranwala reached Nankana Sahib. Later the Commissioner of the division with a military force consisting of 100 Europeans and 100 Indian soldiers, and DIG Police and many Sikh Sardars reached Nankana Sahib by a special train. The military was posted all-round the gurdwara. The gates were locked by the mahant from within. He claimed the burning bodies belonged to his sadhus killed by the Akalis.

After hesitating for a few minutes, Mahant Narain Dass came out of a small room where he had locked himself. He had a gun in his hand which was taken from there by the District Magistrate, Mr. Curie. Two disciples (Chelas) of the mahant and 26 Pathans were arrested, once the mahant was captured. The government took the gurdwara under its protection. At Nankana Sahib many Sikh leaders and Sikh Sardars from Amritsar and other places arrived. The 29 persons arrested at Nankana Sahib were despatched to Lahore by a special train where they were kept in the Central Jail.

The Governor of the Punjab, Sir Edward Maclagan, reached Nankana Sahib on February 22, 1921 accompanied by a large number of officials.

Two days later, the Sikh 'Sangat' was permitted to visit the spot and February 23 was fixed for the cremation ceremony. A huge funeral pyre was erected to cremate the remains of the Sikhs. Finally, order was restored by drafting large bodies of police and troops into the disturbed area. In fact, for the murder of nearly 130 Akalis, 3 men were sentenced to death and 2 including the mahant for transportation for life.

The new mahant was murdered. The attitude of the government did not satisfy the Sikhs. Mahatma Gandhi with leaders like Maulana Shaukat Ali, L. Duni Chand, Dr. Kitchlew, Malik Lal Khan, S. Harchand Singh, S. Prem Singh Sodbans, etc., went to Nankana Sahib on March 3, 1921 and a Diwan was held there. Nankana Sahib Martyrs' Day was fixed on April 5, 1921 and the incident of Nankana Sahib was narrated by Bhai Kartar Singh Jhabbar, Jathedar.

The Taran Taran Tragedy

The mahants of the Taran Taran Gurdwara were notorious for a life of vice and corruption. They looked upon the gurdwara with its large daily offerings as their hereditary personal property. Bhai Mohan Singh Vaid, wrote to the Commissioner at Lahore but to no avail.

The SGPC sent an Akali Jatha under the control of S. Kartar Singh Jhabbar, Jathedar, to Taran Taran. It reached there early in the morning on January 26, 1921. The 'Pujaris', who were 70 in number remained inside the Durbar Sahib, Jathedar Kartar Singh Jhabbar on arrival sent word to the *'Pujaris'* that the objective of the Jatha was peaceful reformation without using force to take possession of the gurdwara. Peaceful negotiation was desired by some of the 'Pujaris' who were willing to settle the affair.

As a matter of fact, such negotiations had actually started with the Akali leaders offering some conditions on which a settlement could be reached. 'Pujaris' wanted time and were told to give their final reply at 10 am January 27, 1921.

The 'Pujaris' hatched a plot ostensibly showing their readiness to accept the terms offered to them and Bhai Mohan Singh Vaid was asked to bring pen and paper. Suddenly, the 'Pujaris' with the help of some mercenaries attacked the Akali Jatha and the Sikh Sangat with their lathis and axes. Fifteen Sikhs were wounded and removed to the Hospital. Two of them died later.

The mahants fled from the scene and on January 27 the Akalis held a big Diwan when a temporary Committee of the 13 was formed to take charge of the gurdwara, till more permanent arrangements were made for the proper management of gurdwaras.

Ejecting the 'Pujaris', the Akalis were already taking over gurdwaras by persuasion or by applying force and after the happenings of January 26, 1921, the mahants were terrified.

Under the changed circumstances, the 'mahants' were glad to occupy a subordinate position in the gurdwara that the SGPC assigned to them.

Guru Ka Bagh 1922

In March 1922, the Punjab High Court delivered judgment on the Nankana massacre case, acquitting 27 accused and reducing the capital sentences to three years, causing deep resentment among the Sikh ranks.

The Guru-ka-Bagh Gurdwara was erected to commemorate the visit of Guru Arjan. There was a plot of land close to the Gurudwara on which acacia trees were planted to provide firewood for the 'Gurdwara' kitchen. The Udasi Mahant Sunder Das was aware that the government sided with the 'Mahants' in their fight with the Sikhs. He claimed that the piece of land known as Guru-ka-Bagh attached to gurdwara was still his property. In the first week of August 1922, he lodged a complaint that some Akalis were cutting wood from his land and the police arrested five Sikhs on August 9, 1922 who were sentenced to six months' rigorous imprisonment.

SGPC Launches Agitation

SGPC determined to secure the land sent a Jatha of five Akalis to cut down some wood. On a complaint being made by the 'Mahant', the Akalis were prosecuted and convicted of theft, once again. The SGPC protested against the conviction and claimed that land attached to the gurdwara was the property of the gurdwara and that trees growing there-on were the property of the Sikh community and could be cut down by them for use in the public kitchen for feeding pilgrims, but the government stood by the 'Mahant'.

The Akalis continued to proceed from the Akal Takht to the Guru-ka-Bagh to cut wood for Guru-ka-Langar and were attacked by the Police till they became unconscious or were unable to stand on their legs.

Next, Jathas of 100 Akalis were formed. They first took an oath to remain non-violent; then they proceeded towards Guru-ka-Bagh. The police would beat them mercilessly but for 19 days this continued and this was observed by many Indian leaders as to how the Sikhs suffered silently with resolute will.

An appeal to the leaders of other communities was issued and a number of pressmen from all over India hurried to the scene of the Akali struggle. Prof. Ruchi Ram Sahni and Mian Fazal Din, two of the members of the Punjab Provincial Congress Committee were deputed by it to proceed to Amritsar to see the situation.

On those days when the Jatha was stopped from proceeding forward at one place or another on the road, barbarous treatment used to be meted out to the Akalis. Policemen under a European officer would routinely administer the beating to the Akalis who would generally squat down on the bare ground with joined hands as if in prayer singing hymns all the while. Measures against the Akalis were tightened. The agitation gained momentum. The black-turbaned Akalis were now being routinely hunted in the villages around the Guru-ka-Bagh.

The Gargajj Akali Jatha

The Jatha came into being on April 19, 1921, after separating from the parent body Central Majha Khalsa Diwan. The Akal Takht Jathedar Teja Singh Bhuchchar, then under detention, was elected its its life president, in absentia.

A severe trial awaited the Gargajj Akali Jatha on September 1, 1922, when about 120 men were on the way to Guru-Ka-Bagh. Near the Gumtala Bridge the Jatha was surrounded by the police who succeeded in breaking the Jatha into several small parties. The beating continued until the whole batch lay prostrate to a man. The Sikhs displayed unique self-control and resolution. They were later chased on either side of the road in different directions into the fields.

Beating of Akalis Stops

Once the Governor of Punjab, Sir Edward Maclagan visited Amritsar on September 13, 1922, the thrashing of the Sikh volunteers stopped. Four days later, the Police withdrew from the scene. Arrests began to be made instead. Now the Akali Sikhs stepped up their campaign. Jathas became larger in size. The government at last gave in. The good offices of iconic Sir Ganga Ram, a rich and influential citizen of Lahore, were secured. He obtained the Guru-ka-Bagh land on lease from the mahant and wrote to the government that no police protection was needed. To cut wood in the jungle for their community kitchen, the Sikhs could now go fearlessly to Guru-ka-Bagh.

The difficult times of the Sikhs were not yet over. On October 13, 1923 SGPC was declared an unlawful association by government for protesting against the deposition of the Sikh Maharaja of Nabha, known for his sympathy with the Akalis and other nationalist elements. SGPC leaders and active members were tried on charges of sedition against the King. For the restoration of the Nabha Ruler the agitataion continued with strength. The small town of Jaitu, in Nabha State, became the scene of a long and dramatic struggle.

Babbar Akali Movement 1922-26

The recent events of struggles of the Ghadarites, the massacre of Nankana, the Jallianwala Bagh holocaust and the Guru-ka-Bagh tragedy inspired a movement which was started in 1921, by Sardar Krishan Singh Binag and Sardar Dhanna Singh of village Bahalpur (Hoshiarpur) which came to be known as *Babbar Akali Dal* or 'Chakkravarties'. Sardar Krishan Singh Binag was a man of reckless courage who delivered fiery speeches and undertook free distribution of a highly seditious leaflet, 'Babbar Akali Doaba'.

Sardar Kishan Singh Binag and his comrades were able to establish branches all over Punjab with Jalandhar as a centre. The members started to collect arms and ammunitions.

The government got alerted and some of Sardar Krishan Singh's trusted comrades were arrested and imprisoned. But he himself escaped and he transferred his activities to Doaba where he got new support.

For the purpose of a conspiracy to eliminate the opponents of gurdwara reforms, arms and bombs were obtained from the NWFP and smuggled into Punjab. From the Armoury of the Air Force in Ambala Cantonment, 7 revolvers were stolen in December 1920 and by the arrests of two conspirators named Sardar Bela Singh and Sardar Ganda Singh on May 23, 1921 at the Lahore Railway Station, the conspiracy came to light.

Toadies Warned

There was no shortage of the British sole-lickers also called 'Jholi-Chuks', that is tail-bearers, toadies or sycophants. If such persons did not pay heed to the warnings given to them, declared the *Babbar Akalis*, their ears and noses were to be chopped off and if such measures also failed, they were to be 'reformed' or simply, murdered.

At the same time, Sardar Karam Singh alias Sardar Narain Singh of Daulatpur, Sardar Ude Singh of Ramgarh Jhugian and Sardar Asa Singh were spreading hatred against the Raj by means of speeches in the adjoining district of Hoshiarpur. Sardar Karam Singh of Jhingar, an emigrant from Canada, joined both parties.

Eventually the two parties met and a campaign against the Government was launched. Special measures were taken towards the end of September 1922 by the British when C.W. Jacob, DC, Jalandhar found the situation rapidly worsening. He wrote to the DIG, CID Punjab apprising him of the situation and requested special measures or else the murders of loyalists might be anticipated before long.

A conference at Jalandhar took place in November 1923 and it was then decided to adopt more rigorous measures for the suppression of this movement and offer higher rewards for the arrest of Sardar Kishan Singh Binag, Sardar Karam Singh and other leading Babbar Akalis who were hiding. A special Police Staff from the two districts concerned was deputed for the purpose of securing the arrest of these revolutionaries.

The situation worsened and there was escalation of terrorism in the two districts of Jalandhar and Hoshiarpur. The activities of the Babbar Akalis also extended to the Kapurthala State. The opinion prevailing amongst the Sikhs of the Doaba was that a few days had remained before the British Rule would end and establishment of a Sikh Raj would take place.

Searches at the various places were conducted by the Police on March 23, 1923 at many places and various documents were recovered.

Revolutionary Conspiracy by the Babbar Akalis

The evidence summarised by the Add. Sessions Judge, Lahore proved the existence of a revolutionary conspiracy aimed at the ultimate subversion of the British Raj and the establishment of a Sikh Rule in the Punjab and Swaraj in India.

The Babbar Akalis aroused the religious feelings of the Sikhs and showed the British Government as tyrannical and oppressive and tried to create a strong antipathy on the part of the Sikhs. They reminded the Sikhs of their past sovereignty of the Punjab and efforts were made to dilute their loyalty towards the British which had lasted for more than fifty years. They were told that the time had come to draw the sword against the enemies.

Domeli, Pragpur and Pallahi Tehsil Phagwara in Kapurthala State and other places in the Jalandhar and Hoshiarpur districts were centres of the activities of the Babbar Akalis. To get arms, the Babbars sent agents to NWFP and also tried to persuade soldiers to steal them from army arsenals.

The Babbar Akalis like the Ghadarites suffered from two shortcomings a) inability in securing arms; and b) ineffective organisation in so far as keeping secrecy by the members was concerned c) allowing personal spite to mingle with revolutionary zeal. The Punjab CID infiltrated the Babbars' inner circles. Babbar violence was of short but intense duration. For a few months they were effective in the Jalandhar Doaba and Hoshiarpur.

By the summer of 1923 most of the Babbars had been captured and the wave of violence was over. Of the Babbar Akalis put up for trial, 6 men, including Kishan Singh Binag, were condemned to death, and, apart from 23 who were acquitted, the rest were sentenced to varying terms of imprisonment. The condemned men did not appeal for mercy and preferred to get hanged.

The Sikhs' Struggle in Retrospect (1916-22)

The Sikhs tried to forge a separate identity in the British Raj to gain advantages for their community as the Muslims were doing in the same British province of Punjab.

The Sikhs were absent at the Lucknow session of INC as well as at previous sessions. They were ignored by the Congress as a minority community but they claimed the same proportionate representation as had been allowed to the Muslims in the Lucknow Pact. The Congress leaders were in a quandary.

The Sikh claim to the weightage was limited to their representation in the Punjab Legislative Council and the Municipal Bodies within the province and it can be said that they made out a very good case for themselves within the territorial limits of the province.

Although the Sikhs were one of the smallest communities in India, they contributed no less than 40 per cent of combatants to the Indian Army. They were the ruling community not so long ago and they owned the highest ratio of the agricultural land. They formed about 10 per cent of the population and claimed 30 per cent of the representation in the Province. Chief Khalsa Diwan the body of the land-owning aristocratic Sikhs was blamed by the politically awakened Sikhs for ignoring the Sikh rights.

Within a few days of the adoption of the Non-Cooperation Resolution by the Calcutta Congress, the Central Sikh League, a political body was formed under Sardar Kharak Singh. A Sikh Conference was held at the Bradlaugh Hall, Lahore where a number of important resolutions were adopted.

The Sikhs and the Montford Reforms

The Montford Report left the working out of the details in the hands of the Franchise and Subjects Committees and the Sikh community found the Lucknow Pact had proved a great impediment, so far as their interests were concerned. A Sikh Deputation, appointed to represent the case of the community in England talked about the serious harm that the pact had done to the interests of the Sikhs and other minorities, which was hinted at by the joint Report also.

The Franchise Committee ignored the Sikhs in allocating the proportion of Muslim representations in the Councils, as per the Lucknow Pact. The Franchise Committee's action reduced the share of the Sikh representation in the Punjab Legislative Council.

After the Minto-Morley Reforms were announced, the Punjab Government remarked *'in the Punjab, the Sikh community is of the greatest importance and it should be considered if any and what measures are necessary for its adequate representation'*. Nothing fruitful for the Sikhs came.

The Lieutenant-Governor of the Punjab, O'Dwyer in his speech in 1917 remarked *'whereas all the Provinces had their Hindu-Muslim problems, in the Punjab one had 'the very important Sikh interests to consider as well'*.

The Hon'ble Sardar Bahadur Sunder Singh Majithia, as Secretary of the Chief Khalsa Diwan demanded a one-third share in the representation of the Punjab Government as the 'absolute minimum', when the question of political and legislative reforms came up for consideration in 1916. Similarly, Majithia added, their share in the Viceroy's and the Secretary of State's Councils should be fixed on likewise principles.

On November 22, 1917 a strong Sikh deputation represented to the government. They informed the British that as per the census figures of 1911, the Sikhs numerically were 12 per cent of the population of the Punjab. The Sikh strength in the Indian Army was 20 per cent while from those who were recruited from the Punjab, the figure was not less than 60 per cent.

The Sikh claim was recognized by the Montford report which said that the Sikhs were a distinct and gallant people and a valuable element to the Indian Army. It further said that everywhere (in civil administration and councils) they were in a minority and go unrepresented. The report wanted to extend the system already placed in the case of the Muslims.

In September 1918, the Chief Khalsa Diwan of Amritsar convened an assembly of the whole community and a memorandum was prepared in which they submitted that they were entitled to an equally effective role in the administration of the country.

The Punjab government in 1918 asked the Franchise Committee to consider the case of the Sikhs liberally. But the Franchise Committee only proposed 'a separate electoral roll and separate constituencies' but did not suggest the exact proportion of seats to which the community was entitled. Based on the weightage allowed to the Muslims, the Sikhs claimed that a share of 30 per cent of seats would be their due. The example of Bihar and Orissa was cited where the Muslims with a population percentage of 10 per cent had got 27 per cent seats.

Finally, the Punjab Government recommended only 19 per cent of the non-special seats for the Sikhs and it was still further reduced by the Franchise Committee which instead of increasing this percentage, as they should have done, reduced it to 8 seats out of 54 or approximately to 15 per cent. The Sikhs conveyed to the Secretary of State for India their extreme disappointment and in August 1917, Sardar Bahadur Sunder Singh Majithia submitted a memorandum to the Secretary of State through the Government of India.

Regarding the Sikh representation in the Council the whole community in the Punjab was quite bitter at the time the deputation to the Secretary of State was preparing to start. The deputation tried its best to get there as early as possible but it could not reach England before July 11, 1920, when they were disappointed to learn that six days before their reaching, the Joint Committee had passed the rules and made their Report to Parliament.

Golden Temple Keys Affairs

On November 7, 1921, a few government officials visited Vice President of the SGPC, S. Sunder Singh Ramgarhia, and the Golden Temple treasury's keys were taken away by them. The treasury contained the jewels and other valuables of the Temple and this action of the British caused widespread indignation among the Sikh ranks.

On November 14, the DC of Amritsar informed the SGPC that the government had appointed Captain Bahadur Singh, Manager of Durbar Sahib and batches of non-violent Sikh Panth Sewaks were ready for arrest rather than submit to the authority of the new manager. In the meantime, the *Sarbarah* took away the bundle of keys. The government did not allow meetings protesting against its action and applied the *Seditious Meetings Act* to some of the central Districts of the Punjab. This could not break the resolute Sikhs.

Baba Gurdit Singh of Komagata Maru fame who had defied police for many years, also addressed a Diwan at Nankana Sahib. The offer of handing over the keys via a court was rejected by the Sikhs who demanded that the keys be handed via Akal Takht.

The government said that it was unable to acquiesce in the control of the Golden Temple by the SGPC because it had mixed political affairs with religious and did not fully represent all the Sikhs. But on the other hand, the government was anxious to maintain the old relations of mutual trust with this community.

The government took the wise step of releasing the Sikh prisoners on January 12, 1922. They were sentenced under the Seditious Meetings Act. At the same time negotiations started between the government and SGPC and on January 19, 1922, the keys of the Durbar Sahib were delivered to S. Kharak Singh by an agent of the government.

Now issuing a circular, the government decided to take action against the Akalis. The circular reached the District Officers on March 7 and by the first week of April 1922, over 2,000 Akalis were arrested.

Gandhi Arrested

Gandhi with his supporters was arrested on March 10, 1922, tried and sentenced to 6 years imprisonment on March 18, 1922, for what the government called their turbulent attitude, and because they had associated themselves with the destruction of the existing system of government.

Gurdwara Bill

Government invited the SGPC on April 3, 1922, to take part in drafting of the Gurdwara Bill. Since there was maltreatment and torture of Akalis in parts of the province, SGPC refused to cooperate with the government which pressed for a conference. A joint meeting did take place. The prevailing atmosphere for a mutual settlement was however extremely unfavourable and on May 15, the Conference failed. The government in no mood to listen to threats or advices, drafted the Bill and introduced it in the Council.

SGPC launched an agitation against the Bill and sent deputations to tour the Province to create public opinion against the authorities. Simultaneously, protests were made by non-Sikh bodies against the indiscriminate way of arrest of the Akalis.

The indiscriminate repression of the Akalis only benefited the surviving mahants who wanted to grab the gurdwaras and the associated properties. Ostensibly they behaved as they were under the SGPC but at the first opportunity, they would break free from it only to turn against it.

The Sikh members of the council also opposed the draft of the Bill and Sir John Maynard informed the Punjab Council on July 31, 1922 that the government had dropped the idea of gurdwara legislation.

The Jaito Massacre in July 1923

Jaito is a municipal council in Faridkot district in the Indian Punjab. It is a subdivision in Ferozepur Division. It was founded by Jaito, a Jat of the Sidhu Clan. Close to it is a gurdwara of the Tenth Guru popularly known as Gangsar.

Maharaja Ripudaman Singh of Nabha had a dispute with the Maharaja of Patiala, not with the Government of India. He was quite concerned about affairs of the community and the government knew about his sympathies with the nationalist and Akali movements. The government appointed a court of Inquiry against him and its finding was against the ruler of Nabha; thus, Ripudaman Singh had to abdicate in favour of his minor son. Exhorting the Sikhs to observe September 9, 1923, as *'Nabha Day'*, the SGPC passed a resolution.

Col. Minchin the AGG and Mr. C.M.G. Ogilvie ICS acting Administrator arrived at Nabha with two hundred strong Gorkha and Dogra soldiers on the morning of July 8, 1923 and surrounded the Hira Mahal. The Maharaja was packed off to Dehra Dun.

SGPC considered it a challenge to the community and made serious allegations of arbitrary conduct and high handedness against the Political Agent.

Call for Sikh Demonstration

On August 2, 1923 the SGPC telegraphed to the Viceroy informing him about the developments, praying for the appointment of a Commission of Inquiry to find the truth. The only indication received was that the Viceroy was considering the appointment and personnel of a Council of Regency for the Nabha State.

The atmosphere cooled down after the Guru-ka-Bagh affair and there were bright prospects of peace between the Government and the Sikhs. But by deposing the Maharaja of Nabha in July 1923, the British Government again plunged the Sikh community into a turmoil of agitation.

The SGPC took up the matter, but the Sikhs were getting arrested for making speeches and taking out processions in sympathy with the Maharaja on the charge of disobeying the government. While the Sikhs were being arrested when *'diwan'* was being held at Jaito in the Nabha State, the Sikhs sat down to recite the *Akhand Path* (continuous recitation of Holy Granth). They were also denied this right. The gurdwara as well as the place of meeting were both blockaded and no food or water was allowed to go in. The Sikhs began to starve. Such was the situation on September 14, 1923.

The British officials were determined not to allow even holy reading and arrived with a military force and arrested the whole congregation assembled round the Holy Granth outside the gurdwara. Then the armed soldiers in uniform were taken into the gurdwara itself, where the Sikhs sat listening to the Akhand Path and the whole congregation including the reciters and the attendants was arrested. It was an act of sacrilege; the *Granthi* was caught hold of by his arms and dragged and arrested.

The news of this desecration drew the very next morning a party of Sikhs to restart the Akhand Path. The prohibition from September 14 was made absolutely rigid. Sikh pilgrims from every area began to pour in to assert their religious right of freely visiting the gurdwara and performing the Akhand Path and other acts of worship.

From Septmber 11, 1923, Akali Jathas of 25 each marched daily on foot to Jaito, after taking a pledge of non-violence before Shri Akal Takhat at Amritsar. The government arrested and removed the Akali Jathas only to set them free at distant places. Once freed, the Jathas travelled back to Muktsar to court arrest again. The stopping of the Sikhs from praying at the gurdwara of Gangsar continued for the last five months and about 5000 Sikhs suffered untold hardships.

The INC Notices Jaito Morcha

At the special Indian National Congress Session at Delhi in 1923, stirring accounts from some Sikh visitors as well as from Diwan Charnan Lal were narrated. The Congress leaders showed deep sympathy with the Akalis. At the same time, Principal Gidwani, Mr. K. Santanam and Pandit Jawaharlal Nehru left for Jaito to take a first-hand stock of the situation but they were arrested upon reaching there which stirred the whole nation. The Congress Civil Disobedience Committee issued a Nabha bulletin.

The Agitation Intensifies

The government was unmoved and the Sikhs decided to end the agony. It was decided that a congregation of 500 Sikhs was planned and they would follow the path of non-violence in their mission and those Sikhs would walk to Jaito to visit Gangsar and resume Akhand Path. Men were drawn from all districts from all walks of life even including a number of peaceful Sadhus. Extension of Nabha Morcha to neighbouring states entailed.

But all this put a great strain upon the resources of the SGPC. Their leaders were arrested and tried. The Akali ferment soon engulfed the neighbouring Sikh States of Patiala, Jind and Faridkot as well.

At Patiala, however, the agitation was opposed and precautions were taken to prevent any Sikh Diwans to be held or Nagar-Kirtan processions to pass through streets.

Jathas were active at Patiala; at Sirhind about 200 Akalis were arrested in an attempt to take part in the Nabha Day demonstration. At Bhawanigarh, the Police came into conflict with the Akalis.

The excitement at Barnala was even greater and a large Dewan was held in the gurdwara at Thikriwala near Barnala where 250 men including a Jathedar was taken into custody. Women of the place formed a procession, marching through the streets of Barnala singing hymns (shabds). Seeing them, hundreds of Sikhs who had not so far participated in the demonstrations came out and joined in the Nabha Day celebrations. A Jatha from Rajpura, on its way to Patiala, was intercepted and arrested.

At Sunam (Patiala State) the local gurdwara was locked up to stop the Akalis from celebrating the Nabha Day. The Pujari-in-charge, however forced open the door and allowed the Sikhs to assemble in a Dewan. A procession was afterwards formed but it was forcibly dispersed.

Despite the precautions taken by the Faridkot state by the President of the court of administration, several hundreds of Sikhs assembled at the Faridkot railway station carrying the Granth Sahib. They were ordered to disperse but they refused and were detained upto midnight. Similar Jathas of Sikhs coming from the adjoining villages were arrested while proceeding to Faridkot.

Brars belonged to the same Jat *gotra* as the Maharaja himself and they lived in this tract in large numbers and therefore Jaito was selected as the venue of the Dewan. The main reason was that the famous Gurdwara of Gangsar was situated there. The

Dewan lasted for three days. The Dewan commenced on the 9th Bhadon (August 25, 1923) and continued for several days with the Akalis being the chief organisers. On the 5th day, August 29, 1923 the Secretary, of the Dewan S. Jiwan Singh along with two other leaders was arrested and taken by the Police to Nabha.

On September 9, 1923, a barefooted procession was formed. This was done in obedience to the instructions of the SGPC which had issued a communique to the effect that the processions of the barefooted Akalis should.

First Jatha Leaves Amritsar

On the Basant anniversary on February 9, 1924, the Shahidi Jatha or the 'Band of Martyrs' took a solemn pledge before the Akal-Takht at Amritsar to restart the interrupted Akhand Path at Gangsar. The Jathedar of the Akal-Takht asked them to remain perfectly non-violent in thought and the Jatha left for Jaito on foot on February 9 evoking tremendous enthusism wherever it went. Sikhs always marched along with the Jatha after coming from long distances.

The Jatha halted at Bargari in the Faridkot territory on the evening of February 20, 1924 and left for Jaito at about 12 noon which was six miles from Bargari. 'Sowars' had been stationed at short intervals all along the way and when the Jatha and the Sangat arrived on the Nabha boundary, they were told by the state officials to go in a batch of 50 men to Gurdwara Gangsar and leave the Nabha territory as soon as they had finished their bath. The Jatha took this as an unreasonable restriction on their religious liberty and refused to bargain for the God-given right of entering a Sikh temple for worship.

Shahidi Jatha Trapped

The state authorities had very mischievously narrowed the passage leading to the Gangsar Gurdwara and the fort by a barbed wire barrier on one side and nearly 200 chained bullock carts formed a long row full of thorny bushes and masses of barbed wire on the other side near the end of this passage.

Also, the state government had recruited many local toughs under the threat of confiscating the property and turning to beat up the Akalis severely, once instructed. The men were prepared for their brutal work and were quite drunk by then. Amongst them were a number of Muslim policemen from Jhelum and Attock Districts, who had done such nasty work before in connection with the *Guru-ka-Bagh* affair.

The *Jatha* and the *'Sangat'* moved in the direction of Gurdwara Tibi Sahib which was about 800 metres away. In the front was half of the Jatha in rows of four, *Guru Granth Sahib* was in the middle and the rear comprised the other half. The Sikh Sangat walked behind the palanquin of *Guru Granth.*

The Administrator with some officials encountered the Jatha and literally asked them to disperse else he would order firing. The Jatha continued its march towards the Tibbi Sahib, followed by a *Sangat* among whom there were ladies, who were distributing food and drink.

Much before the Sikhs had actually entered its territory, the Administrator had made up its mind to beat and shoot at the Sikh 'Sangat'. What followed was an unprecedented human butchery. The big procession of Sikh devotees including women and old men came under a shower of bullets. Many dropped dead or were seriously wounded. But not a single person wavered. They marched for the sacred mound of Tibbi Sahib, after lifting their dead or the wounded. Many went to the neighbouring fields to bring the dead and the wounded to the gurdwara. Soon the Military arrived and snatched the bodies of Sikhs from there. Many of the wounded died for lack of attention and water. The neighbouring fields densely littered with the dead or wounded Sikhs. The Sikhs marched towards Gangsar Gurdwara after depositing the dead and the wounded in the Tibbi Sahib.

The march of the Shahidi Jatha was checked by a detachment of cavalry, which blocked the way and rushed on the Sangat about Tibbi Sahib and the sowars chased Sikh parties scattering them in all directions. This relentless hunt of old men, children and women must have resulted in heavy casualties and many were trampled under the horses' hoofs. The Shahidi Jatha was next surrounded by the Cavalry, other policemen and local Muslim ruffians.

Every Sikh was surrounded by a group of five or six Muslim ruffians who encouraged by the state officials used their sticks freely to beat up the heroes of the Shahidi Jatha to senselessness.

The few Sikhs in the vicinity of Tibbi Sahib, and some ladies who served the wounded Sikhs were abused by the soldiers and ordered to leave the place.

Casualties

As the scene of tragedy was inaccessible the exact number of casualties could not be ascertained. While on the one hand the SGPC reports mentioned that there were 300 casualties including 100 deaths, on the other, the Government reported the figures of 21 dead and 33 wounded. More than 7,000 people were arrested at Jaito on this occasion.

The movement dragged on for some time more until it was brought to an end by a compromise by some moderate Sikhs; both the parties were tired of the long-drawn struggle. In 1925 the Gurdwara Act acceptable to the Sikhs was passed and the Akali leaders were released.

The consequence of this agitation was that the 13th Jatha was left untouched and it marched triumphantly to the gurdwara at Jaito. At the same time Sir Malcolm Halley, the Governor began negotiations with the Akalis so that the latter could take possession of all the important gurdwaras in the Province. After the Gurdwara Bill was passed in 1925, all the important Gurdwaras in the Punjab passed into the hands of the SGPC.

The Sikhs triumphed in their agitation but the relation between the Sikhs and the Government were strained and British confidence in them was shaken. By 1930, the Sikh representation in the Armed forces was reduced to 13.58 per cent and the government's confidence shifted towards Muslims who in 1914 were only 11.1 per cent but in 1930 they rose to 22.2 per cent in the Indian Army.

The Punjab Farmer in Debt

The Extent of Agricultural Debt in the Punjab

In the Punjab, though agriculture was the still the only industry of importance in the 1920s, there is almost no information available as to the extent to which the cultivator was in debt although periodically the British India's settlement officers endeavoured to collect figures for the districts, they served in. But their study was handicapped by the accuracy of their collected data. The same is true for the provinces outside the Punjab.

Till 1917, no one had any information as to how far or to what extent the debt prevailed. About the same time, to assist village banks in making advances to their members, a register was introduced in which the assets and liabilities as well as the debts of each member were recorded and thus it was a rather simple matter to ascertain the extent of debt of each member.

This was done in 1918-19 (i.e. 100 years ago) in the case of 55,308 members belonging to 2,106 societies. The returns were prepared according to a prescribed form to produce results which could be trusted as these were prepared under well-educated officers. The details compiled include all sections of the agricultural community whose members were classified in three categories, viz. proprietors, occupancy tenants, and tenants at will, farm servants, etc. Another distinction was made between proprietors who owned or cultivated 8 acres or less and those who had more than 8 acres.

In the 1920s, Punjab was a province of peasant proprietors, and the problem of how to maintain the peasant proprietor upon his land in freedom and comfort manifested itself as the problem of debt.

We come now to the figures themselves regarding *indebtedness*. There are four salient points for 43,733 proprietors analysed:

Only 17 per cent were free of debt.

Net mortgage debt was not more than 40 per cent of the whole.

For an indebted proprietor, the average debt was Rs. 463.

Total debt is represented by 12 times the land revenue which was paid by all concerned, whether under debt or not.

It was found that over 80 per cent of the proprietors of the Punjab were in debt and this percentage emphasises the truth of Sir Frederick Nicholson's dictum, that 'the necessary complement of the peasant proprietor is the moneylender' and it explains, too, why there were innumerable moneylenders in the province. The province was divided into six circles for the purpose of this enquiry and no circle was more than 26 per cent free of debt, and in two districts of the sub-montane area all but 5 per cent were involved.

Punjab of those days was compared with the rest of India and the few figures available are presented below:

Table 6.1 From Darling's *The Punjab Farmers in Prosperity and Debt* (1928)

Year	*Province*	*Percentage Free of Debt*
1874	Central Provinces	60
1888	The tenantry in the Agra District	22
1894	Nagpur (18,000 tenants)	40
1901	Baroda State	40 (of all landowners)
1907	Faridpur (Bengal)	55 (of all cultivators)
1919	Mysore State (24,350 cooperators)	37

These figures suggest that debt was more widespread in the Punjab than elsewhere. Whether the conditions in the Punjab were better or worse than in the rest of India, it is clear that the moneylender had spread his wings all over the country.

The net mortgage debt was only 40 per cent of the whole, and, though it varied from district to district, in Hoshiarpur and Jullundur it was more than 50 per cent. A non-agriculturist was not allowed from holding a mortgage for more than twenty years under the Land Alienation Act.

The mortgage loan appears to be commoner than anywhere else as proved by 9,000 cases belonging to Jullundur and Hoshiarpur. In these two districts, the net mortgage debt is over 60 per cent of the whole against only 37 per cent in the north (Rawalpindi, Jhelum and Attock) and less than 30 in the south (Rohtak, Karnal and Hissar). Based on this, the gross mortgage debt of the province can be estimated to be at 45 per cent of the whole; and, allowing (at a guess) another 5 per cent for other forms of security, like jewellery, one can draw the conclusion that half the total debt of the Punjab is unsecured.

It is hard to fathom as to why the money-lender would advance large sums to cultivators without a genuine security. These cultivators had many more traits of careless planning rather than punctual dealing, and moreover Punjab often had drought and disease. This was not a major disadvantage to the money-lender since being a non-agriculturist, he was after the produce and not the land itself and he took payment in grain. Moreover, by not demanding security against the loan, he levied a higher rate of interest. An unsecured loan cost was twice as much as one secured by mortgage.

As per the prevailing custom of those days, the cultivator loved his land and soil and only in exigency the peasant parted with his land, and to save his land from sell-out, he had to part with his land sooner or later. Nor did the cultivator want to mortgage his land, fearing always that in the next stage, he might have to sell it. A mortgage might lower his social esteem, as he thought in that eventuality, he might face trouble in marrying off his children. He was, therefore, trying to conceal the debts he had incurred and this was a serious obstacle to the spread of co-operative credit in India.

Later the peasant began to realize that it was better to borrow on a mortgage at 9 or 12 per cent, even though the fact may be public rather than to pay twice this amount for the doubtful advantage of keeping his land untouched and his debt concealed.

A high proportion of unsecured debt indicated that the rural finance system was primitive, good neither for the borrower nor for the lender. There the borrower readily accepted a loan by the simple process of his thumb impression on a bond but thinks twice before pledging the land he loves.

The temptation to make reckless advances is very high for the moneylender at the high rate of interest when no security is taken. It was considered to be a positive sign that in some districts the proportion of secured to unsecured debt showed a tendency to rise.

The three-quarters of those who cultivated in the Punjab on an average ten acres or less, had Rs. 463 per indebted proprietor and was a considerable amount by any means.

For the province as a whole, debt was twelve times the land revenue and the total debt of the proprietors of the Punjab was about 55 crores. The total mortgage debt of the province was estimated to be 34.5 crores in 1921, which was 45 per cent of the total debt of 77 crores and it was 15 times the land revenue.

This gives us some idea of the pressure of debt upon the individual proprietor. The land revenue demand took away nearly one-fifth of the net income of the land. Accordingly, a multiple of 15 means that the average proprietor's debt was equal to about three years of his net income. Although the burden was hardly light; on the other hand, the burden can hardly be regarded as heavy, if debt and sale value are compared. That is because in the four years ending 1926 the average price fetched by land amounted to 288 times the land revenue payable upon it.

Table 6.2 From Darling's *The Punjab Farmers in Prosperity and Debt* (1928)

Year	*Land Value (Cr) (1)=288x (3)*	*Land Income (Cr) (2)*	*Land Revenue (Cr) (3)*	*Net Land Income (Cr) (4) = (2) – (3)*	*Debt (Cr) (5)*	*Debt Recovery time (yrs) (6) = (5)÷ (2)*
1921	1440	25.0	5.0	20.0	75.0	3

It is more prudent to express debt in terms of net income and not sale value, as the sale value has practically no relation to yield.

The dividing line between larger and the smaller proprietors has been taken at eight acres. Those who owned or cultivated more than this have been classified separately from those who own or cultivate less. The results may be summarised as follows:

Table 6.3 From Darling's *The Punjab Farmers in Prosperity and Debt* (1928)

Prop-rietor	*Number*	*% Free of Debt*	*% of Mortgage Debt to Total Debt*	*Average Debt*	*Debt's Multiple of Land Revenue*
Large	25840	18	40	570	10
Small	17380	17	40	310	27

It is seen that the larger proprietor is both more highly in debt and less seriously burdened than the smaller. Though he owes Rs. 570, his debt is only 10 times the land revenue, while the same for the smaller proprietor is Rs. 310 and 27.

Indebtedness of the Tenants

Tenants fell into two main classes: *the ordinary tenant at will* and the *hereditary tenant* who, had a permanent right to cultivate his land, provided he had paid the rent. The latter was called an 'occupancy tenant' and had the status close to that of a small proprietor. The data obtained is as follows:

Table 6.4 From Darling's *The Punjab Farmers in Prosperity and Debt* (1928)

	Occupancy Tenants	*Small Proprietors*
% free of debt	20	17
Average debt per indebted tenant	Rs 290	Rs 310
% of Mortgage debt to Total Debt	25	40

The figures show that there was not much difference between either class. Undoubtedly, by mortgage, the small proprietor raised rather more as he owned his land, and was somewhat more in debt, but debt was almost as widespread in the one case as in the other.

The main interest of these figures lies in the fact that they illustrate the truth of the statement, that debt follows credit. This will be seen from the following table:

Table 6.5

Average Debt	*(Rs)*
Large proprietors	570
Small proprietors	310
Occupancy tenants	290
Tenants at will	135

The larger proprietor borrowed more than the smaller, and the small proprietor more than the tenant. The tenant at will and farm servant borrowed little, because they had no security to offer; the large proprietor borrowed much, because he had ample land as security to offer. No doubt his needs were greater, but where resources were ample, his needs went beyond the mere necessity.

The existence of debt was due to necessity, and its volume dependent upon credit, and the link between the two was the *moneylender*. This was the fundamental fact of rural finance and it possibly explains the intimate connection between prosperity and debt.

From the census report of 1911, there appear to be about one million families of tenants and the farm servants, etc., who owned no land and the average debt of tenants was Rs. 150 per family. A total debt of 15 crores may, therefore, be assumed for non-proprietors. Adding this to the 75 crores estimated for the proprietors, we get (75+15) = 90 crores, for the agriculturists of the province.

For the three years ending 1922-23, the average annual gross value of the agricultural output was estimated at 128 crores (86 millions), which was 42 per cent more than the total debt. The Punjab figure of 90 crores was 19 times the land revenue of the province. The number of moneylenders, were three times as many in the Punjab as in the rest of British India, and the special legislation had to be passed to protect the cultivator against the money-lender. A large part of the debt was unproductive and 33 to 50 per cent of it was possibly due to compound interest made even worse for the borrower who was entrapped in the vicious cycle of moneylending. A substantial amount was also the result of extravagant expenditure upon marriages.

The average rate of interest was possibly above 15 per cent in Punjab. On a debt of 90 crores this involved an annual charge of 13 crores (90*0.15), an amount nearly thrice the whole land revenue of the province (4.86 crores). From 1900 onwards the debt increased considerably till the 1920s.

Land revenue was quite low in comparison to the burden of debt. Land revenue averaged only Re. 1-13-0 per cultivated acre and less than Rs 4 per head and it was no important cause of debt.

Muslim Angle to Debt

There was another angle with regard to the debt in the Punjab. Though almost the whole amount of the required debt was being advanced by Hindus or Sikhs, well over half was incurred by Muslims. Forming 56 per cent of the rural population, the Muslims must have owed at least fifty crores and that was not the right thing for that community to forge ahead of the Hindus and the Sikhs.

The Remedy to Debt

Fortunately, there was a comparatively simple remedy available. A person who took up the membership of a cooperative credit society could pay off his whole debt in 10 to 20 years and also create enough capital to support his basic system of farming. Debt could be converted into a productive debt, with which the whole province could prosper.

The Cunning Moneylender

The loans for drought and disease, uneconomic holdings and the extravagant obligations of marriage, all sprang from necessity and the debt was greater where need was high and the security was better.

The ubiquitous moneylender manipulated the necessities of the cultivator to his own advantage and dominated the complete chain of production and distribution of wealth.

Moneylending is one of the oldest trades in the world, and even today all trade, national or international is based upon it. But the moneylender has had a bad name over the ages. Till the 1920s, men mainly borrowed for grain. In those days, in any province in India, everyone knew that sooner or later famine would return and everyone agriculturist could forward to his only source, i.e. the moneylender. In all agricultural countries famine and moneylending coexisted.

Hunger would compel the ordinary mortal at the shortest interval of time to seek the help of the moneylender and the latter would always be ready to exploit this situation.

The moneylender was clever and well-versed in numbers and he dealt with a person who was ignorant and simple-hearted. It led to the latter's exploitation and moneylending, therefore, was fraught with grave danger to the state, and was usually controlled by law, custom or authority.

Pre-Muslim India had a much more tolerant attitude towards the moneylender as compared to the Western world and we hear of wives and children being sold against debt in the Buddhist period. The interest rate varied from 15 to 60 per cent according to caste, and security. The moneylender often stood between the cultivator and his perishing and he financed the village, marketed its produce and supplied its necessities.

Thus, when agricultural conditions were insecure, the moneylender came into the picture and he was essentially a very powerful and an indispensable person in India's provinces. In the annexed Punjab of 1849, security and credit were not available in the modern way and exploiting the situation, the moneylender was established all over the towns and larger villages.

During the Sikh rule, in the central Punjab, as a result of the Sikhs collecting the revenue before the crop was cut, the zamindar was forced to borrow money from the bania at 25 per cent per annum interest. Amritsar used to have two or three shops reportedly of village grocers and moneylenders infamous as *great extortionists*. In Narowal, the cultivators were in a high degree of indebtedness. Sialkot, at the beginning of British occupation was one of the most indebted districts in the Punjab where about 5.0 million were invested in loans and dealings in grain in 1853.

During the same time, the cultivators of Gujranwala were found to be entirely in the hands of their 'shahs' (moneylenders). In Gujrat under Sikh rule each cultivator always found himself in debt to his Khatri for at least a six months' supply of household necessaries. Similarly, in the Western Punjab, of 1848, there were few proprietors in Shahpur who did not have an account with the Khatri moneylenders of the district.

In nineteenth century Afghanistan also, the moneylender was a necessity but he was not so powerful as he subsequently became under British rule.

During the Sikh rule, the moneylender had to manipulate his customers under two restraints:

Existence of a vigorous village community, which held him in partial check. Even in the 1920s, in parts of Dera Ghazi Khan, where the Baloch tribes maintained their unity, the moneylender had to be watchful of what and how he did. But the tribe could not get without him and so the moneylender had to be treated fairly.

The second check was the apathy of the state towards recovery. There were no formal courts of justice as they existed in the British times and, if a man owed a Kirar money and matters could not be arranged, the case went before the Kardar who could curtail any amount of interest claimed by the usurer. But if the Kardar was corrupt, harsher means might be adopted.

For some time after the establishment of British rule these satisfactory conditions continued but the cases were too often rushed through and decided on unreliable evidence by overworked munsiffs, helped by under-manned, under-paid, and corrupt establishments, almost all city born men unaccustomed to rural affairs. The cultivator lamented that the law instead of being used as salt became the whole diet.

With the decline of the village community and the establishment of civil courts during the British period immediately after the annexation, the reign of the moneylender slowly began. His power was first established in Eastern Punjab's sub-montane tract where the village community was beginning to decay. In the Western part of Punjab, tribal ties were strong enough to hold him in check for another decade till 1870, while across the Indus the rough and ready methods of the Frontier still made him tread with caution. So, his ascendancy may be said to date from the 1870s and typically, it began with a series of famines, which gave him the opportunity he needed.

Under the Sikh rule the cultivator and his dependents lived in penury. Now under the British revenue assessment, the cultivator knew exactly what he had to pay and had substantial surplus when the harvest was good and this could always be marketed under the better communications and growing towns. In the Sikh days, the produce could not go far as the roads were unmetalled and sometimes the harvest rotted in the godowns of Amritsar.

In 1861 came the Railways from Amritsar to Lahore and the great change from medieval to modern conditions began. The same year the opening of the Upper Bari Doab Canal took place and by 1870 goods could be booked to Bombay, Calcutta and Karachi; by 1872 there were over 400 miles of railway, 1,000 miles of metalled roads, and 2,750 miles of canal; trade increased manifold; wealth followed and in the village a money economy began to replace the old system of modified barter.

Land which had been almost unsaleable, during the Sikh rule, now began to have value. Now, due to fixed assessment and rising prices, it became an object of general desire. By the 1870s, the peasant proprietor of the Punjab found himself in possession of this valuable asset. A few acres of land, which earlier looked after him had now appreciated in the British period and his standard of living began to rise and the moneylender began to tighten his hold.

The moneylender was always prepared with his offer for advances and few land proprietors could resist this temptation and the small holder began to borrow with enhanced carelessness. The mortgage which was unheard of in the Sikh rule, was now popular in every village, and by 1878, 7 per cent of the land of the province was pledged.

By 1880, the peasant proprietor was in the grip of the moneylender who ruled strongly for the next 30 years, i.e. up to 1910 or so and the number of bankers and money-lenders proliferated from 53,263 in 1868 to 193,890 in 1911.

After the passing of the Land Alienation Act in 1901, the power of the moneylender was under challenge throughout the Punjab. For the next twenty years, the moneylender could not dispossess an agriculturist from his land since the cultivator's legal position had been strengthened. Moreover, when he died, his ancestral land was not liable for the payment of his debts.

Since 1901, not only the agriculturist's legal position but also his economic position was much stronger. The co-operative movement was started three years after the passing of the Land Alienation Act and the first village bank was subsequently established. The moneylender was not the sole lending source now and the loans were available at 12 per cent from village banks instead of up to 75 per cent charged by the moneylender. However, the peasant was ignorant of law and cooperative movement till the First World War and the moneylender still dominated the village freely.

The First World War of 1914 awakened the villager and he was no longer an ignorant character. The province sent thousands of its men to every part of the world to fight for the British and now regarded moneylenders as nothing more than a parasite. Now, the cooperative banks in 13,500 villages became a formidable rival to the moneylender all over the province.

In the 1920s, the cooperative movement attacked the moneylender. There were now commission shops to oust the middlemen, and arbitration societies ensured the non-requirement of the lawyer. In parts of the central Punjab, the professional moneylender was surely defeated. In Lahore, Amritsar and Hoshiarpur his power was a fraction of what it was and he had almost vanished from villages around Jalandhar, where he was replaced by village banks and the agriculturist moneylender. In Multan also, where he was quite strong, the moneylender was not strong anymore and in Rohtak in the east, he was a shadow of his past.

In the central Punjab, capital was going out from moneylending into trade and these people were migrating from village to town, and in Jhelum and Multan some were finding that farming was more fruitful than lending.

The success against the moneylender was temporary as in the year of 1920-21 Punjab was drought-affected and the money-lender made a comeback of sorts.

In the prosperous district of Lyallpur large sums were being borrowed to buy land and in the adjacent district of Jhang and throughout the Western Punjab the moneylender continues to dominate, and in Multan he still tried to exploit the agriculturists. But in the districts away from the central Punjab, the moneylender remained strong. However, his number was being reduced in the central districts, in Rawalpindi, Ferozepur and Karnal there had been an increase of over 10 per cent and in Rohtak and Hissar of over 50 per cent.

Punjab had three times more moneylenders as in the rest of British India.

Caste of the Moneylender

Most of the moneylending of the Punjab is in the hands of three castes; the *Bania* or *Aggarwal*, the *Khatri* and the *Arora*, all necessarily Hindu and some Sikh among the last two. Apparently, they divided the province amongst themselves. The *Bania* prevailed in the south of the Sutlej or in the Malwa region; the Khatri was dominant in the central and the Arora had his dominance in the west.

Bania

Malcolm Darling called the Bania *'the most subtle and insidious* while Tavernier wrote disparagingly in *Travels in India* about them 350 years ago:

> .... this caste are so subtle and skilful.... could give lessons to the most cunning Jews.... train their children at an early age .... teach them

> arithmetic, which they learn perfectly, using ....the money alone, so that in a moment they will do a sum, however difficult it may be. ... they listen with patience without replying anything to an enraged person....not returning to see him for four or five days, when they believe his rage to be over.

Darling further says '*It is characteristic of the Bania that in times of scarcity his superstitions are as much directed to prevent a fall of rain as the cultivator's are to secure it.*'

Khatri

Akbar's famous minister, Todar Mal, and the great governors of Multan, Sawan Mal and Mul Raj, were all Khatris, and so was the founder of the Sikh religion, Guru Nanak, and the nine Gurus that followed him. The caste was still the most influential in the Punjab before 1947, both in administration and trade, and is noted for its capacity and shrewdness. A proverb in Punjabi said that 'Even if a Khatri puts ashes on his head....he will make a profit.'

The Khatri moneylender's interests varied and he was perhaps less exacting than his rivals and more human. He mixed with his fellow villagers in daily life and as prosperity spread, he tended to prefer the financing of trade to the financing of agriculture.

Arora

If the Khatri was the best of the three moneylending castes, the Arora, or the Kirar, as he was commonly called, was considered the worst. 'Even if they sleep, do not trust a crow, a kirar or a dog', says another proverb. He had a tenacity and thoroughness with the craft of the Bania and the enterprise of the Khatri.

He had made his presence felt in Muzaffargarh and Dera Ghazi Khan, and had a strong hold over both cultivator and land. He often brought in considerable improvement in the vicinity of area he lived in through his interests in capital, industry and thrift. He did not consider any work menial and turned his hand to anything that promised sizeable returns.

He was found all over in the Western Punjab and the Frontier and all down the Indus and the lower reaches of the Jhelum, Chenab and the Sutlej. He even penetrated into Afghanistan, and even further afield into Central Asia.

The Arora was considered to be a useful servant, but an exacting master. For centuries he was nothing but a servile adjunct to the Muslim cultivator, who despised him for everything.

Moneylender's *Modus Operandi*

For the first twenty years of the British rule, the moneylender was satisfied to accept the produce of the agriculturist as his interest for the debts advanced. It served two purposes a) He got a handsome return for the advance provided and b) He sold the produce at a profit to the buyers. He did not show much interest in the land as a security as the land prices till 1870 were not very high. The situation changed in 1870 when the prices of land under the modern British system began to rise. Now, the clever moneylender wanted to have a share of the land by his dubious ways of trapping the landowner or the agriculturist.

The Bania took great advantage owing to a series of famines and would see to it that a mortgage would invariably end in sale. In less than 20 years (1875-93) the moneylender succeeded in acquiring 11,79,000 acres in different parts of the province, and in Gujranwala, he purchased over half the land sold during this period. This culminated in the passing of the Land Alienation Act.

Rates of Interest

Rates of interest depended on the amount of money available and with the risk incurred in lending it. Before British rule, money was never in plenty and the risk in lending was great and it involved the poverty of the borrower and the insecurity of the harvest. In case of default the cultivator had not much of value that could be taken by the lender and by custom his land could not be occupied either. Repayment depended entirely upon the harvest, and, if a series of harvests failed, recovery was impossible. Compared with Western Europe the rates of interest, therefore, were always high.

These varied from 15 to 60 per cent in ancient India, as known to us. Prior to British rule, the rate was 25 per cent for cash and 50 per cent for grain. As more money came into supply and agriculture more secure 18¾ per cent came to be generally adopted for cash and 25 per cent for grain. In districts like Jalandhar and Lyallpur, where the money supply was even greater, this fell to 12 and even 6 per cent; conversely, in the more backward districts it did not fall at all.

Even if we are considering 1920 as the year for discussion in this case, no country in the world would have developed if it had to pay 15 per cent for its capital. Such was the demand for land that the people were borrowing at 18¾ per cent to get a footing in the new canal colonies, with the result that money that should have gone for development, rather went to the money-lender.

But matters were worse than they seemed. In the pre-British period, compound interest was limited by custom to 50 per cent for cash and 100 per cent for grain and under British rule custom was replaced by law and interest was allowed to accumulate without limit. So, it was not surprising that the accumulated outstanding principal with compounded interest galloped in two or three years!

Dealings in Grain

Nearly all the dealings between a moneylender and his clients were in kind, and the practice continued till the war, as it gave many advantages to the moneylender. A) It gave him the produce he wanted for his dealings as shopkeeper and grain merchant. B) it yielded a higher rate of profit, for the account could be manipulated with ease. Such practices were drastically reduced when the village banks challenged the moneylender.

Agriculturist Moneylender

He was not the typical type but an agriculturist, normally a Jat of the sub-montane or central Punjab who had amassed some capital for two reasons: a) either he went to war and spending two to three years, he brought in his savings from pay and b) Due to spiralling prices and surplus of his output, he had some extra money. This money was being lent to other agriculturists. He benefited mostly from the Land Alienation Act of 1901. However, the Jat lender showed no mercy even to his fellow caste agriculturists while extracting his dues.

Prosperity and Debt: In Retrospect

Prosperity Comes to Punjab

Seventy years had passed since the annexation by the British and there was a marked change in the income of the peasants. Only the south-west of the province remained poor. The change has been more noticeable in the central districts and the canal colonies. The peasant enjoyed the luxuries, once available in the town only. Gold was being purchased and the people were having some basic transportation and the lorries had started to arrive.

Twenty thousand miles of canals had ruled out the fear of famine and starvation was now to a minimum. There was an immense development of trade. In fifty years (1870-1920), cultivation increased by 50 per cent and the value of what was produced rose from 35 to over 120 crores (valued in 1920). The canal colonies alone produced 20 million in a year.

Another significant improvement has been the rise in the value of land. In 1866 it sold at about Rs. 10 per acre but the price in 1926 soared to an average of Rs. 238. In the 1860s, land in Ferozepur was hardly saleable but in the 1920s the irrigated land sold at Rs. 600 an acre which was higher than what good land fetched in Britain!

The Rise in Debt

If prosperity increased from 1870 to 1920, so did the debt; and the increase in the one was not directly proportional to the other. At the beginning of British rule, mortgage was rare and the money-lender was weak but by the 1870s, mortgage was common and the moneylender powerful. By 1874, over one million acres were mortgaged, and by 1891 the figure reached four million. In 1891, the mortgage debt of the province (including the NWFP was estimated at 7.83 crores and assuming it to be 45 per cent of the whole, total debt in that year would be about 17 crores. The corresponding figure for 1922 (excluding the Frontier Province) is at least 82 crores, or 65 crores more than in 1891 and it should be more, considering the fact that the figure of 1891 also included data of NWFP.

Therefore, it can be safely said that in the 32 years (1890-

1922), debt was five times as great as it was 32 years ago. Rural debt increased by at least fifty crores.

Debt followed Credit

Debt follows credit and this was the core of the dilemma. In 1873, five out of the seven most heavily mortgaged districts of the province were 'the most prosperous and wealthy' too and in the period of ten years (1912-22) debt increased at a much faster rate in the richer districts than in the poorer. It was aptly said that a zamindar limited his borrowing not by his wants but by his opportunities.

Effect of High Prices

The main factor in the increase of debt undoubtedly was the expansion in credit that followed the rise in the value of land. High prices were good for the cultivator, on the assumption that it brought him more returns and is correct as long as he has more to sell than to buy. But if he had more to buy than sell, the situation was such that he benefited no more than any other class of consumer. In the good years, high prices were an obvious advantage for a farmer having good land area and if water was plenty. In bad years he had to buy the very grain at a higher price for his consumption.

The Rise in the Standard of Living

The rise in the standard of living can be explained by the fact there was an enormous increase of debt in the last 30 years before 1922. The rise in standard was facilitated by the rise in incomes due to the spread of the canal combined with escalated prices; but the percentage of people who benefited was small and they acted as the trend-setters for the villages.

The rise in the value of land made getting money against mortgage very convenient. It was seen that the expenditure and standard of living were based on the income of good years and there were no provisions to meet the exigencies of bad years. Thirty years earlier the borrowing was beyond their thought process and they were compelled to live on what was actually produced in the previous years. As they had no credit to supplement it. In 1922 the peasants found it easier to borrow rather than to alter their scale of living.

Often the rise in the standard of living was achieved more by an increase of debt than by an increase in production.

Increased Cost of Marriages

At the beginning of the twentieth century in the 1920s, the people in north Punjab who were educated gave indications for austerity measures for marriages: the nautch and the firework display were condemned and jewellery was less costly.

But in the central and more prosperous districts, where the increase in debt has been greatest, there was a shortage of women, and money was being spent for a bride, even by those who could ill-afford it. During Sikh rule, there was less to spend by many but with increasing prosperity in the years from 1850 onwards, expenditure rapidly grew, and by 1870 the peasant spent not less than Rs. 165 on his wedding, and the bigger cultivator spent Rs. 545 for the same.

From Rohtak to Amritsar, the usual expenditure was Rs 100 but in the canal colonies and the central Punjab the cost was rarely less than Rs. 500, and might run into thousands.

Land Revenue and Debt

The first point to notice is that under the Sikhs the land revenue demand was 30 to 40 per cent and occasionally even 50 per cent of the gross produce. There was no scope for debt. The land revenue was nearly always taken in kind and was related to the state of the harvest. Although it left minimal surplus in the hands of the cultivator, the system was not oppressive, and in the Lahore district there were more wells in the 1850s than in 1920 and this shows that people found it useful to sink capital in the land.

There are four main reasons why the peasant was obliged to borrow:

1. The small size of his holding and the way it was split up made it almost impossible for him to live without getting into debt unless he had some extraneous source of income.
2. His repetitive losses of cattle from drought and disease.
3. His lack of foresight and being extravagant; the effects of which are greatly aggravated by insecurity of crop; and,
4. His marriage and other domestic ceremonies related extravagant expenditure.

There were two other causes that made borrowing easy, namely:

- The ubiquitous moneylender and his vicious ways and,
- The great increase of credit availability due to high prices of land.

Punjab Irrigation Developed by the British

In India irrigation was in vogue along the banks of the rivers and in the Punjab, irrigation along the banks of the rivers can be dated to the Mughal reign and these are the testimony:

- The Western Jamuna Canal.
- The Hasli Canal from the River Ravi
- Some canals in the Multan district.

The Western Jamuna Canal

At the time of the annexation of the Punjab, the Inundation canals of the riverain tract were the most important. The oldest of the works was the Western Jamuna Canal dating to the Prithviraj Chauhan era or possibly even earlier. Firoz Shah Tughlaq got a pre-existing canal dug out and renovated in 1335 CE to carry water to the Emperor's hunting place at Hissar. In 1568, the canal was renovated by Akbar, but due to excessive silting which caused it to stop flowing in 1750 CE, it fell into disuse and was only reopened under the British Administration.

In 1817, the British Raj undertook a three-year renovation by the Bengal Engineer Group, in 1832-33. To regulate the flow of water Tajewala Barrage dam at Yamuna was built. In 1873, the remodelling of the canal, as a whole, was undertaken and the Western Jamuna Canal is at the present day a modern irrigation work. Somb river dam and Pathrala barrage at the downstream of the canal were built earlier in 1875-76 and Sirsa branch, the largest branch of the canal was constructed in 1889-95.

The Hasli Canal

Constructed in about the year 1633, the Hasli canal was the brainchild of Ali Mardan Shah, the Engineer of the Emperor Shah Jahan. It was a small canal from the river Ravi to bring water to Lahore, and a branch was led towards Amritsar to supply water to the sacred tanks of the Sikhs.

The Upper Bari Doab Canal was one of the first schemes to engage the attention of the administration after the annexation of the Punjab in 1849 and the construction of the canal was considered to be a political necessity.

Lieutenant Dyas of the engineers was instructed to frame plans on the pattern of the Ganges canal, then under construction, and the canal consisting of the main line and the Lahore branch was opened in 1859. The original alignment being used for distributaries and therefore a different alignment had to be adopted for the Hasli canal. The canal was renovated in 1873.

Direct political purpose was also the cause of the inception of the Lower Swat and Upper Swat canals in the North-West Frontier Province.

The British maintained a progressive policy of construction in the Punjab since the 1870s. A table is given below the dates on which the canals of the Province were opened and other data relative to each of them. It is interesting to note that the capital expenditure on all canals excluding the Triple Project amounted in the year 1921-22 to £80,00,000; that the canals of the Triple Project have cost another £80,00,000 and that the total capital expended up to the year 1922 is nearly £1,60,00,000.

Triple Canal Project

The Punjab Public Works Department (PWD) took up the construction work of the 'Triple Canal Project' to link canals. The canals involved were *the Upper Jhelum, Upper Chenab, and Lower Bari Doab* and the scheme was operational in 1917 under the Chief Engineer, John Benton. The scheme involved the construction of three great canals to carry 27,000 cusecs of water per second for the irrigation of 17,50,000 acres. The canals totalled 693 kms in length, 4,800 kms of distributaries and 32,000 kms of water courses. The proposal embodied a bold concept to transport water beyond its natural geographical boundaries by carrying water from the Jhelum river, which was going unused, to the Chenab, and from the Chenab, in its turn across the Ravi river to the lands under-watered.

Table 6.6 Canals in Punjab as in 1920

Name of Canal	*Year of Opening*	*Present Maximum Capacity (cusecs)*	*Area Comma-nded (acres)*	*Area Irrigated in 1921-22 (acres)*	*Length in Kms of Distri-butory Channels*	*Nett Revenue on Capital Outlay (%)*
Western Jumna	1873	6,430	23,24,407	8,55,368	3,022	11.27
Upper Bari Doab	1859 & 1873	6,700	15,04,059	13,43,471	2,510	17.31
Sirhind	1882 & 84	8,541	36,67,221	12,33,619	5,478	12.63
Sidhnai	1886	1,820	2,78,088	2,09,409	402	17.65
Lower Chenab	1887-93	10,853	25,85,458	25,60,932	3,589	44.35
Lower Jhelum	1901	4,200	12,51,900	8,72,215	1,674	19.16
Upper Chenab	1912	4,871** 11,929	15,10,672	6,55,421	2,003	8.64
Lower Bari Doab	1913	7,030	14,27,246	9,93,478	1,923	15.68
Upper Jhelum	1915	2,000** 8,380	5,73,329	3,58,567	1,065	0.25

(From W.P. Thompson's *Punjab Irrigation* & H. Calvert's *The Wealth and Welfare of the Punjab*)
** Utilisable for Irrigation

Rail, Roads and Canals

Until the railway lines were laid and the metalled roads constructed, there was no possibility of sending the agricultural surplus away from the immediate neighbourhood of the towns. In 1856 the first railway line was put under construction in Punjab which opened for traffic in 1861. Wood had to be used as fuel. The line from Lahore to Multan was opened in 1865, which at that time was connected with Karachi by the boats of the old Indus Flotilla. Coal as a fuel was introduced in 1872 when one goods train left Lahore daily for Ghaziabad. In 1883 through communication with Calcutta and Bombay was established. This was a stupendous effort by the British and speaks volumes about their endeavour in modernising Punjab's transportation systems. Simultaneously, they built canals in the nineteenth century which further added to Punjab's prosperity.

Had there been no railways to carry surplus produce to distant markets, it would have been meaningless to increase production; it is obvious that if the surplus foodgrains could not find a market, there would be no profit from the growing of it and it would not have been grown. So, there was a chain between production, surplus, transportation, marketing, profits and attempts for more production. Again, the isolated construction of canals would not yield profits unless simultaneously some advanced transportation system like railways came into being. Also, the reverse was true, i.e. building railways without augmenting agricultural aids and canalisation would mean all dressed up and nowhere to go, so far as Railway Rakes were concerned!

The two works were inter-dependent, and their construction caused the rapid development of the Punjab province which is such a unique feature of the history from 1870 to 1920.

The Bari Doab Canal was opened in 1859; water was admitted but regular irrigation did not appear to have commenced before 1860. The Sirhind Canal was opened in 1870. So, merely 10 years after the annexation, the British had launched massive riverine modernisation in Punjab.

Thereafter progress was as per figures shown:

Table 6.7 From H. Calvert's *The Wealth and Welfare of the Punjab*

Year	*Railway Mileage*	*Canal Mileage*	*Metalled Roads Mileage*	*Cultivated Area (million acres)*	*Land Revenue (Rupees—Million)*
1872-3	410	2,744	1,036	18.8	20.1
1882-3	600	4,583	1,467	23.4	20.6
1892-3	1,725	12,368	2,143	26.7	22.3
1902-3	--	10,893	--	26.8	23.0
1912-13	4,000	16,935	2,614	29	36.0
1919-20	4,441	19,664	2,938	30	40.0

The progress of the railways was under one system called the North-Western Railway, the largest under single management in the world in those days. Till 1918-19, the outlay was Rs. 1,001.6 million and further economic progress of the province depended on the extension of such transportation facilities.

The major irrigation works involved a capital expenditure up to 1920-21 of Rs. 24 crores and the length of channels in operation in March 1921 was 19,632 miles in all. The net revenue was Rs. 32.68 million which was 14.51 per cent on the capital outlay. In 1920-21, the canals and distributaries covered 10.25 million acres out of a total cropped area of 17.18 million acres. The province was saved from famine by the extensive canal system.

In the case of metalled roads, the stimulus of direct profit was absent but their utilitarian value in protecting the population from the periods of scarcity cannot be undermined. However, in the 1920s, the benefits which could be derived from roads was overshadowed by the demand for railways. One need not re-emphasise the fact that the great savings to the agriculture is obtained via good communications; but till the railway line laying plan was finalised, it was not possible to design roads which would remain functional after new railways had been opened. The result was that the Punjab was inadequately provided with metalled roads—about one mile to ten villages.

Good roads would have facilitated transport of manure to the farmer's fields and of the produce from them. But it was not until the early nineteenth century that railways and metalled roads were laid in Great Britain and this technology could in no way reach Punjab or India before the death of Maharaja Ranjit Singh.

Wheat Production

Punjab started to produce more and more wheat, thanks to the canalisation and its transportation. In 1900-01, its wheat production was 2.623 million tonnes which increased to 3.884 million tonnes in 1919-20. However, it fell in the next year due to famine. The average exports from the production between 1900 and 1920 was 28 per cent.

State of Industries in Punjab

In the 1920s, the following steps were being analysed for the development of industries in the Punjab province:

Improvement in Existing Industries

The existing industries obviously offered great scope for improvement and these include *weaving, dyeing, tanning, iron work and wood work*, and in these much could be done:

(a) by improvement of technical skill of the workers in their craft;
(b) by introducing more capital, in the way of improved machinery, implements etc.;
(c) by providing the element of intelligent enterprise to enable the workers to use the capital employed to the best profit.

Development of Agricultural Industries

Making oil pressing, flour milling, cotton ginning, rice hulling, sugarcane crushing, wool washing, etc., more efficient and taking the labour required from agriculturists themselves as done in sugarcane crushing. The best part was the introduction of more efficient machinery and power, and the elimination of waste, and the value addition for the articles of export.

New Industries Based on Agriculture

The possibility that the climate and soil of the province may be found suitable for other crops, not at this time grown, of great industrial value was thought to be quite prudent and appeared to be futuristic like: some source of sugar other than sugarcane, sericulture and silk; the manufacture of straw board from wheat stalks (*bhusa*); of paper from rice stalks and hulls; vegetable and vegetable desiccation; alcohol, as a source of power, from potatoes or cellulose; bees and honey ; fruit and fruit preserving, canning and drying; castor oil and castor cake manure ; poultry and poultry products; and dairying and dairy products. All these seemed possible to be within the capacity of the agricultural classes.

New Industries Not Based on Agriculture

This was the manufacture of improved agricultural implements. Examples of the class are petroleum and its derivatives; cement making; glass making; salt mining (not, of course, new); iron (Kangra); coal (Mianwali); gold washing (Indus) and industries based on the utilisation of forest products.

These industries would have needed labour who would have been specially trained. Considerable amounts of capital and highly skilled management would be necessary.

Obstacles

The extent to which industries could be effective depended on the development of communications and transport facilities within the province. In 1920, it might have actually cost less to transport goods from Lancashire to Amritsar than to distribute these from Amritsar to the local villages. The obstacles to an export trade was to prevent the Punjab manufacturer from expanding his business to achieve fullest benefits and due to its isolated geographical position, it was unlikely that the Punjab could develop industries on the scale attained by Japan.

The second limit to industrial development was the capital required and there was ample wealth in the province and further could be raised to the extent of 40 crores for industries.

The scarcity of men trained to perform the duties of supervision and management was a more serious obstacle to industrial development.

The next impediment to industrial work was the availability of labour. Already the greater part of the unskilled labour employed in the province on earth-work of canals and railways came from outside. There were very few surplus labourers; although a large number might not have been fully employed all the year round. Again, lack of business experience was another important limitation.

Of 79 companies in the province in 1919-20, 14 were under British management with a paid-up capital of Rs. 24.7 million; 65 were under Indian management with a paid-up capital of Rs. 7.8 million. Only 20 companies existed in manufacturing sector with a paid-up capital of Rs. 4 million.

The following table indicates the slow growth:

Table 6.8 Paid-Up Capital in Industries Over the Years

Year	*No. of Companies*	*Paid-Up Capital (million)*
1889-90	22	39,60,00
1894-95	20	47,80,00
1899-00	52	74,10,00
1904-05	59	1,01,80,00
1909-10	136	1,72,06,00
1914-15	99	1,49,70,00
1919-20	79	3,25,14,00

It is not denied that the state could, by heavy expenditure, bring about a rapid change, but the British never wanted to bring competition to its own manufacturers of England who wanted to use India for inputs and raw materials and sell their merchandise in India at a high price to mint profits.

Punjab had no extensive industries in the past such, for instance, as Bombay possessed for several centuries before 1920. There was no inherited aptitude for massive organisation, no highly developed spirit of enterprise, nothing which could be set before the young mind as an example of a real captain of industry. India, after all, had missed the Industrial Revolution.

Punjab Industries and Technical Education

In 1911 an Industrial Conference was held in Lahore and its proceedings lasted over four days and at that conference the question of Industrial Education came up and a special committee was appointed by the government in 1912 to enquire into and report on this subject.

The Mayo School of Arts and Crafts, Lahore was the only industrial school totally financed by the government and it disseminated knowledge on lithography, book binding, and cotton printing.

'The Victoria Diamond Jubilee Hindu Technical Institute' and the 'Rasul College of Engineering (in present-day Mandi Bahauddin District, Pakistan)' were the only two institutions which could be truly called the technical colleges, established in 1912.

Resolutions passed by the Punjab Industrial Conference on February 18, 1911 specified that the Department of Industry should be controlled by a Director of Industries who should be a full-time officer assisted by an Advisory Board.

The government planned to assist industries by exhibiting and demonstrating the use of improved appliances, machines and industrial processes and publishing documents on industrial processes.

The disabilities and the disadvantages vis-à-vis similar products imported into the Punjab were due to factors combined to create a sort of protection in favour of foreign manufactures. It was therefore recommended that:

(1) freights on raw materials and articles made out of the same should be at the same rates;

(2) freights on the same articles whether made in India or abroad should be the same.

The conference further recommended that the government should inform the committee what funds would be available for industrial education in the near future in order that such a scheme might be prepared and introduced at once. The Industry and Education would cover the following trades as mentioned below:

- Pottery
- Metal work, including cutlery
- Woodwork, including carpentry
- Cotton weaving
- Spinning and weaving of silk and wool
- Knitting and hosiery, particularly for women workers
- Lace and thread work, particularly for women workers
- Kandla and gold and silver lace-work
- Nickel plating
- Lacquer work
- Tanning and use of waste products of tanning
- Oil-Pressing
- Cotton seed processing
- Fibres
- Wood pulping

- Match making
- Glass making
- Hosiery
- Dyeing
- Sugar refining
- Weaving
- Pottery, and crockery
- Gold and silver tinsel
- Metal Foundries
- Chemical industries
- Soap and glycerine
- Industrial alcohol distilling

After the Non-Cooperation Movement

The Punjab Congress as well as Muslim League were essentially urban parties. Punjabi peasants had joined the Amritsar rally of the Congress in 1919 but these two parties had not found many takers in the rural Punjab which was dominated by the big zamindars loyal to the British and those big landlords would assist the Raj in sending troops from peasant families, at regular intervals, as seen during the First World War. The Non-Cooperation Movement somehow could not bring the rural and urban masses on the same platform.

While the Non-Cooperation Movement was useful for the Congress which got 6 million new members in towns and villages, in Punjab it was not the only force. The Unionist Party came up in 1923 and it had strong agricultural ideology well supported by the Raj who after the Land Alienation Act was worried about the welfare of the peasant class which routinely provided soldiers for the army. Two key men strengthened the Unionist Party. A Rajput Mian (later Sir) Fazl-i-Hussain (1877-1936) who was a city man who worried about the destiny of the Punjabi Muslims in Punjab and the other man was Chhotu Ram, a Jat lawyer from Rohtak (now in Haryana) who was a spokesman in the provincial council for Eastern Punjab's Hindu Jat peasantry.

The Unionist Party was created to safeguard Punjab landed peasantry's interests. As Fazl-i-Hussain tried to increase the Muslim percentage in Punjab's colleges and government departments, he became popular among urban Muslims also. He was a guide to the leading personalities of the Punjab, surpassing such luminaries as Firoz Khan Noon, Ahmad Yar Khan Daultana, Makhdoom Raza Shah Gilani, Sunder Singh Majithia, Jogendra Singh and Baba Kartar Singh.

In early 1923, Fazl got Muslim representation increased in municipalities including that of Lahore and his aim was to take Muslim percentage in colleges and municipalities near to the actual Muslim population percentage in the state. Raja Narindra Nath protested vehemently but his motion was defeated for cutting Fazl's salary and he got support only from Harkishen Lal and Majithia.

The Hindu opposition to this increase in Muslim share enhanced Fazl-i-Hussain's popularity among the Muslims and in the 1923 elections, the Unionist Party got the clear majority. Raj rewarded Chhotu Ram by removing Harkishen Lal from the council.

Poet Iqbal or for that matter Jinnah were not yet the torch bearers of the Muslims in the Punjab; Fazl-i-Hussain was the man who really mattered for them. In 1924, Fazl was undoubtedly India's most prominent Muslim leader.

The Hindus of the Punjab were in a dilemma. They did not like Gandhi's pro-Muslim beliefs nor could they digest Fazl-i-Hussain's manoeuvres. Incidentally in 1924, Gandhi visited Lahore and tried to strike a rapport with Fazl but he did not enjoy the support of the Hindus. Conseqeuently, Gandhi could not strengthen his bond with Fazl.

The Muslim percentage increase was being given great importance by the British and it upset Punjab Kesari Lala Lajpat Rai who wrote in 1924 that since the Muslims were unwilling to grant weightage to Hindus and Sikhs, Punjab could be partitioned into Muslim-majority and Hindu-majority parts. The Hindus of Punjab thought that since the Muslims were being patronised by the Raj, it would be a pragmatic idea to move towards the British rulers rather than towards Gandhi. So, many Hindus moved towards the political organisation named the Hindu Mahasabha.

The British were clever people indeed. In order to appease Hindus and get their support to rein in Congress in Punjab, they reduced the powers of Fazl-i-Hussain by sending him to the executive council of the governor as a member for land revenue.

The post vacated by Fazl was filled by Jogendra Singh, a staunch Raj loyalist.

Raja Narindra Nath was not yet out of steam. Opposing the Muslim increase of representation, he informed the governor in 1925 that the Hindus could wait for Swaraj but would not tolerate the Muslim supremacy in Punjab.

Punjab During 1925-32

Sir Malcolm Haily born on February 15, 1872 joined the Indian Civil Service in 1895. He was appointed as Colonisation Officer, Jhelum Canal Colony in 1902 and a Member of the Executive Council of the Governor-General in 1919 till 1924. He succeeded Sir E.D. Maclagan in 1924 to Governorship of the Punjab followed by Sir Geoffrey Fitzbervey De Montmorency 1928-1933.

Sir G.F. De Montmorency was born on August 23, 1876 entered Indian Civil Service in 1899. He was made the DC of the district Lyallpur in 1907 and a Settlement Officer of the Chenab Colony in 1909. He acted as the Member of the Punjab Executive Council; 26, 1923 to 1928; created KCSI in 1928. He was appointed Governor of Punjab from 1928 to 1933.

In the 1926 elections, non-Congress and other Hindus defeated Swarajist or Congress candidiates in the Hindu reserved seats. Manohar Lal, a non-Congress man became the education minister and Chhotu Ram had to make room for him! But to retain the Unionist support, Firoz Khan Noon, a Rajput Tiwana was made a third minister.

In 1924, the Unionists mounted pressure on the British to reduce the canal water rates. Fazl-i-Hussain was knighted in 1926. There were many holes/gaps in the Land Alienation Act of 1901 and Unionists led by Fazl-i-Hussain got them closed. The effect was such that in 1928-29 moneylenders accounted for more than one-third of the total income tax from industry and business in Punjab.

In 1928, Fazl, continuing his journeys with landowners of all religions and urban Muslims, pressed for a Land Revenue Act to reduce the land tax. Fazl was promoted to the *Viceroy's Executive Council* in Delhi in 1930 and he occupied that post till 1935.

Men like Zafar Ali and Kitchlew were still the members of INC and Muslim League and the Punjab Congress was polarised into two groups: one led by Lala Lajpat Rai, sympathetic to the Hindu Mahasabha and the other headed by Satyapal which leaned on Hindus, Muslims as well as the Sikhs.

Fazl or Jinnah

Fazl-i-Hussain was the most prominent leader of Punjab's Muslims and Jinnah was still around the corner. In 1927 and 1928, Jinnah tried to seal an accord on the logic that the Muslims would accept joint electorates provided Muslim majority was guaranteed in Bengal and Punjab, the separation of Sindh from Bombay Presidency to make it Muslim majority and one-third reservation for Muslims in any central legislature. This was to be accepted by the INC, Hindu Mahasabha and the Sikhs.

Punjabi politicians could not agree upon it. Sir Muhammad Shafi (1869-1932), belonging to the renowned Arain Mian family of Baghbanpura, Lahore headed the Punjab Muslim League and Iqbal was its general secretary. To Shafi, the issue of separate electorates in Punjab was non-negotiable and said that Jinnah did not speak for the province's Muslims. Iqbal was elected the same year, i.e. 1926 as a member of Punjab council and between 1927 and 1930, Punjab Muslim League opposed the all India Muslim league due to differences over Delhi proposals and boycott of the Simon Commission. Hindu Sabha Members were unwilling to give up weightage of Punjab's non-Muslims. Sikhs were opposed to what they perceived as Muslim rule.

A section of INC and Fazl were open to Jinnah's proposal but scepticism crept in and such idealism received a death blow at the INC's Calcutta session of 1928 and adherence to Motilal Nehru's plan was advocated, instead. INC yielded to the pressure by Punjab's Hindus and Sikh politicians. Lala Lajpat Rai was not opposed to Jinnah's plan but he did not live long and died in November 1928.

In 1929, Jawaharlal Nehru was fast emerging as a powerful leader in the Congress. At the end of 1929, a session was held in Lahore and the Congress announced '*complete independence*' as its goal. It was a grand manifestation of anti-colonial sentiments where delegates from all over India had come including many Muslims. Jawaharlal once again stood out as the leader championing it forcefully.

The INC was upbeat after the nation-wide support it got for its opposition to the Simon Commission.

The Communal Riots 1922-32

This period saw communal strife too often and there were at least eighty riots. Maybe, after the arrest of Mahatma Gandhi on March 10, 1922, the nationalist Muslim leaders became weak and the Muslim struggle for its identity began.

The Muslims were backed by the government.

Riots at Multan in 1922

There was a serious riot at Multan linked to the Muharram on 3rd and 4th September, 1922. A *Tazia* struck a private telephone wire and fell on the ground. It apparently belonged to a Hindu whose shop was near the spot. The Muslims attacked the shop and the town was practically under siege, incendiarism was done in many temples and *Dharamshalas* were burnt. The Sikh holy Granth Sahib was also burnt at some places and a number of women and children were kidnapped.

The total number of people hurt were 372—280 Hindus and 92 Muslims, and 7 people were killed, 5 of whom were Hindus. Damage to buildings alone was nearly Rs. 1,00,000 and the estimate of total damage was about Rs. 3,00,000. British Government officials stood as mute spectators.

The Punjab, Provincial Congress Committee ordered an Inquiry and it showed clearly that it was easy to nip the evil in the bud if firm action had been taken in time. The perpetrators of the mischief were the baser elements of the society.

The Hindu-Muslim leaders helped each other's community and at many places Hindus and Muslims even combined together for their protection. But the relations between two communities were quite strained despite the efforts of such Congress stalwarts like Pt. Madan Mohan Malaviya, Hakim Ajmal Khan and others who visited there on September 19, 1922.

Congress leaders such as Pandit Motilal Nehru, C.R. Das and Sarojini Naidu toured the communally disturbed Northern India and encouraged Hindu-Muslim unity but the communal feeling got intensified in 1923. Subsequent to the redistribution of seats in municipalities and the district boards, more bitterness crept in.

Hindu Mahasabha and Arya Samajis

The Hindu Mahasabha movement was started to strengthen beliefs in Hinduism and to organise the Hindu community by promoting Hindu Rashtra, Hindu culture, and Hindu polity and using constitutional means, try to re-establish the integrity of the State of Bharat by constitutional means.

The Arya Samaj took up the work of 'Shuddhi' while the Mahasabha principally devoted itself to 'Sangathan', promoting physical culture among the Hindus and creating a disciplined organisation among them. The philosophy of Swami Dayanand and the principles of the Arya Samaj are detailed in *Satyaratha Prakash* written by Swami Dayanand himself. He believed in one God and was against idol worship and crusaded against social evils like early marriage, enforced widowhood and subordination of women. He was against the caste system and untouchability.

The Arya Samaj became a great education movement for boys as well as girls years after Swami Dayanand was no more and established a chain of DAV educational institutions all over the country.

The Tabligh and Tanzem

The Muslims organised the 'Tabligh' and the 'Tanzim' movements as a counter-measure to the Hindu 'Shuddhi' movement and to enlarge the Muslim community brotherhood by converting people from other communities. Efforts were made by the Muslim community to resist attempts at the reclamation of any number to the fold of Hinduism. In Agra and Mathura, Hindu and Muslim missionaries worked within the same area raising the religious feelings and leading to the battle between rival proselytisers.

Communal Riots at Amritsar in 1923

The feeling between Hindus and Muslims in Punjab were seriously strained. In March 1923, Amritsar was hit by communal strife. When a Muslim young man attacked a Hindu girl while she was on her way home from school, a Hindu passing by remonstrated with the youth but the Muslims came to his assistance. The Hindus also gathered around and the trouble started. On April 11-12, 1923, the clashes took place in several places. No material damage was done, but 15 to 20 men were injured, though, not seriously. It was reported that the Muslims were at the receiving end.

The Akalis helped the Hindus warning the Muslims that if they approached the temple, they would be attacked. The police and military had to be called. Riots also took place at Amritsar for second time, at Multan and Sukha in Jhelum.

On May 3, 1923, an appeal was made by the Congress leaders and a statement was issued under the signature of Mr. C.R. Das, Maulana Abul Kalam Azad, Mrs. Sarojini Najdu, Hakim Ajmal Khan and Pandit Moti Lal Nehru.

It is true that before the advent of the British, there were differences between the Hindus and Muslims but there was never an orgy of riots, loot and arson leading to losses of life and property and this was probably accentuated by the introduction of communal electorates after the Montford Reforms of 1919.

Amritsar was again the scene of rioting on May 8, 1923 which continued for three days, when about 50 persons, mostly Hindus were injured. The trouble arose over the performance of Aarti in a Hindu temple which was near the mosque in Bagh Jhanda Singh which was opposed by the Muslims who prayed at that time. Muslims attacked a few Hindus whom they found in the adjoining street and Muslim men and women threw brickbats, on the victims from the upper storeys of their houses. The police arrived at the scene and more mischief was controlled.

Rawalpindi Riots 1926

A serious riot occurred at Rawalpindi on June 14-15, 1926 between Sikhs and the Muslims after two phases of the Calcutta riots in April. For quite some time violence and anti-Hindu and anti-Sikh propaganda had been going on in Rawalpindi and the neighbouring villages. There was enormous Muslim rage over the building of a Cinema Theatre towards the back of the Jama Masjid.

On June 13 as the Sikhs took out annual procession on the martyrdom anniversary of Guru Arjan Dev, the Muslims in front of the mosque had some arguments with the Sikhs resulting in breaking out of a riot and property worth Rs. 1 crore mostly belonging to the Hindus was burnt down. The casualties were about a hundred.

At Calcutta as well as Rawalpindi the riots were the outcome of the music-mosque controversy. On behalf of the Lahore Hindu Sabha, Narendra Nath and Dr. Gokal Chand Narang visited Rawalpindi on June 16. It was a one-sided order of the Government of Bengal which issued a communique on June 6, 1926 that no music was to be played before the mosque. The year 1926 had been one of the worst years so far as communal ill-feeling and religious orthodoxy were concerned.

Riots at Multan 1927

A serious riot occurred in Lahore between May 3-7, 1927. A small quarrel between a Muslim and two Sikhs escalated into a riot over the alleged insulting of a Sikh girl by a Muslim near Dabbi Bazaar. It resulted in 27 deaths and the wounding of 300 persons. Isolated and sporadic attacks on individuals took place.

As many as eight communal riots occurred of which the most serious occurred at Sholapur and Multan in July that was the time of Muharram. At Multan, there was a Hindu Muslim riot in which three Muslims were killed and several people were injured on both sides.

The Rangila Rasul

In 1926, a book entitled *Rangeela Rasul* (*The Pleasure-Loving Messenger of God*) was published by Mahashe Rajpal, containing a derogatory attack on Prophet Muhammad. It greatly exacerbated the relations between the Hindus and Muslims in the Punjab. Rajpal was sentenced on January 18, 1927 to eighteen months imprisonment and a fine of Rs. 1,000 for provoking enmity between Hindus and Muslims. In the Sessions Court the sentence was reduced to 6 months. The High Court Judge acquitted the petitioner.

Throughout the Muslim community in India it caused great unhappiness among those boiling with rage against the judgment. The Muslims of Lahore were not placated. Ilam Din, a young man of 18–19 got enraged and on April 6, 1929, stabbed Rajpal to death. In Rajpal's funeral procession a very large number of Hindus of Lahore took part.

However, the real author of the book was another Hindu, Pandit Chamupati and not Rajpal. He had written it in retaliation for one written by a Muslim in 1920 denigrating Lord Krishna and Swami Dayananda, the founder of the Arya Samaj. Rajpal had attracted the wrath of the enraged Muslims, as he refused to divulge the details of the actual author.

As the body of Ilam Din was lowered into the grave (*Supurd-e-Khak)* Allama Iqbal tearfully said: '*This uneducated young man has surpassed us, the educated ones*'. Possibly Iqbal meant that it was the responsibility of all the Muslims to kill Rajpal but it was Ilam-din who had surpassed them all. Such a reaction from one of the founders of Pakistan made people remember Ilam-din as a 'Ghazi' and 'Shaheed'.

Risala Vartman case

An article titled *Sair–i–Dauzakh* by Devi Sharan Sharma was published in the monthly *Risala-i-Vartman* in May 1927.

As soon as the article was published by *Risala-i-Vartman,* Hazrat Mirza Bashiruddin Mahmud Ahmad, asked Muslims to voice their hurt feelings so as to be heard by official authorities. An article was printed in poster form and exhibited all over India. It was also seen in Amritsar. It drew the attention of Muslims to apparently the objectionable portions of the article. The Mirza or leader of the Ahmadiyya Muslim sect at Qadian was the attributed source of the poster, which provoked noticeable unrest among many of the Muslims of the city. In June a Muslim DSP brought the article to the attention of the local government which resulted in proscription of the May issue of the journal *Vartman*. The editor, printer, and publisher of the *Vartman* journal named Gian Chand Pathak and the alleged author of *Sair-i-Dauzakh,* Devi Sharan Sharma were arrested and the Amritsar District Magistrate began to hear testimony within days of their arrest.

Having heard the case thoroughly, Justice Broadway found both the author and the publisher guilty. The author was sentenced to a year of rigorous imprisonment and the publisher was sentenced to six months rigorous imprisonment. The case was concluded on August 6, 1927.

Consequences of Malicious Publications

There was definite deterioration in communal relations. Economic boycott of the Hindus was now being advised as a repercussion due to the *Rangeela Rasul* case across the NWFP, especially in Peshawar. The Hindus were maltreated in the villages. In many areas, Afridis and Shinwaris expelled Hindus living in their neighbourhoods in the tribal area, with Multan riots still fresh in their memories. Later under the pressure from the Political Agent, an Afridi Jirga ended the Hindu boycott and 400-450 people came back to Peshawar.

Amendment to the Criminal Law was being done as an after-effect of the Rangeela Rasul and Risala Vartman cases. A bill was introduced on August *'with the object of making it a specific offence intentionally to insult the religion, or outrage, the religious feelings of any class of His Majesty's subject'*.

The saner elements in both the communities realised the utter futility of the riots which occurred too often and caused injury and losses to the Hindus and the Muslims. Therefore, in the latter part of the year 1927, attempts were made by the leaders of both the communities to come to a mutual understanding on the issues of discord through the unity conferences. But the problem was complex and no solution was forthcoming.

Riots at Ambala, Gurgaon, Kharakpur and Daska Follow

The year 1928 augured well but unfortunately, this happy state of affairs ended soon and two cases of serious rioting happened. The first riot took place in a small village of the Ambala district in which 10 people were killed, and 9 injured; while the other riot took place in the Gurgaon district's Softa village in the present-day Haryana. The village was inhabited by Muslims but surrounded by Hindu cultivators, who raised serious objection to the sacrificing of a cow.

A free fight ensued between the two communities. Police immediately arrived on the scene and brought the situation under control after opening fire. Some Hindus set fire to the Muslim villages. Fourteen persons were killed while 53 were injured.

Two riots took place at Kharakpur (now in Haryana), the first on the occasion of the Muharrarn celebration at the end of June and the second on September 1, 1928, when killing of a cow was done. In the first riot 15 people were killed and 21 injured and in the second riot the casualties were: 9 killed and 35 injured.

Hindu-Sikh Acrimony at Daska

An unexpected acrimony developed between the Hindus and Sikhs over the possession of a religious institution at Daska, Sialkot. Attached to this institution there were 13 shops, 10 out of which were in the possession and occupied by the Hindus; remaining three were with the Sikhs of Daska. Some Sikhs had forcibly occupied the shops attached to the gurdwara during the Akali movement of 1928. On May 22, 1929 the disgruntled Hindu tenants filed a civil suit and obtained a permanent injunction restraining the Akalis.

Some Akalis put their own locks on June 2, 1929 on the disputed shops already locked by the Hindu shopkeepers. These Akalis were sentenced to various terms of imprisonment after arrest. The Hindus got the decree passed in their favour and removal of the locks put on these shops by the Akalis was ordered. This led to a serious riot on July 2, 1929 when the Akalis attacked the shopkeepers. However, the police arrived on the scene and arrested four Hindus and six Akalis. After obtaining a fresh warrant on September 9, 1929, Hindu tenants were given possession of the shops.

On April 3, 1930, Baba Kharak Singh set up a morcha and started sending 'Jathas' to demolish the shops in dispute. On May 14, 1930, Sikhs filed a civil suit in the court of the Senior Sub-Judge at Sialkot. On July 24, 1931, Sayyed Rafiq Ahmad, Sub-Judge dismissed the suit filed by the Sikhs who later held diwans from August 15-17, 1931.

A Jatha under Master Tara Singh on September 13, 1931 with Akalis set out from the Sri Akal Takht Sahib, Amritsar on foot and arrived outside Daska on September 29, 1931. The Siaikot Magistrate met the Jatha and declared. them an unlawful assembly and ordered them to disperse quickly. Upon refusing, they were all arrested and sentenced to imprisonment on October 1, 1931.

7

The Punjab from 1930 to the Lahore Resolution

Riots at Sikandrabad in 1930

A very serious riot occurred on July 3, 1930 at Sikandrabad in Multan District causing a huge loss of property and life. Sikandrabad had always remained free from communal troubles. But in the district some people were fomenting trouble between the Hindus and Muslims but the chief Commissioner and the Government ignored it. A Muslim who had been a loan defaulter of two years for land revenue took a loan of Rs. 10,000 from the Hindu moneylender which led to argument between the two and the small altercation led to a bigger clash between the Hindus and Muslims.

About 1,000 rioters collected to loot and do arson, damaging about 106 houses and shops in the process. The *'Bahis'* (the account books) and other valuable securities of the Hindus was burnt. Property robbed and burnt was worth Rs. 1,30,000.

When the police arrived, already four hours had passed and it made no attempt to recover the looted property. Loot and arson began at Mauza Chak, some 5 kms from Sikandrabad.

Shaheedgunj Mosque/Gurdwara Controversy

Outside the walled city of Lahore, in an area called Naulakha this gurdwara is located. The Sikhs believed that at this location, the Governor of Lahore Mir Mannu, ordered the massacre of thousands of innocent men, women and children from the community.

During the rule of Maharaja Ranjit Singh in Punjab, the entire complex was granted to the Sikhs and a gurdwara constructed here in memory of the killed. It is said that Mir Mannu himself allowed them to set up a gurdwara after they agreed to help him in capturing Multan, at the behest of Diwan Kaura Mal who was a Sehajdhari Sikh himself.

The local Muslims, however, maintain the Sikhs forcibly took over the mosque once the Sikhs were in power. The Sikhs announced on June 29, 1935 that they would demolish the Shaheedgunj Mosque. To protect it, many thousand Muslims assembled in front of the mosque and an organisation for the protection of the Shaheedgunj Mosque named Anjuman-i Tahaffuz-i Masjid Shaheedgunj was formed. The Governor of the Punjab Sir Herbert Emerson tried to mediate but on July 7, 1935 the Sikhs demolished the mosque leading to riots and disorder in Lahore. The Muslims of Lahore who were expecting a peaceful solution were shocked and the British authorities imposed a curfew in the city and the situation was controlled.

Haji Hafiz Pir Syed Jamaat Ali Shah led a movement Shaheedgunj Mosque movement. On July 19–20 the Muslims held public meetings at the Badshahi Mosque, and marched towards the Shaheedgunj Gurdwara/Mosque. Police opened fire on the crowd on July 20, dispersing the Muslims on July 21. More than a dozen Muslims died from police gunfire.

On May 2, 1940 the Bombay High Court gave a ruling on 'Masjid Shaheedgunj Mosque vs SGPC' and recognized the building as a mosque. But it maintained that property has been occupied by the Sikhs for worship for more than 170 years.

Riots at Dera Ismail Khan

A very serious Hindu-Muslim riot occurred at Dera Ismail Khan on August 12, 1931. A small ordinary dispute between a Hindu shopkeeper and a Muslim customer brought on an attack by a mob. The shopkeeper had abused the Muslim and the Prophet of Islam (PBUH). Four Hindus were murdered and many injured. Between 300 and 400 shops and serais were looted and all goods and account books were burnt with the loss exceeding 2.5 million. The DC and the SP failed to control the mob. The DC found to his chagrin that the constables allowed the loot to go on, saying that they were overwhelmed by the number of the looters.

Causes of the Communal Riots

There were four principal causes for the riots which took place in Punjab and elsewhere in India, much before 1947.

The memories of Malabar and the Multan riots;

The *Shuddhi* and the Hindu organisational movements on one hand and the Muslim *Tabligh and Tanzim* movements created enough friction between the two communities which were keen on proselytising. This spread the hostility throughout the province.

The local newspapers reported news after exaggerating happenings on the ground level using strong language to arouse communal passions.

Another factor of inter-communal strife was the communal representation in the Councils, Municipalities, District Boards and even University.

Naujawan Bharat Sabha (1927-31)

By bringing together worker and peasant youths, Naujawan Bharat Sabha, a left-wing Indian association supported a revolution against the British Raj. A more public face of the Hindustan Republican Association, it was founded by Bhagat Singh in March 1926.

It organised lectures, public meetings and protests and had members from the Hindu, Muslim and Sikh communities and due to its radical ideas about religion and agrarian reforms, it could not gather widespread support. After the killing of J.P. Saunders in late 1928, people would shun its public meetings. Saunders was killed following a protest by Naujawan Bharat Sabha against the Simon Commission in Lahore. The popular and Congress supported opinion was that non-cooperation was preferable to violence as a means of achieving change.

The association was banned in 1929 during a period when the government had imposed Section 144 to control gatherings as huge masses campaigned under to release imprisoned Bhagat Singh and his fellow hunger-strikers. NBS led that campaign.

Sohan Singh Josh (1898-1982), an NBS activist, was imprisoned for his role in the Meerut Conspiracy Case; he was released in November 1933. He and some other men were leaders of the NBS as well as the Kirti Kisan Party, which were separate entities.

Later, NBS became one of the three significant left-wing groups in the Punjab, apart from the banned Communist Party of India and the Kirti Kisan Party. Under the Criminal Law Amendment Act (1908), all associations considered to be left-wing were declared illegal in September 1934.

The Hindustan Socialist Republican Army

A revolutionary organisation HSRA (Hindustan Socialist Republican Association) with another name as the Hindustan Socialist Republican Army, was started in 1928 at New Delhi by Bhagat Singh, Chandra Sekhar Azad, Sukhdev Thapar and others. Earlier, it was known as the Hindustan Republican Association (HRA).

During the late 1920s, great freedom fighting activities were carried out by Chandra Shekhar Azad, Bhagwati Charan, Bhagat Singh and scores of other revolutionaries.

The revolutionaries in Bengal, UP and Punjab were contacted by Bhagat Singh, Shive Varmanand and others and on September 8 and 9, called a meeting at Delhi of the workers of the secret societies all over the country. This meeting, was held at the ruins of Kotla Ferozeshah.

HSRA spoke of a revolution drawing its inspiration from the HRA manifesto, involving a struggle by the masses to establish the dictatorship of the proletariat and the removalt of 'parasites' from the seat of political power. Seeing itself at the forefront of this revolution, it acted as the armed section of the masses. Its ideals were visible in incidents of communist-inspired industrial action by workers and also in the rural kisan movement.

In 1928, the British government had set up the Simon Commission to report on the political situation in India. It did not include a single Indian in its membership and it resulted in the galvanisation of various activist factions in opposition to a common cause.

The newly-named HSRA resolved to bomb members of the Simon Commission, at the request of Bhagat Singh,

Arrival of Simon Commission and Death of Punjab Kesari

This was named after a British jurist and was given the task to tour India and propose constitutional reforms. Lord Irwin, the

Viceroy suggested the inclusion of one or two Indian members but Malcolm Hailey, the Punjab Governor dissuaded him from doing so.

On October 20, 1928 a large procession greeted the commission with black flags when it reached Lahore. The Police resorted to a baton charge. Lala Lajpat Rai was surrounded by some young revolutionaries and it angered one James A. Scott, the SP who gave orders for a ruthless caning on the protectors. Saunders attacked Rai with his baton aiming blows at his head and chest.

Seeing the seriousness of the situation, Lala Lajpat Rai asked the people to disperse. At a public meeting held in the evening to protest against the lathi charge, Lajpat Rai spoke against the British. Sadly, due to the injuries suffered by him he died away on November 17, 1928.

Meanwhile, while the whole of India boycotted the Simon Commission, the Punjab legislative council which was influenced by Fazl, Chhotu Ram and Sikander Hayat Khan assisted Simon. A committee headed by Sikander Hayat Khan recommended the retention of separate electorates in Punjab and for 83 Muslim and 82 non-Muslim seats in a house of 165.

In 1930, Fazl-i-Hussain became a member of the Viceroy's executive council and was quite close to the Raj.

Members of the Commission

The following were the team members of the Simon Commission:

Sir John Simon, Clement Attlee, Vernon Hartshorn, Edward Cadogan, Harry Levy-Lawson, George Lane-Fox and Donald Howard

Avenging Punjab Kesari's Death

The revolutionaries, in a meeting held at Lahore, decided to avenge the murder of Punjab Kesari by planning the killing both Scott and Saunders. Chandra Shekhar Azad, Bhagat Singh, Kailashpati, Mahavir Singh, Kundanlal, Shivram Rajguru, Yashpal and others participated in the meeting.

On December 17, 1928, Saunders was killed in front of the police station near the DAV College, Lahore. The action was carried out by Azad, Bhagat Singh, Rajguru and Jai Gopal.

Bombs Thrown into the Assembly

Sardar Bhagat Singh came in contact with Shri Jitendra Nath Dass at the Calcutta Session of the Congress and the latter agreed to train the members of the Central Committee in the making of bombs and explosives. Bhagat Singh, Kamalnath Tiwari, Vijay Kumar Sinha and Ajoy Ghosh went through the course and started a bomb factory at Agra.

In 1929, Bhagat Singh wanted to perform a dramatic act to gain massive publicity for HSRA's aims. And for this he planned to explode a bomb inside the Central Legislative Assembly.

Taking the bombs produced in a bomb factory at Lahore, Bhagat Singh and Batukeshwar Dutt threw them in the Central Assembly. These were exploded to warn the British rulers against their proposed Public Safety Act and the Trade Disputes Act. These bills had been rejected by the Central Assembly but were enacted by the Governor-General by the use of his special powers.

George Ernest Schuster, the finance member of the Viceroy's Executive Council and some other members were injured.

Trial and Hanging of Bhagat Singh, Sukhdev and Rajguru

In the first week of June, the trial began after a preliminary hearing in May. Dutt and Singh were sentenced to life imprisonment on June 12. Asaf Ali defended Dutt while Singh defended himself. Even though some witnesses testified that Bhagat Singh had fired some shots too, the police sergeant said that the gun was pointed downwards.

In Lahore and Saharanpur, the HSRA had set up bomb factories in 1929. The discovery of the Lahore bomb factory on April 15, 1929 led to the arrest of other members of HSRA, including Sukhdev, Kishori Lal, and Jai Gopal. Soon, raids were made on the Saharanpur factory leading to some conspirators becoming informers and the police were able to connect the three incidents of the Saunders murder, Assembly bombing, and bomb manufacture. For the murder of Saunders—Bhagat Singh, Sukhdev, Rajguru, and 21 others were charged.

Based on substantial evidence against him, Singh was re-arrested for murdering Saunders. Hans Raj Vohra and Jai Gopal, his associates issued statements against him and that did him in. He was shifted to the Central Jail of Mianwali from the Delhi jail.

Special Tribunal

Viceroy, Lord Irwin, declared an emergency on May 1, 1930 and to set up a special tribunal composed of three high court judges for the case, he introduced an ordinance.

It was decided by the tribunal on 10 July 1930, to press charges against 15 of the 18 accused only. It allowed their petitions to be taken up for hearing the next day. The trial ended on September 30, 1930. Dutt was among those three accused, whose charges were withdrawn. He had already been given a life sentence in the Assembly bomb case.

The 300-page judgement was delivered by the tribunal on October 7, 1930. It concluded the participation of Singh, Sukhdev, and Rajguru in Saunder's murder. Bhagat Singh, Sukhdev and Rajguru were sentenced to death in this Lahore conspiracy case. Their hanging was scheduled on March 24, 1931. However, the hangings were moved forward by 11 hours and they were hanged on March 23, 1931.

Aftermath of the Simon Commission

Proposing the abolition of dyarchy the Commission published its report in May 1930. It. It also proposed the establishment of representative government in the provinces. Another of its recommendation was that separate communal electorates be retained after tensions between Hindus and Muslims had died down. Birkenhead in 1928 dared Indians to come up with their own proposal for constitutional change for India; in response, the Congress convened a committee under the leadership of Motilal Nehru. On the ground that being dependent on each other for election would bind the communities closer together, the Nehru Report favoured constituencies based on geography. Earlier, Motilal Nehru presented his Nehru Report which advocated that India be given dominion status of complete internal self-government.

Jawaharlal, son of Motilal Nehru joined as secretary of the committee formed under his father to propose a constitution for India. The Motilal Nehru Report of July 1928 recommended among other things:

1. There will be no state religion

2. Men and women will have equal right to vote
3. India will be a federation with an effective centre
4. It contained a Bill of Rights.
5. All power of government was to be exercised through organisations established by, or under, and in accord with, this Constitution.
6. It included a proposal for the creation of a Supreme Court and a suggestion that the provinces should be linguistically determined.
7. However, it did allow for the reservation of minority seats in provinces having a minority of at least ten per cent, but it agreed to reserve seats for Muslims and other minorities in proportion of their percentage of population.

It was believed by it that separate electorates would be a major hurdle to the evolution of an Indian nation. The Nehru Report found support in the Punjab among anti-colonial Muslims. One of the signatories to it was Maulvi Abdul Kadir Kasuri (grandfather of former foreign minister Khurshid Mahmud Kasuri of Pakistan) from the Punjab. Many Khilafatists were also in its favour.

But, Sir Shafi and Sir Fazl-i-Hussain, the Unionist Party founder were opposed to it. Jinnah was invited but he instead sailed to England to join his ailing wife. Jinnah's political career would be in the doldrums till he made a glorious comeback in 1930s.

Had Jinnah taken part in the deliberations of the committee framing the Nehru Report, he might have influenced the discussions and won some of his demands. His friend Raja Sahib Mahmudabad, was in favour of accepting the Nehru Report.

The British government opted for another method of dealing with the constitutional issues of India once it had noted that the educated Indians opposed the Commission and also that communal tensions had increased instead of decreasing. The British government stated before the publication of the report, that henceforth Indian opinion would be taken into account, and that the dominion status for India would be the natural outcome of the constitutional process.

The Government of India Act 1935 was the outcome of the Simon Commission visit. It advocated a 'responsible' government at the provincial level, not at the national level. It meant a government responsible to the Indian community rather than London.

For the Indian independence as a dominion, Clement Attlee was the most sympathetic British leader and it prepared him later for his role in deciding on Indian independence as British Prime Minister in 1947.

More Revolutionaries of the 1930s

The feeling of patriotism and expelling the British was gaining ground. A function had been in progress in Khalsa College at Amritsar and the lights went out. A bomb meant for the Princinpal of the College exploded. He had helped the police by supplying information about the revolutionaries. But unfortunately for the conspirators, a student named Partap Singh died instead, from the explosion.

Sardar Ujjagar Singh was arrested in this connection and on July 29, 1930, he was an accused person, among many. For this, he was condemned to death by the Session Judge.

After the end of convocation of Punjab University, Lahore on December 23, 1930, a young man Hari Kishan from Mardan, NWFP fired at the Governor and Chancellor Geoffrey de Montmorency who was injured and a constable was seriously injured who later died. A Police Sub-Inspector and a few others chased and eventually overpowered him. He was committed to the sessions on January 5, 1931 and he blamed the Governor to be responsible for severe repression. Harikishan was sentenced to death and hanged on the June 9, 1931 at Mianwali Jail.

Basheshwar Nath belonged to a middle-class family of Kaneha in Rawalpindi District. A mere lad of twenty, he was wanted by the police for a long time and on November 4, 1930, Police reached Dharmpur, in Lahore Cantonment area to apprehend him. Basheshwar Nath and another patriot came out and began firing at the search party but a bullet from one of the constables wounded Bisheshwar Nath in the back. Despite being operated upon in Mayo Hospital, he died on November 5, 1930.

Sardar Sajjan Singh of Valtoha was quite disturbed at the incidents in the Punjab and he joined the training battalion of the Punjab Regiment in 1930, to murder a British officer. He waited for a suitable chance. He came to kill the Colonel of the Lahore

Cantonment. He was told that the residence of the Colonel was the bungalow of Capt. Curtis at Mughalpura. Sajjan went to his house and entered it in the afternoon of January 13, 1931 and inflicted several blows on Mrs Curtis and her two young daughters at home. Mrs. Curtis died in the hospital and the two children escaped death. He was sentenced to death on February 7, 1931 and was hanged in the Lahore Central Jail on April 8, 1931 shouting Sardar Bhagat Singh Zindabad as he mounted the scaffold. Jagdish and his comrade, in connection with the Lahore conspiracy case were wanted people and were seen on May 3, 1931, going towards the Shalimar Gardens, Lahore. A large number of policemen surrounded them. Suddenly, a policeman in the garb of a lady in 'burqa' with a view to keep a watch on them, aroused their suspicion and they were prepared for an open encounter. There was a sharp exchange of bullets, in which Jagdish was hit and he fell into the stream and died immediately. His friend was seriously injured and arrested.

A Babbar Akali convict, Sardar Rattan Singh, escaped from custody on April 23, 1932, with ten others by attacking their escort in the train near Bhatinda. He was found on July 15, 1932, in the village of Rurki, Hoshiarpur District where the police assisted by the villagers surrounded the house in the evening and a regular fight ensued. Rattan Singh engaged the police for three hours and he killed three police constables and one villager. In the end Sardar Rattan Singh died of a police bullet and thus he escaped arrest.

Declaration of Sovereignty and Self-Rule

The Indian National Congress raised the tricolour flag of India at midnight on December 31, 1929, on the banks of the Ravi at Lahore. The INC led by Gandhi and Jawaharlal Nehru, publicly declared Purna Swaraj or the declaration of sovereignty and self-rule on January 26, 1930. The declaration included the readiness to withhold taxes.

The CWC gave Gandhi the responsibility for organising the first act of civil disobedience. Gandhi wanted to commence civil disobedience with a satyagraha aimed at the British salt tax. The British had a monopoly on the collection and manufacture of salt as per the 1882 Salt Act. Moreover, the British limited its handling to government salt depots by levying a salt tax. Violation of the Salt Act was deemed a criminal offence. The salt was freely available to those living on the coast (by a simple process of evaporation of sea water) but the Indians were forced to buy it from the colonial government.

Civil Disobedience Movement, 1930-34

There was going to be a reaction to the repressive policy of the government. Some other factors were equally contributory. There was acute economic depression just like in other parts of the world and the condition of peasants and the workers was quite pathetic. Communist workers and peasant associations were coming up. The British were just exploiting Indians for selling their own products and kept the industry at a lower level of advancement so as not to allow these to compete with the European Industries. Communist leaders were arrested in 1929 and illegally kept in jail as under-trials for nearly four years. The British had formed the Simon Commission, denied the dominion status to India and arrested the social revolutionaries; all these did not go down well with the Indian masses.

On Fenruary 11, 1930, the Congress Working Committee authorised Mahatma Gandhi to start the Civil Disobedience Movement.

Dandi March

The movement started on March 12, 1930 with the famous march of Gandhi and his 80 elected followers to Dandi. Sarojini Naidu was one of them. The target was to break the Salt Laws. Salt tax had been doubled in 1923 and this troubled the poor man the most. Salt could not be made even from the sea water. Not surprisingly, Gandhi thought of getting this law repealed.

Gandhi and 80 satyagrahis started the march on foot on March 12, 1930 from Sabarmati Ashram for the coastal village of Dandi, Gujarat, over 390 kilometres away. The people joining the procession wore white khadi and this march was also called the *White Flowing River*.

The road that separated Sabarmati from Ahmedabad had a crowd of 1,00,000 people. As the march crossed village after village, the volunteers registered new satyagrahis, collected donations and persuaded village officials to resignations from British services. Crowds greeted the marchers at each village, beating drums and cymbals. Each night they slept in the open. The villagers were merely requested to give food and water.

Every day, more and more people joined the march and soon the procession became at least two miles long. Thirty thousand people greeted them at Surat and by the time they had arrived at the railhead at Dandi, no less than 50,000 people had gathered. All along his journey, Gandhi wrote articles and gave interviews. *Time* magazine made him 'Man of the Year'. Gandhi declared as he was nearing the end of the march, *'I want world sympathy in this battle of right against might.'*

Satyagrahis reached Dandi on April 5, 1930. Gandhi raised a lump of salty mud after a prayer on April 6 and announced, *'With this, I am shaking the foundations of the British Empire.'* It was then boiled in seawater, producing illegal salt. He then requested his followers to make salt along the seashore and asked them to instruct villagers in making salt whereever and whenever. Gandhi thus broke the Salt Law.

Qissa Khwani Bazaar Massacre (1930)

Khan Abdul Ghaffar Khan led the *Khudai Khidmatgar* who were a group of Muslims of the frontier region, committed to the removal of British rule through non-violent methods. Ghaffar Khan gave a speech in Utmanzai on April 23, 1930 and urged resistance to British rule and he was arrested soon.

A cross section of civil society was led by Maulana Abdur Rahim Popalzai in and around Peshawar to demonstrate against discriminatory laws like the Frontier Crimes Regulation against the people of the province.

A large crowd of the group gathered at the Qissa Khwani bazaar after other Khudai Khidmatgar leaders were arrested. Soon British Indian troops moved into the bazaar and stones were thrown at them. A British Army rider was killed and his body burnt. Consequently, two British armoured cars rammed into the square at high speed, killing several people.

The crowd showed their commitment to non-violence, ready to remove their dead and injured, provided the British troops left the square. The latter did not leave, so the protesters remained there. The British then ordered troops to open fire with machine guns on the unarmed crowd. Many died in the firing.

The official figures reported 20 dead while nationalist sources claimed that several hundred were killed, with many more wounded. Two platoons of the Royal Garhwal Rifles were to be taken to Peshawar to tackle the situation but they refused to board buses.

Boycott of foreign Goods

In Lahore in July, 1930, more than 35 volunteers of the Congress and Bal Bharat Sabha were arrested while picketing Liquor shops. The picketing of foreign cloth shops was done by the lady volunteers the next day. A striking procession of over 200 ladies, carrying National Flags and banners which asked the people to boycott foreign cloth was taken out on July 7 under Mrs. L.R. Zutshi and Mrs. Pooran Devi.

As a result, all the prominent shopkeepers signed the Congress foreign cloth boycott pledge forms. By July 23 the declaration of the SGPC to resort to picketing of foreign cloth and liquor greatly boosted the picketing at Lahore. This action of the SGPC resulted from the unsatisfactory response to their representation regarding the Police firing at the Sisganj Gurdwara Delhi.

Repression and New Ordinances

The government increased its repression all round and released ordinary prisoners to make room for political prisoners. About 1,500 prisoners were reported to have been released from the different jails in the Punjab during the fortnight ending July 31, 1930. But by the middle of August, in the Punjab alone, over 4,000 persons had been arrested for participating in the various activities of the Civil. Disobedience Movement.

The Viceroy promulgated on May 30, 1930 two Ordinances: *(i) the Unlawful Instigation Ordinance and (ii) the Prevention of Intimidation Ordinance* to counteract such activities of the Civil Disobedience movement as related to picketing, non-payment of taxes and tampering with the loyalty of government servants.

The Press Ordinance was already in place. The Viceroy's justification for the promulgation of the ordinances failed to convince the masses. Indian members at a conference of businessmen held at Delhi on June 12 disapproved repression for the present movement. Merchants opined that they could not ruin themselves and face the social Indian boycott simply to honour their commitment for selling goods brought from abroad. The government should open negotiations with Mahatma Gandhi who alone could deliver the goods; they felt.

In its meeting at Allahabad from June 4-7, 1930 the CWC passed a resolution condemning the repressive policy of the government.

Effect of the Ordinances

Picketing of foreign cloth and liquor shops was intensified in every part of the country including the Punjab where volunteers were sent out to picket liquor shops from morning till night. Social boycott of those who wore foreign cloth and were addicted to drink was encouraged. A campaign was started by the Satyagraha committee to popularise spinning. The Congress was busy organising a campaign for non-payment of land revenue.

INC's Waning Influence in Punjab

Punjab played a modest role during the phase of the Civil Disobedience Movement which had brought Congress to the forefront. There were some reasons behind Punjab's lukewarm response to this movement: Good rapport between the Unionists and the Raj; INC's failure to woo Muslim Punjabis; appreciation for the Empire by Sikh and other Punjabi farmers; a number of Lahore's prominent Hindus being pro-Raj.

In 1931, an agitation was launched by Kashmiri Muslims against the Maharaja Hari Singh but the Congress did not support them. As a result, those Punjabi Muslims who had joined Congress, left in hordes to join the newly launched Ahrar Party.

INC was in no position to compete with the Unionists in the Punjab. The left-wing Kisan Sabha was hugely popular among the Sikhs in the central districts. Unionists, in their turn were challenged by the Akalis, the Islamic Ahrars and to some extent by the Kisan Sabha. The Urban Punjabi Hindus, in any case, were drawn more towards the Mahasabha.

First Round Table Conference

It was held between November 1930 and January 1931. HMG had invited the INC, the Muslim league, the Unionists, the Sikhs, the Hindu Mahasabha, the princes, leaders of the so-called 'untouchables' and other political entities for a series of talks in London. While the INC alleged that the British were adopting a technique of Divide and Rule, its opponents claimed that the INC was not a true representative of the whole of India. The British were opposed to Congress, its principal adversary.

In the Royal Gallery House of Lords at London His Majesty George V officially inaugurated it on November 12, 1930 and it was chaired by the Prime Minister Ramsay MacDonald. Lord Hailey, an Indian civil servant with thirty years' experience was one of the main advisers.

The three British political parties were represented by 16 delegates and there were 58 political leaders from British India and 16 delegates from the princely states. Seventy-four delegates in all from India attended the Conference. However, for their participation in the Civil Disobedience Movement the Indian National Congress leaders were in jail and along with Indian business leaders, they were away from the conference. Lord Irwin proposed dominionship to India. Gandhi had refused to attend the London meetings after a discussion in Delhi in December 1929. The Viceroy arrested Gandhi and sent him to prison as per the provisions of the law. It was attended by M.A. Jinnah, Md. Zafarullah, a Muslim Jat of Sialkot and an Ahmadiyya, Maulana Muhammad Ali Jauhar, Mian Muhammad Shafi, Fazlul Huq of Dacca, all Muslim stalwarts. Also attending were Raja Narindranath, Tej Bahadur Sapru, B.R. Ambedkar, S. Ujjal Singh, Begum Shahnawaz, Shahnawaz Bhutto and others who represented minorities, pricely states etc.

Federal structure, Provincial constitution, Provinces of Sindh and NWFP, Minorities, Defence services, Franchise and Executive responsibility to the legislature were the issues discussed at the First Round Table Conference. Dr B.R. Ambedkar demanded separate electorates for the untouchables. The idea of an All-India Federation was floated by Tej Bahadur Sapru. This was supported by the Muslim League. On the condition that their internal sovereignty should be maintained, the princely states also supported this.

Demand for Azad Punjab

The militant mass struggle period saw a scramble for jobs and more share in the administration. At the Round Table Conference, the demand for territorial redistribution of the province arose. Dr. Iqbal's claim for a consolidated North-Western State consisting of the Punjab, North West Frontier, Baluchistan and Sind, greatly disturbed the Sikhs as it would lead to the division of the Sikh population.

In a memorandum the Sikh delegate, S. Ujjal Singh, stated that in case the Muslims got a reserved majority on the basis of separate electorates, they (the Sikhs) would, then, press for a *'territorial rearrangement'* of the province to consolidate the Sikh population. So they demanded that the Rawalpindi and Multan divisions (excluding Lyallpur and Montgomery Districts) which were overwhelmingly Muslim and were racially akin to the North-West Frontier Province should be excluded from the Punjab. This would leave a Punjab of about sixteen million in which no single community would have an absolute majority and each community would be obliged to conciliate the others. Unfortunately, such a proposal was not acceptable to the Muslims who wanted the whole of Punjab for their future country.

A counter-proposal by Sir Geoffrey Corbett aimed at the separation of Ambala Division from the Punjab which was totally unacceptable to the Sikhs and Hindus of the province as it would drastically reduce the population percentage of the non-Muslims in the Punjab.

S. Ujjal Singh compared the Sikhs of Punjab with Muslims in the Hindu majority provinces, where the Muslims enjoyed heavy weightage. He argued in Bihar and Orissa where the Muslim population was 11 per cent and 14 per cent only but enjoyed 25 per cent and 30 per cent representation in the provincial legislature and therefore the Sikhs should get logically a similar percentage in the Punjab provincial legislature.

Even the Anglo-Indians with a population of 0.2 per cent in the Punjab got as much as 4,000 per cent weightage in the Punjab Legislature and the Europeans got a weighted representation varying from 3,000 to 9,000 per cent, Ujjal Singh argued.

Effects of the First Round Table Conference

On January 19, 1931 the First Round Table Conference came to an end. Not much was implemented although many principles on reforms were agreed upon, and the Congress Party carried on its Civil Disobedience. The Conference can be regarded as a failure. The British government understood the importance and the need for the Congress Party to make any decision on India's political fate. However, the Mahatma's presence was necessary. The culmination of events was settled by the Gandhi–Irwin Pact (1931). As demanded by the Viceroy and his Council, Gandhi wanted a peaceful end to Civil Disobedience.

Gandhi-Irwin Pact (1931)

The Viceroy, Lord Irwin, was taking very harsh repressive steps against the Indian nationalism but the British-run Indian Civil Service and the commercial community wanted even harsher measures. Ramsay MacDonald, the British Prime Minister, and William Benn, His Majesty's Principal Secretary of State for India, were keen for peace without weakening the position of their Labour government in Whitehall. They knew that in the absence of Gandhi and the Congress, such meetings carried little meaning even though they wanted to see the success of Round Table Conference. Ramsay MacDonald expressed hope in the Round Table Conference's closing session to see Congress at the next session. Sensing the urgency, the Viceroy ordered prompt release of Gandhi and all members of the CWC without any preconditions. Responding to this gesture, Gandhi agreed to meet the Viceroy.

Tej Bahadur Sapru, C.Y. Chintamani and Srinivasa Sastri, the pro-British members of the Indian Liberal Party appealed to Gandhi to talk to the Viceroy, once the First Round Table Conference had failed. The talks between Gandhi and Irwin were arranged.

On March 5, 1931 the much touted 'Gandhi-Irwin Pact' was signed. In 1929 the Viceroy Lord Irwin had proposed 'dominion status' for British India but he had not clearly spelled out the dates. Also, he called for a Round Table Conference to discuss a future constitution.

The Congress agreed to the discontinuation of the Salt March and participation in the Second Round Table Conference. INC asked for the withdrawal of all ordinances issued to curb its activities, withdrawal of all prosecutions relating to non-violent offences, release of prisoners who marched to Dandi and the removal of the tax on salt.

There was outrage in Britain over the proposed pact with a party which wanted the end of the British Raj. Winston Churchill was disgusted at the mere thought of watching a half-naked Fakir pacing up and down the stairs of the Viceroy's palace.

As a response, HMG agreed to withdraw all ordinances and end prosecutions. It also decided to release all political prisoners barring those arrested for violent acts. Also, the properties of the satyagrahis which were confiscated were to be given back to them. HMG planned to permit free collection or manufacture of salt by persons near the sea-coast and also agreed to lift the ban over the Congress.

Second Round Table Conference (September to December, 1931)

The Second-Round Table Conference commenced on September 7, 1931. The Labour government had been replaced by the Conservatives just two weeks before the Conference convened. The Indian National Congress was solely represented by Gandhi whereas Sarojini Naidu represented Indian women. M.M. Malaviya, Allama Iqbal, Sir Mirza Ismail Diwan of Mysore, G.D. Birla, S.K. Dutta and Sir Syed Ali Imam also participated in the same.

Also present in great strength was the Muslim contingent which included Jinnah, Iqbal, Maulana Shaukat Ali, Muhammad Shafi, Md. Zafarullah Khan and Fazlul Huq. Loyalists, communalists, careerists, big landlords, representatives of the princes comprised an overwhelming number of Indian delegates. The government claimed that the Congress did not represent the interests of all Indians due to wide scale participation of heterogeneous groups. But, Gandhi claimed that Congress represented India. Gandhi emphasised the need of a partnership between Britain and India as between two equal nations.

Gandhi's demanded that a responsible government be placed quickly in full strength, both at the centre and in the provinces. He had the following views a) Congress solely represented political India, b) the untouchables were Hindus not a 'minority' and c) there should be no separate electorates or special safeguards for Muslims or other minorities. But the other Indian delegates rejected these claims of Gandhi. Minorities like Muslims, Dalits, Christians, Anglo-Indians, and Europeans were demanding separate electorate and the conference was deadlocked. There was a sort of stalemate and the Conference ended on December 11, 1931 and Gandhi returned to India with marginal achievements.

The conference resulted in the widening of the gap between the Congress and the minorities. All of the minorities (including Dalits) but barring Sikhs wanted to get their own separate electorates. The antagonistic British Government was for anything opposed to the Indian aspirations. Thus, Gandhi came back, disappointed, without any achievement.

Throughout India, civil unrest had spread again and upon return to India, Gandhi was arrested along with other Congress leaders. Sind, a separate province was created and the interests of minorities were safeguarded by MacDonald's Communal Award.

Governors of Punjab

H.W. Emerson was the Governor of Punjab from 1933 to 1938 and **H.D. Craik** from 1938 to 1941.

Communal Award (August 1932)

The British Prime Minister MacDonald announced the Communal Award on August 16, 1932. Thus it is also known as the MacDonald Award. The proposal of the Communal Award mainly dealt with the minority representation. The communal demands of the Muslims as embodied in Jinnah's 14 Points were fully conceded, giving separate electorates and reservation of seats in the provincial Legislatures

Major proposals were as follows:

1. The provincial legislatures' number of existing seats were to be doubled.
2. The minorities' separate electorates were to be retained.
3. Wherever they were in a minority, the Muslims were to be granted a weightage.

4. Except NWFP, 3 per cent seats for women were to be reserved in all provinces.
5. The minorities would also include the depressed classes, Dalits or the untouchables.
6. Labour, landlords, traders and industrialists were also to be given allocations.

So the communal award gave provisions for separate electorates for Muslims, Europeans, Sikhs, Indian Christians, Anglo-Indians, Depressed Classes, and even Marathas. (Some seats in Bombay were given to Marathas).

The depressed classes were given seats which had to be filled by election from the special constituencies in which only they could vote; however, they could vote in the general constituencies as well. Special electorates were also given to the labour, Commerce and Industry, Mining and Planting and Landholders. Sikhs were 13.2 per cent of the population in Punjab and they were given 32 (or 18 per cent) seats out of the total 175 seats. Their expectation was 30 per cent. They felt the weightage not commensurate with their importance in the state or in comparison to the Muslims. The Sikhs opposed this award and on July 24, 1932 they pledged in a convention to stop its enforcement.

Jinnah demanded the following 14 points:

.... future constitution should be federal with residuary powers vested in the Provinces;

.... for the provinces a uniform measure of autonomy to be ensured;

.... without reducing the majority of any Province to a minority, all legislatures to have adequate representation of minorities;

.... one-third or above representation in the Central Legislature shall be Muslim;

.... representation of communal groups shall continue by means of separate electorates;

.... Muslim Majority in the Punjab, Bengal and the North-Western Frontier Province shall not be affected by any territorial re-distribution;

....Guarantee of full religious liberty to all communities;

.... if three-fourth of the members of any community in the particular body oppose No bill or resolution shall be passed;

....Out of the Bombay presidency, Sind will be cut out;

.... in NWFP and Baluchistan as in other Provinces, reforms shall be introduced;

.... For giving an adequate share in all services and in self-governing bodies to Muslims, provision should be made in the constitution;

.... for the protection of Muslim culture, education, language, religion, etc. the constitution should embody adequate safeguards;

.... without a proportion of Muslim Ministers of at least one-third, no Cabinet, either Central or Provincial, should be formed;

.... except with the concurrence of the states, constituting the Indian Federation no change should be made in the constitution by the Central Legislature.

Meanwhile, the Sikhs and Hindus received reports in July 1932 that the Muslims in the Punjab were going to get statutory majority in the future and this naturally alarmed the former. A conference comprising Sikhs of various schools was organised and held at Lahore. On the other hand, meetings were held by Muslims at various places to counter any attempt to reduce their representation below their entitled level in the province.

This resulted in a great tension among the communities and warnings were issued to the editors of newspapers by the district magistrate to desist from writing inflammatory texts. Attempts by leading Hindus, Sikhs and Muslims to bring about reconciliation proved fruitless. Hindus joined Sikhs in opposing statutory majority for the Muslims.

Response to the Award

Only the Muslims welcomed the outcome of the award which was declared on August 17, 1932. The working committee of the All India Muslim Conference expressed disappointment at the award for being denied the right of a statutory majority in Punjab and Bengal. Congress members were in Jail and those who were outside, received the news with less enthusiasm, having apparently lost faith in the British.

The Hindu Mahasabha met in Delhi and adopted a resolution strongly criticising the award on the following grounds:

It established an unalterable Muslim majority in Punjab and Bengal by giving the reserved seats through separate electorate.

Representatives in Punjab and Bengal of Hindu minorities were less than what their population strength would entitle them to.

Muslims have been given undue weightages in other provinces also, besides the provinces of Bengal and the Punjab.

New communal constituencies have been created.

Contemplation that Sind be made a separate province.

The Sikhs vehemently condemned the communal decision. Issuing a statement from Simla, the Sikh leaders such as Sir Joginder Singh and Sir Sunder Singh Majithia declared that *'the faith of the Sikhs in the British Government sense of justice and fair play has been shaken by the decision of HMG's Government'*. Sardar Ujjal Singh and Sardar Sampuran Singh resigned from the membership of the consultative committee.

Considering the decision to be grossly unfair, Raja Narendra Nath representing the Hindu community in the Punjab requested the Viceroy, the Earl of Willingdon, not to nominate him to attend any conference or committee. Sir Sivaswami Iyer termed the decision as being a triumph for Muslim agitation.

The communal tensions were running high and the kirpans of the Sikhs and swords were taken away but they complained that the Muslims were resorting to violence and were not being apprehended by the police, the majority of which were Muslims, in any case.

The Hindus and Sikhs had a feeling that the officials were unfriendly and hostile to them.

Reaction of Gandhi

Gandhi always maintained that the separate electorate for the depressed class was an attempt to divide and distance the depressed classes from the main body of Hindus. He thought the British were out there to disintegrate the country along communal lines and he wrote a letter to the Prime Minister that if the award related to the depressed class was not changed, he would sit on a fast unto death. In the Yerawada Jail Gandhiji sat on the fast unto death on September 20, 1932 in which he was lodged at that time.

Poona Pact Signed (1932)

The Hindu leaders woke up and went to Dr. Ambedkar, to negotiate on this matter and the result of these negotiations was the Poona Pact of 1932 which was basically an agreement between Mahatma Gandhi and B.R. Ambedkar over the issue of reservation of electoral seats for the Dalits in the British Indian legislature.

B.R. Ambedkar felt that his group's special interests might be advanced by the government's system but as Gandhi's health deteriorated, he and the Hindu leaders then agreed to the pact. The separate electorates were done away with but increased representation to the Scheduled Castes for a ten-year period was agreed upon. The start of the movement against untouchability within the Indian nationalist movement was thus marked by this pact.

The final settlement took place on September 24, 1932 at Yerawada Central Jail in Pune, India. B.R Ambedkar signed on behalf of the depressed classes and Madan Mohan Malaviya on behalf of the caste Hindus. They finally agreed upon 148 electoral seats.

A *unity conference* was called at Allahabad on November 3, 1932 to minimise communal antagonisms. The Conference having the presence of Hindus, Sikhs, Muslims and Christians, progressed well when Sir Samuel Hoare made a sudden announcement declaring that His Majesty's Government had decided to reserve 33 1/3 per cent share in the Central Legislature for Muslims. This was slightly more than already agreed upon and it easily weaned away the Muslims from that conference.

Third Round Table Conference (November – December 1932)

The Third Round Table Conference (November 17, 1932—December 24, 1932) was a damp squib. It was not attended by the INC and Gandhi. Jinnah was a delegate to the first two conferences, but was not invited to the last; nor was Gandhi. Many other Indian leaders were also absent. Like the two first conferences, it had little to show. In March 1933, its recommendations were published in a White Paper and debated in the British Parliament afterwards. To analyse the recommendations and formulate a new Act for India a Joint Select Committee was formed. In February 1935 a draft

Bill was produced by the committee which was enforced as the Government of India Act of 1935.

Jinnah in the Wilderness

The great iconoclast Jinnah also passed through a lean patch. Jinnah had left Congress long back in 1920 after being heckled by the INC members at the Nagpur session. For many years since 1928, Jinnah was in the political wilderness. But he attended both the Round Table Conferences. Jinnah got elected as the Muslim member for Bombay in September 1923 in the newly formed Central Legislative Assembly. He rallied many Indian members around the Swaraj Party, which was formed by C.R. Das, Kelkar and Motilal Nehru in 1922. Demands were pressed for full responsible government. In 1925, Jinnah was offered a knighthood by Lord Reading but he declined.

A minority of Muslims welcomed the Simon Commission rebuffing Jinnah. However, most members of the League's executive council attended the League meeting in December 1927 and January 1928 remaining loyal to Jinnah who denounced the all-white membership of the Simon Commission.

In the three Round Table Conferences, Jinnah was a delegate to the first two conferences, but was not invited to the last. For most of the period from 1930 through 1934, Jinnah remained in Britain, practising as a barrister before the Privy Council, where he dealt with a number of India-related cases. There is considerable difference of opinion among the biographers of Jinnah as to why he remained so long in Britain—Wolpert emphasises that had Jinnah been made a Law Lord, he would have stayed in Britain all his life and that Jinnah was even eyeing a parliamentary seat. Others, disagree. Perhaps he was wedged in between the time of early struggle and the final storm of conquest.

In 1931, Fatima Jinnah lived and travelled with him, and became a close advisor.

The Thoughts About Punjab Partition

Allama Iqbal, Rahmat Ali and Bhai Parmanand

Sir Muhammad Iqbal was knighted in 1922. In 1930 he circulated a wish when he presided over the Lucknow session of the Muslim League: *'I would like to see the Punjab, North-West Frontier Province,*

Sind and Baluchistan amalgamated into a single state. Within or without the British Empire, self-government by the formation of a Muslim State in North-West India.... appears.... the final destiny of the Muslims....' Iqbal did not spell out in any case the Eastern boundary of the 'amalgamated' state he had in his mind.

In 1933, Rahmat Ali (1897-1951), a Punjabi Gujar born in Balachaur, Hoshiarpur in Eastern Punjab gave a clearer picture of a Muslim homeland. He was studying in England and circulated a pamphlet on January 28, 1933, titled 'Now or Never; Are We to Live or Perish Forever?'. 'Pakstan' as a word referred to **P**unjab, North-West Frontier Province (**A**fghan Province), **K**ashmir, **S**ind and Baluchi**stan**' which were the five Northern units of India. By the end of 1933, 'Pakistan' had become a popular word; an 'i' was added for easier pronunciation. Stressing the differences between the Muslims and the Hindu, he wrote:

> ....Our religion and culture.... history and tradition ... laws of inheritance, succession and marriage are fundamentally different.... social code and economic system the ideals which move our people....are essentially different from....Hindus to do the same. These differences .... extend to the minutest details of our lives....we do not inter-dine; we do not inter-marry....our national customs and calendars, even our diet and dress are different.

Bhai Parmanand said in December 1932 that he would not mind *'even statutory majority for Muslims'* in Punjab provided the Hindu majority areas were separated and linked to Delhi or the United Provinces.

Government of India Act, 1935

Although partial responsibility was introduced for the provinces under the Government of India Act, 1919, the Act of 1935 made a clear advance in this direction. The provincial executive was now responsible or removable by the legislative assembly of a province. Under the charge of popular ministers all provincial subjects were placed.

Provincial Curbs of the Act

Provincial autonomy was curbed and the provincial legislature could not do many things. Governors were given powers which clashed with the provincial autonomy. The subjects which were of common interest for the entire country, demanding a uniform treatment were a part of the *Federal List* which had 59 items. The subjects which were not of common interest for the entire country and did not, demand a uniform treatment were a part of the *Provincial List* which had 54 items.

A third list was also prepared which contained items which although primarily were of provincial interest, these could need a uniform policy all over the country.

Ministers were appointed by the Governor who could dismiss them. He was to call the leader of the majority party in the legislative assembly to become the chief minister and to name the remaining ministers. Also, the governor was given special powers to control the police department in the province. It was also a special responsibility of the Governor to safeguard the legitimate interests of the services. He had the power to summon and prorogue the legislative houses in his discretion. He could send a bill for reconsideration.

For taking care of the failure of the constitutional machinery to work as per the provisions of the Act, Section 93 of the Act gave the Governor the power to assume to himself all or any of the powers vested by any provincial body.

Reactions to the Act

From the Muslim point of view, Fazl saw it as a distinct improvement and he returned from the Viceroy's Council in Delhi to Lahore with something to offer for his co-religionists. He asked Punjab's Hindus and Sikhs to accept the minimal majority for Muslims with a broad vision as the latter could have asked 57 per cent or equivalent to their actual percentage in the state, as per the latest census figures. He said that the Punjab's Muslims were *a majority only in name, not in voting strength.... a civilised government should not let a minority be depressed, but what about the....majority to be depressed?* Sounding almost a sycophant, Fazl said about the act that *it was up to the Indian politicians to make the best use of the 1935 Act which the British Parliament has been graciously pleased to give to India.*

Unionists thought that they would use the Government of India Act 1935 to further increase their influence in Punjab.

INC rejected the Act as the powers of intervention given to

the Governors in the provinces was not to its liking. Congress planned to contest the forthcoming provincial elections of 1936-37, despite its disapproval of the large role given to the unelected princes in a federal assembly. The Muslim League reserved the right to try out the provincial scheme for what its worth was. The Muslim League, under Mr. Jinnah also decided to contest the elections.

The princes who had shown promptness in accepting federalism were a worried lot now with the prospect of their sovereignty under a cloud.

The Sikhs, still smarting from the unhappiness over the Communal Award of 1932, added their own quota of unhappiness.

According to this Act of 1935, the Punjab Legislative Assembly was allocated 175 seats with the allocation as listed in the table below:

Table 7.1 Allocation of Seats to the Punjab Legislative Assembly, As per the GOI Act 1935

Category	*No. of Seats*
General Seats	42
General Seats for Scheduled Castes	[8]
Sikhs	31
Muslims	84
Anglo-Indians	1
Europeans	1
Indian Christians	2
Commerce, Industry, Mining, Planting	1
Landholders	5
Universities	1
Labour	3
Seats for Women	
General	1
Sikhs	1
Muslims	2
Total	175

Emerges as a Top leader

"Jinnah comes back from England (1934); Emerges as a Top Leader"

The story behind Jinnah's return to Indian politics in 1934 makes interesting reading. The man responsible for persuading Jinnah to return to politics, was neither Liaqat Ali Khan nor Muhammad Iqbal but Abdur Rahim Dard—an Ahmadiyya missionary in London.

Muhammad Ali Jinnah was disillusioned with Indian politics after the Round Table Conference of 1932. Feeling 'utterly helpless' before the hardline Hindu 'attitude' and Muslims who were either 'flunkeys' of the British, he decided to quit Indian politics for good. Taking up residence at Hampstead Jinnah began his legal practice and his exit seemed to be irrevocable and final.

A.R. Dard met Jinnah in March 1933 and tried to inform him about the lack of good leaders among the Indian Muslims who desperately needed a sincere politician like him. He convinced Jinnah that his abandonment of politics at that juncture would make him a 'traitor' for the Muslim cause. Before the force of Dard's advocacy, Jinnah relented. Dard arranged for a lecture on the future of India at a Mosque in London in April 1933 to symbolise his return to politics. Speaking about 'the eloquent persuasion of the Imam', Jinnah criticised the recent white paper on Indian constitutional reforms and advocated self-government by Indians.

Jinnah biographers, Stanley Wolpert, Hector Bolitho and Jaswant Singh, have not mentioned Dard in their works. Dr. Muhammad Iqbal has not been mentioned debating Jinnah about his future plans. None of Iqbal's correspondence with Jinnah on the issue either exists. However, Liaqat Ali Khan seems to have facilitated the logistics of Jinnah's return. He and Begum Ra'ana met Jinnah in July 1933 and extended an invitation which was the groundwork for his eventual arrival. However, Liaqat Ali Khan's efforts were subsequent to Dard's meeting with Jinnah (in March 1933).

Perhaps hidden by Jinnah's intense loyalty to his homeland was laid bare through Dard's probing.

A.R. Dard had been deputed as the Ahmadiyya Missionary in London only weeks earlier and he received advice from the

Head of the Ahmadiyya Community, Mirza Mahmud Ahmad, to meet and convince Mr. Jinnah to return to India. Therefore, the Ahmadiyya community's spiritual leader used his influence to bring Jinnah back to India. The rest, as they say is history.

The death of Muhammad Shafi occurred in 1932 after a brief illness. With his passing away only Sir Fazl-i-Hussain from the Punjab was left who could assert the leadership against Jinnah but Sir Hussain neither had the large image of a Pan-India leader nor did he feel comfortable outside Punjab affairs. So, he concentrated on the Punjab where mainly because of his efforts the Punjabi Unionist Party was formed in 1923.

Now a resurgent Jinnah after coming back from England in 1934 wanted to forge an alliance with Fazl-i-Hussain and his unionists in Punjab. He wrote rather flatteringly to Fazl that no one could give a better lead to the Muslims in India than Fazl himself. But Fazl refused, to the great disappointment of Jinnah to preside over the 1936 session of the Muslim League in Bombay.

Not losing heart, Jinnah went to Punjab to generate independent support for the Muslim League but Fazl (a Bhatti Rajput) who was sick since 1934 and Sikandar Hayat Khan (a Khattar Jat), both from the so-called martial races and close to the British, were of the view that no one would be allowed to damage the provincial autonomy.

After returning to Lahore from Delhi in 1935, Fazl-i-Hussain sought to prepare the Unionist Party for the forthcoming provincial elections. He made concerted efforts in reorganising, financing and allotting tickets for his party. Jinnah was asked to maintain a distance from the Punjab.

Jinnah's visit to the Punjab was not quite encouraging and he left Punjab with a vow never to come back which he called *'such a hopeless place'*. Fazl-i-Hussain, then 59 years old, died in 1936 after having successfully thwarted Gandhi and Jinnah. Fazl was successful in creating a Muslim-Hindu-Sikh team in Punjab, even though in the higher segments of society.

When addressing students at Town Hall, Lahore Jinnah showed his nationalistic side on March 1, 1936:

> *....there has been no change in me, not the slightest, since the day when I joined the INC. It may be I have been doing wrong on some occasions.... never been done in a partisan spirit...only object has been the welfare of*

my country....India's interests is and will be sacred to me and nothing will make me budge an inch from that position.

After Fazl's death, Sikandar Hayat Khan was chosen by the Unionists to succeed Fazl as their leader. His father Muhamamd Hayat had served as Nicholson's aide in 1857 before becoming a big zamindar. The elevation of a Khattar Jat did not go down well with the Rajput Muslims, namely, the Tiwana-Ṇoon clans of the then Shahpur. Fazl was also a Rajput.

Provincial Elections (February 1937)

Under the new Government of India Act, 1935, the first elections were held in the winter of 1936-37. The Sikhs had the option of choosing either the Unionists or the INC as their election partner but they chose none of them. They had apprehensions about the Congress in Punjab which was dominated by the Arya-Samajis and the Unionists were looking after the interests of the Muslim Jats in particular. The Sikhs were further divided into Akali and anti-Akali group (known as the Khalsa National Party).

The following was the result of the election:

Table 7.2 Result of the Provincial Elections Held for the Punjab Legislative Assembly, 1936-37

Party	*Seats Won*
INC	18
Unionist Party	95
Akalis	10
Khalsa National Party	14
Ahrar Party	4
Hindu Election Board	11
Independents	22
Total	175

The provincial elections of 1937 saw the Muslim League do better in Hindu-majority provinces as compared to the Muslim-dominated provinces of Punjab, Bengal, Sindh and NWFP. The Congress formed its ministry in 7 provinces: UP, Bihar, Central

Provinces, Orissa, Bombay, Madras and NWFP. Immediately Jinnah launched a massive tirade against the Congress ministers as anti-Muslim and the Muslim League as the only protector of Muslims of India.

The INC party lost majority in the Punjab and it got just 10 per cent of the votes. Incidentally, the Muslim League won only one seat and Malik Barkat Ali (1886-1946) was that lucky man who won there and stayed in the assembly for 7 years as the sole representative of the Muslim League. On liberal communal lines, both the Muslim League and Hindu Mahasabha ran the election campaign of 1937; both performed poorly. On the whole, the Muslim League won 109 out of 482 seats earmarked for the Muslims in the whole of India and got 4.8 per cent of the total Muslim votes.

The Punjab Ministry comprised the following:

Table 7.3 Punjab Ministry

Sl	*Name*	*Ministry*
1.	Sir Sikandar Hayat Khan	Premier
2.	Sir Chhotu Ram	Development
3.	Sundar Singh Majithia	Revenue
4.	Shri Manohar Lal	Finance
5.	Major Khizr Hayat Khan Tiwana	Public Works
6.	Mian Abdul Hayee	Education

So, the ministry comprised 3 Muslims, 2 Hindus and 1 Sikh (3 Jats, 1 Khatri, 1 Rajput and 1 Awan). The course ahead for the Unionists was going to be turbulent. The Muslim League was to become very strong. People knew that the British would leave India, sooner or later but who would be the kings in Punjab–Muslims, Hindus or Sikhs or a combination of them?

Jinnah-Sikandar Pact (October 1937)

Fazl-i-Hussain died in 1936 and that created a sort of political vaccum for the Muslim Punjabis of Punjab.

After the February 1937 provincial elections, Allama Iqbal wrote to Jinnah in May and June 1937, urging him to make the Muslim League stronger in Punjab by holding the 1937 convention there and by linking the League to 'the law of Islam' to make the League appear appealing to the Muslim masses. Jinnah was not comfortable choosing Punjab as the venue, considering the recent experience which he had, since it would have meant challenging the Unionists in their own stronghold; he chose Lucknow instead. He, however, invited Sikandar Hayat Khan and the Bengal Premier Fazlul Huq, a leader of the Krishak Praja Party of Bengal.

In May 1937, Ahmed Yar Khan Daultana (father of Mumtaz Daultana), a Johiya Rajput, a big landlord and a prominent member of the Unionist Party felt that all Muslims of the Punjab were with Jinnah so far as all-India matters relating to the Muslims were concerned. Jinnah wanted to remove Sikandar Hayat from Punjab but he was advised to build cordial relations with him. Removing him was not easy. He was a legally elected leader of the Punjab and enjoyed the full support of the British. Daultana wanted to establish cordial relations between Jinnah and Sikandar. He went on to call himself an 'ardent Jinnahite'. He went so far as to submit to Jinnah a list of members who could be enlisted in the Muslim League council.

After the Jinnah-Fazl, Jinnah-Sikandar negotiations had failed; Ahmad Yar Khan Daultana once again approached Jinnah and assured him of his 'devoted loyalty.' He assured Jinnah that like him, Sikandar Hayat Khan was also a great admirer of his (Jinnah's) statesmanship and other unique qualities. He requested Jinnah to have no hostility and ill-will between the League and Unionists' top notch leaders.

For Jinnah, the Congress Party was the main foe and not the Unionist Party. Iqbal wanted to strengthen the League in Punjab as the Muslims were entirely dependent on Hindus; as he saw it. The Lucknow session of the Muslim League took place in October 1937 and Jinnah resisted the temptation of equating the 'League as the Law of Islam', for the first time in his life he appeared in Islamic attire, shunning his Western dress.

The League demanded that the Muslims should be recognised as a force by the British as well as the INC and this session had *Jinnah-Sikandar pact*, as a by-product. This pact recognised the Unionists as the autonomous party but they would be affiliated with the all India Muslim League, henceforth.

Sikandar Hayat Khan was, however, watchful of Jinnah's

activities and wanted to protect his political domain in the Punjab. He was aware of Jinnah's stature which was becoming bigger and bigger and even in Punjab, Jinnah was seen as a protector of Islam against the onslaught by the Congress.

The leaders of the Muslim League in the Punjab including Allama Iqbal were displeased about the freedom being enjoyed by the Unionists, following the Jinnah-Sikandar Pact. The alliance between the Unionists and the League was also not liked by Sir Chhotu Ram, the non-Muslim member. The British were wary that henceforth the Unionist premier would be extraneously influenced by the League members and dilute the strong bond between them and the Unionists. Sikandar Hayat Khan had to be very careful in maintaining a balancing act.

Although India was partitioned in 1947, activities relating to the consolidation of the Hindu and Muslim communities for their ambitions were taking place soon after the 1920s when the Non-Cooperation Movement was called. While the Poona Pact brought Gandhi and Dalits closer, the Jinnah-Sikandar Pact literally merged the Unionists with the Muslim League and Jinnah emerged as the Numero Uno and was universally accepted as a messiah of the Muslims.

Sikandar-Jinnah Reconciliation and the Watchful British

When Sikandar came back from Lucknow after the pact with Jinnah he informed the latter about the Unionists becoming the members of the Muslim League.

The Muslim masses across the country welcomed this new development of consolidation of the Muslim League and the Unionists at Lucknow. Jinnah was a satisfied man as the last session strengthened the League and the Muslim unity aspired by Jinnah was slowly becoming a reality.

The British were wary as they drew their soldiers from the countryside of Punjab and Jinnah was a leader whose loyalty towards the British was nowhere near that of a committed loyalist like Sikandar Hayat Khan. The soldiers were supplied by the zamindars and the DCs whom the Unionist Muslim leaders often consulted for even petty matters. Jinnah lamented this fact and called these Muslim leaders 'spineless'.

Therefore, the British did not like the idea that these martial classes should get entangled in the current political struggle or the communal politics of Jinnah's Muslim League. In early 1935, Jinnah was told to keep 'his finger out of the Punjab Pie' and Aga Khan, the pro-British leader gave financial support to the Unionist Party and not to Jinnah's Muslim League.

Sikandar followed more or less Fazl's and Chhotu Ram's policies.

Jinnah vs Nehru Diatribe (1936-38)

The rise in Jinnah's popularity was accentuated by none other than Jawaharlal Nehru who was fast rising out of Gandhi's shadow to be the foremost leader of the INC. Nehru was INC's president and in 1936 and 1937, he had sharp exchanges with Jinnah. Nehru publicly stated that in India only two forces mattered: British imperialism and the Indian nationalism, as practised by the Congress. Jinnah begged to differ and pointed out that there was a third force: Indian Muslims. Nehru accused Jinnah as the proponent of communalism and that the Muslim League represented a small fraction comprising the Muslims of higher echelons, who practised no social contacts with the general Muslim mass.

Jinnah even called Nehru a *'Peter Pan'* who never grew up and that 'he [Nehru] always poked his nose into others' business. Nehru felt that the Muslims in the INC could provide inspiration equal to *a thousand Jinnahs*. Nehru announced that for the ordinary Muslims the Congress would launch a 'mass contact' programme and it annoyed the Muslim League, a great deal.

A very harsh correspondence happened when Nehru wrote a letter on behalf of INC to Jinnah on April 6, 1938. He wrote:

> *....the Muslim League is an important communal organisation ....and we deal with it as such. But we have to deal with all organisations and individuals ....we do not determine the measure of importance or distinction....the more important the organisation, the more attention paid to it....**this importance does not come from outside recognition but from inherent strength**....the other organisations.... might be younger and smaller cannot be ignored.*

To this Jinnah replied:

> *....Your tone and language.... display the same arrogance and militant*

> *spirit.... Unless the Congress recognises the Muslim League ....on equality and ....negotiate for a Hindu-Muslim settlement. Will wait and check our* ***inherent strength*** *which will* ***determine the measure of importance or distinction*** *it possesses.*

The Virulent Communalism: Jinnah and Golwalkar

Communalism started assuming a virulent, extremist or fascist form in 1937. Jinnah had a view that India consisted of distinct religion-based communities having separate interests which generated conflicts. Jinnah demanded before 1940, within the single united free nation of the future, separate communal rights, safeguards, reservations and so on. Such liberal communalism was dependent mainly on the upper and middle classes.

Communalism after 1937, increasingly acquired a mass base centred around the urban lower middle classes. This also required an issue or a slogan and inevitably, an appeal was made to religious sentiments out of fear and hatred. Slowly, the liberal communalism gave way to the extremist communalism for several reasons. Congress had emerged as a major political force in the elections of 1937.

The zamindars and landlords—the Jagirdari elements—found that their zamindari could be at stake if the socialist ideas percolated to the grassroots level, as the Congress Party often claimed to resort to it in future. The defence of landlords' interests would as such no longer be possible and many of them switched over to communalism for the defence of their ownerships.

In Punjab, for example, the big landlords of West Punjab and the Muslim bureaucratic elite had supported the Unionist Party which was surely communal and casteist to some degree. But the zamindars felt that the Unionist Party, being a regional party, would not be able to hold against the Muslim League on its own which was becoming stronger, every day. So, in the period between 1937 to 1945, they shifted their allegiance to the Muslim League which promised to protect their interests. Hindu zamindars, landlords, merchants and moneylenders in Punjab started to move towards the Hindu communal parties like the Hindu Mahasabha.

Communalism also became, after 1937, the only political weapon for the Raj to use to deploy their policy of divide and rule.

The British threw their weight behind Muslim communalism, even though it was headed by M.A. Jinnah whom they disliked but pampered.

The outbreak of the Second World War, on September 1, 1939 further strengthened the reliance on the communal card and reliance was placed on the Muslim League whose politics opposed the nationalist politics and demands. The League had emerged as the sole spokesperson for Muslims under Jinnah and it agreed to collaborate with the colonial authorities.

To support the Raj the Hindu and Sikh communal organisations had also expressed their desire but the British gave preference to the Muslim point of view of communalism during the Second World War, and later. The election campaign of 1937 was peppered with liberal doses of communalism by both the Muslim League and the Hindu Mahasabha but they fared poorly in the elections.

The communalists now felt that they would lose ground soon if they did not take to militant, mass-based politics. Further, the need to shift to extreme Muslim communalism became a sort of urgency for the Muslim League because the Congress decided to initiate the Muslim Mass Contact Programme.

In 1932, the Communal Award and in 1935 the Government of India Act of 1935 accepted nearly all the communal demands. The INC did not oppose the concessions to the communalists.

Similarly, the Hindu communalists had failed to grow. Moreover, the Congress had permitted both Hindu and Muslim liberal communalists to work within the Congress organisation till 1937. The Congress under Nehru and under pressure from the left was frontally attacking the communalists who were expelled from the Congress in 1938. The Hindu communalists faced political extinction. They had to devise a new programme for their survival and growth.

The so-called 'Ambassador of Hindu-Muslim Unity' ended by demanding Pakistan. By the time the Simon Commission came to India, Jinnah's social base comprised communal minded persons. During the discussions on the Nehru Report in 1928-29, Jinnah gave in to the more reactionary communalists like the Aga Khan and M. Shafi, and ultimately became the leader of Muslim communalism as a whole. He became the author of the famous 14 demands.

In 1936, he had stressed his nationalism and desire for freedom and spoke for Hindu-Muslim cooperation. The poor election results in 1937 showed that none of Jinnah's assumptions were correct. Jinnah had to now stick to his liberal communal politics which seemed to have been fruitless or to abandon communal politics. Both would mean going into the political wilderness. To do mass politics based on the cries of Islam in danger and warning the people against the danger of a Hindu Raj was the third alternative. Jinnah decided in 1937-38 to opt for his last option and undertook the politics of extreme communalism putting all the force behind the new politics based on hate and fear. He would appeal to his co-religionists' fear and insecurity and communicate that the Congress wanted a Hindu Raj in cooperation with the British and domination over Muslims and the destruction of Islam in India. At Aligarh in March 1941 he said:

> If you want to save Islam from complete annihilation in this country, Pakistan is not only a practicable goal but the only goal.

In his presidential address in April 1941, Jinnah declared that in a united India *'the Muslims will be absolutely wiped out of existence.'* The Muslims in the 1938 session of the League were told by Fazl-ul-Huq, the Bengal Premier : *'....riots had laid the countryside waste (in Congress Provinces).... Muslim life, property have been lost....blood had freely flowed.'*

In April 1943, speaking as the president of the Muslim League, Jinnah charged Khan Abdul Ghaffar Khan for his *'....Hinduising influences and emasculation of the martial Pathans.'*

Hindu communalism did not lag behind. Its political path was different. Lajpat Rai and Madan Mohan Malaviya were the two main liberal communal leaders during the 1920s. Lajpat Rai died in 1928 and Malaviya retired from active politics. But Hindu communalism was not dead; it too advanced to the extremist phase. Communalism brought communal leaders to the fore. The Hindu Mahasabha made a sharp turn towards the fascist direction under V.D. Savarkar's leadership. The RSS (Rashtriya Swayamsevak Sangh) now began to carve a niche for itself beyond Maharashtra.

V.D. Savarkar launched a tirade against the Muslims and

warned Hindus of the dangers of being dominated by Muslims. He said in 1937 that Muslims *'want to reduce the Hindus to the position of helots in their own land.'* It was the RSS which now became the chief ideologue and propagator of extreme communalism. The head of the RSS, M.S. Golwalkar, laid down the RSS doctrines in a booklet *We, or Our Nationhood Defined*.

In 1939 Hedgewar announced that Golwalkar would be the next general secretary of the RSS. He gave Golwalkar a sheet of paper asking him to be the RSS leader, a day before he died on June 21, 1940. On July 3, five state-level *sanghchalaks* in Nagpur announced Hedgewar's decision.

He declared in 1939 *'If the minority demands were accepted.... Hindu national life runs the risk of being shattered.'* Attacking the nationalists, Golwalkar charged them for *'hugging to our bosom ... most inveterate enemies (Muslims) and .... endangering our very existence.'*

The following advice to the minorities was given by Golwalkar: *'The non-Hindu peoples in Hindustan must either adopt the Hindu culture and language, must ....respect and ....in reverence Hindu religion....wholly subordinated to the Hindu nation.'*

The RSS

It launched an even more vicious attack on the Congress leaders during 1946-47 accusing them of asking Hindus to *'submit meekly to the vandalism and atrocities of the Muslims'*. *'Those who declared no Swaraj without Hindu-Muslim unity have thus perpetrated the greatest treason on our society.'* The Hindu communalists also tried to raise the cries of 'Hinduism in danger...Hindu faith in danger....Hindu culture or *sanskriti* in danger.'

The campaign of fear and hatred culminated in the Calcutta killings of August 1946 in which over 5,000 lost their lives within five days; there were mass killings of Hindus at Noakhali in Bengal. Subsequently the Muslims were massacred in Bihar and then there were massive partition riots and the assassination of Gandhiji by a communal fanatic followed.

Some authors observe that had Jinnah been conciliated during 1937-39 by forming a coalition government with the Muslim League in UP in 1937, the communal problem would have disappeared or would have been solved. The refusal by Congress for sharing power with the Muslim League annoyed Jinnah and made him turn to separatism. But before he was denied power, Jinnah was already a full-fledged liberal communalist. Although Congress tried from 1937 to 1939 to conciliate him, Jinnah had adopted the philosophy of communalism. He agreed to start negotiations with the Congress leadership provided it renounced its secular character and declared itself a Hindu communal body and accept the Muslim League as the sole representative of the Muslims. The Congress rejected these terms.

Based on the theory that Hindus and Muslims were two separate nations, Jinnah and the Muslim League took the ultimate step in early 1940. Hindu communalism also marched in the same way asserting that Hindus were the primary citizens in India and the Muslims should either live in it as second-class citizens or be expelled from India.

Something similar was involved in the UP decision of 1937. Being opposed to the mass politics, Jinnah and the League even before negotiations for the formation of a Congress Ministry in UP had begun, the Muslim League had cried about 'Islam in Danger' in its campaign against Congress candidates in the by-elections to the UP assembly during May 1937. Jinnah personally issued appeals to voters in the name of Allah and the Quran.

The ideology of communalism needed to be opposed and the Congress and the national movement's failure in this regard proved to be their inherent weakness. The Communists who tried to wean away the communal elements from the Muslim League from 1942 to 1946 failed and instead lost some of their best cadres to Muslim communalism. It was a fallacy that the liberal communalists could be taken along and then persuaded to fight extreme communalism. After 1937 communalism was firmly opposed only by the nationalist Hindus and Muslims. Malaviya, Shyama Prasad Mukherji and N.C. Chatterjea, the so-called 'liberal' communalists failed to rein in Savarkar or the RSS.

In the same manner, the liberal Iqbal or other liberal communalists could not oppose the campaign of extreme communalism unleashed by Jinnah, Fazl-ul-Huq and others after 1937.

By 1947, communalism had already advanced too far and perhaps there was no alternative to partition. The Congress failed to evolve a strategy to combat communalism at the political, ideological and cultural levels and therefore its leadership has to be faulted on this count.

Jinnah Becomes Bigger and Bigger

Iqbal died in Lahore on April 21, 1938 after suffering for months from his illness. Iqbal was a major Sikandar critic and now there was none.

When war loomed large in Europe, Sikandar Hayat Khan as well as Jinnah realised that they could bargain with the British. The acting Viceroy, Lord Brabourne invited Jinnah and Sikandar, one after another for a tete-a-tete in Simla on August 16, 1938. Both spoke about the Raj-Muslim deal.

Jinnah informed Brabourne that if the Raj Congress majority politicians had any major say and protected Muslims in the Hindu (or Congress) majority provinces, he and the Muslims would protect the British at the centre.

Sikandar, on his part assured Brabourne if given a fair deal, he would stand by the British; meaning thereby that the supply of soldiers for the British Army from his province would not be a problem.

These offers of Jinnah and Sikandar Hayat Khan were sent to the Secretary for India in London, Lord Zetland. In September, Sikandar literally guaranteed HMG that the manpower and resources of the Punjab would be placed at the disposal of Great Britain and her allies, in case a world war broke out.

In August 1938, Jinnah had sought the help of Lord Linlithgow indirectly for the League's struggle against the INC and he stepped up his campaign against the Congress. In October 1938, he went on to charge the Congress ministries for adopting 'a most brutal, oppressive and inimical attitude' towards the Muslims. Jinnah gave a call for direct action and was supported by Fazlul Huq and Sikandar Hayat Khan. The special committes set up by the Muslim League seriously indicted the INC.

Jinnah clearly spelt out that to fight the Congress, support from the British could be taken. He went on to say in December 1938 that in the interest of the Muslims of the Congress majority states, the League *'would be the ally of even a devil....'*.

Continuing his vicious attack on the INC in the December

1938 session of the Muslim League in Patna, Jinnah said:

> The Congress is nothing but a Hindu body.... a few misguided Muslims and those with ulterior motives, does not make it a national body.

He further blamed Gandhi for turning the Congress into 'an instrument for the revival of Hinduism, the ideal of which was to revive Hindu religion and establish Hindu Raj in the country.' As the year 1939 rolled in, Jinnah started thinking about the partition of the country. In March of that year Jinnah's confidant Khaliquzzaman (UP born; 1889-1973) met Lord Zetland and told him:

> You may partition the Muslim areas from the rest [of India] and proceed with your federation of the Indian provinces without including the Muslim areas.

Khaliquzzaman told Zetland that the Muslim League would announce its demand for partition at its next annual meeting. Returning to India, he gave feedback to Jinnah on May 12, 1939 that he had the impression that the British *'would not oppose the demand (for partition) seriously.'* Zetland went on to utter in the House of Lords, *'Hindus as represented by the Congress, Muslims as represented by the All-India Muslim League.'*

INC, Muslim League and the War

The war encouraged the hardliners of the Raj who cared for security but not the political progress in India. Jinnah refused to talk to Gandhi on the war. Gandhi could not meet Sikandar either, who was well guarded by the officers of the Raj. Subhas Bose was the INC president for 1938 and 1939 and he demanded that no Indian men and resources should go into the 'Imperialist War'. Soon, Subhas Bose was edged out of the Congress.

Sikandar Hayat Khan, the prime minister of Punjab province informed Sir Henry Craik, the Punjab governor in August 1939 that if need be, he would supply half a million soldiers within weeks! He even said that he would induct Mian Iftikharuddin, the president of the Punjab INC into his ministry if the INC supported the British war effort. His statement did not go down well with the Muslim League whose Syed Muhammad Ali Rashidi recorded his sense of regret in a resolution of which an amendment was proposed by Sir Raza Ali.

Daultana and other Unionists opposed the amendment but it got passed and the statement read *'that the opinion and sentiments expressed by Sir Sikandar Hayat Khan in his statement to the press on August 25, 1939 in no way represent the views of the Muslims in India.'*

Although Jinnah was becoming bigger and bigger every day, Sikandar's influence and grip over Punjab remained firm till he was around. A new Muslim League formed at his house was questioned by Barkat Ali and the question of its validity came up in Delhi on August 1939 when it was declared that if by November 15, 1939, the Punjab Muslim League was not organised, the organising committee of the Punjab Muslim League would stand automatically dissolved. Mian Barkat Ali asked the new committee to be dissolved subsequently. The formation of the new Muslim League was termed illegal on January 10, 1940 and Barkat Ali appealed to Jinnah to rein in Sikandar as the situation was serious with the new session being planned in March 1940 where the presence of rival factions would create problems galore.

Jinnah met Lord Linlithgow on September 4, 1939 while the Second World War was already on and told him that the ultimate solution of the Indian problem had to be solved by partition and the Viceroy should do something so that the Muslim support could be rallied by Jinnah in favour of the British.

The Muslim League passed a resolution on September 18 spelling out that it could support the British if the government recognised the Muslim League as the sole representative of the Muslims in India; a demand soon accepted by the British. As far back as 1937, Churchill advised Linlithgow to use Muslims as a counter-check on Congress by bringing all the Muslims into the same fold.

Gandhi and Nehru, in the meantime hoped for a joint INC-ML front against the British but literally the carpet was pulled from below their feet, rather cleverly, by Jinnah. When Vallabhbhai Patel, INC's top-notch leader met the Viceroy in October, he was told that in the absence of INC support, the British would seek the Muslims' help.

The Congress protested against the dragging of India into the great war and withheld even the moral support to the empire, despite Gandhi's suggestion. On October 17, the Empire informed the INC that Indian independence was not on its war agenda, the situation became tricky for the Congress ministers who did not want to be mere British puppets. It was objecting to the Empire's silence on the issue of Indian independence. On October 22, the CWC called its ministers to resign; a move gleefully enjoyed by Jinnah who thought it would be good riddance and he said the same publicly. By November 27, 1939, all Congress ministries were out including that of Khan Abdul Ghaffar Khan in NWFP.

Gandhi lamented on October 30, 1939 that Jinnah looked to the British to safeguard Muslim rights and nothing that the INC could do or concede to him would satisfy him. Jinnah was now in top gear so far as anti-INC and pro-British stance of his was concerned. He announced on December 2 that the resignation of the Congress governments would be celebrated by Muslims on December 22 as the 'Deliverance Day', a day of freedom from so-called Hindu domination and Congress tyranny. Even the progressive or the moderate elements among the Muslim League were taken aback by Jinnah's excessive abrasiveness, fearing this would create more sycophants within the party. Ironically, the call was backed by the anti-Congress leader, B.R. Ambedkar, the leader of Dalits.

Proposal for a Separate Muslim State

When the Viceroy suggested to Jinnah at the end of 1939 that the stand which the latter had taken indicated the formation of a separate Muslim state, Jinnah blushed. Zafrulla Khan, a member of the Viceroy's council was told by Linlithgow to draft a note for a proposal advising the Muslim League to demand a separate nation.

In January 1940, Jinnah stated openly that the Muslims and the Hindus were two different nations and the Muslim League announcement for formal separation or splitting of India was just being awaited.

Jinnah the Muslim Icon

Jinnah was undoubtedly the most prominent leader of the Indian Muslims in 1940. He was now big enough to challenge the Unionists of Punjab in Punjab. His newly acquired image of the messiah of the Muslims would allow him to overcome the initial rejection that he had received at the hands of the Punjabi Muslims like Fazl-i-Hussain and Sikandar Hayat Khan. He had not forgotten the bitter election defeat of 1937 and his earlier side-lining in 1920-22 by the Ali brothers and Azad, which compelled him to go into hiding for a long period.

The historic **Lahore Resolution** was passed by the Muslim League in 1940 and the coming years saw the bitter acrimony between the INC and Muslim League on one hand and the Hindu-Sikh combine versus the Muslims on the others. This was true for India as well as Punjab. This paved the path for the division of British India into two independent states namely India and Pakistan.

Conclusion

After Ranjit Singh's death in 1839, the Sikh Empire crumbled slowly but surely. Who was to blame? There was no democracy or bureaucracy in his time and the Army was all the more powerful and the power was centralised in the hands of the Maharaja. His successors were not up to the mark and the in-fighting among the Sardars brought the English home. Chaos followed in the Lahore Kingdom. Ranjit Singh, by his wisdom, had kept the English on the other side of the Sutlej river.

When the British found the situation favourable to them, they slowly entered into the late Maharaja's domain. There followed the Anglo-Sikh wars and luckily for themselves, the British prevailed over the very spirited and courageous Sikhs who were led by opportunists and traitors. Maharaja Duleep Singh and Rani Jindan were made captives and the Lahore throne as well as the Kohinoor diamond was gone.

Soon after the annexation in 1849, the British put in place their own board of administration. The board had its own achievements. After the British took over, there was rapid development of the Punjab. Educational institutes came up. Lahore was spruced up. The British introduced the Railways, Postal system, improved roads and almost performed a miracle for the peasants in the Punjab. They developed the canals and the irrigation system and Punjab became one of the best irrigated lands in the world. It had more irrigated land than even the USA.

But the prosperity of the farmer also brought in a new mercantile class in great numbers: the moneylender who would liberally dole out money at compound interest as the capital was needed by the peasant for all the activities of the cultivation. Slowly, most of the peasants found themselves in some sort of a debt trap. This generated some communal animosity as most of the moneylenders were either Hindus or Sikhs.

The British reduced crimes and introduced their own legislation in Punjab. The new land-tax, friendly, to the people was put to place. Judicial administration was introduced with the establishments of courts. A Census was started in 1854. The population of British possessions in the Punjab was found to be nearly 13 million which was about three million more than the rough estimates of 1849.

The Mutiny of 1857 affected the Punjab too. When the British annexed Punjab, the *purbias* or the Eastern UP and Bihar army men fought against the Sikhs. But now the reverse happened. Using the Khalsa army, the British quelled the Mutiny and killed the purbias. While Punjab's Sikhs did not desire Mughal rule, Punjabi Muslims did not want Sikh rule again and the British rule was acceptable as an alternative to most Punjabis. Peace was now being maintained in the Punjab from 1860 onwards. Canals built between 1860 and 1920 brought close to 10 million acres of new land under agriculture.

Punjab saw a severe famine in 1868-69 and relief works were started by the British. The senate established an oriental school and college at Lahore, started lectureships, literary scholarships and conducted examinations. On February 9, 1870 the Duke of Edinburgh and second son of Queen Victoria visited Lahore.

The communal relations before the mutiny were good but after 1857, there was emphasis on purity in all religions and the communities would slowly but surely drift apart in the decades to come. The British duly pampered the minorities.

Simla was made the summer capital in 1876 with the Delhi Durbar taking place in 1877. In 1871-72, there was this famous *Kuka Movement* of the Namdharis which was one of the first tussles between the British and the Sikhs after the British annexation. Soon, the Singh Sabha Movement was started by the Sikhs in 1873.

While the Sikhs and Muslims were striving to become 'purer', Hindus were not left behind. They thought that Swami Dayanand Saraswati would be the perfect foil for this purpose. The Arya Samaj became popular with the Hindu masses. Aimed at proving Islam's superiority over Christianity, Hinduism and

Sikhism, Qadiani Ghulam Ahmad's writings and speeches made him famous all over Punjab in the 1870s and 1880s.

Sir Ganga Ram played a pivotal role in the modernisation and upgradation of the basic facilities in Lahore which was the provincial capital of Punjab.

The communities were greatly divided over the language. Competence in English was essential for getting a certain class of jobs. The use of Persian in West Punjab had been discarded and as in the north Indian areas ruled by them before 1849, Hindustani was favoured, Urdu was implemented in Punjab for official usage.

The British Army chose certain martial races from India and specifically from Punjab, the Sikh Jats from Central Punjab, Muslim Gakhars, Janjuas, Awans, Tiwanas and Khattar Jats from North-Western Punjab, Hindu Jats from Hissar and Rohtak and Hindu Dogras from Jammu and Kangra were preferred.

The population of Punjab rose to 25.1 million in 1921 from 17.6 million in 1855. The most populous areas were around Lahore, Amritsar, Gurdaspur and Sialkot and the Jalandhar Doab. In the countryside, census figures confirmed that fertile lands close to rivers contained more Jats and Rajputs (whether Sikh, Muslim or Hindu) than members of other rural communities. The Muslim percentage in Punjab rose from 47.6 in 1881 to 51.1 in 1921.

Agriculture prospered in Punjab under the British and the year 1881-82 was a landmark period in the development of wheat trade in India and by 1883, the Punjab had seven million acres under wheat cultivation and the yield was equal to that of the United Kingdom.

Muslim, Sikh and Hindu Jats comprised two-thirds of the canal colony migrants in the new Canal colonies which further increased the prosperity of Punjab.

On the political front, the Congress Party was formed in 1885. Punjab's Muslims got their inspiration from Sayyid Ahmed Khan (1817-98), the founder of Aligarh's Mohammadan Anglo-Oriental College (MAO) in 1875 which became AMU later on. The period between 1887 and 1892 saw the commencement of the Chenab Colony, founding of Lyallpur and the launch of the Ahmadiyya movement.

In the 1890s, starting from 1878 onwards, the districts of the

North West Frontier were quite disturbed because of the forward policy adopted by Lord Lansdowne and Lord Elgin and the intrigues of the Amir in Afghanistan. By 1889, the British control had extended over Bori and Zhob Valleys, in the south of the Gomal pass. Between 1897 and 1902, there was the commencement of the Chunian Colony and the establishment of Khalsa College, Amritsar and School of Medicine for Christian Women.

Punjab had to suffer the attack of *plague* in 1897 which hit Jalandhar and its adjoining areas in 1897. Later it reached Gurdaspur in November 1900 and soon spread to Sialkot. In 1901, the plague outbreak occurred in several districts and spread rapidly. Till 1901 about 21,000 deaths were reported and in 1902 it was ten times. The epidemic was still in full strength. The deaths in 1905 were close to 4,00,000.

The *Punjab Land Alienation Act, 1900* was put to place under Lord Curzon. It came into operation in 1901 and the Act prevented the sale of agricultural land to persons of non-agricultural tribes. Thus, this act categorised Punjabi castes into agriculturalist and non-agriculturist. Consequently, the power and influence of the rural agricultural classes and castes in Punjab increased manifold. They in return helped supply soldiers to the army from their villages.

In 1901, a new province called the North-West Frontier Province was carved out of Punjab. It was created for the Pashto-speaking frontier places and including the districts of Hazara, Peshawar and Kohat and the trans-Indus portions of Bannu and Dera Ismail Khan. The frontier was to be managed directly from Calcutta, with no controls from Lahore.

Via the Colonisation Bill 1906, the government wished to convert these lands into plantations as done in Assam and thereby reducing the farmers from owners to cultivators. The settlements at Rawalpindi took place at higher rates and the water coming in from Bari Doab was levied at a much higher cost thereby agitating the farmers even more. If a person at the time of death had no heirs, the Bill provided for transfer of property of that person to the government. The property could be sold to any public or private developer by the government. This was completely against the social norms and was summarily rejected by all the sides.

Meanwhile, on the April 4, 1905, a massive earthquake shook Kangra causing serious damage to houses and public buildings at Lahore, Amritsar, Sialkot and other important towns.

The agrarian movement in the Punjab dispelled the British notion that the Punjabis would be loyal to them, come what may. There was more disappointment for the British as the Sikhs also joined the agitation, rather led it in a big way. The Sikhs proved their loyalty to the national cause as the subsequent turn of events would show. The bill was accordingly amended.

Infused by the Bengal Agitation the Jat Sikhs fought against the higher taxes and the land tax and the water rate were reduced.

Revolutionary activities started in Punjab at the turn of the century and the Swadeshi movement gained ground. It was important to achieve the Hindu-Muslim-Sikh unity but it must be said the Muslims in Punjab were looking for a favour from the British, considering their backwardness. In 1906, the demand for 'Separate Electorates' had been made by the Muslim deputation and the Muslim League had been created.

Both the Viceroy and the Secretary of State for India decided to reform the legislative councils. So the name came up. This culminated as Indian Councils Act 1909. At the central as well as the provincial level, the expansion of legislative councils was undertaken. This was known as the Minto-Morley Reforms, 1909.

The chasm between the elites of the Hindus and Muslims continued in Punjab. INC was unable to gain ground in Punjab where it faced competition from the Arya Samajis. Also, the Hindus and Sikhs of Punjab realised that separate electorates and weightage formula could be deployed in Punjab to their advantage.

While India had a Muslim leader of national stature in Jinnah, Punjab had its own Maulana Zafar Ali and Fazl-i-Hussain. The Muslim League had not made many inroads into Punjab.

The period from 1913 to 1919 saw the political awakening and has been of great political awakening in the history of the Punjab. Punjabis including the Sikhs had to face stern tests by the British Government. The major events which took place were a) The Ghadar Movement b) the Komagata Maru or Nanak Jahaz disaster c) the Jallianwalla Bagh Massacre and d) Agrarian uprising of 1915.

The Ghadar Movement was at its peak in 1914-15. The Khalsa Diwan Society was was organised in Vancouver in 1907. The other societies like (1) The United India League in Vancouver (2) The Hindustani Association also came up. Indians met at Gurdwaras and papers were published in Gurmukhi, Urdu, and English. The Punjabis who had a very high percentage of Sikhs were disillusioned with the Raj and got drawn towards men like Lala Lajpat Rai who visited them in Canada and the United States. Sohan Singh Bhakna of Oregon and Hardayal emerged as new leaders as they were elected President and Secretary respectively. The party began publishing a weekly paper called *Ghadr* (revolution) in Urdu from San Francisco and soon it was being read by Indians abroad.

In 1919, the British introduced the Government of India Act, 1919 or the Montagu-Chelmsford Reforms and some changes were introduced in the administrative system.

An event of national importance occurred in 1920 when Jinnah left the Congress to be permanently with the Muslim League till his death in 1948. Gandhiji started the Non-Cooperation Movement in the whole of India but its impact over the Punjab province was lukewarm. Two leaders who could have bridged the chasm between the Muslims and the non-Muslims in Punjab were Fazl-i-Hussain and Allama Iqbal. But they made no effort in that direction.

An assembly of Sikhs was called by the new Jathedar of Akal Takht on November 15, 1920 who laid some terms for the creation of a central committee of administration comprising baptised Sikhs or those Sikhs who followed all the tenets of Sikhism including wearing all its symbols. On December 12, 1920, the first session of the SGPC was held at Akal Takht Amritsar. This way the Sikhs were united and the First Gurdwara Bill was passed in 1922, the second bill was passed in 1923 and SGPC became the powerful body of the Sikhs. There was this sad Nankana event involving the Udasis vs baptised Sikhs in November 1921. It was followed by the Tarn Taran tragedy and the *Guru Ka Bagh Morcha*. The Babbar Akali movement continued from 1922-1926. In July 1923, there was this *Jaito* massacre which drew everyone's attention in the Punjab.

In the meanwhile, the Punjabi peasant continued to be bogged down by debt with only 17 per cent free of debt. The tenants were also under the debt. The whole amount of the required debt was being advanced by Hindus or Sikhs; well over half was incurred by Muslims.

In the 1920s, the British tried to develop the economy of the Punjab by building industries. It had already built canals over the last 50 years from 1870 to 1920 and irrigation facilities in Punjab were excellent. Weaving, dyeing, tanning, iron work and wood work got a boost from the British.

While the Non-Cooperation Movement was useful for the Congress in Punjab it was not the only force. The Unionist Party came up in 1923 and it had a strong agricultural ideology. Two key men strengthened the Unionist Party; they were—a Rajput, Sir Fazl-i-Hussain (1877-1936) a messiah for the Punjabi Muslims and the other man was Chhotu Ram, a Jat lawyer from Rohtak.

Communal disturbances took place in those times also, e.g. Multan riots in 1922 and Amritsar riots in 1923, Rawalpindi riots in 1926 and again at Multan in 1927.

In 1926, a scurrilous attack on Prophet Muhammad was made in a book entitled *Rangeela Rasul* which was published by Mahashe Rajpal who was stabbed to death by Ilam din. This created bad relations between the Muslims and the non-Muslims. Almost similar was the Risala Vartman case.

The year 1928 augured well but unfortunately, this happy state of affairs ended soon with riots at Ambala, Gurgaon, Kharakpur and Daska.

Relations between the Sikhs and Muslims of Punjab were cordial before 1935 despite the competition for getting favours from the British including suitable representation in the assemblies. The ignition point was the Shaheedgunj Gurudwara/ Mosque controversy which permanently marred the relations between the Sikhs and the Muslims.

In the meantime riots at Sikandrabad in 1930 and Multan in 1931 further vitiated the atmosphere between the Muslims and the non-Muslims.

Bhagat Singh, Chandra Sekhar Azad, Sukhdev and others launched a revolutionary organisation Hindustan Socialist Republican Association (HSRA) in 1928 at Feroz Shah Kotla, New Delhi.

The Simon Commission was given the task to tour India and propose constitutional reforms. Due to the injuries suffered by Lala Lajpat Rai during demonstrations against the Commission, he died on November 17, 1928. The Punjab legislative council influenced by Fazl, Chhotu Ram and Sikander Hayat Khan assisted Simon. In 1930, Fazl-i-Hussain became a member of the Viceroy's executive council.

Bhagat Singh, Rajguru and Sukhdev were sentenced to death in the Lahore conspiracy case as they protested by throwing bombs in the assembly. Orders were issued for their hangings on March 24, 1931.

The Indian National Congress raised the tricolour flag of India at midnight of December 31, 1929 on the banks of the Ravi at Lahore. On February 11, 1930, the CWC (Congress Working Committee) authorised Mahatma Gandhi to start the Civil Disobedience Movement.

Gandhi and eighty satyagrahis started a march on foot on March 12, 1930 for the coastal village of Dandi, Gujarat, over 390 kilometres (240 mi) from their starting point at Sabarmati Ashram. On the road that separated Sabarmati from Ahmedabad 1,00,000 people had gathered.

The year 1930 was marred by the Qissa Khwani Bazaar massacre when Khan Abdul Ghaffar Khan led the Khudai Khidmatgar who were a group of Muslims of the frontier region. They were committed to the removal of British rule through non-violent methods.

Punjab played a modest role during the phase of the Civil Disobedience Movement which had brought the Congress to the forefront.

On January 19, 1931 the First Round Table Conference ended but not much was implemented despite many principles on reforms having been agreed upon, and the Congress Party carried on its civil disobedience.

Before the start of the Second Round Table Conference in London the 'Gandhi-Irwin Pact' was signed on March 5, 1931. Earlier, a vague offer of 'dominion status' in future for British India was given by Lord Irwin in 1929. HMG agreed to withdraw all ordinances and end prosecutions, release all political prisoners.

On September 7, 1931 the Second Round Conference opened.

The conference resulted in the widening of the gap between the Congress and the minorities. All of the minorities (including Dalits) except Sikhs desired to get their own separate electorates. This increased the drift between the INC and the minorities.

On August 16, 1932 the British Prime Minister MacDonald announced the *Communal Award* which was nothing but a proposal on minority representation. On the issue of reservation of electoral seats for the depressed classes in the legislature of British India government *Poona Pact* was signed between Gandhi and Ambedkar, the same year i.e. in 1932.

Between November 17, 1932 to December 24, 1932, the third Round Table Conference was held but it turned out to be a damp squib and it was not attended by the INC and Gandhi. Jinnah was a delegate to the first two conferences, but was not invited to the last; nor was Gandhi. For many years since 1928, Jinnah was in the political wilderness so far as India was concerned.

Gradually, the thoughts about the *Punjab Partition* started to develop and the initial hints in this regard were floated by Allama Iqbal, Rahmat Ali and Bhai Parmanand.

The Government of India Act 1935 was soon passed. The provincial autonomy was curbed and the provincial legislature could not do many things. Governors were given powers which clashed with the provincial autonomy.

Jinnah returned from England in 1934 and emerged as the top leader of the Muslims in India. Fazl-i-Hussain was to die soon and also Allama Iqbal. The only leader in Punjab left was Sir Sikandar Hayat Khan.

The provincial elections of 1937 saw the Muslim League do better in Hindu-majority provinces as compared to the Muslim-dominated province of Punjab. In Punjab, the unionists won 95 seats. Muslim League was yet to develop into a major force in Punjab in 1937. The *Jinnah-Sikandar Pact* in October 1937 bolstered the Muslim League in the Punjab province and Jinnah.

The Jinnah-Nehru diatribe in 1938 further alienated the Muslims from the INC. The loss of INC was IML's gain. Jinnah was growing in stature every day.

Communalism started assuming a virulent, extremist or fascist form in 1937. Jinnah's two communities – two Nation theory generated conflicts.

In Punjab, for example, the big landlords of West Punjab shifted their allegiance to the Muslim League and the Unionist leaders, one after another, started to join the IML. In 1938 Jinnah termed Congress a Hindu body and blamed Gandhi for turning the Congress into an instrument for the revival of Hinduism. As the year 1939 rolled in, Jinnah started thinking about the partition of the country. Jinnah met Lord Linlithgow on September 4, 1939 while the Second World War was already on and told him that the ultimate solution of the Indian problem had to be solved by partition.

Jinnah was undoubtedly the most prominent leader of the Indian Muslims in 1940 and the historic resolution which laid the path for the creation of Pakistan, as envisaged by Choudhary Rahmat Ali in 1933, was passed at the Muslim League session at Lahore in 1940. This is famously known as the *Pakistan Resolution.* Soon, the Muslims were classified as a separate nation. Hindus and Sikhs had their own reactions but they were quite concerned, needless to say, regarding their own future in such a proposed Islamic state.

Bibliography

Anand, Sushila, Alexander, Michael, *Queen Victoria's Maharajah Duleep Singh, 1838-1893*, Vikas Publishing House Pvt. Ltd., New Delhi (1980).

Badenoch, A.C., *Punjab Industries, 1911-1917*, Superintendent, Government Printing, Punjab (1917).

Bell, Major Evans, *Annexation of the Punjab and the Maharajah Duleep Singh*, Trübner & Co, London (1882).

Bellew, H.W. *Kashmir and Kashgar*. London, 1875, Reprint: Sang-e-Meel Publications, Lahore (1999).

Calvert, H., *The Wealth and Welfare of the Punjab: Being Some Studies in Punjab Rural Economics*, Civil and Military Gazette (1923).

Caroe, Sir Olaf, *The Pathans*, Oxford University Press, Karachi (1958).

Chattha, Ilyas, Economic Change and Community Relations in Lahore Before Partition, *International Journal of Punjab Studies*, 19(2): 193-213, September 2012.

Cunningham, J.D., *History of the Sikhs*, first published (1849).

Dalrymple W., Anand, A., *Koh-I-Noor, The History of the World's Most Infamous Diamond*, Bloomsbury, New Delhi (2017).

Darling, Malcom L., *At Freedom's Door*, Oxford University Press, London (1949).

Darling Malcom L., *The Old Light and the New in a Punjab Village*, Oxford University Press, London (1930).

Darling Malcom L., *The Punjab Peasant in Prosperity and Debt*, Oxford University Press, London (1928).

Dhillon, Gurdarshan Singh, *The Sikhs and the British (1849-1920)*, Guru Nanak Dev Mission Series, Patiala (1991).

Gardner, Alexander, *Memories of Alexander Gardner*, William Blackwood & Sons, Edinburgh & London (1898).

Ghose, Sankar, *Jawaharlal Nehru: A Biography*, Allied Publishers Pvt. Ltd., Kolkata (2006).

Griffin, Lepel H., *Panjab Chiefs*, Kapurthala (1890).

Honigberger, Johann Martin, *Thirty-five Years in the East, Adventures, Discoveries, Experiments, and Historical Sketches, Relating to the Punjab and Cashmere; in Connection with Medicine, Botany, Pharmacy, etc.*, R.C. Lepage & Co., Calcutta (1852).

Horniman, B.G., *Amritsar and Our Duty to India*, T. Fisher Unwin, Ltd, London (1920).

Hugel, Baron Charles, *Travels in Kashmir and the Panjab, Containing a Particular Account of the Government and Character of the Sikhs*, John Petheram, London (1845).

Ibbetson, Sir Denzil, *Panjab Castes, Being a Reprint of the 'Chapter on The Races, Castes and Tribes of the People' in the Report on the Census of the Panjab Published in 1883.* Superintendent, Government Printing, Lahore, Punjab (1916).

Jalal, Ayesha, *Self and Sovereignty: Individual and Community in South Asian Islam Since 1850*, Oxford University Press, New Delhi (2001).

Kohli, Sita Ram, *Sunset of Sikh Empire* edited by Khushwant Singh, Orient Longman, New Delhi, first published (1967).

Latif, Syed Ahmad, *A History of the Punjab from the Remotest Antiquity to the Present Time*, Central Press Company Limited, Calcutta (1891).

Lawrence-Archer, Capt. J.H., *Commentaries on the Punjab Campaign 1848-49, Including Some Additions to the History of the Second Sikh War, from Original Sources*, WM. H. Allen & Co., London (1878).

Login, Lady, *Sir John Login and Duleep Singh, with an Introduction by Colonel G.B. Malleson*, W.H. Allen & Co., London (1890).

Mahajan, Jagmohan, *Circumstances Leading to the Annexation of the Punjab, (1846-1849), a Historical Revision*, Kitabistan, Allahabad & Karachi (1949).

Malik, Ikram Ali, *A Book of Readings on the History of the Punjab*, University of the Punjab, Lahore (1970).

Mathur, Y.B., *British Administration of Punjab (1849-75)*, Surjeet Book Depot, Delhi (1973).

Michael, Brecher, *Nehru: A Political Biography*, Oxford University Press, London (1959).

Mujeeb, M., *Dr. Zakir Husain, A Biography*, National Book Trust, New Delhi (1972).

Nijhawan, P.K., *The First Punjab War, Shah Mohammed's Jangnamah*,

Singh Brothers in Association with Maharaja Duleep Singh-Raj Mata Jind Kaur Foundation, Patiala (2001).

Nijjar, Bakhshish Singh, *Origins and History of Jats and Other Allied Nomadic Tribes of India, (900 B.C. to 1947 A.D.)*, Atlantic Publishers and Distributors (P) Ltd, New Delhi (2008).

Nijjar, Bakhshish Singh, *Anglo-Sikh Wars (1845-1849)*, K.B. Publications, New Delhi (1976).

Nijjar, Bakhshish Singh, *Punjab Under the British Rule, (1849-1947)*, Volume III, 1932-1947, K.B. Publications, New Delhi (1974).

Osborne, W.G., *The Court and Camp of Runjeet Sing*, Henry Colburn, publisher, London (1840).

Qarmichael, Major G., *A History of the Reigning Family of Lahore, with Some Account of the Jummoo Rajahs, the Seik Soldiers.*

Rai, Satya M., *Punjabi Heroic Tradition*, Publication Bureau, Punjabi University Patiala; Second Edition edition (1995).

Rashid, Harun-or *The Foreshadowing of Bangladesh: Bengal Muslim League and Muslim Politics, 1936-1947*, Dhaka (1987).

Roberts, Sir William, *A Text Book of Punjab Agriculture*, Civil and Military Gazette (1947).

Shaw, Isobel, *Pakistan Handbook*, The Guidebook Co., Hong Kong, (1989).

Singh, Kirpal, *Evolution and Brief History of the Sikhs*, Guru Nanak Dev Mission, Patiala (1995).

Swynnerton, Rev. Charles, *Romantic Tales from the Panjab*, Archibald Constable & Co. Ltd, Westminster (1903).

Thompson, W.P., *Punjab Irrigation*, Civil and Military Gazetteer, Lahore (1925).

Thorburn, S.S., *Mussalmans and Money-Lenders in the Punjab*, William Blackwood & Sons, Edinburgh and London (1886).

Trotter, Captain Lionel J., *The Life of John Nicholson Soldier and Administrator Based on Private and Hitherto Unpublished Documents*, Thomas Nelson & Sons, London and New York (1897).

Watson, Andrew, *The Story of Bamba*, Women's Ceneral Missionary Society of the United Presbyterian Church of North America, Pittsburgh (1893).

Wikeley, Lt. Col., J.M., *Punjabi Mussalmans*, The Book House, Lahore and later published by Manohar Publishers and Distributors, New Delhi (1991).

Wolpert, Stanley, *Jinnah of Pakistan*, Oxford University Press, New Delhi (1984).

Internet Sources

https://amolak.in/web/the-last-mahantof-nankana-sahib/

http://pakteahouse.net/2011/10/05/the-return-of-jinnah-1934/

http://pu.edu.pk/images/journal/studies/PDF-FILES/Artical-15_v16_1.pdf

https://scroll.in/article/860430/ayodhya-parallel-a-gurdwara-in-Lahore-was-at-the-core-of-a-bitter-battle-between-Sikhs-and-Muslims

https://shodhganga.inflibnet.ac.in/bitstream/10603/172251/7/07_chap.-iii..pdf

https://shodhganga.inflibnet.ac.in/bitstream/10603/8011/10/10_chapter%203.pdf

http://www.alhakam.org/blasphemy-and-the-ahmadiyya-response-a-brief-case-study/

https://www.dawn.com/news/1403799

http://www.global.ucsb.edu/punjab/sites/secure.lsit.ucsb.edu.gisp.d7_sp/files/sitefiles/journals/volume16/no1/2-John%20Webster16.1.pdf

https://www.independent.co.uk/news/people/obituary-niranjan-singh-gill-1542353.html

http://www.iosrjournals.org/iosr-jhss/papers/Vol.%2022%20Issue7/Version-16/A22070160104.pdf

http://www.Sikhs.nl/downloads/English/The%20Sikh%20Generals.pdf

https://www.tribuneindia.com/news/sunday-special/kaleidoscope/-sati-choice-before-Maharaja-ranjit-s-ranis/99411.html

https://www.theSikhencyclopedia.com/the-British-and-Sikhs-1849-1947/sikandar-baldev-singh-pact

Others

Gazetteer of the Amritsar District 1883-84, Compiled and Published under the Authority of the Punjab Government.

Gazetteer of the Amritsar District 1892-93, Compiled and Published under the Authority of the Punjab Government.

Index